THE ALTERNATIVE 39 STEPS

Jane Spurr

First edition June 2009
ISBN: 978-0-9561768-2-0

Set in Gill Sans MT 11 pt and published by
Greenman Enterprise
Greenman Farm
Wadhurst
East Sussex TN5 6LE

Printed by The Ink Pot
Southbank House
Victoria Road
Southborough
Kent TN4 0LT

THE ALTERNATIVE 39 STEPS

CONTENTS

For my dear husband, Howard,
without whom these journeys,
and consequently this book,
would never have happened.

PREFACE

IN THE DEPARTURE LOUNGE

Be honest - does your heart sink when you are threatened with 'the holiday snaps'…or, more often these days, 'the holiday *videos*'? This book plumbs new depths - it's 'the holiday *diaries*'!

I am sure all of us has a story to tell about holiday snaps. Mine is 'in this wise'. I was being shown photos of my friend's recent holiday; I knew none of her fellow travellers - and a surfeit of images of people you don't know can become the teeniest bit tedious. Each photo merited a three or four minute dissertation on each of its numerous subjects - indeed, nothing less than a potted biography of every one of them. The photos were many and various - if somewhat lacking in scenic content. I was not entirely riveted by the commentary - especially 'since I knew not the folk'.

My mind was in danger of wandering when, after about thirty minutes, what joy - the next photo was of a stone shepherd's hut - or should that be a shepherd's stone hut? There's not a lot of call for stone shepherds these days. Also in the photo was a goat - not a shepherd in sight, not the slightest vestige of any human being. My heart leapt, since I knew there could be *nothing* to say about this particular exposure. How wrong could I be? It turned out that this was the *very* hut where Neil (remember him? - *No!*) sat in the shade ("the sun doesn't agree with him") while the others explored the sandy margins of the lake - the Big-Sea-Water - as Coleridge-Taylor might have said - and it sounds more romantic than 'the beach'. The 'stream of consciousness' rolled on. "Neil was the one whose wife used to work with my niece's friend in Selfridges - the one I told you about who had two Labradors." The characters were becoming something of a blur. My powers of concentration were receding at about the same speed as the outgoing tide. Nieces with Labradors merged into neighbours with various ailments, and others who used to work with 'Tim'…"whose brother has got a job as a chauffeur to a pop group and had the girl-friend who could only eat gluten-free things and whose stepmother ran a massage parlour…". By now, I was losing the will to live.

When Howard and I were both working, we were able to afford some remarkable holidays - to places like America and China - and many shorter breaks nearer to home. One of Howard's (many) strong points is planning journeys. This stood him in good stead in his work with, first, the Central Office of Information and, later, the Visits' Section of the Foreign and Commonwealth Office, as his job entailed planning trips for foreign visitors and dignitaries. Those he planned for us were no less meticulously arranged. Howard's grasp of geography is far superior to mine - all the more reason for him to make the arrangements. I find it so easy to mistake place names in the heat of the moment - after all Warsaw *sounds* like Walsall on a dark night, with a following wind. Howard is a fearless person; his fearlessness extended to organising train journeys - even though he knew that the British Rail Timetable had won the Booker Prize for Fiction for more years than either of us could remember.

Some of the holidays took us to towns - and even capital cities. I am glad to have these memories because now I avoid towns altogether and 'city' is a word I have deleted from my dictionary - so now 'citrus' is followed by 'civet'. The countryside is where I long to be.

We made six visits to Paris and I feared they might become too repetitious but, as we did different things on each visit, I decided to include all six. We took a number of package holidays which was a good way of dealing with the basic arrangements, whilst leaving us free to 'do our own thing' on arrival.

We are no longer able to afford holidays but, as we never cease to remind ourselves, living in Wadhurst is 'one long holiday' - especially after a thirty-six year 'stretch' in South London - with no parole or 'time off for good behaviour'. During the period covered by this volume, we lived in Jennifer House, Reedworth Street, Kennington.

A word of explanation as to how the diaries 'came to be' might not be out of place. For many years, I had a long and very regular correspondence with Charles and Rosemary Proctor. I had got to know Charles when I was a student at Trinity College of Music, in 1963, and the story of my musical involvement with him and my part in the Proctors' life is told in my book *A Song of Farewell*. Over the years, the correspondence became a record of the lives of our two families. (Because Charles was an organist, we tried to obtain for him postcards and other information about the organs which we encountered on our travels - hence the references to this in the following chapters.) Charles and Rosemary were always very interested in what we had done and seen on our holidays so these accounts started life as long letters to them. I have done much editing and re-writing for the purposes of this book as the material, in its original letter form, was not appropriate for this purpose.

In these pages, there is no in-depth information about the places we visited; that can be found in myriad guidebooks. There are no deep insights either, so if that is what you seek, this book is not for you! These diaries are nothing but a light-hearted record of where we went and what we did, lightly seasoned with our own (quirky?) observations and comments. Howard was well-travelled *before* 1983 but holidays had not been a part of my life as I couldn't afford them.

2

Consequently, all the experiences we had were new to me. It's worth remembering that, twenty-five years ago, things like air travel, computers, mobile phones and 'all that goes with' were not commonplace, as they are today. To most people, marvelling at the computerized departure boards at airports is about as scintillating as watching paint dry - but to someone who had never experienced it, it was a huge 'learning curve'!

Recently I unearthed the diaries from their rather dusty A4 ring binder. The contents seemed as fresh as when they were first written so now, some years 'down the line', I thought it might be worth sharing them with others who might derive some similar enjoyment. I have tried hard to ensure that all details are correct but can only crave your indulgence if errors have crept in unnoticed. (I do hope these accounts won't end up being quoted in a holiday equivalent of Simon Hoggart's Christmas letters!)

To say we had 'wonderful times' would be an understatement - but all good things must come to an end. We are just so thankful that we were able 'to do what we did, when we did it'. And no matter where we had been or what we had done, 'coming back home' was always something to which we looked forward and for which we never ceased to be thankful.

In these rather gloomy times in which we live, I thought there could be a place for a book that might bring a smile to your face and maybe inspire you to sally forth 'into the bright blue yonder'. I hope that you will enjoy travelling around the world in your armchair as much as we did in real life.

AUSTRIA - IN SEARCH OF THE SOUND OF MUSIC
August 1983

Monday 15th

A trip to Austria was a tempting prospect as we boarded the coach in central London. First stop, Catford - not a lake or mountain in sight - but the coach was changed as neither the brakes nor the microphone were functioning adequately. Not the most auspicious start, but ever positive thinkers, we decide that things can only get better. Eventually, we set off for Dover. We used the channel crossing to good effect, having lunch of roast beef and beaujolais, and purchasing our duty free drinks for the trip. We rejoined the coach on Level WHALE 4 (three cheers for the pictorial symbols!) ready for disembarkation. After a long drive, we arrived at Charleville-Mézières for dinner, which proved to be very disappointing. The service was so slow (we are still waiting for our wine!) but the hotel was very comfortable and we were warned about the most amazing alarm 'event' that would rouse us from our slumbers next morning.

Tuesday 16th

At 0615, our slumbers were interrupted by the most unexpected harmonic sequence (see alarm 'event' above), interspersed with 'voice-overs' in French and English. The English version was so threatening that we had no choice but to leap from our bed. By 0730 we were on the road and at 1015 we arrived in Luxembourg. A sighting of the EEC complex was followed by the legend of a nymph, now hiding in a rock. (If you believe that, you'll believe anything. We believed it.) We don't *think* she is anything to do with the EEC - but we couldn't be sure. The Ducal Palace was somewhat 'minimalist' and there was not much room for proclamations from the balcony as it overlooked a tiny street...but then, not many people live there so perhaps the Duke doesn't need much room. Indeed, it might be easier to invite them all into his Palace. We stopped for some Moselle in a local café and we met a super little dog. The owner's dog, on the other hand, was very unfriendly - as was the owner. At 1100, we left Luxembourg for Germany where we arrived at 1500 at Karlsruhe, for lunch at the station restaurant. What a meal! British Rail could learn a thing or two from this eatery. Our comments on the meal read "very, very tasty, very efficient service and very nice wine". OK - it's not quite Fay Maschler but it 'went down a treat' after a long journey. The 15-star loos were something to behold. Since I am not a German speaker, the advice on the door passed me by. As I fell into the entrance, I thought that must be as good a way as any of learning the German for 'Mind the Step'.

Perhaps our first purchase should have been a phrase book. Whilst we didn't anticipate being in any 'postillion struck by lightning' situations, I was the first to admit that the four phrases I know in German were not likely to be terribly helpful to us. They lose something in translation - but, broadly speaking, they are:

1   Thank you for your letter of the eighteenth.
2   Have you a double room with bath, please?
3   I love you.
4   All is transitory. (I came across that in Mahler's Eighth Symphony.)

We arrived at Munich around 2100 where a meal awaited us. Consommé, beef and macaroni, salad and fruit salad. (It was certainly different....) Thence to a Bierkeller - though it was on the first floor (?). Howard drank a whole stein but I was more cowardly and only managed half one. A traditional Bierkeller-type band was giving its all but we could not appreciate it to the full, thanks to a group of very noisy Americans who appeared to have downed rather more steins than was good for them.

Our hotel was very comfortable and next morning we were offered the first of our continental breakfasts. The vast choice included boiled eggs, cold meat, cheese, bread, coffee, tea, (not quite like we make it). We left Munich in pouring rain and in the hands of our excellent courier Christine, from the North of England.

Wednesday 17th

At 1115, we arrived at our destination, St Gilgen. As soon as we had unpacked, we had (what was to be) the first of many Wienerschnitzel lunches before ascending 1,522 metres in a cable car. I was a quivering wreck at the beginning and Howard was very bruised from where I clung to him for dear life. I got better during the ascent - there was a discernible *diminuendo* in my screams. When we arrived, we were about 5,000 feet (no, I don't know what that is in metres either) above sea level. Another couple of steps from the cable car to the summit and we'd walked off our lunch. We took a stroll around the summit. The views were spectacular and the freshness of the air was something I had not experienced. (Perhaps because I had never been higher than 1,325 feet, on the Worcestershire Beacon.) I recall that the air seemed to 'go to my head', like sparkling wine. It was a very strange and pleasant sensation, but we were exhausted quite quickly. More refreshments seemed to be the answer and, this time, I *did* drink a stein of beer.

We descended (via the cable car) to the town of St Gilgen and took a walk around to familiarize ourselves with what it had to offer. A fountain, the church and the cemetery all got good marks. Over dinner in the hotel, we met Michael and Ruth from Israel and Graham from Glasgow. Michael speaks heaps of languages and has written books in Polish on Criminology. After dinner, we returned to 'downtown' St Gilgen (avoided the disco in the hotel) and the fountain was illuminated. We tried to fathom out the sequence of the continually changing patterns of lights and colours - but failed - so we gave up the unequal struggle and had a early night, as we were very weary from our mountain meanderings.

Thursday 18th

At breakfast, we met Betty and Joan, who we were to meet back at home after our holiday. Before setting off by bus into Salzburg, we did the obligatory postcards so that our consciences would be clear for the rest of the trip. The journey to Salzburg was very scenic, but then, everywhere we looked was scenic!

First stop, the Mirabelle Gardens, which came up to expectations - and were slightly bigger than our equivalent back in Reedworth Street. Howard said that a bishop had this made for his mistress! (We bet the General Synod would have something to say about that if it happened in 1983!) In the old part of town, we found the beer garden which Howard had frequented some years earlier. Fortified by another beer, we embarked on the first of the musical pilgrimages, to Mozart's birthplace. Here were models of opera sets from 'days gone by', scores of Mozart works, a leaflet for the first performance of The Magic Flute, with Mozart's name in such small letters that it was hardly noticeable. Emanuel Schikaneder's was there 'in neon lights' - or the eighteenth century equivalent. There was a piano and a square piano on which, according to his widow, Mozart composed The Magic Flute. (Can we believe her?) Places where composers have lived and worked never fail to move me and are the highlight of any visit, anywhere. Knowing his great love of Mozart, we sent a special postcard to Peter Gellhorn.

After a very good lunch in the beer garden, our next visit was to the fortress. The first part of the ascent was made on the funicular railway but, even after disembarkation, there was still a long way to go on foot - at least, it seemed a long way for unfit types like us. There was a guided tour - in German - though each piece of commentary ended with 'Any questions?' - in English. We didn't like to ask anything as we would not have understood the answer (we were convinced the answer would not be one of the four sentences I knew) so we merely laughed when everyone else laughed and nodded or shook our heads similarly.

Salzburg Cathedral (very large) was next on the agenda. Apparently the outside of it was used in The Sound of Music, though the indoor scenes were filmed in another church which we would see later in our stay. In the pretty square adjacent to the 'Dom' (we've learned another word) were a number of horse-drawn carriages. (Very well drawn they were too - no mean artists, those horses.) Our way back to the bus took us back through the Mirabelle Gardens, with just time to buy the obligatory Mozart chocolate balls - which are hard to avoid in this town.

In the evening, we were promised a free welcome drink - and music. (What sort? Mozart? Somehow we doubted it.) The free drink was Schnapps for the gentlemen and Apricot Brandy for the ladies. The owner's son, Herr Frisch, played the 'organ' - one of those instruments of torture with pre-set rhythms and flashing lights. We stayed no longer than was absolutely necessary to be polite and spent the rest of the evening watching the coloured fountain, of which we never tired.

Friday 19th

Today was a lazy day. We sunbathed on deck chairs provided by the hotel on a wooden platform at the side of the lake. At one point, we had a swim (or, in my case, a 'flail about in the water' as I can only do a quarter of a width on a good day, with a following wind). More enticing foods and drinks throughout the day and, on the way to supper, we noticed that the hotel had a fitness room, as well as a solarium and sauna. We failed to find an *un*-fitness room, so we had to get unfit as best we could.

Saturday 20th

Another lazy day spent by the lake. We had a picnic lunch, after which and when we felt it safe to do so, we attempted another 'swim'. This time I managed eight strokes...is this a record? After dinner (which included one of our favourite things, onion soup), we went into the town with our new-found friend, Graham. The town Festival was in full swing. A band was playing, stalls were doing a roaring trade - and we bought some nougat. Such was the quantity we purchased that we were able to give it away to others on our tour whom we met during the evening. We wound up the day with some *gluwein*. Graham was a bit elderly so we thought he would need a rest before we returned to the hotel - at least that was our excuse.

Sunday 21st

Today we took a coach trip around the Salzkammergut area. Our first stop was in the town of St Wolfgang - at the White Horse Inn. Our comment was 'Too tourist-ified for words'. That said it all. The church had to be seen but, as we entered, a rather strangulated tenor was carving his way through Handel's *Largo*. We had been told the rare altarpiece would be illuminated for a few minutes at

8

the end of the service. While we waited for this to happen, the strangulated tenor seemed to have disappeared (had he finally been strangled?) and the organist was now 'in full swing'. He didn't sound *too* bad - until he started on the first of the JSB *Eight Short Preludes and Fugues*. We revised our opinion of his capabilities. The illuminated altarpiece made up for the temporary assault on our ears. It was indescribably beautiful. The high altar was extremely ornate too.

Our next stop was Bad Ischl and coffee and cake at the world famous *Zauners*. Then came one of the highlights of the trip. We arrived at the church as the congregation was leaving and, here, the organist was 'quite something'. How thrilled CP would have been to hear this - especially as it was the church, and the organ, where Bruckner had played. (The organ may have been rebuilt since Bruckner's day, but we liked to think it had not.) We took a photo of the Bruckner bust on the wall of the church - the best we could do for CP.

Next stop Trauenskirche, with its marvellous fisherman's pulpit and the house where Wolf had lived for quite some time. The graveyard was particularly attractive so we all 'booked our spot'. A boat trip took us across the lake to Gmunden and, en route, the guide pointed out the villa where Wagner had written *Tristan und Isolde*. The marble table near the lake, at which he had sat to do this, was still there. For me, that was a 'gold star' moment. This was my first sighting of real mountains and the sheer size of both the mountains and the lakes was overwhelming. It made me understand the size of Wagner's music in a way which I had never done before.

Gmunden's church had another wonderful golden altarpiece - and a large organ, though it was silent. Back in the square there was a china glockenspiel - also silent, as someone had smashed one of the bells. Several swans were in evidence, waiting to be auditioned for *Lohengrin*. Our next stop was Mondsee, passing a place where 'Schubert stayed a lot'. When we arrived at Mondsee, the first thing we saw was a procession of Alsatian dogs and their handlers. Our first thought was that perhaps this was a very crime-ridden place and these were police dogs being prepared for their next duty. We visited Mondsee's church, another enormous edifice, with yet another beautiful golden altar. *This* is the church where they filmed the interior scenes for *The Sound of Music*. Just as we were leaving Mondsee, the Alsatian dogs were being put through their paces by their handlers in a demonstration of their skills.

We returned to St Gilgen by way of many beautiful villages (Festinau, Thalgau etc.) and we passed the racing driver, Nikki Lauda's house (must have cost a bob or two). The scenery was quite breathtaking and the trip would have been worth it for this alone - the scenery, that is, not Mr. Lauda's house.

Monday 22nd

The Ice Caves at Dachstein are our first destination today. Initially, the journey was by cable car to Schönbergalm at 1,350 metres, but that was followed by a steep walk, carrying the warm clothing which we had been advised to bring. On arrival at the caves, we donned the warm clothing. We were already wearing the 'stout footwear' that was also recommended for the visit. There was an immediate difference in temperature as soon as we entered the caves though, as yet, there was no sign of any ice. Suddenly, there they were - the ice statues. The caves are over a million years old. The ice statues were lit from behind and it was an unbelievable sight. The guide switched off the lights for a time so we could have an idea what it must have been like when the statues were first discovered. In complete darkness, it was a very spooky place indeed. We would not have missed this 'for the world' and the visit was well worth the hard climb and subsequent descent.

Back at the cable car station, we had a memorable Schweinerschnitzel lunch. As there were long gaps between the arrival of each cable car, there was no time to go up to the next level so we returned to the coach and proceeded to Hallstatt for the afternoon. Yet another marvellous gold altarpiece in the church - we were getting quite blasé about them now.....We visited the charnel house which, unsurprisingly, was full of bones and skulls. The ladies' skulls were painted with flowers. We learned that, as they are rather short of burial space, after ten years they dig up remains and remove them to the charnel house - having painted the skull first! We witnessed what appeared to be a funeral but we couldn't make out what was happening. People were carrying (what looked like) urns - but perhaps they were skulls. Whatever they were, the bearers looked remarkably unconcerned about it. We returned to the village and took another funicular railway up to a twelfth century house - for refreshments. To entertain us while we ate, we watched a helicopter collecting something in a bucket - we knew not what - then returning to ground level with the bucket dangling underneath. We were not able to see the end of the mission as the landing site was out of view. Even as we were contemplating what might be happening on the ground, an Alpine storm arrived. It was a storm the like of which we had never seen. Thunder, lightning and torrential rain were its main components - did it need any more? We secured the cameras and my handbag in all available plastic bags and ran...as quickly as our unfit legs would carry us. By the time we got back to the funicular railway, we were 'soaked to the skin' - but the cameras and my handbag were as dry as the bones that we had seen in the charnel house. We sat in our sodden garments during the return journey to the hotel. The driver told us we were going back by 'the pretty route', but we had to admit there were no ugly routes around these parts. A shower had never seemed so good. We donned dry clothes and treated ourselves to a pre-prandial whisky - to stave off any colds that might have tried to take hold.

After dinner, we were treated to a 'folk evening' which featured lots of yodelling. Yodelling consists of vocal exercises up and down tonic and dominant arpeggios - occasionally a sub-dominant crept in when we weren't looking. The novelty quickly palled (though Frank Ifield put it to good effect all those years ago). Much to my relief, Howard did not express any interest in working towards Grade Eight Yodelling. As far as we could make out, all the 'songs' were variations on *The Happy Wanderer*.

After a polite interval we left, as the next day, we had to make a very early start for Vienna. Breakfast was brought to our room at 2330...an odd arrangement but done to save the staff having to rise at the crack of dawn to prepare it. The downside was that we had to rouse ourselves from our slumbers at 2330 to let in the waiter with the breakfast!

Tuesday 23rd

This was our penultimate day and would prove to be one of the longest and most interesting. We had to leave the hotel at 0630 so we were up, dressed and breakfasting at the crack of dawn. Only coffee had been provided in the overnight thermos flask - no tea, for which I was desperate. The magnificently modern and luxurious coach on which we travelled soon made me forget my tea craving. Herbert, the guide, was immensely knowledgeable and did not stop talking for the whole journey. It was almost 'information overkill' and I found it hard to take in everything we were being told - especially as I was drifting in and out of consciousness...

Our first stop was Schönbrunn - a sort of mini-Versailles - but not mini-enough for us to take in anything more than a small percentage of it. Indeed, there was time just to see part of the gardens and the Schönbrunn statue in a little 'chapel-like' place, where an old lady was selling glasses of water from the fountain in the statue. Our last treat was a sighting of the Imperial Carriages; the 'Coronation' carriage was superb.

We arrived in the city of Vienna by way of ever-decreasing circles on what is the Ring Road. (It was strange to think that this had been in Russian hands not too long ago.) We lunched at the *Augustinerkeller* to help regain our concentration. Our brains were saturated with places, dates and names and they needed some sustenance to set them back on an even keel. Thus fortified, we made our way to St Stephen's Cathedral. Their Cardinal had died on August 14th and was lying in a coffin in a side chapel. His Requiem Mass was to take place that evening, followed by burial in the crypt. It gave us great pleasure to be able to buy postcards of the St Stephen's organ for CP and we much looked forward to telling the Proctors about this particular visit, as Charles had been a student in Vienna in the 1920s.

Our next stop was a guided tour of the Vienna State Opera. This was a most impressive place, as we would have expected. It was amazing to think that much of it had been destroyed in the war(s?) but it had been rebuilt to the original designs. We *had* to go to the Sacher Hotel for *Sachertorte, apfelsaft* and wine (served in a glass jug on a silver tray). This little treat cost the earth, but it's just one of those things we *had* to do. The hotel was not unlike the George V in Paris - so we had to investigate the loos. Vases of carnations and pretty tiled walls greeted me in the Ladies - as did Alison and Zena, two of our fellow travellers.

Our next stop was the Prater and, *en route*, we passed the house where Strauss wrote *The Blue Danube*. It's now a MacDonald's Hamburger emporium! There was just time for a ride on the (huge) ferris wheel, immortalized in the film *The Third Man*.

All too soon, it was time to leave Vienna for the long return journey. We left the city, passing the St Francis of Assisi church, to the accompaniment of ... *The Blue Danube* (what else?) on a tape. Our stop on the way home was at Durnstein, a most attractive place. We bought a very unusual wine container for Howard's parents' Golden Wedding anniversary present. Then, just to make sure that the contents would be acceptable, we drank some new wine at the Richard Lionheart restaurant, in the company of Alison and Zena. A photo of us all, taken in the early evening sun, bears witness to the beauty of the setting - and you can almost *taste* the wine. During the final leg of the return journey to St Gilgen, I concluded that all the houses round about looked like musical boxes and all the churches must be made of marzipan. (Twenty five years on, I can understand why I thought the houses looked like musical boxes but can't think why I thought the churches must be made of marzipan?)

Wednesday 24ᵗʰ

This was our last day so, before saying goodbye to St Gilgen, we had one last walk into town where we bought a furry dog (who still has pride of place in our house), a book about the Salzkammergut region (with glossy pics.) and, as they were so cheap, some Gluwein sachets - ready for winter.

The coach arrived from England with our 'replacements'. (For a few moments, we must admit we were envious of them.) At 1115, we set off on our homeward journey. Innsbruck was our lunch stop. Though there was no time for sight-seeing, Howard disappeared to take a picture of a golden roof. I was worried, thinking he would never be seen again and the coach would leave without him. As usual, my anxiety was misplaced. After lunch, our route took us over the Arlsberg Pass - highest point 6,000 feet. A short stop gave an opportunity for us to taste the freshest of fresh air. (Was that Julie Andrews in the distance?) Our next stop was Leichtenstein, arriving in Vaduz at 1930. Leichtenstein is another 'minimalist' place and as both the inhabitants of Vaduz were out, we saw no one. There was time for a quick walk into town before dinner. A service was just ending in the local church - perhaps that's where the two inhabitants had gone? Outside was a bust of Rheinberger. We couldn't understand the German inscription and I was ashamed to say that I didn't know whether he was born there, lived there, played there, or *what* he had done there. I looked him up when we got home. He was born there...three cheers for Leichtenstein! After our evening meal in a local restaurant, we returned to our hotel room where, from our balcony, we could see the Duke's castle - wonderfully illuminated.

Thursday 25th

After a terrific breakfast, we made an early start as there was still some distance to cover before we reached Calais. We left Leichtenstein at 0730, though our departure was delayed by a party of geese who chose that moment to stroll along the highway. Then followed a long drive to the outskirts of Basle and on to Strasbourg for lunch. An even longer drive took us to Reims where Howard had stayed for some months in 1975/76 whilst taking a French course. The coach had to double park in a very precarious position so the men helped the drivers to unload the luggage. We dined in a nearby restaurant with a group of our new friends and promised them a visual treat at the end of the meal - but didn't tell them what it would be. Howard led us to the front of the Cathedral which, being illuminated, produced a real 'fairy tale' effect. Indeed, it looked like a set from a play - it was hard to believe it was a Cathedral at all. Howard gave us a guided tour of the exterior of the Cathedral and told us lots of things about Reims - the jackdaw only having a small supporting role. Our final treat was to stop at a nearby bar and share a bottle of champagne, in sight of the illuminated Cathedral - a memory which will stay with us for a very long time.

Friday 26th

This really was the last lap today and another early start was needed to make sure we got to the coast in good time. There was a stop at St Quentin for everyone to stock up at the hypermarket. Duty-free wine and mouth-watering French cheeses were the order of the day. An uneventful return crossing (with just time to consume our last meal in the restaurant on the ferry) and very soon, we were back in London. Graham came back to our flat as he had five hours to wait before getting his overnight train to Scotland. Friends had left us some fresh food - more than enough to share with Graham.

And so to bed...with plans to emigrate to Austria as soon as possible...

WILD WEST - HERE WE COME!
September - October 1984

Sunday September 16th

It was time to prepare the inevitable list of all the things we needed to do, take, arrange, before setting off on this marathon. The 'Wild West - Here We Come' file (yes, it really did exist) had a thorough looking-over to ensure nothing was overlooked. One thing that helped us enormously in the preparation of this trip was the amount of advance information Herbert and Isabelle (Howard's uncle and aunt in California) had sent us. It started to arrive in January and continued in a steady stream. We realized that we could not take all of it so some serious weeding was needed. This would be the first transatlantic journey I had made, though Howard had been there some years previously.

Thursday September 20th

Mrs. Proctor telephoned to tell us about her friends in Scottsdale and to suggest we made contact with them. We typed a letter to the Oettings and took it with us to post on arrival, since Scottsdale was early in the trip. Time for the Big Pack - followed by supper and an early night. The excitement was palpable.

Friday September 21st

0600 - early morning tea as we tried to convince ourselves that we really *were* going today. Countdown to departure - gas off? plugs out? spare food given away? passports packed? The list was endless - but we left Jennifer House at 0930 and our neighbour took the first of the many photos for 'The American Collection' - us and the luggage - really original...

There was a delay at the British Caledonian Victoria check-in as the computer had broken down, so we couldn't get our seat reservations. Eventually, the computer was fixed and we were able to check in our luggage. Hopefully we wouldn't see it again until Los Angeles. Equally hopefully, we *would* see it at Los Angeles. (Or would it be a 'breakfast in London, dinner in LA, luggage in New York' syndrome?) Time would tell. At Gatwick, I was amazed at the television sets which changed continuously to update the flight information. Howard was used to this as he went to Gatwick very often with official visitors - either to meet them or to say 'goodbye' to them. Our flight, BR223, moved up the chart like a pop song. Half an hour before departure, the last call was made. I started to get very anxious - in case we missed it. Howard reassured me that it was quite normal for the 'last call' to be so (relatively) early and there was no need for us to rush to the departure lounge. I decided I had time to go to the loo. A lady standing near the entrance warned me "There's a man in there doing

15

maintenance, love". "I don't mind, as long as he's handsome" I quipped. When I came out, I had to admit to the same lady "He wasn't exactly Paul Newman, was he?" to which she replied, "He's my husband"…we beat a hasty retreat before I managed to 'put any more feet in it'. We were not to know there would be free newspapers on board so we stocked up with adequate reading material, including a book written by our downstairs neighbour, Alan Judd. *A Breed of Heroes* was now on sale in paperback.

The plane turned out to be a DC10. I fell to wondering what DC stood for - District of Columbia, Direct Current, *Da Capo* - would I ever know? And why 10? Are there DC9s and 11s? We rented the headphones, which offered twelve channels including pop music, comedy, sound tracks for the two in-flight films and two classical music channels. We took off to the Rachmaninov *Paganini Variations*, followed by pre-lunch drinks to the accompaniment of Brahms' *Second Symphony*. (Was this *real* or were we dreaming?) "Steak or chicken?" they asked. I suggested chicken as steak would be difficult to eat with plastic cutlery. Howard's thinking is more advanced. He concluded that the steak would *have* to be tender to cope with the plastic equipment. In the event, the cutlery turned out to be *real* - not a plastic knife or fork in sight. We feasted on steak, roast potatoes and red wine, 29,000 feet above Scotland, the Hebrides and a stretch of water, which preferred to remain anonymous. We were heading for Greenland.

We settled down to sleep until it was time for the in-flight film. We'd been going for two hours, so only nine more to go. It was strange to think that we would not have a night time. It would be 1600 (local time) when we arrived (but 2300 London time - on which we were still operating) so the whole flight would be in daylight. We asked if we could look in the cockpit (see what 'amateurs' we are when it comes to flying!) and our request was granted. Even Howard had not seen anything like this, though he was well travelled. There was not a sqare inch of 'wall' that did not have a dial, switch, knob, lever or computerized screen - but, as everything was 'on automatic', the Captain was free to explain a few things to us. Mind-boggling was the word that sprang to mind.

At the end of eleven hours, we arrived at Los Angeles at 1615 local time. To us it was midnight. Howard changed his watch so he could 'acclimate to the new schedule' straight away. Life was not so easy for me as, for some reason, I could not change my watch so I had to stay either eight hours ahead or four hours behind. Los Angeles airport was very modern as it had been 'done up' in living memory for the Olympics. But the passport queue had to be seen to be believed. We fell to thinking that we would be spending the whole three weeks in this queue. Everyone was suspected of being a terrorist (though this was twenty-five years ago!) or a smuggler - not of drugs necessarily, but of *food*.

WILD WEST - HERE WE COME!

After what seemed like one and a half lifetimes, we met up with the Thomas Cook representative and the Greyhound coach which was to take us to Anaheim - forty miles away. At the Holiday Inn, a message awaited us from Herbert, asking us to 'call collect' - which meant 'reverse the charges' in English. (What had we done with the phrase book?) The hotel was very comfortable and, after only half an hour, we had already had a heap of "Have a nice day"s - even "Have yourselves a good time"…yes, they really *did* say these things. We spent our first American money buying a stamp to post the letter to the Oettings in Scottsdale.

Saturday September 22nd

By 0800 we were breakfasting 'across the freeway'. (Breakfast did not seem to be included in American hotel reservations.) This was our first encounter with eggs 'sunny side up' or 'easy over'…and hash browns…and the bottomless coffee cup. 0830 was the time for the very thorough and informative briefing from the Thomas Cook representative, Elizabeth, after which we went straight to Disneyland, right opposite our hotel. Initially, I was not too sold on the idea, but having seen it, I was totally converted. It was unbelievable - for adults as well as children. There was so much to see and do that we could have spent the whole three weeks in this attraction alone! A selection of the things we did included 'Pirates of the Caribbean', the monorail, New Orleans Steamer, Mark Twain Riverboat, Bear Jamboree, the submarine and the Haunted House.

Back at the hotel, the 'information lady' had details of how to get to the Hollywood Bowl by bus, as we had tickets for the concert later that day. We hadn't appreciated the fact that the Hollywood Bowl was about the same distance from Los Angeles as Anaheim - but in the opposite direction! Before setting off on that big adventure, we called the Oettings and arranged to meet them on Monday. Peter Wearing, a school friend of mine from Cannock Grammar School days, was a Professor at the University of Arizona at Tucson, so we arranged to meet *him* on Tuesday.

The trip to the Hollywood Bowl was long, involving two bus journeys. (I was worrying already that we would never find our way back!) When we arrived at the concert venue, there were somewhat peculiar instructions about where we should rejoin the bus at the end of the evening - "by the fourth ivy"? No one seemed to understand this - least of all us - but with 17,000 people coming out at the same time, we knew we *had* to find the right place as the bus would only wait for twenty-five minutes. We acquired our four-dollar supper and sat, with everyone else, on a kerbstone by the roadside, to eat it. The cognoscenti had Glyndebourne-style picnics, complete with candles, tablecloths and wine. Our more meagre fare was barbecued chicken with coleslaw, a plum, and a plastic cup of root beer - something we had never before encountered and vowed never to encounter again. At long last, we were in the auditorium. I had harboured a wish to come to this place ever since I was a teenager and had bought a 'Golden Guinea' gramophone record of the Hollywood Bowl orchestra. The picture on the sleeve looked so romantic.

The concert opened with a 'performance' (I use that word loosely) of the American National Anthem. The conductor did not seem to be too well versed in his craft - and we were rather shocked. Not one first beat of a bar ever coincided with a down beat - the reason being there were no down beats, only beats that went from left to right - and back. We learned that the 'maestro' had won the chance to conduct the orchestra because he had donated a large sum of money. (We were beginning to realize how money-conscious America is.) Someone should have told him *something* about the basics of conducting - because not to put too fine a point on it, he made a fool of himself.

We breathed a huge sigh of relief when James Loughran mounted the podium and took control of the LA Philharmonic. The whole evening was full of superlatives of every kind - not least the fact that there were 17,000 people in the audience. (It was a sell-out.) The amphitheatre was very well lit and the sound, though amplified, was good. The main work in the first half of the programme was a performance of Beethoven's *Third Piano Concerto*, given by an inscrutable oriental gent. The second half was a watered-down version of the Last Night of the Proms. (I felt proud to be British, especially as I was wearing my Elgar tee shirt.) We thrilled to *Land of Hope and Glory*, *Greensleeves* and *The Royal Fireworks Music*, the latter ending with a spectacular pyrotechnic display, the fireworks going off in time to the music. Only the Americans could think of *that*.

During the last two movements of the *Fireworks Music*, we shuffled along to the exit, trying to look inconspicuous, so that, when the concert ended, we could beat the other 16,998 people to the bus. Had we missed it, a taxi back to our hotel would have cost around £80. We arrived at the Fullerton 'Park and Ride' (now commonplace in England, but new to us in 1984) at midnight. Two local people, who 'just loved our English accents', offered to drive us back to Anaheim - about five miles - because they pointed out that it might be very dangerous to do the journey by taxi (?). We were extremely grateful to them though, in retrospect, since we knew nothing at all about them, we might have been in just as much danger as if we had taken the taxi. To be fair, they seemed genuinely pleased to be able to help and kept telling us how much they *loved* our Prince of Wales. It seems that most Americans think that most British people are on first name terms with the Royal Family…

Because we had not yet bought a phrase book, we thought we should compile our own 'glossary of terms' to help us get around this vast country. Some excerpts:

Bathroom/Restroom	Toilet
Chips	Crisps
French Fries	Chips
RVs	Recreational Vehicles
Campers	Caravans
Strollers	Push Chairs (that *really* had us foxed)
Furdal	Fertile
De*bree*	Debris
De-bus (pronounced the opposite way to De*bree*)	Get off the bus
Movie	Film
Parking Lot	Car Park
Locked out	We're lucky with
Missals	Used in war - NOT prayer books
Hang a left	Turn left
One dollar	You don't get a lot for it

Sunday September 23rd

This was the day for the Universal Studios visit. We were to be driven right around the studios in the 'glamour tram'. Even allowing for the fact that everything in America is huge, this was - well - huge. We thought the site covered some few square miles. We had not gone very far when we were hijacked by aliens from another planet and forced at gunpoint into their spaceship. It looked like 'curtains' for us all but, just in the nick of time, we were rescued by a laser-toting earthling. After that narrow escape, the next stop was the Special Effects department. What we saw here was something of an eye-opener to us computer-unfriendly people. For instance, a rocket, which looked very impressive on film, turned out to be tiny - propelled by sparklers issuing from its rear end. An impressive-looking submarine in a war 'movie' had been filmed in a small fish tank. We were shown how bits of a picture could be blocked out and replaced by something else. The computer effects were endless - and, looking back on it, they were 'in their infancy' compared to what happens now. What was that about 'seeing is believing'?

Still reeling from our close encounter with the aliens and not knowing what, if anything, is real in the world of films, the next stop was the Props. Department, which housed over five *million* items. They never throw *anything* away. The film sets were next - masses of them, from Wild West towns to modern cities, to 'Jaws' … and many many more. These were the ones we saw and we got the impression that they were just the tip of the iceberg. Then the action 'hotted up' somewhat. We were attacked by a submarine, driven through a lake where the waters divided as they did for the Red Sea, over a collapsing bridge which put itself together again after it had collapsed, through an avalanche (we stayed at 180 degrees while the walls rotated - but it was very convincing) and, finally, into a tropical storm. 10,000 gallons of water were used for the tropical storm - but they were immediately recycled into a huge tank, ready for the next time. Collapsing trees sprang back into their original positions too! At the end of the Studio Tour, we were taken to the Entertainment section, to watch animal training and to learn the tricks of the trade of stunt men - rather them than us!

The last part of the day took us by bus to Hollywood town. Outside a certain cinema, over the years, film stars had put their footprints and handprints in wet concrete so they are preserved for posterity - even Roy Rogers and Trigger got in on the act. The bus took us on to Sunset Strip (remember '77'? You won't unless you are 'of a certain age' - or older), Beverley Hills (is that where the Beverley Sisters lived?) and Rodeo Drive - reputed to be the most expensive shopping area (mall?) in the world. Men's ties *started* at $100 (£80) so we didn't get any for Christmas presents. Finally, we were taken to the Hollywood Bowl (now empty and very quiet), back to City Hall, from which Superman jumped, and last of all, a little Mexican market.

Back at the hotel, we were glad of the Happy Hour - and a rest. This had been a very exhausting day, especially after the long transatlantic journey and the concert not many hours before - but we were not complaining. We knew this would be a very demanding trip - but we had come a long way to see a lot of things so we were prepared for anything.

Monday September 24th

This was to be our first day 'on the road' and there were many miles to cover - indeed 400 miles were 'scheduled' for today - from Anaheim to Phoenix and on to Scottsdale. Scottsdale is the posh part of Phoenix and we were staying in the Hilton! (We were not doing things by halves here…) The long drive took us through desert-type terrain and past an Indian reservation - where they have Bingo…another illusion shattered! (Wonder if they thought 'white man speak with forked tongue' where 'legs eleven' or 'key of the door' are concerned?) We arrived at the Hilton at 1800. The cold water was very warm but reception told us there was nothing they could do about it - it was because of the heat! The swimming pool looked inviting so we made a note to try it out. I wondered if I would be able to improve on my 'quarter of a width on a good day' record. By now, the arrangements for the next day had altered somewhat and we were to meet Peter Wearing for lunch and the Oettings for supper. To round off this long day, we ate at the *La Lunt Marble Club*. (A strange name for a restaurant, we mused.)

Tuesday September 25th

We made an early start for Tucson but just fifteen minutes out of Phoenix, it started to rain. Nothing remarkable for us, but, for the locals, for whom rain was an extremely rare event, it was good news indeed. The only snag was that there was no adequate drainage on the roads - so they flooded. Our first stop was the Sonara Desert Museum, where there was a wonderful array of plants, animals and fish. We had time for a very swift glance at a few selected exhibits only as we were due to meet Peter at 1100.

He was waiting for us, in his large, air-conditioned Pontiac car. It was so hot everywhere that everything had to have AC - as it is more commonly known. Peter took us to a Mexican restaurant for lunch. If we learned one thing from this, it was that Mexican meals tend to be 'on the large side'! For me, who has a very small appetite, it was a challenge indeed. I did my best. After lunch, Peter drove us to the University of Arizona where he taught and then to his house, where he showed us the collection of books he had written on London Theatre History up to 1929. (Since our visit, he has completed this series, bringing it up to date, and has written many more books.) It was indeed a whistle-stop tour as he drove us back to Old Tucson to rejoin the coach at 1430. On our return to Phoenix, the torrential rain continued unabated.

The Oettings arrived at our hotel at 1815 and drove us to *Garcia's* Mexican restaurant (!) - passing their church *en route* - congregation approximately 1,000. The evening began with Marguerita cocktails but I was very anxious about how I was going to cope with another Mexican meal. Mrs. Oetting chose a salad, so, thinking that would be something I could manage, I opted for the same thing. We could not have known that it was to be the most gargantuan salad either of us had ever seen. It was encased in an enormous hollowed out water melon...I tried my very best and was glad to see that our hostess had as much trouble as I did in getting through it. Both of us left a considerable amount in the hollowed out shell. This meeting gave us the chance to show the Oettings some recent photos of the Proctors and to bring them up to date with their news. At the end of the evening, we were driven back to our hotel by a route which allowed us to see the lights of Phoenix and Scottsdale.

Wednesday September 26th

The itinerary for today included Montezuma's Castle, a Sedona Jeep Tour, Pine Forests and The Grand Canyon. Our courier, Elizabeth, told us that the Sowaro cacti (of which there were many in evidence) were about one hundred years old but apparently it takes them fifteen years to grow just one foot. They act as protection for some animals who nest in them.

Montezuma's Castle was 'very old and interesting'. We recorded no more than that - so perhaps it wasn't so interesting after all (?) Who was Montezuma? Why did he have a castle here? An information vacuum, I'm afraid. The rain continued to pour down, but we put on a brave face.

Sedona proved to be a magnificently scenic location and, after lunch, we took the Jeep Tour almost to the top of the mountains - 7,000 feet. We were prohibited from reaching the actual summit as it was shrouded in cloud. We drove in and out of more cloud during our descent.

The Grand Canyon was *the* most spectacular sight we have ever seen - and have *still* ever seen to this day. We agreed that it would have been worth all the money this trip cost us just to see this one thing. It was indescribable - like trying to tell someone what the *Ninth Symphony* is like - you can't - you've got to *hear* it for yourself. With the Grand Canyon, you've got to see it. Our first sighting of it was in the wind and rain and it was very cold. Just five minutes later, and from another viewpoint, the sun was moving slowly over the landscape. It looked for all the world like a film set, being gradually illuminated by a master lighting engineer. We were convinced it was a cardboard cut-out model. The ensuing sunset was 'out of this world'. We took many photographs, one of which was so successful that we framed it and it hangs in a place of honour in our house to this day. Back at the hotel, we had steak for supper. Luckily, before we ordered, we saw the size of the steaks which others were eating and decided to have 'one between two' - and even *that* was a struggle for us. Other members of our party followed suit - the restaurant staff were none too pleased!

Thursday September 27th

Our day began with another typical American breakfast, which included bacon, eggs, hash browns, a slice of orange, and the ever-present bottomless coffee cup. (We were on holiday and this was a novelty to us, but we wondered how Americans cope with this amount of food every day...might go some way to explaining the fact that so many of them are 'on the large side'?) Next stop, the Grand Canyon airport, where we caught a nineteen-seater plane (it looked like an overgrown hairdryer) for the 217-mile journey along the length of the Canyon, to Las Vegas. The statistics about the Grand Canyon are mind-boggling. Suffice it to say it is one mile deep and its width varies from four miles at its narrowest point to eighteen miles at its widest point. The Colorado River runs along the bottom. The eighty-minute flight was fascinating and the scenery was ever-changing - bare rocks, forested areas and, finally, lakes, as we approached the end of the Canyon. This 'wonder of the world' is truly a sight to be seen.

When we landed at Las Vegas, I spotted a record of Ferde Grofé's *Grand Canyon Suite* and made a mental note to get a copy when we got home. (I fell in love with it from the very first note and it rarely left our turntable for many weeks after our return.) Grofé is one of those composers who is known for only one piece - or, in his case, one and a half pieces. The *Grand Canyon Suite* was his 'greatest hit'; his other claim to fame being that he orchestrated Gershwin's *Rhapsody in Blue*. (Never let it be said that our diaries don't have some educational element to them...) Grofé's entry in the 1960 edition of *The Oxford Companion to Music* revealed that "...he makes more money than all American symphonic composers put together".

We were taken to the Golden Nugget Hotel and our room was number 1719 - on the seventeenth floor! The swimming pool looked very inviting in view of the heat that was prevalent in these parts. We spent the afternoon there, sipping Tequila Sunrises, followed by a spell in the Jacuzzi, which was *very* hot. While we had been flying to Las Vegas, our driver, Paul, had taken the coach round the rim of the Canyon so his journey had taken much longer. Elizabeth had warned us to take our swimming things in our 'hand-carry' so we would not have to wait for the arrival of the luggage before being able to use the pool. This we had done - but what we had *not* done was remember to take the suntan lotion - an absolutely essential item in the temperatures that prevailed. The suntan lotion arrived around 1600.

Everyone was gambling - and slot machines were *everywhere* - even in the most unlikely places, like the 'restrooms'. The food and drink were 'dirt cheap' - to encourage everyone to patronize the venues. Clearly, the management made so much money from the gambling that they were able to charge 'peanuts' for the refreshments. And when we saw the amount of gambling that was happening, we could understand this. We had our first drink - $1 for anything we wanted - then ventured into a place across the street for lunch (Fremont) and had as much as we wanted from a buffet for $2-25 (approx. £1-80) - for three courses! Drinks in *this* establishment were a mere 50 cents. Apparently some people save all year to come to Las Vegas for their 'vacation' and spend the whole time playing the machines and indulging in other forms of gambling. What a waste of life!

In the evening, we went to the Flamingo Hilton (opposite the famous Caesar's Palace) for dinner and the 'City Lights' show. It was a pity there had not been enough material to finish off some of the ladies' costumes...they must have been rather chilly. A short drive around Las Vegas in our coach brought the evening to a close - almost. We decided to take a short walk around our immediate neighbourhood, just to get a 'feel' of the place on foot. We chanced our arm with one dollar on one of the thousands (really!) of fruit machines - but Lady Luck was not smiling on us so we could not afford to retire.

Our thoughts on Las Vegas? What a sad, depressing place.

Friday September 28th

The best thing you can do with Las Vegas is to leave it - so we did. What's more, we left on an empty stomach because a visit was planned to *Whisky Pete's* - in the Nevada Desert - for breakfast at 95 cents! And what a breakfast...it made all the others look like snacks. It was sheer 'death by cholesterol' - with *three* fried eggs, fried potatoes, myriads of other 'naughties', toast and unlimited coffee. To walk off the effects of this 'less than good for us' feast, we strolled around the parking lot - taking photos of the huge trucks that we had seen on our travels. We were joined by some huge beetles so, rather abruptly, we stopped strolling around the parking lot. The temperature everywhere was uncomfortably hot.

Our next stop was Calico Ghost Town - which lived up to its name - except for the Calico, of which we saw none. The temperature was now 90 degrees (Fahrenheit - we hasten to add). We had lunch in *Lil's Saloon*, a real old cowboy saloon, complete with swing doors. We half expected them to swing open and a gun-totin' type to announce "This town ain't big enough for both of us" - but it wasn't to be. Perhaps it was as well ... Outside, a large number of chipmunks waited to greet us, but lost interest when it was clear we had no food to share with them. We would have liked to have lingered in Calico - but our 'skeduel' did not allow for that.

Bakersfield was where we were to lay our heads at the end of the day. Bakersfield had nothing to commend it at all - but the Ramada was the best hotel yet. It was the complete opposite of the Golden Nugget - especially in size - and the hotel had laid on a reception for us - probably to encourage Thomas Cook to continue to use it. They could not have made us more welcome - and our windows opened on to the swimming pool.

Saturday September 29th

Our destination today was Yosemite (pronounced Yos-emm-itty, rather than rhyming with Marmite) National Park. Elizabeth told us we should "get our 'ooo's and 'aaahh's ready for this" and Nancy (a fellow traveller who had done this trip last year) seconded that. We took the bus tour along the valley floor. The 'ooo's and 'aaahh's were not long coming, with spectacular views of woods and mountains. 'El Capitaine' is the biggest granite monolith in the world. It takes about five days to climb up its sheer face. What a pity - we just didn't have those five days to spare.

Our accommodation was in Pine Lodge at Bass Lake, in pine log chalets. There was a certain amount of 'weeping and wailing and gnashing of teeth' from some members of our party. The exact reason for this eludes us at this distance of time but it was something to do with the room allocations. In all the hotels so far, we had had two double beds in each room. Here we had *three*. We were given a coupon which allowed $5 off the cost of our meal - to make up for the fact that we were not accommodated in the 'other part'. Something had gone wrong with the allocation of rooms and it was thought somewhat 'fishy' that these coupons were already prepared. An explanation was that the hotel was double-booked. We were not complaining as we were quite satisfied with our room. We ate with Joan and Harry (from Wolverhampton). Yet more steak - but this time, it was served on skewers. The restaurant was in semi darkness, which was very romantic but made it difficult to see what we were eating. (You can't have everything in this life…)

Sunday September 30th

San Francisco was today's port of call. (By now, it was getting a bit like "It's Sunday so this must be San Francisco".) The coach took us on the City Tour, followed by the Golden Gate Bridge, a sighting of Alcatraz, the Pacific Ocean - and much more. This was the only way to see all these things in the limited time available to us. We ate Pacific seafood in *Castagnolas* - a real treat for Howard for whom seafood is a particular delight.

Monday October 1st

This was a free day in San Francisco. *En route* to breakfast, in *Buena Vista*, we came across a road closed off and two burly policemen - armed to the teeth just like on TV. They told us they were making a film but we didn't know whether they were real policemen or actors. Yesterday, at the Golden Gate Bridge, we had seen a fire engine that would appear in the next James Bond film. There certainly was a Buena Vista at the breakfast place - of both food and scenery - and we could have had Irish coffee, but we eschewed it. We thought it was a *bit* early in the day - even for us.

We made our way down to Pier 39 for the seventy-five minute trip on the Blue and Gold boat. The trip took us right *under* the Golden Gate Bridge, so we were in the Pacific Ocean. We sailed round the bay (somewhat bigger than the Aberystwyth equivalent) around Alcatraz. It ceased to be a penitentiary in the 1960s, but it still looked very bleak. The commentary told us that Al Capone and his chums were 'guests' here and only five people ever escaped, though no one knew what became of them; it was thought they drowned in the attempt. It was not so much the distance from the mainland that was the problem for the escapees (though they would have to swim undetected) but the water was very, very cold. From the boat, we had excellent views of the Bay Bridge and the skyline of San Francisco.

Back on *terra firma*, we caught a cable car to Chinatown. I was very surprised at this as I was expecting something like the ones in Austria in which we would be suspended in mid air once again. (I had promised myself I would not scream this time.) These cable cars were nothing like that. They travelled along the *road*, attached to a continuously moving cable under the street. They were very 'clanky and jerky' and it seemed hard work for the driver, who had to pull back with all his weight on a handle, every time the car stopped. Stopping often took place in the middle of a crossroad - and cable cars had the right of way over all other traffic.

Chinatown did not disappoint us. It felt very Chinese as there were no Europeans (or Americans) in sight. We went to the *Golden Dragon* for lunch of Dim Sum - including Shark's Fin…The waitress didn't exhibit an enormous command of the English language and our Chinese was not all that it might have been - indeed, it might not be too far from the truth to say that it was (and still is) non-existent. Ordering was effected with lots of grinning and pointing to the menu, which was in Chinese and English. (The Chinese seem to be grinning, permanently. Funerals must be quite happy affairs.) Having fed the inner man/woman, we wended our way to the American Express offices in the financial quarter of the city - to get more money! On the way to the American Express building, we went up to the fifty-second floor of the Bank of America. We took the express lift, which was non-stop to the fortieth floor - but stopping after that. We left our stomachs behind on the twenty-sixth. On the fifty-second floor, we pretended not to notice it was a 'Members Only' place and we swanned into a very plush lounge and admired the view of San Francisco and the Bay, until a very smooth man respectfully pointed out that "it was a private club and didn't open until 1500". We couldn't imagine why he thought we weren't members - maybe it was the hats, cameras and open-neck casual appearance of us…? We professed ignorance, apologized and descended. This time, our stomachs stayed on the fifty-second floor, as it was 'express' all the way! What a wonderful thing is gravity…there was certainly a lot of it about that day.

From the American Express building, we went in search of the Hyatt Regency Hotel (with its lifts on the *outside* of the building) which we understood was the one used for shooting *Towering Inferno* - a film to which we were not attracted when we lived in a twenty-three storey tower block. We had some trouble locating the entrance so we asked a lady selling jewellery from a little street stall. She had a wonderful dog, called Angel, who was nothing but a bundle of fur. The 'love at first sight' was mutual - between us and Angel, not the jewellery seller… The lady loved our English accents - we found we only had to speak and people would go into transports of delight. She directed us to the most futuristic place we had ever seen. Classical music was playing over the tannoy system - an improvement on almost anywhere else you can think of - but why must the human race have music every minute of every day in every situation? The next thing that caught our eye was an extraordinary modern sculpture - and then we realized that the whole of the facia of the hotel was surrounded by greenery. The glass lift *didn't* go up on the outside of the building after all. It went up on the inside, but, as we ascended, we were able to watch the futuristic entrance hall receding. The lift went literally through the roof to the revolving restaurant at the top. We were not allowed to walk around, unless we were patronising it (and, at the prices they charged, we certainly were *not*) but we *were* allowed to stand and admire the view.

We returned to thank Angel's owner for her help, before embarking on a close encounter with BART - the Bay Area Rapid Transport system. This was San Francisco's answer to London's underground system, but that's where the similarity ended. They just hadn't got the hang of the graffiti on the walls and the general dirt and filth that is all part of the rich tapestry of London's system. But then, they were rather newer at it than we were, but we reckoned that they would get the idea in time. This was another futuristic experience as the whole system is run by computers - there were no human beings to be seen. Tickets were purchased from computerized machines, with instructions posted all over them. There were choices…a) if you had a ticket already…b) if you wanted to change…c) select price of ticket and proceed to 2. It was all rather threatening and woe betide you if you didn't do it! The trains themselves were *very* posh, with wall-to-wall carpets.

America is all commands: Walk! (pronounced Wark) Don't Walk! Wrong Way! Yield! (to what?) Enjoy! (or else?) Have a nice day/evening/pretty well anything! Right lane must turn right!…and, yes, the exclamation marks are theirs!

Once we had fathomed out how to buy the tickets, it was easy to find our way. It was like the Paris Métro, in that you need to find the final destination of the line - and there were only four destinations from which to choose. The BART took us to the City Center and City Hall. After a beer on the UN Plaza, we 'did' City Hall, but when we tried to get into the Museum of Modern Art, we found it was not open on Mondays. (Over the years, we made a habit of visiting places that were *closed* on the day we went there.) The Opera House wanted to remain anonymous as there seemed to be no indication that that was what the particular building contained. (That being the case, I wonder how we knew what it was, since we saw it only from the outside?) Our next stop was St Mary's Cathedral, which was *very* modern and *very* big. The guidebook told us that it was 'a fantastic example of modern architecture'. As we approached it, someone closed the only open door...but all was not lost. A sign proclaimed 'When closed, use entrance on Geary Street', which we tried to do - but every 'entrance on Geary Street' seemed firmly locked. We wandered round to the third side of the building - same notices, same situation. We wondered why they didn't have a notice which said 'Cathedral closes at 1700'.

We walked back to our hotel - a very long way indeed - but a good way to see the city. Our route took us through Polk Street, which was considered a 'not very desirable area', but we were brave. A shower was most welcome on our return to the hotel. Our feet were really complaining as they had put in some really hard work today. In the evening, we tried to locate *The Magic Pan* in Ghiardelli Square. Howard had been to a *crêperie* here ten years ago and was anxious to find it once more. We were not sure whether or not *The Magic Pan* was it - but, as it had an excellent menu, and the specials were very good, we ate there anyway. Howard had one of his very favourite things - *Crêpes St Jacques*. Both our meals were wonderful - and not expensive. To walk off our meals before bedtime, we went back to Broadway and tried to find another old haunt of Howard's, a place where his friend David Peterson had taken him ten years before. We were unsuccessful - and the area was distinctly unpleasant ('sleazy and horrid' were what we wrote about it) so the only thing to do was to get out, which we did.

Tuesday October 2nd

Once again, we patronized Pier 39 for breakfast. Two (real) policemen came for the same thing. We didn't get used to the sight of armed policemen for the whole of our trip. We met up with the other sixteen members of our party who were going to Muir Woods. To reach our destination, we drove over the Golden Gate Bridge. The woods had spectacular trees which were between 400 and 800 years old; some were 2,000 years old! We went along Bohemian Grove and Cathedral Grove with James and Danielle and ended up at the inevitable gift shop, where we bought a deer. We had met some real ones who had licked our fingers and let us stroke them. We were surprised at this as, usually, deer are so very timid and will run a mile at the approach of anyone. (Well, those in Richmond Park did when I had tried to engage them in conversation some years before.) We lunched with Tony and Rosemary in a basement of a book shop. It took forever to get our orders but, when they *did* arrive, they were *very* good and plenteous. Before returning to Fisherman's Wharf, we had time for a little rest by the Pacific Ocean - and did some bird watching.

Back in the city, we went to the *San Francisco Experience* - a 'movie' about the history of the city, including the 1906 earthquake - all to the accompaniment of a souped-up version of Mahler's *Eighth Symphony*. After our own Happy Hour (duty free drinks now running low), we dined at the *Hungry Tiger* - overlooking the bay. We saw no tigers, so they must have eaten earlier in the evening.

Wednesday October 3rd

A train ride took us to Roaring Camp, so-called because the lumbermen who worked there drank lots of whisky and got...roaring drunk. Howard asked if there were any vacancies, but they told him it was all some time ago. On to Cathedral Grove, where six or seven redwood trees grow in a circle and, looking skywards, where their branches seemingly met (they don't - it's an optical illusion), it looked like the ceiling of a cathedral. At the end of our train journey, we were provided with a steak lunch, cooked on an open range, eaten by real log fires and washed down with hot cider, serenaded the while by a folksy-guitar-playing singer - who *wasn't* so hot. For pudding we toasted our own marshmallows over the open fire. Back to the bus via a close encounter with some very tame geese, to whom we fed the spare bread. We journeyed on to Monterey and Cannery Row - the actual Cannery Row about which John Steinbeck had written. To get there we went through a fertile (pronounced 'fertul') Californian valley where artichokes, sprouts (their word for 'cress'), pumpkins and many other goodies were growing. We were told that Marilyn Monroe was the Artichoke Queen in the 1940s - but no one seemed to know what that meant, least of all us.

The last journey was along the 17-mile Drive. As our American cousins would say..."Wowee!" - or even "Real Neat"! We saw some millionaire-type residences before stopping for photos of seals, birds and squirrels - the latter were very tame and took monkey nuts out of our hands. (How come we were carrying monkey nuts?)

Our last stop was Carmel, where we left the Thomas Cook Tour and said goodbye to all the new friends we had made during the last couple of weeks. Howard's uncle and aunt, Herbert and Isabelle, were waiting for us. At last we were to see them 'in their natural habitat'. They took us back to their condominium ('Hacienda') where we had our own little apartment. When we had unpacked (the first time in two weeks because we had been travelling continuously), we joined Herbert and Isabelle for supper. It was lovely to eat in a house once again, after so many meals taken 'on the road'. Isabelle thought that the rash, which I seemed to have collected, was poison ivy.

Thursday October 4th

After a leisurely breakfast, I went to the infirmary (which was part of the condominium) where the nurse declared that my rash was insect bites and gave me medication. We did our washing in one of the launderettes - a treat as, by now, we had two weeks' worth of dirty clothes. We took coffee on the patio, then visited the hospital where Isabelle worked as a volunteer. Herbert had to return to Hacienda for a meeting of the Finance Committee so Isabelle took us to the Carmel Mission - very old and interesting - thence to the supermarket for the first of many hunts for the skin cream that I had promised to find for a friend in London.

Friday October 5th

As we drove to Carmel Beach and Point Lobos, we spared a thought for our Thomas Cook friends who would be heading back to England today. At the beach we watched wonderful breakers in the Pacific Ocean and walked in the egg-timer-like sand, as far as the shore - and paddled. For posterity, I took a photograph of my feet standing in the Pacific Ocean, though how anyone could identify that it was that particular body of water, I was (and am) not sure. At Point Lobos we met some divers and pestered them with lots of questions about diving. They had been down to seventy-five feet and had been in the water for thirty-seven minutes.

Back to Hacienda for lunch on the patio (was this all a dream - it was so warm?) and, after a suitable interval, Isabelle joined us in the swimming pool. The afternoon passed with lots of lying in the sun and reading our books, before making short work of steak in the Hacienda restaurant in the evening. (Steak had certainly featured prominently on this trip.)

Saturday October 6th

A bus journey to Nepenthe (sounds like something you would rub on your chest for a cold) took us along the cliff top, a bit too near the edge for comfort. Clouds separated us from the sea for part of the trip. It was good that we did this journey by bus because, if Herbert had driven, he would not have been able to enjoy the scenery - which was in the 'not to be missed' category. After lunch in the open air, we took the bus back to Monterey where Isabelle and I made another attempt to track down the elusive skin cream, while Herbert and Howard picked up the car. There was some confusion about where we had arranged to meet. The ladies were *sure* it was Lucky's while the gentlemen were *sure* it was Thrifty's - so we waited for each other in different parts of the parking lot. On the way back to Hacienda we were taken to see Herbert's church, before returning for more sunbathing and swimming. Herbert attended the Episcopal Church and Isabelle the Roman Catholic one. In the evening, we went to an 'ethnic supper' at Herbert's church, where the Reverend Doctor Charles Taylor talked about stewardship. (Nothing changes, does it...)

Sunday October 7th

Isabelle's birthday - so there was much excitement. We had taken a present from England - a table mat made of Nottingham lace and a tea towel showing historical sites in Britain. We went to the Episcopal Church with Herbert while Isabelle went to the Carmel Mission. After lunch on the patio, when the temperature crept up to 80F, there was more swimming, but when the temperature dropped to 70F, the other swimmers rushed for their bathrobes - and shivered. They thought we were quaint because we remained in the sun, reading our books. 70F to them was 'quite nippy'.

In the evening, we donned our best clothes (such as we had with us) for dinner at the Country Club, Herbert's Golf Course. An excellent meal was provided to celebrate Isabelle's birthday and, at the end of the evening, we even danced a little. I didn't have suitable shoes for dancing (and, even if I had, I am no Ginger Rogers) but I gave it a whirl with the best of them.

Monday October 8th

We did some gift shopping in Carmel before setting out on the 17-Mile Drive once more. Our route took in the Pebble Beach Golf Course (which we had seen so many times on British television). We had a sandwich lunch at Pacific Grove and the rest of the day was spent relaxing. Though this might not seem very exciting, after the long travels we had done with the Thomas Cook tour, we needed to recharge our batteries - not least to prepare for the long journey home, which was not far distant.

Tuesday October 9th

We returned to Carmel for some window-shopping and, more importantly, to get our 'thank you' present for Herbert and Isabelle. We took the Hacienda bus into town so that we could shop on our own and buy the present, which we would present to them on our last evening. We arranged to meet at noon for a picnic - which we arranged. Herbert and Isabelle had told us where the relevant food stores were located where we could purchase the wherewithal for lunch. With difficulty, we remembered where we had seen the shop from which we bought the jade vase, the present for our hosts.

We met up at noon and, as Herbert predicted, had a 'sand sandwich'. It was beautiful white Pacific sand though, so we could not complain...After lunch, we had another Pacific walk-about before driving to the Carmel Valley. At suppertime, we had 'squash', which, to our surprise, turned out to be a vegetable. (We were expecting a fruit drink!) This squash was acorn and banana flavour (eaten with butter and sugar), with an accompaniment of orange jelly and veal. A fresh fruit salad ended the repast - and the day.

Wednesday October 10th

We returned to Monterey in the morning, where we fed the sea lions (what a noise they made!) with real sea lion food purchased at an adjacent shop. The Greyhound station was our next port of call as we had to buy our tickets for the bus the next day. We found it hard to believe that this was our last day in this idyllic place. In the afternoon, we did our final sunbathing and swimming - not a moment too soon as, at 1640, the swimming pool was covered - because it was getting cold!

We took advantage of the launderette once again and washed our clothes so that we would have clean things when we arrived home. Our final meal with Herbert and Isabelle was pork chops with peppers and rice and carrot salad (must make it), followed by cake, ice cream and sparkling wine. They had spoilt us 'something rotten' for a whole week! Our gift of the jade vase was much appreciated by our hosts.

We retired early, having done 'the big pack', because the next day we would start on the return trip and would be 'in transit' for two days and nights - one of which would be on the plane, when we knew we would not get proper sleep.

Thursday October 11th

All good things must come to an end and we left Hacienda at 0930 to drive to Monterey to pick up the Greyhound bus at 1015. We had to change at Salinas (I worried whether our luggage had changed with us) and from there we headed for Santa Barbara. The El Prado Motel was just a few blocks from the Greyhound bus station. Having deposited our worldly goods, we took a long walk to the ocean and another *Castagnolas Lobster House*. We didn't think it was *quite* as posh as the one in San Francisco but there *were* live lobsters in a tank! Howard had a whole lobster…while I had a more modest portion of fresh salmon. It was a memorable meal and our view from the restaurant was of the moonlit Pacific Ocean. It was very romantic. Another early night, to prepare for the last and longest leg of the return journey.

Friday October 12th

Fortified by breakfast in a little Mexican restaurant opposite the Greyhound terminus, we boarded our Greyhound bus for Los Angeles. Some American ladies were so thrilled that we were English. The dialogue went something like this: "Which Queen was it I saw some years ago? I went to a castle with Henry Eight written above it when I was last in England. Where would that have been? I think the Queen goes there." We suggested Windsor.

In Los Angeles we took another bus to the airport, where we arrived in very good time. I breathed sighs of relief as I always worry about missing things….We made some duty free purchases but we were given a receipt for them, not the goods themselves. We were told that they would be given to us either when we got to London or maybe 'in flight' after Dallas. Dallas? Why Dallas?

Surprise, surprise, as soon as we took off we were told we were going to Dallas. They said it was due to mechanical things with the plane - but we suspected that it was more to do with the fact that the plane was not fully booked. We took off to Brahms *Second Symphony*. (Seemed to remember that from the outward journey.) Soon, there was sunset behind us and night time ahead. (If those early sailors could have flown, they would have known the world was round!) We stopped for one hour in Dallas and, though we were not allowed to leave the aircraft, we could walk around, as the plane was empty. As time for take-off approached, the plane filled up with a large party of Americans heading for England for a vacation…our suspicions were proved right.

Another snack arrived, but it was too soon after the last one for me so I eschewed it. We slept through the film and, when we awoke, dawn was breaking. First it was just a glimmer of light but we watched it through to the full sunrise when it became much too bright for comfort. In no time at all, Gatwick was just ahead - so too was disembarkation (de-plane?) and all that that involved. As we had not left our return rail ticket in the States, we took a train into London and a taxi to Kennington. Though we had enjoyed every minute of this marathon trip, it was just wonderful to be home.

"We went round the world last year but didn't like it"

TO THE DORDOGNE
or
HOW WE SOLVED THE PROBLEM OF THE EEC WINE LAKE...
WE DRANK IT!
September - October 1985

This holiday was shared with a few friends. We travelled by car, with Janet. We were to stay in *La Tourette*, St Julien de Lampon, Dordogne, in a spacious stone-built eighteenth-century farmhouse, which we rented from the Laws, some friends of Howard. The house was about one mile from the village of St Julien de Lampon and adjacent to a farm. The fact sheet about the house told us "The village of St Julien de Lampon has two good grocers, a butcher, two bakers, a bank, a modern chemist's shop and a resident doctor. Excellent shops abound in Sarlat (15 km) and Souillac (12 km) and there are plenty of good cheap restaurants in the area." (It all sounded too good to be true.) Joy Law had written a book about the area (*Dordogne*: Macdonald Futura 1981 ISBN 354 04602 0). We took a copy with us.

Friday September 27th

It was a working day so we could not leave until 1830 but we arrived in Portsmouth by 2100. For once we were too early (a very unusual occurrence for Janet, who was known to all as 'the late Miss Wells') so we patronized a very welcoming-looking nearby pub, advertising meals - which we wanted. What a mistake! It was most *unwelcoming* and we were told that it was impossible to get a meal in a short time as they were all 'freshly cooked'. To add insult to injury, we were 'shooed out' of the eating area by the unfriendly landlord for even contemplating entering the 'holy of holies', where other mortals were actually eating. Downcast, we returned to the port and joined the queue to board the car ferry. Our food cravings were satisfied very soon by some fish and chips. After a swift turn round on deck, we headed for bed; it had been a long day. Our sleeping accommodation contained four berths so we had more room than is usual on these occasions. A view of the English Channel from our porthole induced sleep in a very few minutes.

Saturday September 28th

Dawn was breaking as we disembarked at Le Havre. This was Janet's first experience of driving on the other side of the road - so the mantra for the fortnight became *Think Right*.

We set out for Chartres in an abundance of fog. Our first stop was Pont Audemer, where we purchased the wherewithal for a picnic at lunchtime - bread,

Livarot cheese and Normandy Cider. (The Livarot cheese continued to make its presence felt for the next two days.)

The Cathedral at Chartres was as wonderful as we had been led to believe. My boss, Canon Eric James, had asked us to locate the statue of John the Baptist. We *thought* we had found it, so we took photographs - but a nagging doubt remained - was this *really* the one? (There was another that *could* have fitted his description.) The sun was streaming through the stained glass as we entered the Cathedral; we could not have seen it at a better time. It was quite breathtaking. We went into the book shop and checked in a guidebook that we had identified the correct statue - and we had. Clever us! We bought some postcards of it for Eric, just in case our photographs did not come out properly.

We ate our picnic in the Cathedral gardens; it was exceptionally hot. The Normandy Cider was very disappointing. The bottle was wired up, like champagne, but the taste was anything but champagne-like. We didn't think it was even very cider-like. We would have taken it back to the shop - but it was a long way back to Pont Audemer. We had to give it the benefit of the doubt and say that was how it was *supposed* to taste - so we put it down to 'local colour'.

Our route took us towards Chenonceau by way of Amboise. We saw the château at Amboise and remembered that, in days gone by, the severed heads of dissidents were displayed on the outside, to deter other like-minded souls. (We didn't *think* they still did this in 1985.) We arrived at Chenonceau with just forty-five minutes to closing time, so there was just time to look around. It was small, as châteaux go, and we took all the standard pictures of the reflections…they were so attractive, we couldn't resist them.

Our overnight stop was the Hotel Colbert in Tours, which Howard had researched in one of his many books on the subject. Though we were exhausted from walking round Chartres and Chenonceau, we just had to wander down to the Cathedral to see it illuminated. Howard and I had lovely memories of it from a few years before - and the music in the Archbishop's garden. Sadly, on this occasion, the building was swathed in scaffolding for much of its height…bit like 'closed on Mondays'. Following the advice of our hotel manager, we headed for the Place Plumereau, which was full of restaurants. We sat outside *Le Tournedos* and had some supper, while watching the world go by. There can be few more pleasant ways of spending an evening…

Sunday September 29th

Breakfast was taken *au jardin*, where we made the acquaintance of the resident dog, Miké. Before leaving Tours, we made another trip to the Cathedral for a look inside. There was especially lovely stained glass in the south transept, though now we compared everything with Chartres. There was an enormous organ too, but no postcards or information which we could collect for CP.

After our 'cultural fix', we were back on the road to the Dordogne. We stopped for lunch at Bellac, a 'dead and alive' (mostly dead) place if ever we saw one. Possibilities for food didn't look too promising until we met an old English sheepdog, whose owner told us of a very good restaurant about two kilomètres along the Poitiers road. The canine's owner was not wrong. We treated ourselves to a very good meal at his recommendation - and Howard had his first snails of the trip. The temperature was in the 90s when we left.

Back on the road, and refreshed by our excellent meal, we came upon Hautefort, the site of a picturesque château high on the side of a hill. (Perhaps that's why it was called Hautefort?) Around 1900, we arrived at our destination, *La Tourette*. Howard's family had stayed there some years before, when it had been rather primitive. It was much more user-friendly now. Our friends Joe and Edna were already there…and it was like a dream come true. They had discovered where everything switched on and they had a meal ready for us. We were very hot, sticky and tired, so the sight of food was just perfect. After a refreshing shower, supper was shared with Joe and Edna with much note-swapping about our respective journeys. They, too, had been at Chartres on Saturday lunchtime.

Monday September 30th

Joe and Edna cycled into St Julien for the breakfast baguettes but, when we tasted them, they were very hard - the previous day's, perhaps? Joe and Edna were very disappointed, but we ate them anyway! After breakfast, Howard, Janet and I walked into St Julien to do shopping for supper. (The arrangement was that we would take it in turns to prepare the meals each day.) It was not the best day to have chosen for the exercise. The butcher was not open, the bank was not open and there was no shoe-mender in the village, so Jo's sandal could not be repaired. We did succeed in getting a large quantity of wine and some paella for supper. (Not typically French, we thought, but in the absence of other things, beggars could not be choosers.) Then it dawned on us just how far back it was to the farmhouse where we were staying. The bag with the wine became heavier and heavier, so we took it in turns to carry it back up the long hill. The suggestion that we should sit at the roadside and drink some of it fell on deaf ears.

We got back to the house in time for our first salad lunch on the patio, after which everyone retired to different parts of the estate, ostensibly to read - but sleeping took over. Aperitifs on the patio (everything happened on the patio -

the weather was so good) preceded the paella supper. The phone rang - what a surprise! Who could it be? We had left the number with friends back home, in case of emergency - but it was a bit early to be having the first one! It turned out to be Megan and Joyce, two friends from London who were to join our party on Wednesday evening. We turned in for an early night as we were on baguette and milk duty the next morning.

Tuesday October 1st

We set off for the baker's at 0730 - but it was nowhere to be seen. The local baker, which only the day before had displayed a notice telling the world that it had changed hands and that the new owners would be starting 'today', now displayed a subsequent notice to the effect that they were not opening until the following *Tuesday*. We had to wait for supplies of bread to be delivered to the *alimentation*. At 0825, we set off up the hill, bread in hand, past a motley collection of dogs, all of whom barked at us. One howled from the comfort of a sun-lounger, another barked at the top of the valley and the echo of his bark could be heard for miles around. We rather thought he did it to impress himself with his own barking. He certainly impressed us.

We knew the others would be wondering what had become of us, but there was no way we could let them know. Our way led to the farm to collect the milk - fresh from the cows. The farmer's wife, Madame Jayle, said something to us but it was at such a rapid pace that neither of us understood it. On the 'action replay', we thought that *'l'homme'* was in the *'grange des vaches'* a few metres up the road. The smell had to be smelled to be believed - but our milk was awaiting collection in its jug, so we handed over four francs - for two litres of milk. Now breakfast could start…

We set out for Groléjac as Joe thought we might be able to use the swimming pool at the camp site there. Doubtless we could have done, if we didn't mind not getting wet. There was no one at the camp site and the swimming pool had been drained. A sign told us *'fermé pour l'hiver'*. *Quel dommage!*

We went on to Sarlat where we stocked up with wine and food for that evening and had time to look into their cathedral. It was a very disappointing site. It was musty and damp and generally looked 'uncared-for'. One of the paintings was hanging out of its frame. There was a small organ displaying a sign that it had been 'damaged by vandals'. The big organ had much to commend it, according to all the information pasted on the door to the organ loft; but, sadly, no information which we could take with us.

We picnicked by the river, before going to Domme - a walled town on a hill, reminiscent of Winchelsea in East Sussex. It was very pretty, with panoramic views in every direction. (Perhaps Winchelsea should be twinned with Domme?) We might have seen some caves, but they were…closed.

Back at *La Tourette*, we had to do something to the clocks (put them on or back?) before tucking into our pork chop and apple supper.

Wednesday October 2nd

Megan and Joyce were due to arrive this evening. Before this, we visited Souillac to buy our picnic for lunch and to look in their church. The Seven Deadly Sins were carved into the West Door - that put us off a bit…When we got back to *La Tourette*, a lawn-mower (*tondeuse de gazon*) delivery man arrived. Joy Law had left us a note to say we should expect him. We did our best to hijack him so we could practice our French but he couldn't stay and he had already had his lunch. So we just read and slept instead…

At 1745, I went to sit by the gate to await the arrival of Megan and Joyce, though Joe had made a big chalk sign on a board reading 'Megan this way'. At that moment, Joe and Edna returned from a bike ride and Edna gave me a lesson in bike-riding. I was still at the stage of trying to stay on the bike when Megan and Joyce appeared. This was fortuitous for Edna and probably saved her bike from a fate worse than death - not to mention Edna who was clinging to it and me for dear life. (The *Tour de France* would have to wait for a few years, I feared.) Supper was a wonderful Boeuf Bourgignon, prepared by Joe, Edna and Janet.

Thursday October 3rd

It was our turn to do the bread and milk collection once again - but we were too late for the milk. The cows only happened at predetermined times - but there was a new-born calf in the *grange des vaches*. It stood on wobbly legs, looking puzzled by the world…don't we all?

The rest of the day was spent lazing by the river, though some of our party went to Roufillac to see a leather and fur shop. Supper was taken at *Le Grilladin* at Groléjac, where we had an excellent meal for fifty francs - though it was generally agreed there were too many courses for comfort…

Friday October 4th

Megan and Joyce did the baguette run and found it was further up the hill than *they* had thought too! Today's visit was to be to the prehistoric Caves of Lascaux. The actual caves are so precious that only five people a day for five days a week are allowed into them. It was discovered that lots of people breathing on the prehistoric cave drawings were causing them to deteriorate, so a second cave was built nearby - Lascaux II - and there the public *is* allowed to visit. The visit would have been much more fascinating in English as the French guide spoke much too quickly for most of us, though he was very enthusiastic and the commentary was accompanied by much arm-waving. Megan was quick to decide that she *wouldn't* take up the study of ancient cave drawings when she retired.

Eager for culture today, we went on to *Les Eyzies* - more very old caves, this time full of stalagmites and stalactites - and statues of Neanderthal and Cro-Magnon man.

Our barbecued pork chop and chestnut supper was interrupted by a thunderstorm. It was *very* exciting and I stood outside in the heavy rain, watching the lightning and making sure the fire was out. The others thought I was doing a rain dance, so I didn't disabuse them. It was all very elemental...

Saturday October 5th

We went to Sarlat today and divided our forces. Janet, Joe and Edna did food shopping while Megan, Joyce, Howard and I searched for a place for Sunday lunch. It was essential to book as the French go out *en famille* for this meal and it would have been difficult to find somewhere 'on spec'. In a very quiet corner, we found the most marvellous little gift shop where we bought rings and a nutmeg grater.

The shopping had included the lunch time picnic which was demolished at a picturesque spot by the river. By now, I was more than engrossed in a book about Wagner. The others were learning snippets about him too, from time to time, as I found out more and more extraordinary things about this extraordinary man. What an odd bod! But did it matter - if he could pen little gems like *Tristan*?

Before supper, we had a little adventure with the *machine à lavage*. The instructions were in French (no surprise there) but we thought we had understood them. The snag was that the washing powder we had brought with us from England was completely wrong for this kind of front-loading machine and Edna assured us that it would wreak havoc with everything if we used it. Joe and Howard were dispatched to the *alimentation* to procure a more suitable brand. It was called 'Skip' and the instructions told us that 'one jar of ordinary mustard (150 ml) was sufficient for one load'. We knew they did things differently in France but we thought this was going a bit far...but we did what we were told...

Sunday October 6th

We went to Sarlat Cathedral at 1100 for the morning service, which turned out to be just like Series 3 at home - even including *La Paix*! The music was very undisciplined. A lady 'directed' the congregation in the responses, using both arms in the manner of a tic-tac man. At the end of the service, we were treated to a nifty bit of JSB and heard the organ 'in the fullness of its glory'. *Still* no information or photos to take back for CP.

Our reward for our church attendance was to sit outside in the sun at one of the many cafés and sip Pernod, until it was time to set forth for the *Auberge de Salamandre* for lunch. Joe and Edna (who had not been to church) were waiting for us. It was a very attractive restaurant with pretty table decorations of real flowers. The food was equally attractive.

Having satisfied the inner man/woman, we moved on to Beynac Castle where we went round with a guide (in French) but with a leaflet in English. Afterwards, a very steep descent and on to Roque Gageac, where we sat on a wall by the river for drinks. Another steep climb took us to the local church, then back home by way of delightful scenery. Supper was artichokes.....were they worth the bother? The general opinion seemed to be that they were overrated.

Monday October 7th

Megan and Joyce left today as they wanted to explore further east and they had to be back at Bordeaux by Sunday. The rest of us picnicked again by the river and, because it was very hot, we were very red - not sunburnt exactly, but nicely sautéed.

Our visit today was to the Château Fénelon, where a French lady took our money, gave us tickets and told us to proceed 'up there' to the gate, which we dutifully did. We waited - and, after a while, the same lady joined us - and asked us for our tickets…She turned out to be the guide and, since we were the only visitors, we had her all to ourselves. Though she spoke quite quickly, we were able to ask her questions or to repeat things more slowly. The château (which was inhabited, though the owners were away) housed a small car museum where old Rolls Royces and Bugatis were on display.

The rest of the day was spent relaxing in the wonderful weather.

Tuesday October 8th

Some went exploring *à bicyclette et à pied* while the rest of us went to Rocamadour, which lived up to its reputation. As we approached, on the Hospitalet Road, there were wonderful panoramic views of the town, set into the hillside. Parking was none too easy but we managed - and then watched in awe as a coach driver turned his huge coach round by the town gate…We went up the Pilgrims' Staircase which, we were told, in the olden days, the pilgrims went up on their knees! It was as much as we could do to go up on our feet…but our

41

destination was the same, the *Vierge Noir de Rocamadour,* which was very old and very venerated. Also here was the site where the body of Zaccheus was found. (?) The *Chemin de la Croix* took us past all the Stations of the Cross, each one carved in a huge stone edifice about ten feet tall. The final one was set in a sepulchre - with life-sized figures. At the top was not only a wonderful view (there were so many of these in these parts) but also the Cross of Jerusalem. This was altogether a very impressive place indeed and we were glad to have visited.

Our next stop was the *Gouffre de Padirac,* more prehistoric underground caverns. We descended by way of a series of lifts, followed by a long walk, through damp walkways which got damper all the time (we might even have called them 'wet') until we arrived at the boats. Eleven people (mostly three in a row) could get into the boats and it was a spooky thought indeed that we would have been in complete darkness (deep underground) had it not been for the electric lights that had been installed. When Monsieur Martel discovered it, it must have been 'quite something'. No wonder he went out and discovered brandy next - he must have needed it! There was another walk at the other end, with a French guide, and between us we thought we had worked out what he was saying. The whole experience was 'out of this world' - both metaphorically and physically.

Back above ground and at Megan's recommendation, we visited Carennac, mainly for the roofs. It turned out to be a good recommendation. Carennac also had a Norman church with a very impressive tympanum. The little town was absolutely deserted - and, consequently, very quiet - and beautiful.

Wednesday October 9th

Our destination today was Bergerac, a journey of sixty miles, by way of a lovely pottery, where we bought *lots* of things. In Bergerac, I was very brave and went into an automatic loo. That was a new experience for me, and others of the party vowed they would never use one - too claustrophobic, frightened of getting locked in...It served its purpose and was very clean and hygienic - but I could not see how to flush it. In the end, I had to give up the unequal struggle and, as I went out, two things happened. The first was that the loo flushed itself and cleaned itself automatically with all sorts of jets of water here and brushes there. The second was that the remainder of the party had decided that this historic event should be captured on film, so, as I came out, I was met by a battery of cameras. It was a 'first' after all, so deserved a photographic record.

We had to see the statue of Cyrano de Bergerac and we sought in vain for a statue of John Nettles - but the weather was not kind to us. The rain got heavier and heavier - the first day that the weather had cramped our style. We decided that discretion was the better part of getting soaking wet, so we made our way back to *La Tourette*, where we occupied ourselves with various activities - indoors. Howard began to plan the route back to England as we were due to set off in two days' time. Supper was pork chops and cabbage, prepared by the master chefs Joe and Howard, followed by Instant Death, prepared by Jane - what can one say?

Thursday October 10th

Howard and I did the baguette run (or *walk* to be more accurate) and we were followed all the way by a magpie. This little feathered friend had hitched a lift on a bike when Janet and Joe had done the same journey on a previous morning. The theory was that it was attracted by Joe's bald patch! Our main task for today was to clean up the house in preparation for our departure. It was very nostalgic to have a bonfire (something we never did in London) and all burnable rubbish was burned on the barbecue fire. We didn't want to use the newly cleaned kitchen again so we lunched in Sarlat after doing some last-minute shopping (mainly for wine). The open air restaurant brought us *two* helpings of soup and *two* helpings of potatoes. We never did find out why - we just ate them. The rest of the day was spent quietly in the sun - our last opportunity.

Friday October 11th

We were packed and off by 0745. Following Howard's carefully planned itinerary, our first stop was Brive, where we had breakfast and bought things for our lunch time picnic. Onward to Argenton where we stopped, unknowingly, behind a factory. The owner said we could picnic there as long as we didn't leave any rubbish (as if we would!). Our overnight stop was at the Hotel Olympia, in Bourges. We set off to explore the Palais de Jacques Coeur and the Cathedral. As the next tour of the Palais was at 1710, we had half an hour to pop into the Cathedral. It had an amazing front door, and, inside, there was lots of glass - not quite comparable to Chartres, but getting on that way. Again there was a very large organ but it preferred to remain anonymous as we could find no information about it. Back at the Palais de Jacques Coeur, we had a guided tour - in French - but Howard found some English translations which seemed to be word for word what the guide was saying in French.

We had a very long walk around the town to find somewhere for supper. For a French town, it seemed to be rather lacking in places to eat until we found a small square, packed with restaurants. We went back to the hotel to recover our equilibrium as we had been walking for three hours. The meal was 'worth the wait' - especially as it included real French onion soup.

Saturday October 12th

After breakfast in the hotel, we were back on the road, stopping at a supermarket for essential picnic supplies and the odd bit of impulse buying - including some Coquille St Jacques. Our picnic was taken at Chartres once again and we had one last look into the Cathedral before setting off for Le Havre, where we would catch the ferry for England. There was time for a last meal in France and Howard had researched a restaurant in one of his many books. We had some difficulty finding it until we realized it had changed its name! The meal was a treat, lamb chops with the thinnest, most delicious chips we'd ever encountered.

We boarded the ferry at 2030 and all five of us shared a cabin! No mean feat...

Sunday October 13th

Howard was first from his bed - at 0500. It was quite tricky - and a logistical puzzle - for five of us to wash and dress in a confined space, but we managed. Very soon, we had our first sighting of Portsmouth. At 0730 we said our goodbyes to Joe and Edna as we rejoined our cars for disembarkation. We had promised ourselves bacon and eggs as soon as we saw a suitable café so it was with sighs of relief that a Happy Eater hove into view. Not only were the bacon and eggs a real treat, but the first cup of English tea got high marks too.

We arrived back in Kennington at 1100 - just in time to have missed church, but we can't have everything in this life, can we?

LE HAVRE AND ITS ENVIRONS
March 1986

The plan was to travel by ferry to Le Havre and explore the area 'round about'. There had been a drama the day before we were due to leave when Townsend Thoresen phoned to say that, due to a twenty-four hour seamen's strike, we would not be able to go on Thursday night at 2300 - as the strike was not due to end until midnight. After a number of frustrating phone calls, speaking to recorded voices and being cut off, eventually I was told that we were booked on the 0900 ferry the next day - but it would be going to Cherbourg, not Le Havre, adding an additional 140 miles to our journey!

On Thursday, Howard spent his lunch hour at the offices of Townsend Thoresen, then rang me to say *the original plan had been reinstated* and, after all, we *would* be going at 2300 that night. I phoned our travelling companions, Janet and Mary, to put them on 'red alert', in case they were busy making some alternative plans for the evening.

We were on the way to Portsmouth by 1830 and our overnight ferry landed us at Le Havre at 0700. We left our luggage at the hotel and, since we couldn't check in until midday, we set off for Fécamp, the home of Bénédictine. The weather was perfect - warm and sunny - and our way took us via Etretat, a beautiful coastal place with equally beautiful views, many of which we photographed. We went up a little hill to look at the church perched on top (no surprise, it was locked...) so, like the Duke of York, we went right down again.

At Fécamp, we purchased our picnic and sat in the sun near the harbour to consume lots of lovely French bread and cheese, washed down with lots of equally lovely French wine. The only things we had been unable to get at the *alimentation* were tomatoes. Imagine my delight when I saw a little shop advertising *légumes*. I emerged from it clutching my prize - but my joy was short-lived. The tomatoes were not very nice at all - even mouldy in parts...but it was a small blot on the landscape of our happiness.

Feeling refreshed in body and mind, we felt we should now attend to the spirit, so we set off in search of the church. Had we not checked with a passer-by, we would have spent ages admiring the wrong church. We found the right one and entered by a side door. From there it was a dozen steps down into the body of the church. The view from the west door to the high altar was very impressive and, much to my surprise, my photograph came out quite well. (My small camera was not very good at taking indoor scenes in indifferent illumination.) There was much to see in this church and, even as we were discovering everything, the great west door opened. We thought there was going to be a funeral - or they were bringing a body to lie in the church - but nothing materialized and we never did find out.

We went to the top of the cliff where we made short work of the pudding from our picnic then looked into another very pretty church, again perched atop the cliff. It was filled with wreaths for sailors and we decided it was all to do with a recent French ship, which had been lost at sea in a gale.

We returned to Fécamp and to the Bénédictine-making place - and the monks. On arrival, we discovered it was *closed* for another week - after which time it would open for the season. We discovered that the brew is no longer made by the monks; it is a commercial enterprise now. The building where it happened was very ornate and really rather horrid...so we drove back to Le Havre and checked into our rooms in the Hotel Mercure, a three-star place. Bearing in mind we had paid £60 each for three nights - that included the crossing, the cabin on the ferry and the car - we didn't think we'd done too badly, as rooms in the Mercure were £35 a night - £45 if you had a *Chambre d'Angle*. We never did discover what that meant but our room must have *been* one as that was the price quoted on the back of our door. (Could it have meant a corner room?) Howard's inexhaustible store of travel books suggested a good eating place for supper - and we were not disappointed.

The next day, we went to Honfleur, a little fishing village recommended by Eric James. He told us how very picturesque it was and how we 'mustn't miss it'. I thought 'his name will be mud if, having gone all that way, we thought it was nothing to write home about' - but I needn't have worried. We all agreed it was a delightful place - as our photos of lots of sailing ships in the basin testify. On the way to Honfleur, we turned off the road and drove over a very muddy and uneven lane to the estuary of the river. A very large boat was going by and it was very reminiscent of Rye Harbour where I had been recently with the Proctors. We decided we should walk back to the main road, leaving Janet to drive her car alone, as we felt the added weight of the three of us might not be good for the suspension, tyres or nerves...

Honfleur is reputed to be inhabited by artists but we saw only one - painting at his window. We took the others 'as read'. I thought we would find a little square like that in Montmartre in Paris, but it was not to be. We patronized the market and wandered about drinking in the local colour - and, eventually, the local wine. There were two exceedingly interesting churches but we knew before we got there that they would be closed...we were right. Both of them opened 'later that day' but our timetable didn't allow us to stay. We had read about them -

one was wooden and the other was in the shape of two ships' hulls inside. Bearing in mind how much time was left on the parking meter, we bought some take-away *crêpes* (filled with ham and eggs) and *frites* and sat dangling our legs over the side of the *bassin* in the *plein soleil* to eat them. Our final task in Honfleur was to buy a card for Eric, a souvenir of one of his favourite places. His birthday was not far away; we thought it could be an original birthday card.

After Honfleur, we made our way to Bayeux to see the famous tapestry. We took the scenic route, dawdling along the coast and, after a while, decided to stop for ice cream and a walk along the sandy beach. Howard and I were appointed ice cream monitors so we set off in search. We had walked for quite some time and had no success. Eventually we found a bar and it did, indeed, sell ice cream - but not to take away. As Janet and Mary were, by now, far distant, we had to return empty-handed.

Time was getting on so we continued on the main road to the Bayeux Tapestry. As we approached, there were numerous signs indicating its location. Obviously it was a big 'crowd-puller' hereabouts - not surprising as it is world famous. Before the sighting of the tapestry itself, there was an interesting exhibition telling us all about it. The Tapestry is about 2'6" wide (high?) and very very long. It was displayed in one continuous piece which 'went round corners' so that the whole thing could be housed in one building. It was behind glass and kept at a constant temperature - like original manuscripts. (We were surprised to find some very *rude* bits on it - but we averted our gaze and concentrated on the aesthetic bits!) Needless to say, the Way Out from the Tapestry took us straight into the gift shop where most of the 'gifts' were very expensive. We settled for an odd postcard or two. There were cushions and cloths to embroider, featuring scenes from the Tapestry, but, despite my prowess as an embroiderer many years ago, it is not something I could tackle now because of my eyesight.

Having 'done' the Tapestry, there was time for a quick look in the Cathedral. It was *very* cold - but there was a large notice board all about the organ - including five photos of the console and an advertisement for a forthcoming organ recital. Our hopes rose, but not by very much. We found a tiny postcard stall, manned by a tiny elderly lady. We managed to get an organ postcard, in the nick of time, because, one minute later, the elderly lady closed her little shopette. Howard and I found two gift shops near the Cathedral and, as was usually the case, some things were cheap and not very attractive and the attractive things were *very* expensive. We did not patronize either of them.

Our next stop was a supermarket as we were in search of some spices for a friend back home. We found a Co-op (of all things) whose sign on the door proclaimed 'No dogs allowed'. This did not surprise us…but what *did* surprise us was that a little bulldog greeted us as we entered. He made a rather feeble attempt at barking and looking fierce, but he wasn't very good at it, so resorted to trying to lick us to death. No luck with the spices but we did get some very good French cheese. In an adjacent pedestrian precinct, we found a shop that sold spices and we paid 'through the nose' for them. They were all spices that could have been bought in England (thyme, parsley, rosemary etc.) but our friend had been very keen that we should buy them in France - so we did as bidden.

As we travelled back to Le Havre, darkness fell and, though Janet was doing well driving 'on the wrong side of the road', she would have preferred the journey to have been completed in daylight. We had supper at another of Howard's 'finds' from his guide books.

On Sunday we went to Rouen. First we had a large breakfast from a rather sumptuous buffet of cereal, fruit juice, ham, eggs, stewed fruit, fresh fruit, French bread, croissants, cheese….the choices seemed endless. We arrived at Rouen Cathedral just as the service was ending. We caught the end of 'something choral' sung by an indifferent choir, then there were the notices and, suddenly it was all over. The speed at which the congregation left the church was extraordinary. It seemed to take about ten seconds to clear the Cathedral. No 'final quiet prayer' here - and we were among the few who remained. We stayed because the organist had 'struck up' and, though he played something very slow, lugubrious and minor, it did show off the machine to advantage. We reflected on how sad it was that his 'audience' was we four English people, plus one and a half locals. *C'est la vie* - we supposed. We were not able to look round the whole Cathedral as the area behind the high altar was closed off for some reason that we could not fathom. There was no gift shop but, just across the square, a little tobacconist's shop sold us a postcard of the organ.

We wandered off to the market square where we found an inviting-looking bar, ordered some drinks and sat in the sun to await their arrival. After rather a long time, an 'east-facing' waiter acknowledged our presence and assured us he was 'coming in a second'. Quite a few seconds went by, during which time we wrote all our postcards - but still no sign of the waiter. We admitted defeat and went in search of lunch at a self-service place. It fitted the bill perfectly. We visited the very modern church in the market square and Howard took a photo of me blowing out the flames at the base of the statue of Joan of Arc. That was a very naughty thing to do and, of course, it was Howard's idea. I would never have *dreamed* of doing anything like that!

Our next port of call was Jumièges, where there was a ruined abbey - another of Eric's recommendations. We arrived at 1538, only to find it closed at 1600. We had not expected a ruin to be 'closed' but the guardian allowed us to take a quick photograph. It was indeed a beautiful place and we made a note that we should return at a future date to do it justice.

All fancied ice cream - again - and we found a bar with a supermarket attached. Howard's request to the patron was turned down as he said he wasn't selling ice creams until the following weekend. (Why? We had no idea.) Undaunted, we patronized the supermarket and, at the checkout, Howard asked the lady there if *she* sold ice cream. She assured him she did and called to someone through a door, asking them to bring four choc ices. Imagine Howard's surprise when the bearer of the ice creams was the man who had said he wasn't selling them until the following weekend! The looks that Howard got were as icy as the confectionery - but we didn't care - at long last, we had our ice creams, so we sat on a wall contemplating the outside of the abbey of Jumièges - humming Fauré's *Dans les Ruines d'une Abbaye*.

We were back in Le Havre in time for an early supper as check in at the ferry was at 0800 the next day, so we did not want to be late turning in tonight. Howard had found us another little place which was excellent. The two waitresses were very amusing and seemed to like us - which was not always the case as not all *les Anglais* are *bonnes nouvelles*. We were joined by three Korean sailors whose knowledge of the French tongue seemed minimal - and their knowledge of English even less. They seemed to be having difficulty understanding the menu so we suggested to the waitress that she should mime the choices for the inscrutable gents. We demonstrated possible versions - for pork, chicken and steak - but this merely reduced the inscrutable gents to tears of laughter. We realized we should have *shown* them what *we* had chosen and pointed to where these things were to be found on the menu. In the end, we left them to their own devices. It sounded as if they had ordered three main courses each - but we agreed that, as they were sailors, they would get very hungry, scrambling up and down sails all day long, so they would have needed lots of sustenance.

On Monday morning, we were back at the ferry at the appointed time. The crossing took about six hours as there was much fog. We went on deck to watch the departure from Le Havre and stayed there until we had gone through the harbour walls, by which time it was very cold and very foggy. The rest of the journey was spent idling the time away with various pursuits like eating and drinking. We were back at Portsmouth by 1500 and, after an uneventful journey, were soon back in Kennington - looking forward to our next jaunt.

Begun in 1126, the Cathedral was still unfinished.

MORE TALES FROM THE VIENNA WOODS
June 1986

Friday 13th

Friday the thirteenth…was this a good day to travel, we asked ourselves. We are not superstitious and, since we had the tickets, we didn't have much choice. After a hectic day at work, we headed off into the unknown (Victoria station) at the start of our journey to the culture-packed city of Vienna. We intended to find all the launderettes where Beethoven *might* have washed his shirts, had he felt so inclined (but, as we know, he never *did* feel so inclined); all the cafés where Schubert had written *lieder* on the tablecloths and all the houses from which Mozart had been ejected.

The Gatwick express whisked us along to the airport. We were amazed to find that there was a telephone in the train and, over the tannoy, the 'public-relations-aware' guard told us that it was for use only with credit cards. (Does money still exist?) At Gatwick we found our way to the Panorama restaurant, with panoramic views of the planes. We were fascinated by all the announcements over the public address system·

"The driver meeting a group of Panamanian seamen travelling on to join a vessel at Tilbury, to Airport Information please." (Too much duty-free rum?)

"Mr John Stonestreet and Mrs Ethel Taylor to Airport Information please." (where *Mr* Taylor would like a word with them?)

"Miss Judy Sparrow, recently arrived from the Canary Islands, to the Special Assistance desk." (to discuss her identity crisis?)

"Mr Booth, recently arrived from Verona and travelling on to Brighton, to Airport Information please." (to meet the second gentleman?)

"Madame Pompadour, travelling Virgin Atlantic…" (and if you believe *that*, you'll believe anything!)

This is 'virgin on the ridiculous' - and must stop.

A comfortable two-hour flight soon delivered us to Vienna airport where we encountered a young man bearing a large sign reading SPURR. We were driven into Vienna in a Mercedes - along with a German lady, who spoke excellent English. (No chance for me to practise my four German phrases on her…) We were to stay at the *Kaiser und König Palais* Hotel, the former town residence of Katharina Schratt, the mistress of Emperor Franz Joseph the First. Our room was very comfortable and overlooked the square which was packed with birds and trees.

Howard had researched a restaurant for supper but, on the way there, we stopped to check we were going in the right direction. A passer-by not only told us the way, but recommended a different restaurant. We took his advice, with profit, and were soon enjoying our first Wienerschnitzel, in the company of a young Canadian assistant professor of Human Resources.

Saturday 14th

After a delicious buffet breakfast (fruit salad, real orange juice, cheese, ham...), we found our way to the Cityrama office to book the two tours we had decided to take - one to the houses of composers and the other to the Wachau Valley and Melk. We found the Cityrama office very easily as it was near our hotel, but we thought it was rather odd that we had to press an entry phone to gain access. We went up a very old-fashioned staircase, encircling a lift; we were in another age - it was all rather reminiscent of the Bluebell Girls. We arrived in an office on the mezzanine floor, where we were greeted by someone who was as surprised to see us as we were to see him. Then the truth dawned - we had gone in *through the back door*. The main entrance was 'round the corner'; we were escorted to it through the back of the Bluebell Girls' place, into the front of the modern Cityrama office. The staff were very helpful; we arranged our tours and collected vouchers for tickets for *The Magic Flute*, which we were to see in a few days' time. As this is Howard's all-time favourite opera, it would be one of the highlights of the trip.

We thought a walk round the city would help to orientate us; we remembered some places from the whistle-stop visit which had been part of our holiday in 1983. First we went to the Stephansdom via the Tiefer Graben, where a huge mosaic on a wall indicated that not only had Beethoven lived there from 1815 until 1817 but he had written opus numbers 101, 102, 106, 137 and 98 - in that order?

At the Cathedral we succeeded in obtaining our first organ postcard for CP. This time, we were able see the Chapel of Prince Eugene. In 1983, this was the chapel that contained the body of a cardinal who was lying in state, so it had been closed to the public. We found out the time of the main service on Sunday and then set off for a walk suggested in our guidebook.

The first stop was a tavern but we had not gone there with the intention of imbibing anything - just to see this *particular* tavern as, in years gone by, its customers had included Brahms, Beethoven and Wagner. However we felt it only respectful to have a glass of Pils, so, while enjoying our liquid tribute to these great men, we made out the shopping list for our lunch time picnic. Imagine our dismay when we discovered that it had just gone noon and all the shops seemed to have closed. We found a small place which was *just* closing - so we shot in and bought basic supplies. We took our picnic to the banks of the Danube Canal where we found a spot with a table and ate in comfort. We were near what looked like a bandstand where people were setting up something (we never did discover what it was but we had a distinct feeling that it might have been a pop group) but, by the time we had finished, whatever it was was not ready to start.

We went in search of a 'tabac' to buy a book of tickets for public transport - bus, tram and underground. It struck us as odd that these tickets couldn't be purchased at an underground station (only much more expensive single tickets could be obtained there) and we felt it did not encourage people to use the system. Armed with our *carnet* (or the Austrian equivalent), we took the underground out to the Schönbrunn Palace, where we arrived just as the next tour in English was about to start. The general public was not allowed to visit without a guide so we were very fortunate to have arrived at that moment. There was only one guide for a very large group and she looked and sounded distinctly bored most of the time. Never mind, we did get to see it - and what a place! The size of it had to be seen to be believed...all those rooms! The thing that struck me was the amount of dusting it involved. After we had 'done' the inside, we walked in the extensive grounds and took a photograph of the Schönbrunn herself. (Howard said she was a little nymph.) We saw their 'Roman Remains' - which has been built in 1778! Exhausted, we returned to our hotel just as a thunderstorm lit up the sky.

Sunday 15th

On the way to the Stephansdom for the morning service, we called into Peterskirche. It was very ornate - every picture and statue was surrounded by metal rays - and two skeletons in glass cases were dressed in ornate jewelled garments. The service was just ending but we were in time for the last hymn - at least we could only *assume* it was the last hymn as no one joined in...The organist's postlude was very short - and very weedy - Lovelock Book One - and the early chapters at that! We didn't think anyone had stayed up all night to write it and ,if the organist was improvising, he had a long way to go...

The Stephansdom for the 1000 service was our next port of call. A small orchestra and choir were singing a setting which we didn't recognize. A cardinal seemed to be presiding and as soon as the sermon started, we left because we couldn't understand it and, more important, we were heading for the Augustinerkirche for 1100. We arrived there at 1040 and it was almost full. We managed to find two seats. As 1100 approached, it was 'standing room only' - and the service was in Latin!

53

The hymns were displayed on a board thus:

290	290
486	491
290	304

They certainly liked hymn number 290....but, suddenly, the board disappeared, never to return. Sadly, just like back at home, the congregation chatted away while waiting for the service to start. (Why can't people be silent?) Two people behind us carried on a conversation all the way through the organ prelude. The orchestra took *for ever* to tune. We couldn't work out why this was. Suddenly, the tuning was drowned out by the organ. For some parts of the service, the music was Bach's *Mass in G* and, for other parts, a Scarlatti *Mass*. The musical forces were in the organ loft over the west door and it was lovely to *hear* the music without the distraction of seeing the orchestra and choir. At 1130, the *Gloria* was still 'in full swing' (if a *Gloria* can be thus considered?) and we realized it was going to be a very long service. There was a collection during the *Credo*. At the end of the service, we were treated to a wonderful JSB *Passacaglia and Fugue* on the 'Bach Organ' in the body of the church. Lots of people stayed to listen, which surprised us as, usually, most people were out of a church faster than you could say 'counterpoint'.

A man sitting next to us during the service had been perusing huge quantities of organ literature and it turned out that he was part of an organ tour, visiting numerous instruments 'round and about'. He had one book which we would have loved to have had for CP, but it was only available if you were part of the tour. We were able to have a copy of a leaflet which gave the specifications of both organs but there were no postcards of them - which struck us as rather odd in view of the importance they placed on these instruments. The foyer of the church was full of recordings of things like Schubert Masses, performed by the local choir, orchestra and organ. There was a notice advertising the Masses for the forthcoming Sundays; it was *very* impressive indeed.

We lunched at the *Augustinerkeller* - right next door - where we had been on that same whistle-stop tour three years ago. It was as good as we remembered it, which pleased us as sometimes, when you 'go back' to places, you can be disappointed. Not so here...

We returned to our hotel and changed out of our Sunday best clothes because we were off to the woods - the Wienerwald. We found our way by underground and bus (thanks to Howard's excellent organisation) and wandered about enjoying the woodland scenery, until we found two damp tree trunks over which we spread our all-purpose plastic bags and sat to write the postcards. We walked for about three miles down a very steep and windy road until we reached Grinzing, where we were going to sample the *Heuriger* - the 'new wine'. The *Heuriger* taverns hang a pine branch outside to show they are the genuine article and when the new wine is finished, the pine branch must be removed.

Monday 16th

We felt distinctly *pianissimo* today but, as it was another beautiful morning, we made our way to the Stadtpark to see statues of famous composers. We found Schubert, Johann Strauss (he is big news in Vienna!), Robert Stolz and Lehár. Bruckner proved to be more difficult. The guidebook assured us it was there, but we were having no luck in finding it. We did find a rather weird statue of two men - very modern and odd - and Howard was convinced that was the Bruckner monument. I was not convinced because all the other composers had statues that looked like them and there was no plaque or other indication to say this was Bruckner (and friend?). We continued our search, retracing our steps, peering into bushes in case he was overgrown. We drew a blank.

Across the road was the Beethovenplatz and underground car park. (Is this *really* where Beethoven used to park his car?) Not only did LVB have by far the biggest and most imposing statue (quite right too!), he had a whole square to himself.

Off we went to the concert hall to get tickets for Montserrat Caballé that evening. We were not sure we would be able to get in but we managed to get two seats - actually on the stage! We took advantage of the shade opposite the *Hochschüle für Musick* to treat ourselves to a pre-prandial apfelsaft before going on to Karlskirche. (More 'gilded rays' abounded here.) Despite the fact that it was a very hot day, it was very cold inside the church. How do they heat the place in winter? It must cost a fortune. Lunch was taken at a little help-yourself place in Karntnerstrasse, then back to the hotel for a rest before our close encounter with Madame Caballé.

We had supper at *Figlmüller* (the Chimney Sweep) where we had the largest Wienerschnitzel in Vienna - at least that's what we thought *beruhmtestes* meant. They were certainly very large indeed, completely filling our plates - a challenge for me.

It was time to find our seats on the stage and await the arrival of Madame Caballé and her pianist, Miguel Zanetti. (Isn't he the one that makes fridges? Perhaps it's a spare time job? Howard said I was confusing him with Zanussi - a natural mistake.)

Madame C looked like a ship in full sail - and the diminutive pianist looked like her breakfast. But they were both absolutely marvellous. The programme included a masterly *Ständchen* (R Strauss version) and an equally masterly rendition of Granados' *Lover and the Nightingale*. We were treated to *five* encores…but we weren't complaining.

Tuesday 17th

The day I had been waiting for most of all - visits to houses of composers. Unfortunately Peter, the guide, was not very pleasant - and was very dictatorial. I got on the wrong side of him straight away as I lost one end of the ticket and then locked the door of the minibus as he was trying to open it…but, to give him his due, he was very knowledgeable about the houses we visited.

The first was the Figarohaus, where Mozart had written *The Marriage of Figaro*. We were told what an unpleasant man Mozart had been (perhaps Peter the guide was a descendant?) and he (Mozart) had squandered his money on prostitutes and drinking. His wife, Constanze, was a 'lousy housekeeper' (Peter's words!) so Mozart had died a pauper. (This tends to be one of the only facts most people know about him, in the same way that everyone knows about Beethoven not washing his shirts.) The widowed Constanze married George Nikolaus Nissen who, with his new wife's help, wrote Mozart's biography. It was a huge tome - and it did not leave out all the unsavoury bits… We saw the actual *Lacrymosa* from the *Requiem* (at least as far as it went - three cheers for Süssmayr) and the facsimile of the *Ave Verum*. Also on display was the certificate of Mozart's entry into Freemasonry, with pictures of his Lodge.

The next visit was to the Beethoven house in Heiligenstadt. Beethoven moved to Heiligenstadt to 'take the waters' in a desperate attempt to find a cure for his increasing deafness. From the window of the house, Beethoven could see the steeple of the church. One day, he saw the bells ringing and realized he could not *hear* them. It was here that he wrote his famous *Heiligenstadt Testament* to his brothers, Carl and Johann, of which we saw a facsimile. Johann was a big businessman and used to end his letters saying he was 'master of this, that and the other house'. Ludwig wrote back saying he was 'master of the brains'. We know which we prefer - and there were no monuments to his silly old brother… but, having written the *Heiligenstadt Testament*, Ludwig then wrote the Second Symphony - which couldn't be a more cheerful work. (Do your best things in the worst times?) I recalled how, in our Musical Analysis lectures at College, Gladys Puttick had pointed out that the second subject of the slow movement bore a distinct resemblance to the tune of *The Lambeth Walk*. (So *that's* where Beethoven got it from!) Peter told us that Beethoven had lived in eighty different places in Vienna - he really *mustn't* have paid the rent. How did he find time to write any music at all when he was so busy moving - let alone write what is some of the greatest music ever written by anyone? The last thing we saw was Beethoven's death mask. I remembered that I used to have a postcard of this on my wall in my student days.

The next stop was Schubert's birthplace. This was a beautiful courtyard and very well kept but we were told that sixteen families lived in this cramped space - and that included forty children. There was no running water - merely a well in the middle of the courtyard. We were shown the kitchen where Schubert was born. Salieri had been his piano teacher. In a glass case was a lock of Schubert's hair and his spectacles. We heard that he, like Mozart, was a most unsavoury character, with red hair (not much of it), small and fat, and, again like Mozart, had problems with 'drink and women'. (Could he have been the original person who, when asked what he would do if he got too old for wine, women and song, replied 'give up singing'? History does not relate.) Again, like Mozart, Schubert died of syphilis. There was a portrait of a very important-looking man and Peter told us that this person introduced Schubert to a servant girl from whom he caught the fatal disease. It is hard to believe something so horrible about someone who could write something as sublime as the *Quintet* - to mention only one of his 'gems'. The guide did tend to dwell on the more sordid side of the lives of the composers. His last pieces of information were that Schubert never had any money and never owned either an apartment or a piano. He would stay with friends and, though we saw lots of pianos on which he had played, he had never owned any of them.

Our last visit was to the house where Haydn died and which had been visited subsequently by Brahms. Haydn differed from the three previous composers in that his genius was recognized in his lifetime. Furthermore, he had a salaried job with the Esterházy Court and he didn't squander his money so when he died, he was a wealthy man. We saw a facsimile of his Will which was some four pages long whereas Schubert's had been less than a page. Amazingly enough, the guide did not tell us that the symphony was not the *only* thing for which Haydn was renowned for being the father...with the guide's propensity for the scandalous, we can't imagine why he overlooked this tasty morsel. When Haydn died, he was buried in a little local cemetery but later it was thought he deserved to be in a more important place. His body was exhumed and his head was found to be missing! Apparently someone had removed it to examine the skull and the brain, in an endeavour to find out how the brain of a genius differed from an ordinary brain. There was a big problem getting his head back. It was finally restored to his body in the 1950s.

We were told that the composition of *The Creation* and *The Seasons* ("mustn't call it *The Four Seasons*" said Peter - as if we would!) really 'burnt him out'. There was a picture of him towards the end of his life (Beethoven was also in the picture) and it was reported that Haydn was carried on to the stage to conduct *The Creation*. Also on display was a piano with pedals operated with the knees. Brahms came to this house many years later so there was a room full of Brahms' things, including his actual furniture and chairs with music embroidered on to them.

At the end of this most memorable trip, we were returned to the *Stephansdom*. We lunched at *Griechenbeisl* - the café where Wagner, Schubert and Strauss had been in their day. We went back to the Figarohaus for a more leisurely look round and, from there, we found our way to the Museum of Fine Art, a huge place very similar to our own National Gallery. It was crammed full of works by Brueghel, Rubens, Rembrandt and Vermeer - and it had the Titian *Ecce Home* - and lots, lots more. Their Crown Jewels were also kept there. To end the day, we had a little meal locally - and an early night. We were very tired and the next day we had to be ready to leave at 0900 for the Danube trip.

Wednesday June 18th

Today was the coach trip to the Danube Valley, to Melk and to see the Nibelungen. Our guide was very humorous. He told us his name was Franz Joseph the Third, because he had three crowns, all in his teeth - but he wouldn't show them to us as he was a Republican. The drive to Melk took us past the place where the horses from the Spanish Riding School go for their holidays.

Our first destination was the Melk Benedictine Monastery. This had been started in 1089 so they were getting ready to celebrate their 900th anniversary in 1989. The Chapel was being re-gilded. Everywhere we looked was covered in gold leaf. We were accustomed to seeing gold leaf in a rather tarnished state but, as this had just been applied, it *shone*. We saw two of the forty-two monks in the Order attached to the Monastery though only fourteen of them lived there; the rest operated in parishes round about. The Library was spectacular. It was full of very ancient books and there was no heating or lighting in the room as the risk of fire was too great. If you wanted to read the books (and you couldn't unless you were someone very important), you had to read them in the Library itself, sitting by the windows. The Guest Dining Room was another splendid place - about the size of the Wigmore Hall - with an extraordinary *trompe l'oeil* ceiling, featuring pillars which appeared to be upright from one angle and sloping from another. A distinctly unhappy-looking man (a Konrad Adenauer look-alike) was trying to organize groups for tours in different languages. He got very upset because people kept asking him where the guide was…The English guide appeared and we spent a good, informative hour with him.

At the end of our conducted tour, we went to the nearby restaurant. We wanted to sit outside but the Konrad Adenauer look-alike insisted that certain tables had been reserved for our party *inside*. We were too frightened to protest, so in we went. There appeared to be no choice of food and what was obviously a set menu was presented. It was a delicious meal so we were not complaining. We met two people from Bristol and, when it came time to pay, the waitress seemed to want money only for the wine. The Bristol people told us that the meal was included in the price of the tour. Clearly we had misread the leaflet. They also told us that we had to be back at the coach at 1400 whereas we thought Franz Joseph had said 1330. Much to our surprise, more wine appeared and we were given a free wine-tasting. Again we did not remember seeing *that* on the itinerary. We recalled that there *was* to be a wine-tasting at Durnstein, so we assumed plans had changed and the tasting was now. Then, to our embarrassment, Franz Joseph appeared - to tell us that the coach and all other members of our party were waiting for us. (It was a very hot day and, for some reason, the engine of the coach could not be turned on until it was moving, which meant the air conditioning could not happen! Our fellow passengers were wilting in the heat… we were not the most popular things since sliced bread…)

It transpired that we had got mixed up with *another* tour called 'Sightseeing Tour' whereas we were on the 'Cityrama Sightseeing Tour'! The *Tourmeister* of the other one was the Konrad Adenauer look-alike. (We had thought he was someone attached to Melk Abbey.) However, it had been entirely his mistake as he had taken us for members of his party and had insisted that we went along with those people. Franz Joseph assured us that we did not need to pay him anything (!) - but we thought we would avoid him at all costs for the rest of the day. Our hearts sank when we boarded the boat that was to take us on the Danube - and there was Konrad again!

The Danube was by no means blue - more of a murky brown - but the boat took us almost all the way to Durnstein, where we had the scheduled wine-tasting, sitting in the evening sun by the river. It was a most beautiful place; Richard the Lionheart had been imprisoned here and subsequently rescued by Blondel. If you've got to be imprisoned, we can think of worse places! Franz Joseph told us that the tourist industry in Vienna (their main industry) was really 'feeling the pinch', especially as regards Americans, for three reasons: 1) terrorist attacks/Ghadafi 2) Chernobyl and 3) the value of the dollar. (Nothing changes does it?) By the end of our trip, not a single Nibelung had crossed our path (perhaps it was their day off?) so we went back to the hotel for a more than welcome shower before patronising a local restaurant for an omelette supper. Before turning in, we watched England beat Paraguay 3 - 0 in the World Cup.

Thursday June 19th

Today's visit was to the Spanish Riding School via two houses in the *Tiefer Graben* - one where Mozart had lived, the other (with mosaics) where Beethoven had lived. We could not go inside but we took photos of the plaques on the outside of the buildings. We spent an hour in the Spanish Riding School, watching the training. Even though it wasn't a performance, we still had to pay and the riders wore very posh uniforms. There was a large number of different coloured horses but we thought it was only the white ones which took part in the actual performances, because they were the only ones on the postcards. (Looks like Equal Opportunities had been overlooked where our equine friends were concerned.)

We called into the Michaelerkirche - another very ornate place - and a sign indicated that they needed £13,000 spent on the organ - *each year!* We made a modest contribution by buying a postcard of it for CP. We had amassed a goodly collection of them by now.

Next stop, *Demel*, for coffee and cakes. This was a very expensive place indeed and we paid £6-50 for two cups of coffee and two cakes. (What is *that* in 2009?) It was like stepping back in time because it seemed nothing had changed in there for years. I imagined it was something like Fortnum and Mason, but as I have never been in F and M, I couldn't really compare it. In no time at all, we decided we would not be lunching in *Demel*, and we fell to wondering who *did* go there in the normal course of events. It was certainly a place 'to have seen'.

We took our opera voucher along to the box office of the *Staatsoper* to exchange it for the tickets for The Magic Flute performance. We returned to the *Augustinerkeller* for lunch (it really *was* worth the return visit) then took the tram to the Belvedere ('a splendid palace built by Prince Eugene of Savoy'). Whilst looking round the Upper Belvedere, it started to thunder, but there was no accompanying rain so we walked in the gardens towards the Lower Belvedere. Half way there, the rain started and, very soon afterwards, we discovered we could not get into the Lower Belvedere as it was closed until 1600! Nothing for it but to go back to the hotel and change into our Sunday best for the visit to the Opera.

We took a leisurely walk in the Stadtpark and had a quick snack before arriving in good time to find our seats in the balcony. There were three rows of boxes and two balconies. We were in the lower balcony and our seats were £15 each. Goodness knows what the others cost - but we did find out that the most expensive were £80! It had deterred no one as the place was packed and people were standing right up at the top of the auditorium. There was a massive chandelier over the stalls, and we were rather glad we weren't there, just in case it had fallen on our heads…In the interval, we mingled with high Viennese society in the bar, where there was a bust of Clemens Krauss and Richard Strauss, who had been Director of the Opera until 1945 - the year I was born. I wonder if that had any bearing on the fact that he stopped being Director in that year. I can't imagine it did…There were many more statues but, as there was just one interval, there was no chance to see them. It was dreadful to think that this opera house had been completely destroyed in the Second World War. We wondered how similar the present building was to the original, which Charles Proctor would have seen when he was a student in Vienna in 1926.

Could this be the subject for my Dimbleby Lecture for the cabaret at the Summer School later on this year? It certainly sowed the seed, as the lecture was eventually entitled *Die Zauberflöte auf dem Nibelungen*. The producer of the performance we saw in Vienna was Joachim Herz and, not long before this holiday, we had seen his *Parsifal* at the Coliseum in London - with odd, extremely minimalist scenery. Tonight's production was not nearly so odd and was much more *Magic Flutable* than the Jonathan Miller production that we had seen recently in London. There was the odd quirk; Tamino's costume was like a dressing gown over a vest - until towards the end, when it was like a judo outfit. (We were convinced it had some great significance in the scheme of things, though what it was rather eluded us.) Papageno's bells resembled a pepper pot on the end of a stick, rather than the usual up-ended glockenspiel.

Friday 20th

We could hardly believe it was our last day. We had to be back at the hotel at 1730 to be collected to go to the airport so, after breakfast, we packed. This was done in record time; doubtless we could claim the Olympic record for packing. We left our luggage at the hotel and set off to visit the Musical Instrument Museum in the Neue Berg. This was full of old instruments - horns, trombones, serpents and the like. In addition, there were keyboard instruments including one from a Beethoven place, one that Schubert had played, one that Haydn owned and one from the home of the Schumanns, on which Brahms had played.

We visited the museum of old weapons and some very ancient sculptures, similar to the Elgin Marbles - the Ephesus Museum. Lunch was taken at *S'Mullerbeist,* and it included French onion soup. We slept off our lunch in the Stadtpark and made a final search for the elusive Bruckner monument. It remained elusive. Finally we stopped for some refreshment at the tourist café, where we were serenaded by a little orchestra playing Strauss - the *other* one - he wears very thin very quickly and we swore we never wanted to hear another piece of music in ¾ in our life - or, at least, not for a very long time!

Time was running out so we headed for a sweet shop to buy the obligatory Mozart chocolate balls, then popped into the *Stephansdom* for one last admire. We used up our last ticket on the métro to take us back to the hotel. Then it was 'Goodbye Vienna' - or, at least, '*Auf Wiedersehn*'.

Vienna had certainly come up to expectations - but we never *did* see any launderettes - so history hasn't been altogether fair to LVB!

VIVA ESPAÑA
January 1987

We got into the habit of having a short break somewhere warm just after Christmas to recover from the festive Season - and 'all that goes with'. In 1987, we chose Benidorm as our destination. Gasps of horror usually greet the mention of Benidorm, but that is 'in season' - when it's full of lager louts and fish and chips. In the winter, it is a completely different place. It is very quiet, not a lager lout or chip in sight, and is populated by OAPs (Golden Age Citizens) who go there to take advantage of the warm climate, while England shivers in its winter attire. As a spin-off, they save vast amounts on their heating bills, ensure they stay cold-free and have all their meals provided for them. The longer they stay, the cheaper it gets. It couldn't be a better scheme.

Saturday 3rd

On our flight to Alicante, two sweet little girls sitting in front of us, loaned us a teddy bear (Big Sophie) for the duration of the flight. At Alicante, a coach was waiting to take us the hour's drive to Benidorm. As we approached our destination, the courier told us that the coach could not go right down to the hotel as the streets were too narrow so we were transferred to a taxi for the last part of the journey. Reception kept Howard's passport! Would he ever see it again - or ever be able to get back to Kennington?

Sunday 4th

Breakfast was taken in the restaurant overlooking the sea, a view of which we would not tire during the next seven days. We took a stroll into the old town before our 1000 appointment with the Thomson representative. We lit upon the church and wandered in. A recording of some Vivaldi sound-alike music was playing but, when it finished, to our surprise, the next offering was a Petula Clark-type pop song. Strange choice, we thought. We couldn't stay to hear more from the repertoire as it was almost 1000. Time for the Thomson representative's 'welcome' meeting for all the newcomers - and it included free champagne - a little early in the day, even for us. We were given some literature about the local 'attractions' and we booked a tour to Guadalest (Eagle's House) on Wednesday. We avoided *like the plague* the 'Pirates' Evening', which threatened to be a meal followed by pantomime-type activities, where everyone was warned to have clean underwear, in case they should be chosen to be a participant! Most of the guests seemed to like that idea…it appealed to us not at all - and we realized we were about the youngest people in the party.

Our priority was to lie on the beach and relax with a book. Just along from where we settled was a group of keep-fit enthusiasts, under the watchful eye of an instructor. We watched them - and decided we must have the fittest eyes on the beach. It was soon time for lunch - a huge buffet - which we ate sitting in the window, overlooking the Mediterranean.

When we had digested lunch, we took the free boat trip to Peacock Island, about fifteen minutes out into the bay - and it was quite blowy. Peacock Island really did boast peacocks but they showed no interest in us since we had no food for them. We *did* see a peahen with five tiny chicks who looked like five balls of cotton wool. After our peacock extravaganza, we caught the last boat back (1630) and rested until it was time for dinner. All this relaxing could be quite exhausting. Dinner was at a paella restaurant recommended by the Thomson representative, and we were not disappointed - except to find that, though the menu promised gazpacho, the waiter told us it was available only in the summer. We tried not to be too sad and, when the paellas arrived, they were 'well worth the wait' so the gazpacho was all but forgotten.

Monday 5th

Today was the Spanish equivalent of Christmas Eve. They don't celebrate Christmas on December 25th but on January 6th - Epiphany. We took a stroll around the town where we discovered the mats we'd seen others using on the beach. As they were only £1 each, we bought two of them so that we were fully equipped for the next sunbathing session.

Lunch time was another buffet, which we thought was very good value for money, especially as it was included in the price of the holiday. Eating lunch was such a strenuous activity that we had to have a lie down to work up enough energy to make the next decision - where to go that afternoon. The temperature was not quite as hot as the previous day so we decided a walk to the one end of the bay was in order. We called at an *Apoteke* as I had contracted a very bad cough. (How can anyone get a bad cough in this sunny clime? We didn't know, but I had managed it.) The cough mixture looked like floor polish and was called *Bronco Formo* (surely it was for horses?). The floor of our hotel room was soon the most highly polished in Benidorm.

Howard tracked down a very promising Italian restaurant for supper - *Il Fratelli* - so we went along to make a reservation. As it was the eve of the Three Kings, the set menu was a nine-course banquet! We didn't think we could do justice to that and we dreaded to think how much it would have cost - a small detail which was omitted from the menu - but the Patron, when he discovered that we wanted to eat at 1930, assured us we could eat *à la carte*, which looked very promising, especially as most of the diners were not expected until 2130.

When we set out in the evening, large numbers of people were lining the streets, awaiting the procession of the Three Kings. We couldn't wait to see it as it would have made us late for our meal. The restaurant did not disappoint us. The food was excellent, beautifully presented with lots of slices of oranges and lemons scattered throughout - and the service could not have been better. Howard gave me a red rose (the age of chivalry was not dead after all!). By the time we left the restaurant, the procession had been and gone, leaving evidence of itself all along the streets, in the form of confetti and streamers. We wondered if Father Christmas would come again in the night - in Spanish? We retired early, just in case...but the people in the next room chose that time to have an argument, which went on for over two hours. Then a gradual *decrescendo* set in, so we were able to sleep.

Tuesday 6th

For the first time, I noticed that the sheets had HS embroidered on them - so, too, did the armchairs outside the hotel. Howard said it stood for Hotel Selomar. (He has no imagination.) Today was the big day - Epiphany. We spent the morning on the beach in the shade of a huge rock as it was very, very hot. The keep-fit contingent arrived and, this time, we were nearer to them so we could hear what the instructor said, though we couldn't understand it as it was in Spanish. His demonstrations were crystal clear however, so we soon 'got the gist'. The participants were all 'tending towards elderly' but they made noble efforts - some more noble than others. One man didn't seem to know his right arm from his left and, as he faced the wrong way throughout, we concluded that he might not be deriving maximum benefit from the sessions. It was fun observing all the different types of mankind on the beach - the 'I was a seven stone weakling until I took the Charles Atlas course' type, the types who were *still* seven stone weaklings - and some who were nearer *seventeen* stone, and a bit moth-eaten.

For lunch, we found a restaurant where we could eat for under 500 psts. (about £2-50). It was very good and it turned out to be where all the locals ate - always a good sign. We couldn't see any other *Inglese* but there were two parrots living there who whistled in reply to us. To walk off our lunch, we took a two-mile walk to the other end of the bay. We met lots of dogs and some wonderful doves - in the local dove-park.

We had noticed that the film of *Amadeus* was on in the hotel that evening so we decided to eat *chez nous* and go to the film at 2100. Imagine our disappointment when we went to the bar for the 'complimentary drink', only to find that the poster now advertised *Rambo 2*! We took our complimentary drink in another lounge overlooking the sea, from where we watched the waves breaking - but no one put them together again...I was convinced that someone switches off the sea at night and starts it up again in the early morning. After all, why would it want to be breaking away all night with no one to look at it? After supper, as there was no *Amadeus*, we retreated to our room and read our books.

Wednesday 7th

We were out early to ensure we got our places under the cliff, where we spent the morning. We were getting browner (or redder?) by the minute. After an early lunch, we set off by coach for Guadalest. The ride up into the mountains was picturesque and included sightings of real orange and lemon trees - with real oranges and lemons growing on them - in that order. Our first stop was a craft shop where we were encouraged to try Muscatel out of one of those flasks with a long thin neck, from which the wine was poured down the drinker's throat. We didn't need much encouragement - and we tried our best not to let it run down our chins - and our clothes.

What remained of the castle of Guadalest was at the top of the mountain and thus, in its day, would have been impregnable. The castle had been all but destroyed by an earthquake in 1644 or 1748, depending on which guidebook you read, but what's an odd hundred years between friends? What few parts managed to survive the earthquake were destroyed by a dynamite blast in a subsequent war. Some people just seem to get all the bad luck, don't they... The cemetery at the top is the site of the Castello San Jose, of which only the ruins of the fortifications remain. We walked to the cemetery, past the Stations of the Cross in mosaics, and were rewarded with wonderful views. There was just time for a little potter round the village, taking in a kiwi fruit cake and a glass of muscatel, before the coach took us back a different, but equally picturesque, way.

By the evening, my cough had really taken hold, so we returned to the *Apoteke* and asked for something stronger. They sold us some antibiotics (without a prescription!) which I took with some hot water, lemon and honey which we had just bought - and whisky. (Come to think of it, that was probably not such a good combination with antibiotics...glad I *didn't* think of it at the time.) Howard had a glass of whisky, purely out of sympathy for my affliction. A Chinese meal provided our supper and we were back in bed with our books by 2030.

Thursday 8th

We set out to explore Villajoyosa, a little town about five miles away. The guidebook told us hat it was noted for its church - a 'jewel set on top of the town'. We had quite a difficult time locating the bus to take us there and, having located it, we were told we had to buy our tickets 'across the road'. This necessitated a mad dash to the ticket-buying place as the bus was about to leave - but we just made it.

The bus journey was a mere ten minutes. Villajoyosa looked a 'dead and alive' place - mostly dead - and we could see no evidence of the 'brightly painted houses' described in the guidebook. We scrambled down to a beach over some nondescript rocks and, on reaching the front, we had to conclude it was even *more* dead than we first thought. No sign of the 'jewel set on top of the town' church, so we made our way right to the end of the front, to a little harbour and marina - where nothing was happening. (There were some men engaged in rock-blasting on the other side of the road but we didn't feel we could count them as part of the local colour.) We retraced our steps and enquired of a local where we would find the *iglesia* - only to be told there were two, each in completely opposite directions. The one we wanted was 'up there' - so off we set again. Eventually we arrived at what was the 'old town'. We had been walking in the wrong direction all the time! There *were* houses painted in bright colours and there was a church but, surprise, surprise, it was locked. A lady told us something very quickly, in Spanish, and we assumed it meant that the church was only open for services - so we smiled, nodded - and left. By now, we had decided that the Villajoyosa was not *that* 'joyosa' at all so we thought we might as well catch the next bus back. Unfortunately, they were every hour so, while waiting for the next one, we tried in vain to obtain some fresh orange juice. It seemed to be unobtainable - we were offered only Fanta. (We had read that, though this was the land of oranges, actual orange juice would be hard to find - but we did not believe it. Here was the proof.) We continued our search until the bus arrived.

Back in Benidorm, we found a café with real oranges on display and we wondered whether there would be the remotest possibility of these being turned into fresh orange juice. Our luck was changing...we could have it here - and we both consumed a glass containing the juice of three oranges *each*. I was trying my best to get as much vitamin C into my system as I could to combat my silly cough and cold.

The afternoon was spent with our books but in the evening we went to another 'find' of Howard's, *El Vesubio*. It was very good indeed and, again, everything was decorated with slices of oranges and lemons. There was pleasant Musak, including the '*Moonlight Sonata*', which interested no one except me because I was immersed in Lucia. Back at the hotel, Howard watched *The Woman in Red* but the room was too smoky for me so I returned to Riseholme and Lucia and friends.

Friday 9th

We paid a visit to Calpe, about fifteen miles north, on the coast, where the father of one of Howard's colleagues had a villa. We took the local bus for the journey of about forty-five minutes. The bus dropped us right at the top of the town so we had a very steep walk down to the front, where it was very windy. We succeeded in buying a couple of real orange juices in a little bar, before walking to the end of the front to the marina where Howard's colleague's father had his villa - though we didn't see him. What we did see was a man windsurfing, very expertly. This was a first for us - and we were impressed by the sight, though not impressed enough to want to try it. We retraced our steps to the *Capri* restaurant and, when we sat on a bench to consult the map, we were joined by a lovely black dog who sat himself down on my feet and put his head in my lap. Then he climbed onto the seat...clearly he didn't want to be left out of anything. Suddenly, the dog dropped a stone from his mouth, but he wouldn't let us pick it up to throw for him, so we made our way to the restaurant, closely followed by black dog. When he realized it was our intention to go in, he dropped the stone and waited, obviously deciding that this was the only way to keep our attention. Obediently, we threw the stone for him a couple of times and each time he brought it back. The third time, Howard threw it further away and, while he was retrieving it, we nipped inside.

We had a delicious meal, starting with gazpacho, a special favourite of ours since we had it every day on our honeymoon in Barcelona in 1980. Howard had his 'all-time favourite' dish, a plate of seafood, while I had pork. Pudding was a calorie-free (?) bread-and-butter pudding with cream for Howard and strawberries in port for me. Because of the antibiotics, I was avoiding wine but I thought the port would not present a problem. What strange logic...Though we declined coffee, the waiter brought us a glass of muscatel and some little sweets and dates. The climb back to the bus stop was a good way to work off all the naughty things we had just consumed.

I missed out on a tablet so that I could have some of the champagne which we had bought in the duty-free shop. It was our last night in Benidorm so this was our little celebration. We put the champagne into cold water in the hand basin but realized that the plug didn't fit, so all the water drained away. The champagne was removed to the bath, where the plug was much more efficient. Our final meal at the hotel was to be the Gala Dinner, so some Welsh ladies had told us. They were here for a number of weeks so they 'knew the drill'. The Gala Dinner turned out to be the same as any other dinner we had had, except that it was eaten by candle light -and we were given a free glass of sparkling wine. Not quite as 'Gala-ish' as we had hoped...

Saturday 10th

Time had flown by and the week was over. The sea was very rough as we packed our cases for the return journey and we were glad we were not going home by boat. We were not due to leave the hotel until 1800 so we made a final foray into the local supermarket where we bought a litre of Grand Marnier for a mere £5. Back to our room to finish off our duty frees then we moved our luggage downstairs at midday, when we had to vacate the room. Our particular deal did not include lunch in the hotel on this final day so we went in search of an alternative eatery. We found one called *Jesus* and we thought we wouldn't get anything better than *that*. Another bit of nostalgia as we had some sangria, something of which we had consumed rather a great deal on our honeymoon. Howard had a fish paella, with large and interesting piscine content; my chicken version was equally tasty. Pudding was some form of ice cream - and whisky! Again, as they brought the bill, they brought a complimentary small glass of muscatel. We reeled out of the restaurant and sat for a while, observing the really bad-tempered sea.

The afternoon stretched ahead so we spent the time reading in the hotel lounge until our taxi arrived to take us to the coach which would take us on to Alicante airport. Our flight was shown as boarding at 2100 for its 2145 departure. We noted with some concern that the 1230 Air Europe Manchester flight was still indicated - and we wondered why. Thinking back, we remembered that this delay had been reported in the hotel before we left. While we were pondering this, an announcement advised the Manchester passengers to proceed to the restaurant 'where a meal would be served' - note the future tense. That added to our concerns as we wondered if we would have a similar lengthy wait.

Our flight was called and we went to the departure lounge, where there was a rather longer than usual delay. A stretcher case was being taken on board and some of the seats were being removed. We hoped they were not 12A and 12B, which were reserved for us. While we waited, the announcement about the meal for the Manchester passengers was repeated. It was still in the future tense and it was now one and a half hours since we first heard it! Not only were they having a long wait for their flight, they were having another long wait for their meal. Our take-off was delayed by one hour (a mere nothing in comparison) and we reached Gatwick just after midnight. The next train to London was in an hour's time so we bought the only paper available and found out about Prince Edward. The Sunday Mirror told us not only what each member of the Royal Family *said* about it, but also what each member *thought* about it. Clearly Her Majesty telephoned the Sunday Mirror on a regular basis to pass on all this information to them.

In no time at all, we were back in Kennington, in a warm bed, counting our blessings and sparing many thoughts for the poor Air Europe passengers.

El Cid driving the Moors out of Castille

LOITERING ALONG THE LOIRE
or
CHERCHEZ LES CHÂTEAUX!
April 1987

A few years earlier, Howard and I had taken a coach tour to some of the châteaux of the Loire. Our friend Janet liked the sound of it and we were more than happy to repeat the trip. Sadly, the tours did not start until later in the year but Janet said she would be happy to drive.

Monday 6th

We took an overnight ferry from Portsmouth to Le Havre and assumed it was a very good crossing as we slept through it - and woke at 0500. Disembarkation was very swift and, in no time at all, we had found the place where we had breakfasted two years ago when we were *en route* for the Dordogne. Suitably refreshed, we made our way to Pont Audemer. Our last visit to this place had been on a very grey, foggy day but, this time, bright sunshine illuminated the very colourful market stalls, selling flowers, plants, vegetables…and much more. We looked into the church, which boasted some beautiful stained glass and, in the morning sunlight, we were able to see it 'at its best'. We bought our lunch time picnic from the market, ensuring we selected some cheese that would *not* make its presence felt in the car for the next few days. Once again, we headed for the garden behind the Cathedral at Chartres. Our way took us through Conches where we stopped to look at the remains of a fortification and a large church with more lovely stained glass.

We made short work of our picnic at Chartres, particularly enjoying the wonderful cheese. History does not record what we drank, but it was certainly not the Normandy cider which had been such a disappointment two years ago. We spent a happy hour in the Cathedral.

Our last stop was to be near Tours, at Mettray, a 'small château-like house' named Belabet, about three miles outside the town. We ended up on a modern housing estate and found it hard to believe that the 'small château-like house' would be there. We were despairing of finding it when a local person directed us up a dirt track road which we had eschewed, never believing that our destination lay at the end of it. But it did! There we found Belabet and Madame Bellanger, a lovely lady who could not have made us more welcome. She spoke no English (except "I love you" - well, it's a start) so we had chance to practise our French on her. 'Fractured' is the word that best described my attempts but Howard, being an 'ace' French speaker, had no such problems. Belabet was a beautiful dwelling

71

(more than living up to its title of 'small château-like house') set in large grounds, in which numerous sheep were making short work of cutting the lawns. Madame Bellanger invited us to join her in an aperitif of *pétillant* Touraine rosé wine - *Methode Champenoise*. (Howard had written to say that we would like to try the local wine.) We were rather taken aback when Madame Bellanger indicated that the whole bottle was for us and if we did not drink it all before dinner, we could finish it with pudding! The meal that followed included cauliflower cheese, chicken, salad, cheese and finally chocolate cake - all washed down with two carafes of Chinon wine - after which we had no difficulty in sleeping.

Tuesday 7th

We woke to find the sheep returning to their lawn-cutting duties. It was a beautiful day and Belabet looked entrancing in the sun, surrounded as it was with flowers.

There was no time to linger as our first château, Chinon, was waiting for us. There was lots of Jeanne d'Arc everywhere, including the spot where she met the Dauphin. I did my (banned!) Jeanne d'Arc impersonation again, much to Howard's horror...A great deal of renovation work was being done on this château. Our lunch stop at a nearby café offered a four-course meal for thirty-seven francs, and that included wine! The food and drink were as much a part of this holiday as the culture...On we went to Azay-le-Rideau, which was very picturesque and here we had a guided tour, in French, but with an English translation on a sheet. The guidebook told us 'it gives an unforgettable impression of elegance and harmony' - and it did.

Next stop Villandry, taking in a view of Ussé (the Sleeping Beauty one) from the approach road. The gardens of Villandry were wonderful and we imagined they must have been even *more* wonderful when all the flowers were in bloom in the summer. (Even now the topiary was a sight to behold.) The gardens were on three separate levels; the top level was the water garden where we found a swan and friends, very anxious that we should take their photograph, for which, obligingly they tucked their heads into their feathers in a somnolent posture. The second level contained the flower beds and the topiary and the third level was made up of more flower beds interspersed with the vegetable garden. At one side was a garden of aromatic and medicinal plants. All these areas were laid out so immaculately that a plant would not *dare* to grow in the wrong place and weeds were unheard of. We sat in the sun and caught up on some French history, courtesy of Howard, who, after all, is an expert on same, having studied it at Oxford (all those years ago).

We returned to Tours where Howard had researched an eatery for our evening meal. (He is an expert on that too!) After our large lunch, we did not want very much so we partook of some crêpes and cider.

Wednesday 8th

We went in search of a supermarket and found a *Mammouth*. It *was* mammoth too, with thirty checkouts, so we made a note to do our returning duty-free shopping there on our penultimate day, rather than leaving it until we got back to Le Havre, just in case we ran out of time - highly likely since we were in the company of our friend 'the late Miss Wells'. We took the opportunity of buying our picnic in this temple to shopping.

Our next stop was Blois where we headed for the Tourist Information office to buy tickets for the guided coach tour in the afternoon. Howard had telephoned Blois from England to confirm that the tour would be happening and that there would be an English guide on the coach and in the châteaux - but he had been misinformed. There was a coach trip - but no guides! We did some quick sums and concluded that we could 'do our own thing' much more cheaply and have our freedom - and our picnic. The only snag about this was that we had promised Janet a driving-free time so she could relax, but she said she was happy to continue to drive - so we set off for Chambord.

We picnicked in brilliant sunshine under the trees in the park at Chambord. Both the park and the château were enormous; the park covered 13,600 acres; the château had 440 rooms, only 73 of which were open to the public - and we didn't see *all* of those! Log fires were burning in some of the 365 fireplaces and the evocative smell permeated the whole building - giving us an idea of what it must have been like all those years ago. What we couldn't get over was that this was just a hunting lodge! We walked up the (very rare) double spiral staircase, and stood where the ladies used to stand to await the return of the men folk from *la chasse*, to see what was going to be for supper. ("Not roast stag *again*?") We found our way to the main entrance and walked back up the 'drive' (I use that term loosely) so we could take a photo of the front of the building. Because of the enormity of its construction, it was not possible to retreat far enough to get the whole thing into our viewfinders. Rarely had we been so tired - the result of walking up and down staircases and into many of the seventy-three accessible rooms.

Our next stop was Cheverny where we arrived only just in time to gain admittance. This was much smaller than most of the others (but then *anywhere* would be much smaller than Chambord!) and it was furnished, so it had a rather homely feel to it. The owners lived there and we assumed they must occupy the second floor as visitors were permitted to see only the ground and first floors. A highlight for me was to see a selection of the seventy hounds which were kept for hunting. We must have been about thirty - perhaps the other forty were out hunting, or maybe it was their day off. The thirty we *did* see did not disappoint. They were beagles and they were extremely friendly, jumping up and down to make sure we didn't miss stroking a single one of them. We looked into the trophy room (which could be hired for private functions) but the heads of wild boar and stags did not endear themselves to us, so we returned to the beagles.

We went in search of *L'Oubliette*, a restaurant Howard had found in his Michelin guide. 'Search' was the operative word as it was very much 'off the beaten track'. Suddenly we wondered if we should have booked - but luck was on our side and we were given the last table. It was a never-to-be-forgotten meal in an extremely attractive setting with its own log fire. It provided an opportunity for some more Chinon wine - and it meant that our early night was 'on hold' as there was no way we could hurry such a wonderful culinary experience.

Thursday 9th

Our first stop was the supermarket to buy our duty-free wine, tasty *fromages* and much more. In 1987, there was a limit to how many litres of alcohol visitors could take back to England, which was just as well as we had to spare a thought for the additional weight in the car. We bought our picnic and set off for Loches. (I decided that, if ever I had a dog, I would call it Loches. How come we called her Millie?)

Loches was a bit gloomy, perhaps because of all the dungeons, but we climbed up some very narrow stairs to the top of the keep. This was a very ruined and broken-down château but it was a lovely 'Des. Res.' for birds. Apparently, a duke, who had been imprisoned there for eight years, came out into the light and promptly died. (Why didn't he put on his dark glasses?) We saw the church of St Ours, which is distinguished by two octagonal pyramids (formed by the vaulting over the nave) which rise between the towers.

We were headed for Chenonceau, but stopped in some woods for our picnic, which included walnut cheese - a 'first' for us. We were pleased that we had visited Chenonceau on our Dordogne trip in 1985 because, on this visit, the river which surrounds it was moving very quickly and there were no reflections to be seen. Instead, men were clearing logs, branches and foliage, which were damming parts of the surrounding water. As with Villandry, the gardens had yet to come to their full majesty. We sat under an umbrella for a *boisson* at the café, but, very soon, we were sitting under *three* umbrellas to avoid a passing downpour.

The last château on our itinerary was Amboise and by the time we arrived, the downpour had passed. This had been the only rain of our trip so we could not complain. There was a very good French guide at Amboise and even *I* could understand most of what he said - but there was an English leaflet to help us. We saw the Chapelle St Hubert, where are buried the remains of Leonardo da Vinci and, in the distance, the house where Leonardo died. The exit from the château was down a long ramp which had been constructed so that horses and carriages could drive right into the building.

We drove back into Tours where we just managed to avoid being locked into the Cathedral. The lady with the key had seen us! For our evening meal, we found the restaurant which we had patronized on our Dordogne trip and we indulged ourselves - with steak and chips!

Friday 10th

We bade farewell to Madame Bellanger at 0745 and headed for Kennington. We bought our picnic at Chartres and set off towards Bernay where we stopped to eat it in a wood. It was rather windy so plastic bags, bits of cheese, pieces of bread and plastic glasses had to be tethered to prevent their escape. In the course of our journey, we had done many sums estimating the fuel capacity of Janet's new car, but everything pointed to the fact that we were about to run out of *l'essence*. It was with some relief that we saw a sign indicating a Fina station, just two kilomètres down the road. Our relief was short-lived because a notice indicated that the machines were *en panne*. We didn't know what that meant but we concluded that we were not going to get any petrol. The garage attendant told us that we would be able to get *l'essence* in Bernay which was not far away. We crossed our fingers - and it worked - we made it to Bernay and a filling station. (Back home, we looked up *en panne* and found it could mean 'plush', 'fat', or 'breakdown' - so we assumed in this instance it had meant the latter. We live and learn.)

We were back at Le Havre by 1530 ready for our 1700 sailing. Dutifully, we joined the queue but our hearts sank when a notice told us that sailing time had been put back for half an hour. So often that can be the precursor to a l....o....n....g wait - but we were lucky. The ferry sailed at 1730. It was 2230 when we disembarked and the long drive to Kennington lay ahead, in pouring rain. SE11 was a welcome sight at just after midnight.

*"Another thing about Liechtenstein - their
road maps are really easy to fold."*

THE FÈVRE WEDDING
August 1987

In 1975, Howard decided to take 'a year out', (a sabbatical?) from work and went to Reims University to study French Language and Civilisation. One of his language teachers was a young man (much younger than Howard) by the name of Jean-Marie Fèvre. Little did either of them know but their meeting was to be the start of a deep and lasting friendship which continues to this day. Jean-Marie's family now numbers five - his wife Mirjam, and three children, Victor (currently at university), Nicole (about to go to university) and Eric, who is not quite old enough to go to university.

We were delighted when we learned that Jean-Marie was to be married in August 1987 and thrilled to receive an invitation to the wedding. It was to be an unforgettable occasion, held in Châtres (no, not the place with the big cathedral). The service was at the church of Saint-Rémi in that village and the reception in a nearby hall. It was the busiest weekend we had spent in a very long time.

Friday 28th

We journeyed from London Victoria to Paris by way of a hovercraft to Boulogne and two trains - one at either end - and we arrived in the capital at 1730. The Hotel Ibis was as anonymous as any hotel in a chain invariably is; it could have been in any city in the world and, according to their brochure, they *are*. It was located next to the Montmartre cemetery, though we didn't think there was any connection - the food wasn't *that* bad. The restaurant we patronized in the evening was in an approach road to the cemetery. We felt it would be very handy if the food *did* turn out to be less than ideal. Montmartre cemetery is huge, though nowhere near as big as the Père Lachaise one which we had visited previously. Despite the fact that Berlioz is buried in Montmartre, it was not possible to look round as it was locked - which struck us as odd as the inhabitants were hardly likely to attempt to leave.

We headed for *Le Grandgousier* restaurant where we met two Americans at the next table, Tod and Nancy, who told us they were 'Mercedes people'. ("There's a six-month waiting list in America to buy a Jaguar"! So what? thought we...) We were sure that they thought we were prehistoric for not even *wanting*, let alone *owning*, a car or a video. They were enjoying their vacation in Europe and did not appear to be the 'It's Friday, this must be Paris' type of American tourists. They were continually amazed at all the *old* things in Europe and explained to us that in America, if something was one hundred years old, it was really ancient - so to see the French *chattoes* (thus pronounced) was just 'something else'.

After supper, we went up to Sacré Coeur and took a little wander around the Place du Tertre, imagining what is was like when *real* artists lived there - when Utrillo had sold a few small paintings for just a few francs in order to get some money to buy something to eat (or drink?). Wouldn't he be surprised now?

And so to bed - we had a very busy, and long, day ahead of us.

Saturday 29th

After breakfast (not the Hotel Ibis's strong point), we had two hours in hand so Howard had programmed a visit to the Parc Monceau, which neither of us had seen previously. The weather was perfect so, taking with us the remains of yesterday's picnic bread (sliced, from England) and bread from breakfast, specially removed *pour les oiseaux* (unsliced, superior *pain français*), we walked to the Parc Monceau. It seemed to be full of joggers and people doing exercises. One oriental lady was engaged in some rather odd activity; we couldn't decide whether it was exercises or some kind of religious ritual. We fed our bread to sundry collections of sparrows and ducks, all of whom seemed very grateful. We discovered two large statues - one of Maupassant (shades of my 'A' Level French exam) and one of Gounod. Maupassant's statue had a rather droopy female attached to it so I sat on her knee and Howard took a photo of G de M and two droopy females.

By now, it was time to make our way to the Gare de l'Est where we bought return tickets for our trip to Romilly. It said *à composter* all over them but, as we didn't understand what that meant, we decided it didn't apply to us. We were to live to regret that decision. We *did* see people hurrying to get their trains and putting their tickets in little orange machines dotted all over the station but we didn't make the connection…where ignorance is bliss…Just time for a meal at one of the numerous eateries on the station. It took three attempts before we understood what the waiter was trying to tell us to do with our luggage trolley. When we had satisfied his demands, we were rewarded with a lovely steak, some Beaujolais and some cheese.

The Romilly train was very modern, quiet and clean - in every aspect. We felt British Rail could learn a thing or two…After a journey of about eighty minutes, we were met at Romilly station by Peter, one of the two other English people who would be at the wedding. He drove us to Châtres, where we met his wife, Mary. We were to spend most of the time with them and travel back to Paris together the next day. One of their daughters was in *Me and My Girl* in London so we were able to enthuse as we'd seen it twice - and loved every minute. It turned out that Peter was an engineer and built 'plants' for things. (We were not quite sure what type of things…) He told us that he had been to Romania for two years to supervise the building of a plant there - 'it's surprising how quickly you pick up Romanian' he told us.

The four of us changed out of our travelling clothes and into our glad rags for the wedding. 180 people had been invited, so we were not surprised when we kept meeting lots and lots of people arriving at the house. It was very different from an English wedding so very interesting for us all - as none of us had attended a French wedding. At 1400, Mirjam and Jean-Marie (the bride and groom) appeared, dressed in all their wedding finery. The next hour was spent in the extensive grounds of the Fèvre house with much taking of photographs. Mirjam is Dutch and we had a long chat with her father. (We felt ashamed as we know not one word of Dutch!) All Mirjam's family and friends had travelled from Holland, and there was a large number of German friends too. As both Mirjam and Jean-Marie are linguists, they had no problem with the various languages.

At 1500 - as laid down in the invitation - the group photograph was taken; first, about twenty-four children were photographed with the bridge and groom - then the whole group. A special stand had been erected in the garden so the 180 guests ranged themselves on it for the photograph. It was rather chaotic and Jean-Marie was issuing instructions in French, German and Dutch. After the official photograph, anyone who wanted a photo on their own camera was invited to hand their camera to the official photographer, who took it for them.

Next, we were told to form ourselves into a *cortège*. We were rather anxious - until someone told us that *cortège* was merely the word for a procession! The order of the *cortège* was: the bride and her father, all the little children (the little girls were all in white dresses and the little boys in white shirts, bow ties and dark trousers), then all the guests *in order of age* (!), starting with the youngest. Needless to say, we were near the back. Everyone worked out how old they were; we weren't asked to give our ages. We stayed with Peter and Mary towards the back. At the very end of the *cortège* came the groom - on his own. The *cortège* then made its way to the *Mairie* (the Town Hall) where the couple fulfilled the civil ceremony. It took only a couple of minutes, during which time the 180 guests waited outside. Apparently in France the church ceremony and signing of the registers are not acceptable as a legal requirement so the law stipulates that you must have a civil ceremony. We think the couple's parents went into the *Mairie* though we couldn't see, as we were at the end of the line. At the conclusion of the very brief ceremony, the Mayor, carrying the Tricolor under his arm, came out onto the steps with the newly married couple.

The *cortège* moved off to the church, in the same order. The bride and groom did not walk together. At the church, all the guests went in first, followed by the bride and her father, followed by the groom *and his mother*! That *did* amaze us - but apparently it is it what happens at French weddings. Sadly Jean-Marie's father had died the previous year but, had he been there, he would not have been in the procession. The remaining parents were seated at the front of the church, awaiting the arrival of the bridal party.

Nuptial Mass followed and the congregation was issued with a printed form of service with the plainsong setting of the Mass printed out - *in Latin* - which we were told is now very unusual in France. The rest of the service was printed in French and Dutch and the readings and sermon were delivered in both languages. The organist was a blind friend of Jean-Marie and at one point, one of Jean-Marie's numerous sisters (who is also blind) played the Bach-Gounod *Ave Maria* on the violin, accompanied by the organ.

At the conclusion of the service, the newly-wed couple, followed by their parents, went behind the altar and shook hands with the priests (two Dutch priests and the local French priest from the village) and also signed something - perhaps some kind of register as we would do, just for the church records (?). As we came out of the church, there was a guard of honour made up of scouts and guides, as Jean-Marie had been involved in Scouting for a long time, and had been the youngest Scout Commissioner in France.

The *cortège* formed once more - but this time the newly-wed couple were together. They led the procession back to the house and extensive grounds for the *vin d'honneur*, which was champagne. Numerous glasses of it were brought round, together with little cakes.

It was now about 1800 and the next thing on the schedule was the meal at 2000 in the village hall. Little did we know what the meal would be like. We saw a rather elderly lady standing on her own and decided to go and talk to her. We were dying to find someone on whom we could practise our fractured French. (Well, *I* was - Howard's French is very good.) We were so lucky because the lady spoke excellent French, at a speed we could cope with and, an added bonus, she was a *lovely* person. We took to her immediately and spent over an hour in conversation with her. Her name was Nelly Hugot and she had taught Jean-Marie when he had been at the Lycée. She was *very* proud of him as he had done so well. She said if ever we were over that way again, we must be sure to call on her and she gave us her little card. We learned that she had a dog and two cats and lived with an elderly friend.

Eventually, the *vin d'honneur* drinking ceased and we made our way to the village hall for the meal. We found our places from the seating plan - a large one to accommodate the 180 guests. It had been worked out very carefully so that those of similar nationality were seated together. Consequently we were sitting with our two new friends, Peter and Mary, and two Americans. In addition we had three French people with us. Howard sat next to one of Jean-Marie's aunts who didn't like speaking in English.

Very soon we realized that this was going to be no ordinary meal, by the array of glasses and cutlery that was laid before us. We had individual menus with our names printed on them, and a booklet entitled *Guide de Fête*, containing a collage of pictures of the couple over the years, together with a 'running-order' for the evenings, songs (in two languages), and amusing articles - not all of which we understood! The menu itself was a masterpiece. It read:

Melon au Ratafia	
Escalope de Saumon à l'Oseille	
Sorbet Champenois	
Filet de Boeuf Périgourdine	Riesling
Garniture Favorite	
Coeurs de Laitue	Côtes-du-Rhône 1985
Fromages de France	
Charlotte aux Fraises et son Coulis	Champagne
(en pièce montée)	
Soufflé Glacé à la Framboise	Café - Liqueurs
Petits Fours	

Between each course, there was either a short speech or one of the songs (in which everyone joined), then dancing. Consequently, each course took almost an hour. The children were becoming very excited and running round the hall at a great rate - the waiters and waitresses were doing sterling work serving food and drinks whilst avoiding *les jeunes* who threatened to trip them up at any moment. We didn't quite understand what all the courses meant - for instance what was *Melon au Ratafia*? It turned out to be a whole ogen melon each, the seeds having been removed, the top cut off in a decorative shape and replaced as a little lid - not before the space in the middle had been filled with a liqueur! The *Escalope de Saumon à l'Oseille* turned out to be salmon in gooseberry sauce and the *Sorbet Champenois* was Sorbet soaked in a very strong liqueur (Calvados?). We were intrigued to know what the *Charlotte aux Fraises et son Coulis* (en pièce montée) would be. (What is a mounted piece? we asked ourselves.) It turned out to be pieces of fruit set into a sort of mousse. Then there was more champagne and finally coffee and liqueurs.

By now it was about 0200 and we were flagging - fast. We remembered that we had a long journey later this day and an early start was necessary. Our train left Romilly at 0913 and, if we missed it, we would have been in great difficulties as we had to catch a connection in Paris to get us back to Boulogne. A German guest had been delegated to drive us to the local hotel which had been booked for us. Peter and Mary had been staying there for the previous two nights and told us it was 'basic but clean' - an accurate description. Jean-Marie had said that he hoped 'the room would be OK'. We didn't know whether he meant he hoped there would *be* a room or that the room provided would be satisfactory. We were instructed to go up some back stairs on the outside of the building (as the proprietor would not be on duty) and we would find a board with the rooms listed - and the keys. The German man and his wife were also staying there so he knew what to do. We were very pleased as, at that time of night, we would have been worried if we couldn't find the room and/or the keys. He showed us the board where, certainly, rooms were 'chalked up' but some were partially or wholly erased; some keys were there and others not. We managed to work out what we thought would be a double room and took the key to Room 18. Finding it involved another flight of stairs. The German was extremely kind and stayed with us until we not only found the room but ensured it was suitable for us. We knew we would have only a few hours sleep, so without further ado, we leapt into bed and into the arms of Morpheus.

Sunday 30th

We were ready for breakfast at 0800. One of Jean-Marie's sisters had been delegated to pick up both us and Peter and Mary at 0850 to take us to Romilly station to catch our 0913 train. At 0800 there was no sign of life at the hotel. It was as quiet as the grave and all doors into what might have been a breakfast room remained firmly locked. After a while, the lady in charge appeared so we were able to have some *petit déjeuner* and settle our bill (£9 for a double room and breakfast for both of us!) whereupon Dominique arrived to take us to the station. She told us the party had finished about 0530 and, when she had got home, her two children (aged 2 years and 3 months) had been rather fractious and demanding attention so we guessed she had had no sleep at all - yet she looked as fresh as a daisy! It convinced us we must be getting old!

At Romilly station, we learned the significance of *à composter* - as Dominique accompanied us into the station to explain that we had to put our tickets into the orange machines to have them cancelled. She told us that failure to do this could incur a fine! We had been lucky on the journey down. Back in Paris we agreed to share a taxi with Peter and Mary to get to the other station - not very far away. We piled all our luggage into a waiting taxi and then piled in ourselves - but when Howard tried to get into the passenger seat at the front with the driver (the other three of us were sitting in the back) we were told that it was *interdit* to travel in the front, so Peter and Mary said they would take a separate taxi. Luggage was then *unloaded* from the boot and they set off on their own. We were rather sad, as we had not had time to say 'goodbye' to them properly. We went to the Gare du Nord, to a restaurant where we have eaten on a number of previous occasions. We noted that they started serving at 1130 so there would just be time to get a meal before checking in at the station for the 1240 train.

The return journey was uneventful and efficient, the sea was very calm, the *aeroglisseur* whisked us from one side of the Channel to the other in thirty-five minutes - then we boarded a Victoria train at Dover station.

Home by 1845 and a very early night, to catch up on our missed sleep - but not before we had made a pot of real tea - the only thing the French don't seem to understand.

Quelle Fête Formidable!

"He really captured her in this one."

MAJORCA? MALLORCA?
However you spell it, we went there!
January 1988

Thursday 7th

We received a note from the travel agent: "There will be minor internal refurbishments taking place". This did not augur well. Was it a euphemism for:

1	The hotel has been stripped and is being rebuilt?
2	They are putting on a new roof - or, at least, that part over our room?
3	The hotel isn't *yet* built?

Wednesday 13th

We collected our Spanish currency from the bank. The crisp new notes bore a picture of a very bad-tempered-looking man on the 2,000 ones, and a very sad-looking man on the 1,000 notes. (Is he sad because he can't be on the 2,000 notes? Perhaps he was once on them and went bankrupt?) It was rather like Monopoly money and we made a note to buy two hotels on Trafalgar Square the minute we arrived. Can Majorca really be in the Balearics? It sounds more like a disease than an area. (I mustn't forget to pack the cream in case I get an attack of the Balearics.)

Sunday 17th

1645 saw us taking off with Britannia Airways. Almost immediately, we were treated to a video to show us what to do should the plane crash. The people in the video looked so cool, calm and collected. (I was convinced that if it *did* crash, I would be in too much of a state to remember where to wind the straps, inflate the life jacket, find the whistle, inflate the straps, wind the whistle round and jump off the wings!) A little panel permanently displayed the altitude and ground speed. (We're not on the ground all the time but they seem to prefer it that way.) At one point, the display indicated 40,000 feet and 500 mph - but, out of the window, the horizon looked stationary. I was convinced we had not yet taken off and someone at Gatwick was pulling a cardboard screen across the windows. There was nothing to see except the sunset - but, I had to admit, that was pretty spectacular! We climbed up to 41,000 feet (by 'we' I mean the aircraft - not us personally) and levelled out at 520 mph. We were eight miles up!

The plastic meal was acceptable and, no sooner was it finished, the pilot informed us that we were just under half an hour from landing, so he wished us a happy holiday and would say goodbye. Where was he going? If he got out now, we would *all* be for it! The descent began - and we monitored it on the display panel.

At first Howard calculated how many feet we were descending every ten seconds but the descent quickly got out of hand - even for Howard's computer-like brain. (I began to wonder whether I should have taken more notice of the escape procedures...) Suddenly the machine switched itself off and said "Thank you for flying Britannia Airways". (Why should they thank us? *They* did the flying. Left to us, we'd have been in one hell of a muddle by now...) We approached the runway at 140 mph. We hoped we would slow down in time - or there would be the quickest customs and passport clearance known to man.

We arrived at Magaluf at 2200 and checked over our room, looking for signs of the leak in the roof or any other indication of the 'minor refurbishment'. We found none - but it was very hot and we discovered that the radiator was set at (what seemed to be) 5,000 degrees Fahrenheit. Our endeavours to turn it down met with no success so we went to sleep with the minimum of bedclothes. From the lounge, we could hear what the brochure described as 'entertainment'. It was not *exactly* our sort of entertainment but, weren't we lucky, we could hear the incessant drum beats - even though we were on the third floor. What it must have been like on floors one and two we could only imagine. We noted that the first floor had a special baby-sitting area where the little ones could go to bed while their parents were being entertained. (Perhaps the tots were terribly into percussion?) Strange noises emanated from the plumbing system but we supposed we would get used to them. There was black soap in the bathroom. Was it joke? No, our faces came up shining white.

Monday 18th

We decided to go to Palma, the capital of the island, to see the cathedral. The bus stop was right outside our hotel and it cost a mere 50p for the eight mile journey. The bus was very old-fashioned, with shiny wooden seats which we slipped off every time it went round a corner - and there seemed to be many corners on this particular journey.

Palma was much bigger than Magaluf - much more city-like. We headed for the cathedral which was enormous. A man was issuing admission tickets, which cost £1, though that did include admission to the cathedral 'treasures'. There were numerous side chapels, stuffed full of artefacts, paintings, gold-covered statues etc. - but all were firmly *locked*. We assumed this was for security purposes. There were two large, rather garishly-coloured rose windows which did not depict religious figures. It wasn't possible to see the most important part - the tomb of the Kings. The 'treasures' did not disappoint. They included a number of relics surrounded by vast amounts of jewels and, believe it or not, they had a piece of the true cross, surrounded by even *more* jewels.

All this culture made us peckish so we headed for the *Sea Horse* restaurant. The meal was excellent but we were slightly uneasy about a tank full of live lobsters, just waiting to be eaten. (We hoped they didn't know…) They are not the most attractive of creatures but we couldn't help but admire the way they are put together. What do all the bits do? After the sangria and the Spanish brandy, a walk by the sea was a *must*. We wondered if it was possible to return by boat, but it didn't look too promising so we made our way back to the bus - meeting two black swans on the way.

Back at the hotel, we attended the (by now predictable) Welcome Party. Most of the things on offer we would not want to touch with half a dozen barge poles, but we did book to go to the Caves of Drach. After dinner, we took a walk round Magaluf in search of possible eateries for the times when we would not eat in the hotel. We found only one that looked viable, serving local food; there were copious 'British Pubs' offering 'Pub Food - Bacon and Eggs - Shepherd's Pie' etc. which made us wonder what it must be like to be there in the height of the season!

Tuesday 19th

We set out to explore the five-star hotel about one mile away round the headland. On the way we passed many new apartments to rent or buy. Presumably this was going to be a very up-and-coming area, though it was very quiet. There were signs to the Royal Savoy Residential Club. We didn't know what it was - but it sounded expensive. When we reached the multi-star hotel, we found it *closed*. On the adjacent road, we discovered supermarkets, ' British pubs' and similar were springing up, so we assumed that, soon, it would be another Magaluf.

We wandered on down to the beach and the bay and came upon a desultory bar. We wondered who went into it at this time of year, since there was not a soul in sight. Just then, one extremely large spot of rain, immediately followed by other similar, made their presence felt. Before I had the chance to say "I think it's about to rain" (always one for the *bon mot*), a huge downpour ensued. We wondered no more 'who went into this bar at this time of year'. The answer was *us*. Two orange drinks and one storm later, we emerged again. We discovered what we thought was the Royal Savoy but it looked 'closed for the winter'. As far as we could tell, they were merely very expensive-looking apartments.

We made our way back to the hotel and, since we had had a rather expensive lunch the previous day, we bought an extremely inexpensive picnic - and some postcards.

The afternoon promised a trip to Marineland, half way between Magaluf and Palma. We were at the bus stop at 1350 for the 1400 bus. At 1440 we were *still* at the bus stop. A fellow traveller had warned us that we should never believe the bus timetables. Another couple joined us and, as they were going to Marineland, we shared a taxi. Marineland was not disappointing. First there were the seals, then the dolphins. The seals were fun but the dolphins were amazing. I thought I would invest in a dolphin and train it to do shopping. After all, they can train them to track down submarines and things, so shopping should be a piece of cake. The penguins won our hearts. They liked being stroked - and even being picked up and cuddled. They were very sweet - and handy sized. We watched the parrots 'do their thing'. How clever they were - but what a noise they made - and could there have been the teeniest bit of jealousy among them?

We returned to the hotel on the most crowded bus we had ever seen. One of the passengers was carrying a vast rubber-plant. As soon as we'd had dinner, we turned in as we had an early start for the Caves of Drach the next day.

Wednesday 20th

Today we tried to work out who everyone was. There was a golf team amassing to our left. Many of them had shirts with messages emblazoned across their chests. A Frenchman's chest proclaimed 'Adventure Equipment'. (What kind of equipment and what kind of adventure?) In the evenings, many of the ladies had glittery, bejewelled decorations all over their bosoms. In certain lights, we were dazzled by the glare! We wondered if they wore this garb 'in flight' and, if so, did it interfere with the aircraft's instruments. Enough musing - the Caves of Drach beckoned.

A comfortable coach ride took us to Manacor and a visit to a pearl factory where they made MAJORICA pearls. These are imitation pearls but, we were told, they couldn't be distinguished from the 'real thing' (except by oysters, we supposed). Nevertheless, they were expensive. The visit was somewhat disappointing as there was no guide. From a balcony, we watched the people (all female) at work, but we could only guess what they were doing. It would have been much better if there had been someone to explain what was happening and to tell us the comparative costs of what we were seeing and the equivalent in *real* pearls. The tour ended in the inevitable shop where there was a huge selection of 'everything pearl'. We resisted the temptation to buy anything as we are not really 'pearl' people.

The next stop was Porto Cristo and the Caves of Drach (caves of the dragon). We deprecated the fact that the guide had not warned people to bring extra warm clothes for the caves. We knew from bitter experience just how cold caves can be. Imagine our surprise when the guide told us these caves are at a constant temperature of 65 degrees all year round. Not only that - we would probably find it warmer *inside* the caves than *outside*. (That'll teach us!) The caves were spectacular - stalagmites and stalactites in abundance. We reckoned they must have been there for a 'good few years'. We were not wrong - between approximately ten and twenty million years apparently. We watched some boats in the 'theatre'. One of them contained live musicians. It was a most attractive spectacle. Musicians that had played here in the past included Sarasate and Pau Casals. The guidebook told us:

> "The small orchestra, on a boat trimmed with tiny lights emerges from the deep darkness of Lake 'Great Duchess of Toscana' and crosses Lake Martel to the strains of *Alborada* (Dawn Song) by Caballero, accompanied by two other illuminated gondolas that throw light upon the most delicate crevices of these crafted scenarios of water and limestone, while the musicians play *Study in E Major* by Chopin (the famous 'How still is the night' piano étude) and *Largo* by Handel, in their boat stationed immobile behind a column." [Should this sentence be considered for 'the longest sentence in the English Language' Prize? Ed.]

> "Later, when the three boats are joined, commence the return to the strains of Offenbach's *Barcarolle*. The Drach's quartet was conducted for forty-seven years by the great musician Jaume Vadell, who professed to have performed more than thirty thousand concerts on the lake. Nowadays all the musicians of the Drach's quartet belong to the *Ciudad de Manacor* Chamber Orchestra."

It was quite a long, but measured, walk down to the level of the lake. We couldn't imagine what all this must have looked like to the people who originally discovered it - without the advantage of electric lights and the steps and walkways that had been built there. It must have been very scary. We decided we would not become speleologists. We were told there were 190 steps to climb to get out and Raphael, our courier (his similarity to an archangel was minimal) warned us to take them slowly and rest if we got tired. (As if we needed this 'warning'…) We counted them as we ascended. Imagine our surprise and delight when, on reaching step number 119, there were no more! We must have misheard.

Howard had researched a restaurant in Porto Cristo for our lunch. We walked up a very steep hill, but failed to find it. Majorca is not noted for its street signs (mostly there aren't any) so there was no way of knowing where the Avenue of the Pines was - and the area seemed deserted. We asked someone - but he was

Scottish. We asked a local builder - but he 'didn't come from those parts' (at least that's what we think he said - our Spanish being non-existent). We had noticed an eatery on the way up the steep hill so we returned to it. Our hopes of having Paella were dashed as, though it was on the menu, it took twenty minutes to prepare and time was not on our side. Nevertheless we had a delicious meal. Howard had fried squid! I didn't.

Back on the road, we stopped at a very touristy ceramics shop which offered 'free drinks'. The glasses were miniscule - but we could refill them time and time again with tastings of numerous Spanish liqueurs and the inevitable sangria. We had to admit the shop had lovely ceramics - so we bought a little bear, just to remind us...

Thursday 21st

We took advantage of the one day free car hire (which was part of our deal) and drove from Magaluf to Palma, then on to Inca via Santa Maria, Consell and Binissalem. Thursday was market day at Inca. In the fruit and vegetable market we bought some oranges - with the green leaves still attached. Hygiene didn't seem to be a high priority - at least as far as the cauliflowers were concerned. They were 'dumped' in a huge pile on the ground and prospective customers picked through them like old clothes in a jumble sale. We tried to look in the church but it was safely locked. A Spanish lady told us (we think) that 'it only opens in the evening tomorrow' (?) We lit upon a leather shop, full of wonderful things, but we asked ourselves "quite honestly, what would we do with them?".

We continued on our way via Alcùdia to Puerto Pollensa. This turned out to be a very pretty place and we noted 'very up-market tourism here'. We tracked down the restaurant that Howard had researched for lunch, only to find it was closed. Indeed, it looked as though it was being refurbished. We soon found another eatery where we had a very acceptable lunch. Howard had *Moules Marinières*. I didn't!

The Hotel Formentor was the next stop. The Hotel and the Cap Formentor were reputed to be 'very special'. What a surprise - the hotel was closed - but we realized that it was not the sort of place we could afford to stay in our lifetime! We turned our attention to the beach. 'Beautiful' really was an understatement. We met some other British people and severally wondered how much it would cost to stay there. The others said that they had been told it was millionaires' paradise, though maybe nowadays the millionaires go to Barbados (?). It certainly looked very luxurious.

We drove up to the lighthouse at Cap Formentor, which took us round windy roads ('windy' as in 'roads with lots of bends' rather than 'lots of breezes'). There were even more breathtaking views at the top. It was very, very windy (this time as in 'breezy' only more so...) and not stiflingly hot so we were glad we had packed extra sweaters. The descent was just as hair-raising as the ascent.

Back at sea level, we headed for the Monastery of Lluch where we had been led to believe there was a sort of Black Madonna and Child - though it turned out to be brown and called 'the little brown lady'. The story of how she came to be there was rather improbable but we located the monastery. The first sign we saw within the monastery, in large neon letters, read 'Bar and Restaurant'. We'd never come across any monasteries with a bar and restaurant before - but then we hadn't been to *that* many monasteries. The brown Madonna turned out to be black (from the candle smoke?) and she was kept behind glass. Apparently she is known as Our Lady of Lluch and is the patron saint of Majorca. The whole basilica was very ornate and, at the high altar, scaffolding was erected and tarpaulins let down from it (?minor refurbishments?). It appeared they were re-gilding the enormous altarpiece. We didn't see any more of the monastery, nor did we sight a monk. We were not sure how much we were allowed to 'wander around' - so we didn't.

Time was getting on and we had yet to drive home. The monastery gift shop was still open, though there was hardly a tourist in sight - except us. The music on the ever-present musak machine was 'pop' music, which seemed very out of place. We eschewed plastic models of the Black Madonna - that lit up!! Similarly a life-sized copy - where would we put it? We were not there at the right time of the day to hear the famous Lluch boys choir (the Blue Boys) but we observed them dragging around large quantities of twigs and wondered if it was for a bonfire. They seemed to live in a choir school and, given that it was miles from anywhere, we wondered if they got lonely. We assumed they sang plainsong (and the like) at the appropriate times, so we were interested when we saw a record of them on sale in the gift shop - but, on the record, they were singing the *Blue Danube* and a Brahms *Hungarian Dance*!

We made our way back via Selva and Inca and were back by 1930. The car was still half full of petrol so we had fulfilled our part of the bargain. We returned the keys to reception and headed for dinner. It had been a long day - especially for Howard who had had to do all the driving - on the wrong side of the road - but it had been well worth it, and having the free car meant that it was very economical.

Friday 22nd

Our destination today was Bellver Castle, so we took the Palma bus. The hotel had advised us to get off at Tony's Night Club. The rather bad-tempered bus driver was not exceedingly helpful about pointing out our stop - but we got off anyway. Though there was no sign of a castle, we made it, with the aid of our map. On arrival at the gates, we discovered they were padlocked, though held open loosely with a chain - enough to gain admittance. We met a lady with a lovely fluffy Alsatian dog and asked her if the castle was open. (We didn't feel inclined to ascend what looked like lots of steps only to find it closed.) The lady indicated that there were two ways up - the stairs and the road - and, if we took the stairs, we would be out of breath. (This was indicated in mime.) She hadn't actually answered our question - was the castle open? - but we decided to ascend the stairs. Even stopping at the Chapel *en route*, there were 487 steps…but at a comfortable incline. The castle really was worth the visit; to think what it must have been like 'in the old days'…the guidebook told us they had bullfights in the courtyard! The little museum, which promised 'olde worlde' things and armour, was very interesting. Though there were lots of 'olde worlde' things (some from as far back as 1700 BC), there was no armour. As we'd only paid 45p to get in, we were not complaining. We were rewarded with lots of wonderful views from the top, but we wondered how anyone ever attempted to invade it. It was such a long climb - the invaders *must* have got a taxi - or they would have had no breath left to invade.

We retraced our steps and proceeded to the sea front, looking for possible lunch places *en route*. We found the place where the boats left for Magaluf at 1630 and we decided to take a boat back to our hotel. We found a good lunch place, but still they didn't have gazpacho. The waiter told us "it was a cold soup and the weather is too cold for it"…Finally, however, we did have paella - and very good it was too. Howard had fish and I had a combination of fish and meat. We noticed under *Postres* (that's pudding to us) that we could have Caramel Casters!

By the time we finished our lunch, the sun was well and truly out, so we went in search of the church of San Francisco. We were not surprised to find it locked - so we thought we'd try the Palacia Vivot. The guidebook told us that we had to 'tug a chain to ring the bell' to gain admission. That had changed to 'press an entry phone' - which we did. A disembodied voice told us that it was closed for restoration! We did manage to see the church of St Eulalia. Nothing is recorded about this particular visit so we can only conclude that it was not very memorable.

We returned to the sea front and the departure point for the boat to Magaluf. A board indicated that the *Flipper Segundo* would leave at 1630 and sail round the immediate bay, dropping people off at Magaluf (hopefully not straight into the water). It was 1610 and while we were waiting, I spoke to a seated lady - wearing a fur coat (?). Her English was minimal and first she told me that the boat would go "tomorrow", then the trip would take "ten hours" (we reckoned it was all of about one hour), then "the boat only goes in September, August and July" (in that order?). While I was having this conversation, Howard had been approached by a man selling contraband gold ornaments 'that he got in Barcelona'...Howard didn't buy any of them. By now, we were thoroughly confused about the possibility of the projected maritime trip and we were convinced no boat would arrive. Imagine our surprise when, just before 1630, the *Flipper Segundo* pulled up! Our joy was short lived. The boatman told us he had finished for the day - "the trips to the resorts are only in the summer" - and what he was doing was "we translate the persons from the ship in the *buy*" (thus pronounced).

We had to retrace our steps to the bus stop and took a bus back to Palma Nova from where we walked the rest of the way along the beach, where possible. Where not possible, we rejoined the road, where we saw what must have been the posh part of Palma Nova; not a fish and chip shop or British pub in sight, but very 'Des Res' everywhere. The last part of our walk took us along the long stretch of beach from Palma Nova to Magaluf, in a beautiful sunset.

Saturday 23rd

A trip on the Glass Bottom boat was planned but we were extremely doubtful that it would happen; we were quite prepared for 'it only goes in the season' - but our luck was in - it was going. Only a handful of people boarded at Magaluf and there was some difficulty in fixing the gangplank so that we *could* board, as the sea was rather choppy. Free wine on board was advertised. The first half hour seemed quite bumpy, as we went around the bay collecting other people. Once we got under way, it became much smoother - or was it that we were getting our sea legs? No sooner had we moved off round the bay than we encountered dolphins who stayed alongside the boat for a while, until they got bored. ("Not *another* lot of tourists?") Our voyage took us in and out of little coves, with the two crew taking it in turns to navigate - though a lot of the time the navigation seemed negligible. They seemed to consume large quantities of beer and, as soon as all the passengers were on board, they announced that the bar was open - and a price list appeared. What had happened to the 'free wine on board'? We stopped for half an hour at Portals Vells where we wandered up to the caves. We found amazing sculptures on the walls but it was not clear what they were.

Back on board we headed straight back to Magaluf and the (by now) very cheerful Spanish sailors told us there was free sangria, dispensed from one of those wine-pouring containers with a very long stem. This was held aloft above our heads and the contents poured down our throats at an alarming rate. The Glass Bottom referred to two observation places through which we could watch the marine life. I had expected that the whole of the floor of the boat would have been made of strong reinforced glass - but it was not so.

We lunched at *Pepe's*, the only restaurant we found in Magaluf that served Spanish food - and not just egg and chips! We spent a long time over lunch, which we took outdoors, the weather having improved sufficiently to allow this. After lunch we made our first trip to the beach; the weather had not been warm enough to permit this earlier in the week. We watched the afternoon departure of the Glass Bottom boat and, when the temperature began to fall, we retired to our room prior to dinner in the hotel.

Sunday 24th

We went to the top of the hotel to see for ourselves what was happening. All we could think was, if that was what they called 'minor refurbishment', what was their idea of 'major refurbishment'? Floors eight, nine and ten were open to the elements at either end and the doors and windows of the rooms had been removed. All three floors had been completely stripped. We were glad we were on the third floor.

Breakfast time and a different selection of people appeared, together with some old faces. There was a woman whose bosom proclaimed HARRODS. (We wondered if her husband would have BROKE emblazoned across his chest.) We had the room until midday so we did some last-minute shopping, where we ran into a friend from Kennington! We took our final meal in the hotel and spent the afternoon sitting in the lounge reading. The temperature outside has dropped again. Just after 1700 we were told that there was an hour's delay. An Englishman, travelling on our coach, told us that he had learned from yesterday's newspaper that there has been snow in England and that airports had been closed. Our hearts sank - but we need not have worried. The return journey went smoothly and uneventfully and we were back in Kennington by 2300.

PARIS IN THE SPRING
April 1988

Friday 22nd

We made a start at 0430 so arrived very early at the new check-in place at Victoria station. We were so early that we couldn't get in but a security guard admitted us, without any checks on who we were or what we were doing. (Perhaps 'security guard' was somewhat of a misnomer?) As soon as the time ticked round to 0600, we were able to check in our case and get our seat reservations and boarding cards, so no need to queue at the airport. One of the incentives to get people to use the new check-in was that they offered free single rail tickets to Gatwick. We caught the 0615 Gatwick Express and arrived in time to buy papers and duty-frees. We were persuaded to buy a different make of cigarette for our friend Val as the lady told us a) they were the same (?) b) they were 60p cheaper and c) we got two free photo albums with them! Can't be bad...

The flight to Charles de Gaulle was a mere forty minutes, but they served breakfast, which consisted of a sweet cake and coffee and tea. We were met at Charles de Gaulle by the Thomson representative who ushered us all into a waiting coach for the journey to the Gare du Nord. To get to our hotel, we were taken by taxi (paid for by Thomsons) so we had a long ride across the city - free. The Hotel Liberia really *did* exist (we had wondered - with such an unusual name) and *Monsieur et Madame les concierges* were much more affable than some *concierges* we had encountered.

We wasted no time in going in search of lunch at the *Polidor*, making our way to it through the Jardins de Luxembourg. We were glad to see that the *Polidor* was still doing very well. (Could it be since people heard that *we* had eaten there?) Fortified by lunch, we took the métro to the Degas Exhibition at the Grand Palais. It was a very comprehensive exhibition indeed. There were over 300 exhibits and it declared that it was the largest exhibition in the world (we presumed they meant 'of Degas things'?). After its sojourn in Paris, it was to go to Ottawa and New York. It included an amazing picture of Manet and his wife - with the wife cut off! Apparently, Manet had done this because he didn't like it. (We imagined that Degas wasn't too keen on Monsieur Manet after that...) As the catalogue cost £30, we didn't buy one, but we did splash out £4 on a smaller version, packed full of information. The Exhibition was well laid out with drawings, sketches, paintings and, in room D, sculptures - including the famous ballet dancer. There were some sculpted horses so we resolved to get some postcards of these for Rosemary Proctor. Sadly there were no postcards of the sculptures.

We walked back to our hotel down the Boulevard St Germain and the Boulevard Raspail, a walk of about two miles. When we had rested (our early start was beginning to catch up on us), we were off in search of dinner. As usual Howard had done his research and the first port of call was *Le Dôme*. There was lots of seafood on offer, but it was an expensive place so we didn't patronize it. *La Coupole* - almost next door - was closed for renovation (April 14th until December - wow! that would be *some* renovation!) The one that Howard had in mind was *Le Bistro de la Gare* - and that *was* open and was where we ate - outdoors. We endeavoured to work out the relationship of the others diners - was that his secretary, daughter, mistress? The inside of the restaurant was spectacular. It was a real olde worlde *brasserie*, with brass railings, enamelled panels and lots and lots of mirrors on the walls.

After dinner, we took ourselves off for a little wander round Montparnasse; where was the famous fifty-nine storey tower? Suddenly we emerged from an underpass to find a glass and metal building and, as we raised our eyes…and raised our eyes…and raised our eyes, eventually we saw the top, towering fifty-nine floors above us. It was a slightly vertigo-making moment.

We returned to the hotel to catch up on our sleep and prepare for the next day when we were going to see the graves of Saint-Saëns, César Franck and co.

Saturday 23rd

The cemetery of Montparnasse was our first port of call. Though we had a map, it was not easy to find the graves we had identified. Eventually we succeeded in finding Saint-Saëns, Vincent d'Indy, César Franck, Guy de Maupassant and a cenotaph to Baudelaire. Two that we couldn't identify but which struck us as strange were a very odd 'Thinker'-like statue coming out of a wall and a full-sized body lying on the ground with OPIUM written on its head.

We had to attend the Thomson Welcome Party. One of the representatives was giving the assembled company riveting information about the Eiffel Tower - literally. Did we know that there were 2.5 million rivets in the Tower and that the weight of it is the same as the weight of seven jumbo jets? Well, we had to say we did *not* know that - and we fell to wondering how it might affect the rest of our lives. We were told that it is possible to see forty-two miles from the top of the Tower. It turned out that trips to Giverny did not happen on any of the days we were there, so we reverted to Plan A, which was to make our own way by train on Sunday.

We set off for the Foire du Trône, the fair in the Bois de Vincennes which we had seen advertised in the métro. We walked to the Porte St Denis where we a) bought a picnic to eat in the Bois de Vincennes and b) booked a table at the *Brasserie Flo* for later that evening. Our visits to Paris *always* include a meal at this restaurant, Sunday lunch at *Chartier* and the organ recital in Notre Dame on a Sunday night. We stopped for some French onion soup - some of the best we've ever had - after putting our noses into St Eustache, where it looked as though they had finished restoring the organ. On our last visit to Paris, there was much information on panels at the back of the church all about the restoration. That had gone and organ recitals were now advertised. Jean Guillou was the organist of St Eustache and the second organist was André Fleury.

We wandered down the rue St Denis to buy our picnic. What a place! There were ladies (?) stationed every ten yards or so along the pavement. It was lucky that it was a warm day as they were not overburdened with clothes. *Chacun à son*…We booked our table at the *Brassiere Flo* where they were already busy serving lunch. This place is like the Windmill - it never stops. The men were outside preparing the fresh fish, as usual.

Now it was time to head for the Bois de Vincennes. Apparently Louis XIV had his honeymoon in this wood. We supposed he couldn't afford the prices in the Paris hotels. We found a good spot, sitting in the sun by the lake, and made short work of our picnic. We were joined by a huge number of dogs out for their walks, some of whom came and talked to us - uninvited. Many joggers were out in force too and we felt very lazy. Nothing for it but to have another strawberry. We fed the remains of our bread to the ducks, who didn't seem particularly grateful. We thought they probably got lots of food.

Off to the fair. Some of the rides were terrifying. Needless to say, we didn't go on them. We really *are* middle-aged (and in the case of me, a congenital coward). Some of the 'attractions' went right through 360 degrees, stopping at the top of the arc so the passengers were upside down! Just to *watch* this made us feel queasy. We didn't enter the competition to win a larger-than-life-sized teddy bear. Our only indulgence was candyfloss; it was like eating pink cotton wool. The noise of the fair was almost unbearable. Every ride was accompanied by very loud, raucous pop music and all the stall holders were doing their best to drum up custom by broadcasting their wares through a microphone. This was not the place for a peaceful afternoon stroll - but it took us back to our childhood. We wondered how much it would have cost to bring two children to this fair. The average cost of a ride was 10F (£1 approximately).

We left the fair and headed for the tranquillity of the zoo, but we realized we were running out of time so we contented ourselves with seeing a few animals through the fence, including some zebras. Howard maintained they were merely horses who had put their pyjamas on for an early night. (I was reminded of the Irishman who had a pet zebra called Spot.)

We returned to the hotel to change into more respectable garb for our visit to the *Brasserie Flo* - one of our all-time favourite eateries. A party of Americans arrived at the table next to us - and their first course had to be seen to be believed. It consisted of two large two-tiered assorted *fruits de mer*. One elderly American looked quite intimidated by it! They couldn't believe it was all for them, so they invited us to help out; it was too late since we had finished our main course. For me there was no decision to be made about pudding as Passion Fruit sorbet was on the menu. Howard was more adventurous - bitter chocolate cake and coffee sauce - calorie free of course. Our meal was washed down with an excellent bottle of Côte du Rhône.

As was our wont, we followed our meal with a walk up to Sacré Coeur and a wander round the Place du Tertre. We didn't think there were as many artists there as we had seen in the past; much more of the area seems to be used for tables from the numerous cafés.

Sunday 24th

First stop was the Gare St Lazare to buy our tickets for Vernon because we were off to Monet-land. There was an hour before the train left so we walked to the Church of the Trinité. The organ was playing as we arrived, but Bach rather than Messiaen. Is it, indeed, Messiaen playing? We couldn't see but we doubted it. Last time we had been here, we were told that he only appears on Grandes Fêtes - and Easter 4 could hardly come into that category. A desultory choir 'moaned' its way through a desultory setting. A cantor appeared from nowhere (maybe the Opéra by the sound of his voice) and led the congregational responses - to not much avail. The congregation wandered in late. It was much worse than at home, where, on the whole, most people were there at the start and a *few* arrived late - here it seemed it was the other way round. The church was very pretty; the sun was streaming in and many chandeliers were lit. We felt the latter were not necessary as the aforesaid streaming sun provided ample illumination. We stayed until the end of the sermon then returned to the station to get our train.

The train was going all the way to Dieppe and was quite crowded. It was very long; if we had walked much further down it, we would have arrived at Dieppe before it had moved. Eventually we managed to find two seats for the very fast (forty minute) journey to Vernon, which was the first stop.

At Vernon we were given excellent directions to both eateries which our food expert had researched. *Les Fleurs* didn't attract us much so we pressed on to *Au*

Beau Rivage. Weren't we glad we did! It was *the* most perfect place, with *the* most perfect food and wine - taken whilst sitting outside in the sun, in perfect weather with a view of the Seine. No wonder the place is in the *Gault Millau and Michelin* guides. According to the sign outside, it had been in the *Chaîne des Rôtisseurs* 'since 1248 - 1950'. (We didn't know they had food critics as long ago as 1248 - and whatever happened in 1950 that meant they had to leave it?) It also featured in *Le Bottin Gourmand* and *Guide Hachette France* 1985. And it deserved them all! If there was ever a more perfect day - and occasion - and with Monet-land ahead, we couldn't imagine what it could be.

The moment was nearly upon us - when we would set off for Giverny and Monet-land. Howard paid the bill and, at the same time, asked them to call a taxi to take us there. That was the only way to get there - except by bicycle, which could be hired. The snag there was that I can't ride a bike - at least not very successfully. I have two problems - one is starting, the other, stopping. Someone has to give me a push to start and the only way I can stop is by falling off (bad for me and the bike) or by running into a wall (not to be recommended). So a taxi it had to be. We would ask it to return at 1445 to collect us and return us to the station to get the 1510 train back to Paris. If that proved impossible, maybe we would have to walk back to the station and therefore catch the 1700 train. We wanted to get back on the earlier train so that we had time to get to the Notre Dame organ recital at 1745.

While Howard negotiated with the restaurant, I sat writing up this diary (in very scribbly note form). The fire engine, which we had seen going out not so long ago with all sirens sounding, returned - with all sirens still sounding. As it rounded the corner, the driver saw a friend and stopped for a chat! While we waited for the taxi, we wrote a few postcards. There was not much room for the message as the details on the reverse of the postcard told us that it was the Hall of Mirrors in Versailles - but in seven languages (including two in oriental characters).

Time went on and no taxi appeared. The lady of the restaurant told us that she had tried three taxi firms, all of whom said they were having lunch and couldn't take us for another forty-five minutes. There was only one thing for it - the lady offered to take us herself - and did! It was *so* kind of her- she was so sweet - as was her little grand-daughter whom she brought along for the ride.

On arrival at the Monet House and Gardens, we enquired about taxis back to Vernon and were told that there was a phone in the garden. A French lady, who had overheard our conversation, told us that she and her husband also wanted to get the 1510 train back to Paris. She offered to phone for the taxi and we agreed to meet at 1430 in the little bookshop. They had seen the garden in the morning so just had to see the house when it opened at 1400. This meant we didn't have to waste any time making phone calls.

We headed straight for the gardens. What a sight! And what scents there were. Everywhere we looked were beautiful flowers of all sorts, shapes, sizes and colours. It was indescribable - and the book we bought did it full justice. On we went to the water gardens and the Japanese bridge - pictorial representations of which we had seen so many times. It was thrilling to see it now 'for real'. We were surprised to find what a huge tourist attraction the place was. The water lilies were not out - but there *were* some green boats moored - and everywhere we looked were more and more flowers. It was idyllic. How we longed for the Proctors to see it. We returned (past some black tulips!) to the house, which looked quite large from the outside. Inside we found that the rooms that we were able to visit were not numerous - and it was very crowded. We crawled around in a conga-like line with everyone else. The kitchen and dining room were blue-tiled and yellow respectively - and we saw Monet's bed - but it was all too crowded for comfort. We were grateful that we had not come one hour later as, when we emerged, the queue to get in was enormous. We met up with the French people (who turned out to be Swiss) in the bookshop where we managed to get some postcards and two copies of a wonderful book about the gardens, one for us and one for the Proctors. We hoped they would not have it already as they seemed to have every word ever written about Monet. We were reasonably sure they would not have this one as it had been published in France.

The taxi returned us to Vernon in good time for the train, which was a double-decker - so we travelled back to Paris upstairs. After a quick turn round in the hotel, we set off for the Notre Dame organ recital, given by Robert Hebble of the USA. As usual, the Cathedral was packed and, as we'd arrived a few minutes late, we could not get a seat. It never ceased to amaze us how in excess of 1,000 people turned up for these recitals. He played some baroque music, JSB, Karg-Elert, and finished with two movements of a symphony which *he* had written and dedicated to the memory of his teacher, Virgil Fox. We feared the worst, but were pleasantly surprised. The Cathedral shop was closed by the end of the recital. It was just as well or we might have been tempted to buy some organ tapes for CP.

We went back via the nearby market selling little birds - which we'd seen on the way. Our day ended at *Le Petit Zinc*. It was thronging with Americans, though a real Frenchman sat next to us - and smoked throughout! The couple who sat opposite us were 'something else'. The wife (?) did not stop complaining. She didn't want any of the sauces; she pointed out to her husband (?) that she would be wearing the same thing on Wednesday and Thursday evening because she wanted to wear the *suit* on Friday night. She couldn't possibly wear it on Wednesday night as those people had seen it already! (What unimportant things concern people!) Despite all this extra-curricular activity, we had an excellent meal.

Monday 25th

This was the day for our return to London, but not before we had ascended all fifty-nine floors of the great Montparnasse Tower. We had been given discount vouchers for this by Thomsons. (It usually cost £3 but we paid only £2-30 - not much of a discount...) We discovered that the fifty-sixth floor was *only* for tourists - and the panoramic view. There the view was from the *inside*. We walked up the remaining three floors where we emerged *en pleine air* to get the unfettered panoramic view - and *what* a view! It was somewhat misty so we couldn't see the forty-two miles which could be seen from the Eiffel Tower (and, therefore, presumably from here too) but we saw wonderful sights nevertheless. We returned to ground level in the lift and counted as accurately as we could. If our calculations were correct, it took thirty-six seconds to descend fifty-six floors! But then, gravity was on our side....

We bought our final picnic, returned to the hotel to collect our things and took a taxi to the Jardin des Tuilleries to eat our lunch, before boarding our coach at 1215 for the return to the airport.

Au Revoir Paris......

"You know, I think you're right."

A FORTNIGHT'S FROLIC THROUGH THE FALL FOLIAGE
or
Why the Gettysburg Address has no postcode
October 1988

Thursday 6th

At 0600, we had tea, followed by a two course breakfast - to get us into training for the breakfasts we would encounter on the other side of the Atlantic. When it was time to leave, I remembered to check that the gas was off. (That would take all the excitement out of the Gatwick Express journey which I usually spent wondering if, indeed, I had turned off the gas.) Which way to America? We were not sure - but we turned left out of our gate.

We checked in our luggage at the special Gatwick place at Victoria station, so no more carrying suitcases until we reach New York. We were shown a diagram of the plane so we could choose our seats. Worryingly, it had no wings. We can't have everything in this life, so we supposed that's what they meant by Economy Class. When we arrived at Gatwick, we found that departure was delayed by ninety minutes. When we enquired why this was we were told there was a technical fault with the boroscope. The British Airways lady wasn't terribly knowledgeable in technical areas and seemed not to know just what a boroscope did. We thought it was the thing that heated up the soup.

A little girl hove into view, writing furiously in a notebook. It turned out she was writing a diary so I admitted I was doing the same thing. I pointed out my writing was not nearly as neat as hers and to prove it, I showed her a page. Her response was "Well, you have to write quicker when you're old". (You don't see yourself as others see you!). We took off in a Boeing 747 - a jumbo jet! We were ninety minutes late and I read in the in-flight magazine that delays are very expensive to airlines. The magazine went on to say "British Airways estimate a loss of £900 for each minute a Boeing 747 is delayed". We calculated that they had just lost £81,000! Motto: A boroscope in the hand is worth two in the 747.

Our first stop was Manchester - that's Manchester England, not Manchester USA - where we collected more passengers. As soon as everyone was on board and we'd taken off again, it was cocktail time, swiftly followed by lunch. (All the drinks were free! We liked the idea of that.) It was 1645 (1145 in the USA) - rather late for lunch, but who cares. We were given posh individual menus from which we chose 'Ballotine of chicken with savoury stuffing, flavoured with fresh herbs, garnished with veal sausage, grilled tomatoes, broccoli spears and fondant potatoes'. We didn't know what Ballotine of chicken was but we liked the sound of the rest.

After a delicious meal (much better than the usual plastic variety), I decided to find out what the upstairs of a jumbo jet looked like. After a few abortive attempts (I couldn't believe I could get lost on a plane!), I found some steps. I followed a man with his children. Onward and upward - only to find myself on the flight deck! Three men - loads of instruments...but I felt guilty as I was there by accident so, before descending the stairs, I took a peek into the 'upstairs'. About twenty people were watching the film and it didn't look all that luxurious. It turned out this was not the First Class compartment. That was at the front of the plane on a lower level. Back downstairs, everyone was looking out of the windows at what turned out to be Greenland. It was very desolate but beautiful scenery.

At tea time, an air hostess said we could go and look in the cockpit. (We'd asked earlier if this might be possible.) Off we went - officially this time. What a sight! The First Officer told us that everything was done automatically all the time but the crew *might* do something for the final two minutes on landing - if necessary!

We arrived at JFK airport in New York where we stood for over an hour in a slow-moving queue for immigration. It was immensely boring and frustrating, especially as we were very tired. Eventually we boarded a bus which took us to the Milford Plaza Hotel in downtown New York, where our room was on the twenty-third floor. (Twenty-second really as Americans count the ground floor as number one.) By now, we had been going for twenty-one hours and all we wanted to do was to sleep so we would be 'all systems go' for the beginning of the great adventure.

Friday 7th

Breakfast was taken across the street at *Camelot*. We knew from past experience that breakfast didn't happen in the hotel - unless we paid a hefty extra charge. The morning was taken up with a guided tour of New York in the coach. New York was founded in 1653 as New Amsterdam, then the English renamed it New York in 1664. We learned that New York City (which is not the capital of the State of New York - that's Albany) had a population of eight million; it was divided into five Boroughs - Brooklyn, Queens, Staten Island, Manhattan and the Bronx; one million people lived in Manhattan and a further one and a half million came in to work there each day. (I wonder what the relevant statistics are now, at the end of the first decade of the twenty-first century.) We passed Central Park - which is twice the size of Hyde Park; the Dakota Building (very expensive apartment block) where John Lennon was murdered (Leonard Bernstein lived there at that time); the Empire State Building which, we were told was built on three layers of foundation and contained 60,000 tons of steel, enough to make a double-track railroad from New York to Baltimore. There were stretch limousines everywhere - in three and four sections - all with darkened windows so that we couldn't see *in* but the occupants could see out. They must have used three or four parking meters! We went by the playground where the final scene of *West Side Story* was shot. (Having seen the film of that ten times, I was particularly impressed!)

Finally we went to St John's Cathedral. The guide told us that it was the largest cathedral in the world - "It is Episcopalian - which is the Church of England's version of Christianity"…(Well, that's one way of putting it!). It could hold 10,000 people and was the length of two football fields. This was the church in which Howard had sung with a small vocal ensemble when he visited the USA in 1976. When the ensemble saw the size of the church, they wondered how their concert would be heard by anyone 'at the back' since there were only ten singers in the choir. It turned out that the concert was to be given in one of the side chapels - which was only the size of a regular English Parish Church.

Saturday 8th

The Circle Line Boat Trip was scheduled for this morning; thirty-five miles in three hours, right around the island of Manhattan. We cruised around Manhattan Island on the Hudson River (which separates Manhattan from New Jersey, the next State). This was certainly a good way to see all the sights of the city and get the general idea of the layout of it. We passed the Statue of Liberty - which was very big - but then *everything* in New York is big. The Statue of Liberty was the world's tallest sculpture (at least it was in 1988), designed by Auguste Bartholdi and the interior designed by Gustav Eiffel (of Tower fame). The Statue was a gift to the people of the USA from the people of France. (What for? we asked ourselves.)

After the boat trip, we headed for the Lincoln Center for the Performing Arts, via the Metropolitan Museum of Art. The latter was a daunting prospect to see it all so we contented ourselves with a 'selection'. In the Lincoln Center were the New York State Theatre, the Metropolitan Opera House, Avery Fisher Hall (where the New York Philharmonic lived) and the Juilliard School. We were able to have a guided tour of the New York State Theatre (where Tosca was due to be performed that afternoon) and the Avery Fisher Hall. We weren't able to get into the Met. as *they* had a matinée too and the guide told us that the Met 'had gone very peculiar about people looking round it'. The Lincoln Center was twenty-five years old and much old housing had had to be pulled down to make the necessary site for it. Just before they started to build the Center - and while the site was still derelict - they filmed *West Side Story* there.

We went on by subway (their word for Underground) to the Cloisters, a branch of the Metropolitan Museum of Art. It was a Museum of Medieval Art in Fort Tryon Park, overlooking the Hudson River. It was opened in 1938 and contained sections from such monuments as a twelfth century chapter house, parts of cloisters from five medieval monasteries, a Romanesque chapel and a twelfth century Spanish Apse. Most of it was paid for by John D Rockefeller Junior. (Seemed like he paid for *most* things in New York.) It also contained medieval tapestries, illuminated manuscripts, stained glass, sculptures and metal work. The Cloisters herb garden boasted more than 200 species of plants grown in the Middle Ages. This was a very beautiful and peaceful place after the bustle of downtown New York.

We took a bus back downtown - much better than the subway as we were able to see many of the 'sights'. We went past the Union Theological Seminary (which I knew of through Christian Action, for which I then worked), and we got off at St Thomas' Church, Fifth Avenue, where there was a wedding in progress - even though it was 1800. We presumed it was John Andrew taking it, as he had a very English accent. John Andrew was a friend of Eric James (my boss) and Eric had been there in May that year. What a large place it was - and what an amazing altar piece. The wedding was a very posh affair, with four best men and hordes of bridesmaids and page boys and girls. A would-be Pavarotti rendered two pieces - the second of which we recognized as *Bist du bei mir*. (Howard remarked that, at such a wedding, 'for richer, for poorer' would probably read 'for richer, for not *quite* so rich'!) This was the church where Andrew Lloyd Webber's *Requiem* had its world première.

We crossed the road for a quick look into St Patrick's Roman Catholic Cathedral. Another 'real biggie' with a huge organ. By now, hunger pangs had set in so we went to a Brazilian restaurant. Saturday night was the night they did the special national dish - so we had it. The waiter was very kind and pointed out that one portion would be enough for both of us. What an understatement! It was enough for about four people. Weren't we glad we'd only ordered one portion! It was a sort of stew (sorry - Stoo) with beef and pork and sausages in a black gravy with black beans and rice and salad. And it was very cheap...a good find which, needless to say, Howard had found in one of the guidebooks.

Earlier in the day we had done the almost obligatory trip to and up the Empire State Building. One of the Eight Wonders of the World - the only one built in the twentieth century - it was 1,454 feet high. (We were not yet metric!) We went to the Observation Place on the 102nd floor - a mere 1,250 feet) from where, on a clear day, you could see for eighty miles! It contained seventy-three elevators (that's 'lifts' to us) and the speeds of them ranged from 600 feet to 1,200 feet a minute! Other statistics to boggle the mind: there were 6,500 windows to wash on a continuous basis, 3,500 miles of telephone and telegraph wires, 1,860 steps from the street to the 102nd floor…and so on…We were getting used to incredible statistics; we needed to - we were going to have many more.

Boston was on the itinerary for the following day - but not before we'd discovered that New York is pronounced Noo Yark.

Sunday 9th

We met up with our tour guide, Robert (Bob) Wagner - not the film star nor any relation to the *Tristan* one - and our driver for the trip, Leon Batchelor. The morning drive was very pleasant (passing road signs to the *other* Rye) and we had our first sightings of the Fall Foliage. Bob assured us that "we ain't see nothin' yet"…but what we were seeing was beautiful.

On arrival in Boston, we were taken straight to the Boston Tea Party ship. There was a token bale of tea which visitors could throw into the water, after which it was hauled in again - ready for the next visitor. Lunch was taken in a Covent Garden-type area - Faneuil Hall - full of restaurants and shops. (Could this be a Mall?) Suitably refreshed, we took a short walk along parts of the Freedom Trail taking in the Old State House, the Old South Meeting House, Old City Hall (with a statue of Benjamin Franklin), the site of the first school, King's Chapel, Granary Burying Ground - where Paul Revere and lots of other notables are buried - Park Street Church (where *America* was first sung) to the State House were Michael Dukakis had his office. (Would he *still* have his office there after November?). Outside Mike's office was a statue of General Hooker - yes, they really *did* get their name from him! He used to import 'ladies' to 'entertain' his troops.

On we went to the Howard Johnson hotel which, compared to the NY Milford Plaza, was very spacious. It had two double beds but we were to find that was not an uncommon feature in hotels. We went in search of a good fish restaurant which Howard had researched but we got somewhat lost and a passing cyclist stopped to help us. He told us we were wasting our time going to that particular restaurant as it was very popular and people came from 'all over' to go there… and we'd have to wait 'in line' for hours for a table. We ignored his advice and went there anyway - but he was right! It was seething with people and already there was an enormous 'line' (their word for 'queue'…how many times we were to hear that word during our stay…) We found an alternative where Howard was still able to have his fish and we suspect we ate more cheaply than we would have done at our chosen place.

Back to the hotel for an early night. Every night will be early on this trip as we have to be up at 0600 each morning ready to leave at 0800 - but we hadn't come 5,000 miles across the Atlantic to linger in bed!

Monday 10th - Columbus Day - National Holiday

We drove to Montreal, Canada, by way of Montpelier. All day we drove through the Fall Foliage which lived up to its reputation. A detour took us to see the bridge where the decisive US/British battle had taken place. There had been 700 of us and only about 350 Minute Men. However, our men had marched for miles with seventy pound packs, in heavy clothing and carrying firearms. The Minute Men (so called because they could be ready in a minute) didn't have *any* heavy clothing and hadn't marched anywhere. Consequently we lost. The Americans say that after the first few British were shot, the rest ran away! (Who could blame them? Though how they could run after all that marching, the seventy pound packs and the heavy clothing...?) It was a historic sight and there appeared the famous phrase "The shot that was heard around the world".

On to Montpelier which was very pretty. Lunch was provided for us all at *The Lobster Pot*. A huge salad was contained in a boat in the middle of the restaurant and we could go back as many times as we liked to help ourselves. We considered purchasing some real Maple Syrup at the adjacent shop (they made a big thing of Maple Syrup in these parts) but we decided against it. Visions of it leaking in our luggage and causing major havoc influenced our decision.

Next stop Canada but the border stop was horrendous. (Bob told us that it was easier to get into Russia than it was to get into Canada.) It took forever. All the coach parties had to get out, go to a separate line and file through a customs shed-type place to have passports checked and stamped. The consequence was that it was 2000 and dark when we arrived in Montreal. (Canada is the second largest country in the world, Russia being the largest.) In the hotel we wondered how we would manage for towels; they had only provided eight! - plus two facecloths, plus two types of soap, plus shampoos, plus bathing hats...we supposed we would have to manage as best we could.

Tuesday 11th

Bob pointed out that Canada is a bilingual country and that distances are measured in kilometres, not miles. We were given a morning coach tour of Montreal which included a visit to the Notre Dame Basilica. We thought it too ornate for its own good. At the high altar everything was illuminated by blue light which made it look like something from a film set. We expected the priest to be lowered from the ceiling to the accompaniment of a ninety-piece orchestra!

Behind the altar was a large chapel which had been damaged by fire. One half of it had been saved so the other half had been rebuilt to match. There was a huge bronze altarpiece (about twenty feet high) which, we were told, had been sent to Basingstoke, England to be cast. As we drove through Montreal, we passed many large transporters carrying squashed cars. Eventually we saw the site where all the squashed cars were dumped at the docks. The metal was then loaded onto ships and taken to Japan where it was recycled and turned into Japanese cars. (Peter, the trainee tour guide, asked if that is what was meant by re-incarnation!)

We were taken to the Olympic Stadium, built for the 1976 Montreal Olympic Games. It cost billions of dollars to build and, at that time, they were still paying for it. They levied taxes on cigarettes and liquor which helped to pay off the debt. The Olympic Village, which had been built to house the athletes, had been sold off as apartments and some of them were for Golden Age people - their version of Senior Citizens. On the Olympic Stadium was the world's tallest Inclined Tower. (We were not told what it was inclined to do.)

The next stop was St Joseph's Shrine, a place of pilgrimage for sick people - their equivalent of Lourdes. We went on to the Observatory for a panoramic view of the city. Back in town we booked a table for our evening meal at a French restaurant which Howard had found. That was to prove a wise move as it turned out to be a very popular place.

We went to the underground city of Montreal. There was a whole city below ground level and, in the winter especially, people go there to do the shopping because it gets so cold above ground. We didn't dally in the shopping area but made our way to the Museum of Fine Art. There were many European works of art including: Millais - *St Martin's Summer*; Pissarro - *The Road from Ennery to Pontoise* and *The Harbour of Rouen*; Monet - *The Cliffs at Pourville*; Renoir - *Young Girl with a Hat*; Pissarro - *Afternoon, Duquesne Dock at Dieppe Low Tide* - and a sculpture by Wilhelm Lehmbruck - *Bathing Woman*. The latter was of particular interest because there is a photograph of a sculpture by Lehmbruck - *Seated Youth 1918* - on the cover of John Robinson's *Honest to God*.

We went back to the hotel for a rest - the first of the trip - but we knew we must take advantage of every opportunity to rest to keep up our stamina. We ended the evening at the French restaurant which came up to expectations. We met two Americans who lived in Massachusetts but had an apartment in Montreal. They were there for their annual health check. (We wondered why they didn't have this closer to home.)

Wednesday 12th

We were allowed the luxury of a 0900 start as we were headed for Ottawa - Canada's capital, where we were to meet the Mounties and their horses. It was only about 100 miles to Ottawa so we arrived there at 1115 - and it was snowing! We learned that Ottawa is the anglicized form of Outaouac, an Indian tribe who traded furs with seventeenth century French voyagers. The city was originally named Bytown, after Colonel John By, supervising engineer of the Rideau Canal. In winter the Rideau Canal became the world's longest man-made skating rink; six miles of ice - and the locals actually ice-skated to work on it.

The coach dropped us at the Rideau Center - another underground city/shopping complex or, as the guidebook described it "a climate controlled, three-level shopping Mall of 220 stores and services, located in the heart of downtown Ottawa". We found a fast food place (that wasn't difficult - everywhere was crawling with them) and had a fast food snack. It came in disposable containers, no knives and forks - yet we have the audacity to sneer at 'backward' nations who haven't yet invented knives and forks and still eat with their hands! From the ridiculous to the sublime was how we described our next visit - to the Chateau Laurier, a very posh hotel. That was where we were to meet up with the coach but, before doing that, we took advantage of their 'restrooms'. We discovered that this hotel was in the same chain as the Hotel Scribe in Paris, in whose restrooms we've rested before now.

Our next visit was to the Parliament Building, much of which had been destroyed by fire in 1916. It had been completely rebuilt. The only part that survived the fire was the Library and that was due to the presence of mind of the staff who closed the steel doors and fixed wet towels round them. There were statues of Queen Victoria everywhere. We saw their House of Commons and the Senate - which were rather similar to ours back home.

We went on to the College of the Royal Canadian Mounted Police where we saw all the horses stabled and, from an observation gallery, we watched the rookies practising dressage. It reminded us very much of the Spanish Riding School in Vienna.

It was still snowing as we rejoined the coach which took us to the Ramada Hotel in Hull, just outside Ottawa. Another problem with the towels - but at least there are twelve this time, so perhaps we'll be able to manage. We set off to walk to the National Museum of Art but it was too snowy and windy and we decided that the bridge over the Ottawa River really was longer than we thought. As the Museum closed at 1700, we realized we would never make it in time so we retraced our snow-covered steps and went in search of the Portage Center. That took us on another space-age walk through corridors, shopping/eating areas. Our quest for our evening meal ended at *Oncle Tom*, where we made a reservation for 1900. It looked splendid in every respect and the guidebook said it *was* splendid. The guidebook was not wrong. Our meal was preceded by a mini drama.

We set out for the restaurant in the early evening. Having carefully researched the space-age walk and decided we would be able to remember the way to the other side through the labyrinth of shops and eateries, imagine our surprise when we encountered locked doors. Undeterred, we braved the elements, convinced this was but a temporary setback. We discovered a way into the underground car park, which we had negotiated earlier as part of our reconnaissance of the route (pronounced 'rowt'). Now the car park looked rather empty; just a few desultory cars parked therein. Furthermore, we couldn't find the way out. (We decided we must have gone onto a different level on our previous visit.) All doors seemed to be locked, including the one we had just come through - it must have been a self-locking affair. All car exists were firmly locked with large pneumatic doors. We were locked in, alone, and with no visible signs of assistance. Were we worried? Us? The intrepid Spurrs? You *bet* we were!! Finally we found a door and out we went. Another door stood in our way but at least these two doors weren't locked. I peered round the corner and saw what looked like a 'push bar to open' device. Howard held both doors open, with arms outstretched and umbrella extended, while I investigated the possibility of escape. Relief - there was the outside world. It *was* a 'push bar to open' so we ran out, as fast as our worried little legs would carry us. (It might have been only one small step for mankind but it was two *big* steps for the Spurrs!) We stuck to the main road for the rest of the walk to the restaurant. Happily the remainder of the evening more than made up for the nerve-racking beginning. We walked home in the open air, eschewing all would-be-covered ways and *certainly* all car parks.

Thursday 13th

We headed for Toronto and Thousand Islands - home of the famous Thousand Island Dressing. Bob, the tour guide, told us that we were to stop for coffee in the middle of the St Lawrence River. We believed him - he'd been right so far - but we couldn't help feeling we were going to have wet feet. We stopped on a bridge, half way across the St Lawrence River from where we had lovely views. After a quick cup of coffee, we walked back to the bridge with Keith the Colonel. Keith (Haycock) and his wife, Norah, were ex-NATO people with whom we had breakfasted on a couple of occasions. They were very sweet and Keith was very funny, in a measured, precise way. Norah didn't venture onto the bridge but we did and we hoped we would be rewarded with some beautiful pictures.

On to Kingston for lunch at *Dukes*, a very English pub, or as near as they get to one. After lunch we visited the tart shop across the street, where we could get real tea in teapots. (Their idea of tea was a cup of hot water into which you dangled the tea bag - it didn't come ready immersed...) Bob had not realized that 'tart' could have two meanings in English and he had told a previous group to "be sure to get some tarts from the very accommodating lady"! Kingston was a previous Spurr family seat, so we looked in the phone book for any Spurrs - but not one was to be found. They must have heard we were coming!

We resumed our journey to Toronto along the shores of Lake Ontario. Bob told us that it would look more like an ocean as you can't see the other side as it was fifty-five miles across - more than twice the width of the English Channel. He was right. The five Great Lakes are Huron, Ontario, Michigan, Erie and Superior. The Huron Indian word 'Toronto' originally meant Meeting Place. Our first sighting of the city was the CN Tower (Canadian National) which was then the world's tallest free-standing structure at 1,815 feet 5 inches. It is twice as high as the Eiffel Tower. (We said there'd be lots of statistics on this trip - and there's still quite a few 'world's largest, longest, deepest' things to come.) We had booked to go to the CN Tower the next evening.

We checked into the Viscount Hotel, the only hotel on the tour which is out of town. To get into the city, we had to take a bus for five miles then a Metro for fifteen stops. At the Viscount hotel, we met Bob's parents who were staying for a few days. They were in the hotel lobby to greet the whole coach!

We went off to find the Chinese restaurant that Howard had selected for us. This involved a thirty-five minute bus ride followed by a fifteen stop subway ride. This deposited us a few blocks ('blarks') from the restaurant. Another disappointment - the menu is only sixteen pages of single-spaced A4 long - and that was just the food. There were another eight pages of drinks. (We wondered if the restaurant is owned by the brother of the person who provides the towels in the hotels.) How could they expect their customers to choose from such a scanty menu? We chose the 'dinner for two' but when it arrived, we thought they had made a mistake and brought a meal for *twenty*-two! Perhaps our Chinese is not as good as we thought it was...We had a good, plentiful and inexpensive meal, with mottos cooked into the little biscuits which arrived at the end. "It is better to have a hen tomorrow than an egg today". We wondered where we would *put* a hen if we had one tomorrow. It was probably something Confucius said - or maybe something he ate? It certainly confused us. On the way back to the hotel we ran into Bob and his parents and Peter the trainee tour guide who is taking this trip with Bob to learn all about it. As we were returning directly to the hotel, we took Bob's parents with us so that Bob and Peter could 'go out on the town' for a while.

Friday 14th

With great daring we traversed the busy highway - to get our breakfast across the street. If you could have seen the width of the road and the volume of traffic, you would realize just how daring we were!

Our next excitement was to take a bus to the harbour. We discovered that tickets for public transportation were strange. All fares were $1.05. On boarding a bus, we put the exact fare only into a box, but we were not given a ticket. If it was your intention to continue your journey by subway or another bus, *in the same direction and within the hour*, you had to ask for a Transfer Ticket and you were given a piece of paper. If, however, you started your journey at a subway, you had to buy a ticket at the subway station and discard it *immediately* at the ticket-buying booth. Failure to do this meant being hauled back - as we were! Why they couldn't just sell a ticket straight away, valid for everything, we couldn't imagine.

The next boat trip was at 1100 so, to fill in the time, we wandered along to Queen's Quay - yet another fountain-filled shopping Mall (pronounced 'Morl'). The boat trip was excellent as it took us right out into the islands in the lake and, of course, from the lake were the best views of the Toronto skyline and one of the few places from which the CN Tower could be photographed - as it is so tall.

We returned to town for lunch and glanced into City Hall. There were no conducted tours available (they told us they were short-staffed) but we were free to look round on our own. We thought we would defer that pleasure until we had had some lunch. On the way, we met some black squirrels and made a mental note to bring a roll or two to feed to them on our return. There were lots and lots of squirrels and they were all very tame. On our return, having had a good lunch, we sought out the squirrels as we were armed with squirrel food. A man was feeling them walnuts, which they obviously loved. When he had exhausted his walnut supply, we thought it would be our turn - but no! The squirrels turned up their noses at our roll and just slunk off! Did they not realize that we had lashed out thirty-four cents to provide their hand-fed lunch? We gave it to the sparrows instead. They were much more polite and gracious about accepting it.

In Nathan Phillips Square (named after Toronto's mayor from 1955 - 1962), outside the City Hall, was a giant reflecting pool. In the winter, the pool became one of the most popular ice-skating rinks in the City. Also outside City Hall was a 2.2 tonne Henry Moore bronze sculpture *Three Way Piece No 2* - known locally as

The Archer. This had been purchased through a public subscription fund in 1966. (We mused on the location of *Three Way Piece No 1* - but got nowhere.) We took a brief look around City Hall, sighting a special tapestry depicting the history of Toronto. It was twenty-four feet wide and six feet high and it had taken 140 people 11,000 hours (over six years) to complete it. In the entrance of City Hall was a fascinating mural entitled *Metropolis*, created by David Partridge from 100,000 nails. At the base of the central support in the Hall of Memory was a cornerstone containing a time capsule of historical artefacts and memorabilia from the era when City Hall had been built.

In the evening, we went for dinner to the revolving restaurant 1,150 feet up in the CN Tower. Before we set out, we were treated to a wine and cheese reception given by our hotel for the Jetsave Tour. (No doubt this was a PR exercise to encourage more business with Jetsave, as the hotel was so far out of town.) Bob's parents came with us to the CN Tower. Bob had already told us that his mother couldn't bear heights or lifts! Oh dear - it was a long way up in the lift! As it started its very swift ascent, (twenty feet per second), Bob told his mother not to look out - so she would miss the sight of the ground receding at a rate of knots…The panoramic view from the restaurant was well worth the ascent. The restaurant made one revolution every seventy-two minutes and we were there for about 1½ revolutions. Bob told us that all the lights in the buildings in the city are left on at night for the benefit of the tourists! We would not have liked to have been responsible for the electricity bill but Bob went on to say that electricity was very cheap as it came from the Niagara Falls. At the end of a lovely evening, we returned to our hotel - but in the comfort of the coach rather than by public transport.

Saturday 15th

Niagara Falls was the destination for today. I fell to wondering whether they would be open or whether it might be half-day closing but Howard pointed out that if they ever closed, even for half an hour, the results would be disastrous. The statistics were really staggering. 70,000 gallons of water tumbled down every second; there are two Falls - one on the American side and one on the Canadian side - the border between the two countries running between the two Falls. The Canadian one is much bigger and is the famous Horseshoe Falls. This is 2,000 feet wide, 176 feet high and 180 feet deep. The American Falls are a mere 1,100 feet but they are 182 feet high. We took the famous *Maid of the Mist* boat ride - which took us right to the base of the Falls. Howard had done this fourteen years before so he knew what to expect. The spray from the Falls was so huge and there was so much of it that it looked like a cloud. We were provided with blue waterproof coats and hoods which were really necessary when we reached the Falls - and even before we got there because of the spray. It was not possible to describe what it was like to be right close up to the Falls. Breathtaking is the nearest we could get - but that was very inadequate. Bob had told us that the water that came over the Falls is only 25% of what *could* come over; the other 75% is harnessed to provide electricity.

The land over which the water passes erodes at the rate of one foot a year. 12,000 years ago, the Falls were four miles away! (Once, the American Falls were stopped temporarily so that scientists could investigate the erosion factor.) When the sun came out, there was a permanent rainbow over the Falls. Our mind boggled at the thought of the people who had gone over them in a barrel - and lived! Then there was Blondin, the tightrope walker, who tightrope-walked over them a number of times - on one occasion cooking an omelette half way. Another time, he walked across with his manager on his shoulders - and had to keep putting the manager down for a rest! Don't people so strange things? We had no desire to emulate Blondin's feats.

To digest all the statistics, we took a drive to the helicopter rides and waited while a few of our party (not including us) took one. It lasted a mere ten minutes - and cost a fortune! We went on to the gorge and the whirlpool, both of which we photographed to excess.

The Best Western Hotel was our destination for tonight. A towel count revealed thirteen - though Howard maintained it was only twelve - plus a bath mat. For dinner, Howard had found *The Old Stone Inn* for us. This was a home-made English baronial hall, complete with family crests and a log fire - and a harpist who played throughout - while nobody listened - except we did - and even asked what one of her tunes (sorry - toons) was! The waiter (who we thought was probably a student) told us he was majoring in Economics at College. (Howard reckoned he was minoring in coal.) Another patron of the restaurant was wearing a backless, frontless creation and Howard observed that she wore no bra..."at least not the conventional sort - perhaps it's one of those stick-on ones"...but it did not detract from our enjoyment of a really delicious meal in lovely surroundings.

To end the evening, we walked down to the Falls to see them in their illuminated splendour. It was an indescribably beautiful sight - so we made no attempt to describe it...

Sunday 16th

We had been warned that the restaurant in the hotel was very slow at serving breakfast - and there were four coach parties all leaving around the same time. The previous evening, we had discovered a hotel (only opened in the previous June) which also did breakfast starting at 0700 - but we decided to keep our secret to ourselves. We presented ourselves at the rival establishment at 0655, only to be informed that they didn't start until 0800. When we told the receptionist that his counterpart the previous evening had informed us 0700 was definitely the starting time, he indicated that they *might* start at 0700, but the previous day, "the lady hadn't turned up until 0730 anyway"! The best laid plans of...we scurried back to *our* hotel, where we were still in time to be first in the queue (sorry 'line').

It was the longest drive of the tour today (349 miles) and, due to seat rotation in the coach, it was our good fortune to be in the front seat! It could not have been a better day for it as we drove for miles and miles through the Fall Foliage. We were en route for Carlisle and, at the lunch stop, Bob organized a little gambling. We all paid one dollar and Bob divided the front coach wheel tyre into segments with chalk. He numbered the segments and gave us all a number. The one whose segment was on the ground on arrival at Carlisle would be the winner. We were very pleased that it was won by one of the single ladies, who became better off by $27.

We arrived at Carlisle, which was some way from Harrisburg. Bob had warned us that there was absolutely nothing to do in Carlisle but it was the evening when we 'rest up'. There was a swimming pool and a restaurant. We eschewed the former and had a good meal in the latter. The hotel was on the main highway and there were alternative eateries 'across the street'. We were not brave enough to attempt the crossing. (The Rubicon would have been a piece of cake in comparison.) If we had for one moment thought we *were* brave enough to go 'across the street', the printed leaflet in our hotel room would have been more than enough to dissuade us. It read: "WARNING - Four tourists have been killed in Carlisle this year attempting to cross Route II on foot. Route II is a very dangerous highway. Please *do not attempt* to cross Route II on foot." Underneath this warning, it read: "For your convenience, our dining room is open from 1900 - 2130." (An eye to the main chance?) Another record towel count: twelve plus a bath mat, two wash basins and two loo roll holders, complete with two loo rolls, both of which seem adversely affected by gravity at the merest touch! There was also a huge Mastermind-type chair in which I sat and the conversation went:

Howard	Name?
Jane	Jane Spurr
Howard	Occupation?
Jane	Minion
Howard	Specialized subject?
Jane	Coach tours of the Eastern USA
Howard	You have two minutes on
	"Coach Tours of the Eastern USA" starting from…..
	…nowwhatisthenameofthetourguide?

We completed the postcards, had a gentle rest and then retired.

Monday 17th

We breakfasted with Keith and Norah. Keith's verdict on the sausages went "There could be many uses for these sausages, but eating is not one of them". When we got underway on our journey, we passed near Five Mile Island - the site of a meltdown in a nuclear plant in 1979. 140,000 people had to be evacuated.

In Harrisburg, we made a quick visit to the State Capitol Building. Harrisburg is the State Capital of Pennsylvania - not Philadelphia, as many people think. The outside of the Capital Building looked like St Peter's, Rome, and the inside entrance hall looked like the Paris Opera. It was altogether an impressive-looking place. In the steps up to the main door of the Capitol Building was a Keystone. Pennsylvania is known as the 'Keystone State' because of its strategic geographical location among the thirteen original colonies, as well as its key position in the economic, social and political development of the United States.

Our next stop was the Hershey chocolate factory - called Chocolatetown - where we took a guided tour round a simulated factory (Chocolate World) on an automatic train. We felt the commentary was aimed at ten-year olds and downwards. At the end of this trip, we arrived in the most enormous shop selling 'all things chocolate' - though how furry teddy bears qualified, we couldn't quite see. (No, they weren't covered in chocolate.)

Lancaster was our next port of call. The Amish and Mennonite people lived around these parts. The Amish were the most distinctive in that they belonged to a very strict religious sect who didn't believe in using twentieth century technology of any description. Consequently they didn't have electricity, telephones or motor vehicles. Their mode of transport was horse-drawn carriages. They didn't believe in any form of ornamentation so their clothes were very simple but made to very strict rules. Unmarried men were clean-shaven but, once married, they had to grow a beard. Ladies wore different apparel depending on whether or not they were married. They held one religious service every two weeks and it took place in someone's house. Benches were 'bussed in' and boys and men sat on one side of the room, girls and ladies on the other. The service lasted three to four hours! The location of the service rotated each fortnight so you got to have it at your house about once a year. In preparation for it, the house had to be spring-cleaned and lunch had to be provided for everyone at the end of the service. We were taken on a trip round a working Amish farm - with a *huge* gift shop attached to it. This was not run by the Amish people but it sold things they had made.

Lunch was taken in a little complex of thirty country gift shops - all of which was a little bit too 'touristy' for comfort. I had a hot dog washed down with root beer - which we both agreed tasted like liquorice-flavoured germolene! I couldn't drink it - so shared Howard's lemonade instead. Bob told us that though the Amish people had these strict rules, they did store food in freezers attached to local shops (for which storage space they paid) and, if anyone was ill, they were happy to be driven to hospital by a neighbour using a twentieth century car and then be treated with twentieth century things at the hospital. We felt that was not *quite* in keeping with their proclaimed lifestyle.

Washington DC was our last stop of the trip. Kennedy Airport was getting horribly close and, even if everything went according to plan with no delays, Wednesday/Thursday would be a twenty-three hour day without sleep - except what we could grab on the coach or plane. Our Washington Hotel was right at the edge of Chinatown so we had an inexpensive but good Chinese meal, followed by a wander down to the White House. No sign of Ron or Nancy so we retired to bed.

Tuesday 18th

This was our last proper day and it started with a coach tour of Washington with a local guide Martha. She was very knowledgeable indeed but did not pause for breath for the duration of the four-hour trip. We saw the White House, Capitol Building, the Pentagon - and much more - all from the outside only.

Our first stop was Arlington National Cemetery where, among others, John F Kennedy is buried. We were taken to his burial place where the eternal flame burns and excerpts from his famous speeches are engraved around the walls of the monument - including "Ask not what America can do for you..." As well as JFK and his brother Robert, who is buried nearby, the cemetery is filled with more than 200,000 veterans and their dependents on 612 acres of land. Other famous people are there - though they are there because they have been at one time in the armed forces - not just because they were famous: John Wesley Powell, the first man to explore the Grand Canyon in 1869; Robert E Peary and Richard Byrd, Arctic explorers; astronauts Dick Scobee and Michael Smith from the Challenger disaster in 1986; Joe Louis, the World Heavyweight Boxing Champion. Though we didn't see it, we learned from the informative guidebook to the Cemetery that there was an impressive 'Tomb of the Unknowns' - like our Tomb of the Unknown Warrior in Westminster Abbey. In the Tomb lies an Unknown Soldier from World Wars 1 and 2, the Korean War and the Vietnam War. The Tomb is guarded twenty-four hours a day, regardless of climatic conditions, by soldiers from the Army's US Third Infantry, 'The Old Guard'. This enormous Cemetery had line upon line of headstones in neat military rows - all exactly the same height and shape. Apparently, if you are buried in Arlington, the Government provides this and there are strict rules about what can be left on graves. Many of the dead were from the Vietnam War and, according to the guidebook, at the height of that war, there were thirty-five burials a day happening here. What a dreadful loss of life! Presumably there were similar losses on the other side. And we had to ask ourselves - what for? Though in a different content, you couldn't help thinking "To what purpose is this waste?"

We went on to the Vietnam Veterans' Memorial, which was then a very recent addition to Washington DC. On this very modern edifice are engraved the names of all those who were killed, taken prisoner or listed as 'missing'. The names are not in alphabetical order but in the order in which news of them was received. Nearby are two books in which the names are recorded in alphabetical order - and giving an exact reference so you can go and find the relevant name on the memorial. There are 58,132 names. There are two symbols next to the names: a diamond indicates that the death was confirmed; a cross (and there were about 1,300 of them) indicates that they were either missing or prisoners of war at the end of the conflict and remain missing or unaccounted for. If someone returns alive, a circle, as a symbol of life, is inscribed round the cross. If confirmation of their death is received, the diamond is super-imposed over the cross. This was a very sad place indeed and the guide explained that, for many bereaved people, this is the only place they can come, as they have never been able to have a funeral. Looking at this memorial, with so many thousands of names, no one could imagine that the human race would ever, even in its wildest dreams, contemplate any form of armed combat again. But history continually proves that wrong.

Up the steps to the Lincoln Memorial; another huge edifice with the seated statue of Abraham Lincoln towering nineteen feet above us, enclosed on three sides by marble and open on the fourth side, facing the Washington Monument and the Capitol. The guide told us that the statue is very conducive to meditation and

John F Kennedy would go there from time to time. President Nixon, at around 0400 on that fateful day, went up to the statue and the secret service men said he stood before it for about forty minutes - then returned to the White House and wrote his resignation.

The next stop was the J F Kennedy Center for the Performing Arts. Another huge place, comprising an opera house, theatre and concert hall. James Galway and Neville Marriner were there and N Marriner was conducting the *Enigma Variations*, amongst other things, so we felt a bit homesick. Our guide was *still* talking - non-stop - and our brains had gone into meltdown. Before they had melted, and as we went by the National Archives, she told us that therein were stored the original Declaration of Independence, the Constitution and the Bill of Rights. Apparently, the Declaration of Independence was stored in a special case, behind bullet-proof glass, enclosed in helium! Each night, it sank into a special hole in the ground so it was protected, in the event of a nuclear war. (Though, as Bob said, who would be left to read it?)

At the end of the guided tour, we headed for the Air and Space Museum (which, all along, we thought was the Aaron Space Museum!). This was a real highlight. Here we saw the history of flying from Day One, including the original planes that undertook many of the early flights. There was the Wright Brothers' original 1903 *Flyer* and Lindbergh's *Spirit of St Louis*. We didn't spend lots of time with the olde worlde stuff as we were headed for ('zeroed in on!') all the space things. There were many of the original nose cones used in early space flights and seen on TV at the time of landing in the sea, just before the crew were fished out. There was not much space inside them - indeed they were immensely cramped. (Perhaps the astronauts should be renamed *Lack of Space* Men?) To say there wouldn't be room to swing a cat would be an understatement - there wouldn't be room to put the cat *in* there, let alone swing it! We went into an Orbital Skylab where we saw how astronauts lived and worked when they were in space for a length of time. On display were lots of things used in the first moon landing, made by Armstrong, Collins and Aldrin in 1969, and loaned by them to the Museum. I recalled how I sat up all night to watch that historic occasion. We saw some actual moon rock which the boffins maintain is 415 billion years old - give or take a year. There was an exact copy of the Lunar Module which made the first moon landing. (Had there been any problem with the actual Lunar Module, this second one would have been used. As it wasn't used, it was in the Museum.) There were many other assorted rockets and capsules (actual ones), together with scale models of things - and an explanation of what went wrong with the ill-fated Challenger in 1986.

Next stop was the National Gallery of Art, where was housed Leonardo da Vinci's *Ginevra de' Benci* - the only Leonardo da Vinci in America. Last time Howard was here, the L da Vinci was not - it was on its holidays, so Howard didn't get to see it. It was doubly good to see it this time around. There was the odd room-full of Rembrandts and more than one odd room-full of Monets. Someone by the name of Paul Mellon seemed to have given a lot of these things to the Gallery. When we went to the East Wing (where all the modern stuff was to be found), a sign indicated that Mr Mellon had financed the building of it - as well! (He must have had a bob or two to spare.) It gave us an odd feeling seeing these European works of art here in the USA. Part of us said "What are you doing over here? You belong in Europe." It was a bit like putting your shoes on the wrong feet.

We didn't have time to go to the American History or Natural History Museums - there just wasn't time to do everything - and it was very tiring. The whole complex of museums is known as the Smithsonian Institution (pronounced Inst-it-two-shun) after someone called Smithson. We had noticed that, whenever there was a chance to elongate words, the Americans did - viz: transportation for transport, burglarized for burgled (there was even a reference to a play which had been 'musicalized'...!). We would probably have called the complex the Smithson Institute.

One of our last visits was to the Washington Monument - right to the top - in a lift (sorry elevator). It was 555 feet 5 and one eighth inches high. Back on *terra firma*, we walked to the Jefferson Memorial, round the side of the tidal basin of the Potomac River. The Jefferson Memorial was very similar to the Lincoln memorial, except that it was open on all four sides. On one wall is carved an excerpt from the Declaration of Independence, which Jefferson drafted.

It was a long way back to the hotel and our feet were already complaining so we took the subway for two stops. It was very smooth, clean and modern, though buying the tickets was something of a brain-teaser. Luckily a local resident came to our aid, which was doubly fortunate as the location of the ticket machines was very dimly lit so it was difficult to read the instructions. We made it back to the hotel - tired, hot and sticky. A shower never felt so good. Thus refreshed we met up with the coach which took us to the Georgetown area of the city, where we had an excellent fish meal.

Wednesday 19th

Today saw the start of the long return journey but there was one more stop before we hit JFK Airport. We still had to visit Philadelphia. There we saw the Liberty Bell - America's second most 'sacred' possession, next to the Declaration of Independence. The bell had been cast in Whitechapel in London but it seemed to have got cracked every time it was used! The only two occasions when it had been used in recent times were at the end of World War Two and at the Bicentennial. We saw the Benjamin Franklin Museum and the remains of his house.

We left Philadelphia at 1300 for the journey to New York. There was a competition on the coach to see who could guess how many miles we had covered in America. The answer was 2,164.

At JFK Airport, while waiting to board our jumbo jet to go home, we saw Concorde land. That was an impressive note on which to quit America. Our flight was uneventful and the plane was not full so the two seats next to us were empty, meaning we could spread ourselves somewhat.

Thursday 20th

As it did going out, our route took us via Manchester. Hardly had we taken off from Manchester than the captain announced "We are now beginning our descent to London Gatwick". We reckoned that Manchester wasn't that far away since we were travelling in excess of 500 miles an hour.

Wonderful though our trip had been - and it really had been wonderful - after all the superlatives of the last two weeks, could there be yet more? Yes! The best was yet to come. It may not have been the tallest, the longest, the grandest , the biggest or the oldest, but it was by far the best - it was home!

VIVE LA REVOLUTION!
July 1989

Thursday 13th

We were at Victoria station in time for the 0715 train to Gatwick, only to find the 0645 train had not yet left. We boarded it, even though all the carriages were in darkness and peopled by shadowy travellers. As soon as it pulled out into the bright sunshine, the lights came on; clearly they were solar powered.

On arrival at Gatwick we made our way to the new North Terminal, which worked well - with the exception of the *Atlas* restaurant, where we breakfasted. (We completed a 'comments' form!) We sought a table, bearing our rapidly cooling breakfast which had cooled while we waited in various queues. We shared a table with three rather elderly ladies, two of whom said not a lot but the third more than made up for the others. She organized everything and everybody - even down to the quantities of milk they should take for their early morning tea. One of them dropped a £1 coin on the floor. We helped search for it (unsuccessfully) and all of us, except the 'organizer' commented on the fact that the carpet was patterned with £1 coin look-alikes. Suddenly, the 'organizer' decided she had spotted the missing coin - then realized it was the pattern on the carpet! (Some mothers do have 'em...) A grumble from the 'organizer' about the piped pop music from the adjacent shop and about the equally adjacent screaming child made us realize it was time for our appointment with Security Control and Passports. I was frisked and one of our bags was searched but Howard was in the clear.

We were met at Charles de Gaulle airport by Alan, the Thomson representative and transferred to our hotel by a black London taxi which we shared with another couple. The man had been in the army fifty years ago and had been in the Champs-Elysées for the July Fourteenth procession at the end of the War. He had been given a free ticket to the Folies-Bergères but had not used it - and he wanted to use it now! He had sent a photocopy of the ticket to the Folies, together with a photocopy of a letter from the then President of France, thanking his regiment. The Folies-Bergères had written back telling him he should go along and they would honour his free ticket.

Our hotel, the Floride Etoile, was very comfortable but we straightway set out for lunch. The place that Howard had researched had stopped serving as it was now 1500 but the adjacent place served us, so we did not starve. It was very hot so we returned to the Floride Etoile for a rest as it was going to be a long evening.

We ate at *Le Bistro de la Gare* at Montparnasse, where we had eaten on our previous visit to Paris. The buses stopped running at 2040 (!) so we had to take the métro. We arrived at the Place de la Bastille and the new opera house, ready to see the concert at 2200 on the large screen in the Square. We became suspicious when there was no sign of a large screen or a 2200 concert. There was a big stage with flashing lights where a pop group was about to 'give its all'. We didn't want to be within a mile (kilomètre) of that. Crowds of people had gathered and fireworks were being let off indiscriminately into the thronging masses - so we decided to retreat. We walked back to the hotel and, walking in the opposite direction, were hundreds of people making their way to the Place de la Bastille. Dancing the night away to the accompaniment of a pop group and laser things was not our scene.

Friday 14th...this is it...Bastille Day

We decided to try our luck in the Champs Elysées to watch the *défile militaire* so we headed off in the direction of the Arc de Triomphe. All the side roads were crammed with tanks and other military vehicles. It was rather a frightening sight. The drivers and associated personnel looked like *children*! (Had they lowered the age at which you can/must join the armed forces?) We managed to find a good vantage point in the Champs and we stood there for a very long time, seeing everything as it passed. The first thing to pass by was a large mounted detachment, accompanying the President, Monsieur Mitterand. Paris was full of assorted heads of state who had come for many and various summit meetings. We wondered if they would all come by - but they didn't - just Monsieur Mitterand. The majority of them were gathered at the other end of the Champs, at the Place de la Concorde. As well as all the processions on the ground, there were numerous 'fly-pasts' of various aircraft - from super-modern military things to planes that had flown in the War. It was all very noisy, but spectacular. We wondered if our photos would come out as it was quite difficult to take photos of planes only inches away travelling on the quick side. We grabbed a quick lunch at a place we had spotted on the way but it was a bit of a disappointment. Though we ordered French onion soup (which we *love*), they forgot to bring it. We reminded them and they *did* bring it - but we wished they hadn't bothered. It didn't appear to have been in close proximity to an onion in its life.

We returned to our room for a rest to prepare ourselves for the *grand défile* in the Champs that evening. We were told it would include elephants and real London fog. (?) Suitably rested, we made our way once more to the Place de la Bastille to see if we could attend the free concert in the new opera house at 1700. When we discovered that we should have obtained our free tickets in advance (we hadn't) and when we saw the masses of people trying to get in (already *munis* with their free tickets), we realized we wouldn't stand a chance, so we headed for the free Barber's Shop concert given by an American choir in the Jardins de Luxembourg. On the way there, we called into *La Coupole* to make a reservation for dinner. The last time we had been in Paris, it was being 'done up' so now we saw it in all its newly-decorated splendour. It was owned by the same people who owned the *Brasserie Flo*.

We were surprised to find that the American Barber's Shop choir was all female - but then we thought that, as barbers' shops are now unisex, this made sense. We enjoyed it and the choir had excellent diction - but we wondered what the French made of it.

We had an excellent meal at *La Coupole* and it was exactly like the *Brasserie Flo* in mme that if any waiter walked at less than twenty miles an hour, he would be sacked. The staff literally slid along the floor carrying enormous quantities of food, drinks and mountains of plates and glasses - all balanced on trays on their shoulders.

After our meal, observing the huge numbers of people heading for the Champs, we decided that discretion was the better part of valour and resolved to watch the procession on TV in our hotel room. If we had had any doubts about whether or not to go to the Champs, they were resolved when we arrived at the Métro station to go home. We had to force our way onto the platform to get on the train. (It made the Northern Line in the rush hour look quite empty.) It was with enormous relief that we arrived at our station, Boissière. We scurried to our hotel and dug ourselves in to watch the proceedings from the comfort of our bed. Were we glad we did! Everything got under way at 2130 and was still in full swing at 0030. At 2330, when the British soldiers left the Arc de Triomphe, Jessye Norman launched into *La Marseillaise*, in full sail - in a weird creation of red, white and blue. Howard maintained that the 'dress' would be hired out as a marquee after the event. This was followed by much more of the procession which included red London buses, fire engines spraying rain onto dancers, milk containers spraying 'snow' onto Russian soldiers, a real locomotive and zebras. We never *did* see elephants or London fog.

Saturday 15th

We walked down the Champs to see what it was like after 'the night before'. Some of the Russian 'snow' was still in evidence but, apart from that, the street cleaners (who seem to be continually on duty in Paris) had been out in force and all had been cleaned. We walked the length of the Champs, pondering on the cost of this extravaganza. Still, it was only once every 200 years.

Concorde Métro was closed and the whole area was crawling with very smartly dressed *gendarmes*. Were they new uniforms or just their summer outfits? Many roads were closed off and there was much whistling at pedestrians and traffic. When we asked why this was, we were told that the high-powereds had passed this way and might return.

We walked on to the Madeleine to find out what the music would be on Sunday. We didn't find it very inspiring, though the Psalm had been composed by the *Maître de Chapelle* and there was to be some organ music by Alain and Dupré. We continued our walk to the *Brasserie Flo* to make a reservation for Sunday evening, and bought our picnic lunch in the rue St Denis. It was an extremely hot day and, as if to underline it, most of the ladies standing around on the street were wearing very few and very flimsy clothes. We wondered why they didn't go inside out of the heat. When Howard suggested we walked in the shady bit, I pointed out that the whole street was shady!

Our picnic was taken in the gardens of the Forum des Halles - the site of their old Covent Garden, now modernized like *our* old Covent Garden. We were not alone with our picnic. The pigeons made it quite plain that they would like some too but we tried to ensure that the tiny sparrows didn't miss out on anything. After lunch, we had a quick look in St Eustache and were pleased to find an organ postcard for Charles Proctor.

We went on to the Tuileries to look at all the stalls that were on offer. It was a bit disappointing and there were huge queues to get into the 'theatre' sections. We decided to return to the hotel to prepare for the evening and the firework display which was not due to start until 2230. As the fireworks were to be held very near to the hotel, we ate at a little Italian restaurant next door, then set off in search of the *feux d'artifices*. We didn't need to consult the map because absolutely everyone was going there so it was just a question of following the crowd. We had thought we would go to the Champs de Mars for one of the best views, but quickly realized that we would never get across the bridge - it was solid with people. We selected a square centimetre of bridge - and waited. There was still an hour to go and it was nowhere near dark so we joined some others sitting on the floor. We met a lovely French lady and her seventy-five year-old mother - neither of whom spoke English - so it was a real opportunity to practise our French on them - and they couldn't escape! Eventually the illuminations on the Eiffel Tower were extinguished and that was considered a sign that something was going to happen - and it did. As firework displays go, it went - but it wasn't nearly as spectacular as we had imagined. Predictably there was lots of red, white and blue but we had imagined there might have been montages of revolutionary people - and similar. Unless you were very tall, it was possible to see only those fireworks that went up very high into the sky. Nevertheless, we had seen it and we were grateful to get back to our hotel safely, away from the thronging masses.

Sunday 16th

Though we had not been terribly impressed by the musical offering at the Madeleine, we decided to go there. Many of the roads were still closed off and the gendarmes told us the same thing - that the high-powereds had gone by and might return.

The Gospel and the theme of the service was The Good Samaritan and we recalled that, back in London, David Sheppard would be preaching on that very theme at Gray's Inn Chapel as he was there to preach the annual Mulligan sermon. The three readings were read in French but the Epistle was read also in English. Intercessions were made in five languages - French, English, German, Italian and Spanish. (A very cosmopolitan place this!) The Mass was sung in Latin. It was Messe sur Les Litanies des Saints - J le Capon and the psalm was Psalm 68 by J Havard de la Montagne (Maître de Chapelle). The leaflet promised Liszt's Variations sur Weinen Klagen, Sorgen but it never happened. We wondered if it had been played before we arrived. Still to come, however, were Improvisation, Deux Danses by J Alain and the final piece, which was to be the Fugue en Sol Mineur by Dupré. This turned out to be Fugue in F major by JSB.

After all that intellectual effort, we headed for Chartier for lunch. Chartier is a cavernous place with very high ceilings which can seat in excess of 200 people. Its other claim to fame was that it was very cheap. The world and his wife went to Chartier. An elderly lady at the next table told us that she had been going there for fifty years, knew all the staff and was ninety years old. She told the waiters that 'life was absolutely wonderful' - and she certainly seemed to be enjoying every minute of it.

Our next port of call was the Louvre and the new Pyramid. It was baking hot but we queued to get in - and did. The Pyramid was a new entrance to the existing museum. We went on to Notre Dame where we checked on the organ recital later that afternoon. There was a concert in progress - an American choir - but not the lady barbers this time.

Notre Dame was packed, as usual, for the 1745 organ recital so we had to sit on the floor - but it was only for thirty-five minutes. The programme was not as action-packed as some previous ones had been. It started with a Scarlatti Toccata but worked up to a good concluding Alleluia by Guiseppe Rosetta, of whom we had not heard - but would like to have heard more.

It was time for the (now traditional) *Brasserie Flo* meal. For the first time, Howard had the *assiette de fruits de mer* - a huge platter of assorted fish on a bed of ice. (Not *quite* the sea food platter he was used to in SE11 - fish fingers on a bed of peas.) After our meal, we made our (equally traditional) pilgrimage to the Sacré Coeur and the Place du Tertre, then home by métro.

Monday 17th

After breakfast, we left for the Porte Maillot to catch the airport bus. It was fortuitous that we left lots of time for this exercise as it was not at all clear from where the airport bus started and we walked a goodly distance underground, carrying all our luggage. When we did find it, all was well and we had a quick and uneventful journey back to Charles de Gaulle airport. The traffic going into Paris, however, had to be seen to be believed. Mile after mile of it was at a complete standstill. At the airport, we bought a paper and read of the dreadful delays in air travel due to a strike of French air traffic controllers. Happily we were not affected. It seemed to be flights to Spain, which had to travel through French air traffic controllers air space, which were badly hit. The paper also told us of the death of Karajan.

Our return journey was unaffected by the strike and within a short time, we were back once more, *chez* Jennifer House - and home.

BACH TO BEIJING - AND BACK
November 1989

The reason for this trip was that the Bach Choir, of which Howard was a member, had been invited to give the Inaugural Concert of the new Hong Kong Cultural Centre, in the presence of TRHs the Prince and Princess of Wales. The Choir members' expenses were met by the sponsors, Hutchison Whampoa. That meant we would only have to pay one lot of fares and hotels - though I have to admit that I was not very keen to go. I found the Bach Choir an intimidating prospect and it cheered me not at all when people kept telling me "you will be able to do things with the other wives while the Choir rehearses". That thought filled me with dread. They were much too 'upper crust' for me and I always felt distinctly uncomfortable in their presence. However, I felt I had to go for Howard's sake so I kept hoping that the trip would be cancelled. There was a chance of that as the Tiananmen Square Massacre had happened in June 1989 and, since Their Royal Highnesses were going to be there (albeit they would be in Hong Kong), it might be thought too dangerous to visit that part of the world. I was clutching at straws.

Arrangements were made to go, so we decided to tack on a week in China after the Choir commitments were over. We thought we would never be as close to China again, so it seemed too good an opportunity to miss to see the mystic Orient.

Sunday 5th

Our flight left one hour late, as the number of passengers and the number of pieces of luggage did not tally. In six hours time, we would be in Dubai. We had our (now obligatory) look into the cockpit. There were so many lights everywhere, it was like Christmas already - except that, unlike those in Oxford Street, each one had some huge significance as regards our safety!

We were given a meal, after which we retired for the night. We were woken at 0330 at Dubai to change planes. It seemed such a pity as we couldn't see anything wrong with the one we were on and being woken from a deep sleep at that hour was horrendous in the extreme. There was a carbon copy British Airways jumbo jet waiting to take us on to our destination. (We couldn't decide what country Dubai was in. Was it the United Arab Emirates? We noticed 'Emirates' on the side of many aircraft - and all the Arabs looked *united* enough - so we supposed it was.) What we saw of Dubai airport - the transit lounge and the tarmac - was full of Arab gents in either security uniforms or sheets - and they were armed! (The Arabs that is - not the sheets.) It was very warm and the local time was 0730.

Monday 6th

We were already four hours ahead of London time. By the time we reached Hong Kong, we would be eight hours ahead, so we assumed we were about half way there. The second half of the journey was as uneventful as the first. Yet more food and drink were provided. I couldn't manage any more. Sleep was what I craved but it was not too easy - and how we *longed* to be lying down after so many hours of sitting. Our route took us over India, Burma and China, arriving at Hong Kong at 1915 local time. Now we really *were* eight hours ahead of London time.

Getting to the hotel from the airport always seems to take an age and this was no exception. (At least they drove on the left - like us!) Eventually we arrived at the Hyatt Regency Hotel where our room appeared to be very spacious. We weren't able to see just *how* spacious it was as we seemed unable to make the lights work. I crawled around the floor with my torch, looking for plugs - or similar - and we had to agree these were not ideal conditions, though we supposed it would improve with the daylight. A passing employee of the hotel put us out of our misery by explaining that the lights operated when we inserted the room key into a slot by the door. Thus illuminated, the spaciousness was confirmed. It was indeed a huge room containing the largest bed we'd ever seen - perhaps the whole choir is to share it with us?

To complement the large bed, there was an equally large rubber plant which reached up to the ceiling, a sofa, a desk, fresh fruit, a Chinese lacquered Ming Dynasty (we think) cabinet which, when opened, revealed an un-Chinese lacquered television - dynasty uncertain. Along with the Gideon Bible was a copy of The Teachings of Buddha. The bathroom was equally lavishly equipped. Apart from the myriad towels, there were things for shoe-cleaning, shampoos, foamy bath stuff, a hair dryer, tissues, fresh drinking water in a silver(y?) jug, sewing kit, telephone, a framed picture and another plant - somewhat smaller than its bedroom counterpart. The only thing that was missing was something to take boy scouts out of horses' hooves. The brochure extolled the virtues of the Hyatt Regency from the minute you stepped through the door - having been greeted by a turbaned Indian gentleman. "The lobby at the Hyatt Regency is considered by many as one of the most attractive of any hotel in Hong Kong. Dramatic yet soothing, it acquires its understated elegance from beautiful Italian and Spanish marbles, natural teak wood panelling, theatrical lighting and a gallery of exquisite antiques." (And that was just the entrance hall!) No wonder the rooms were so posh - and that they "exude a wonderful feeling of warmth and comfort enhanced by subtle earth tone colour schemes". (!) But, for £100 a night, so they should...

There was also a Business Centre and a tariff detailing how much things like typing cost. It occurred to me that, if I got bored, I could offer my services and earn some swift Hong Kong dollars to help pay for the trip - after all, at £3 for an A4 page, that would come in useful. There could have been the teeniest snag if they wanted things typed in Chinese. One look at the 'Restaurants and Bars' list was enough to ensure that we would not be eating or drinking there. A fresh orange juice would set us back £2-30p, breakfast a mere £9 and the cheapest thing in Hugo's restaurant ("one of Hong Kong's première and perennial Continental restaurants…gourmet cuisine and fine wine") was £20 - and that was only the main course. We had a quick snack at a place across the road before retiring to catch up on our long awaited sleep. It was now 2300 local time (1500 back in London) so we had been going for thirty-one hours without sleeping in a proper bed.

Tuesday 7th

We breakfasted with Dai and his room mate Keith (fellow choristers) in *MacDonalds*. (Is there *no* escape anywhere in the world from this chain?) We heard a shattering piece of news. Lesley and Peter Hewetson-Brown were also in the choir. I had been at school with Lesley many years before. When they arrived at the hotel, they had been told that Lesley's father (whom I knew well) had had a heart attack and died while we were travelling out to Hong Kong. After breakfast, Howard and the other choir members had to go off for a photo-call so I returned to our palatial room to start this diary.

Lunch was taken at the *Great Shanghai* restaurant, which had seating for 500. ('Great' was not a hyperbole!) Howard went to his first rehearsal so I returned to our room to read up about Hong Kong. I learned that it means 'Fragrant Harbour' and 98% of the inhabitants were Chinese. Though English was used by all the Government bodies, the dominant language was Cantonese. The guidebook went on "Chinese languages have a few basic words, usually fewer than a thousand, but each word can have up to thirty different meanings, depending on context, combination and, chiefly, intonation. Cantonese has nine tones, more than any other dialect. Greetings are complicated - even 'thank you' is difficult, for there are two forms of thanks and they are not interchangeable. It is usually possible to get by with English." The last sentence pleased me no end but the guidebook was making me rethink those Chinese evening classes.

On return from Howard's rehearsal, we watched on TV the arrival of the Prince and Princess of Wales, who were to open the new Cultural Centre the following night, prior to the Inaugural Concert at which the Choir would perform. Suitably reassured that TRHs had arrived, we took our first trip on the MTR - Mass Transit

Railway - their underground system. It was highly computerized, swift and clean. We bought two Stored Value tickets which meant that each time we took a journey, we inserted them into the entrance machine gate and they were returned to us. On leaving the system at the end of our journey, we fed the tickets into the exit machine and it displayed how much value was left on the tickets. We took a train under the Harbour to Hong Kong Island and sought out the *Jade Garden* restaurant in the Swire building. Dishes on offer included: Double-boiled Snake with black chicken in soup; Pan fried Shredded Squid with Preserved Vegetable and Bean Sprout (just the one?); Deep fried fresh milk with Banana; Boiled Drunken Shrimps in soup 'Cooking in front of table' - and Steamed Carp lips with Soya Beans and Garlic Sauce. We eschewed all of these but we did chew some beef and duck, which were excellent. We ate it all with chopsticks. Howard was very versatile with this equipment and I was to improve my technique vastly during the period of our stay. Something we learned was that rice came as a separate course - unless it was requested with the main dishes.

Toothpicks were brought to us at the end of the meal. There were two in each packet - one for the upper and lower set?

On our way back, we glanced into the Mandarin Hotel - apparently one of the all-time finest and most expensive. Its real crystal chandeliers dripping all over the entrance hall certainly made it look expensive. We went to the twenty-fifth floor restaurant - only for the view. We would not be eating there as we would have needed to have taken out a mortgage on a meal - just for the first course!

We went back home on the Star Ferry. The eight minute crossing of the harbour landed us very near to the new Cultural Centre so we had a quick peek inside. We would see much more of it soon as this was where the concert was due to be held. We reflected on how conspicuous we must have looked in this city as we are so aware of how conspicuous other Westerners look to us, amid the seething crowds of oriental faces. There was an almost total absence of black faces: there were some Indians and Sri Lankans but very few West Indians or Africans. The Chinese really *were* inscrutable. When they talked to each other, apart from the fact that it was not possible for us to understand one single word (unlike in European countries where at least some words *sound* similar), it was impossible to tell, either from their faces or from the inflexions in their voices, whether they were sad, happy, angry, peaceful, arguing or just chatting. Luckily English got us by - liberally sprinkled with much nodding of the head and bowing.

Wednesday 8th

Howard had a morning rehearsal and the afternoon was to be a coach tour of Hong Kong. We agreed to meet in the hotel Coffee Shop as soon after 1300 as possible and I would pre-order the food. The menus were in our room so it was possible to decide in advance. Howard decided on 'sliced beef with asparagus on tomato coriander bread' while I chose 'favourite sandwich selection'. We could have had 'Mandarin Glazed Chicken with Lotus Roots' but we didn't want to appear ostentatious! Life is not always as straightforward as we would wish it to be. When I tried to order my 'favourite sandwich selection', thinking it would be a 'selection' from which I could choose my 'favourite', I was asked what kind I wanted. My reply was "What kind are available?". The reaction of the waitress was an inscrutable smiling "Yes". Undeterred, I suggested salmon (as presumably 'all favourite sandwiches' were the same price - and they probably didn't have cheese and pickle anyway.) 'Salmon' drew a smiling blank stare, so I tried "Egg and tomato?". A similar smiling countenance, which indicated to me that, in the oriental world of 'favourite sandwiches', salmon and egg and tomato were equally incomprehensible. What could have developed into a lengthy smiling encounter was brought to a sudden conclusion when the mystic oriental lady wondered if I would like Tuna fish. This answer to a maiden's prayer sounded too good an opportunity to miss - plus the fact that, prolonging the conversation might have proved very inconclusive. Tuna fish it was - and all was agreed with much more smiling, nodding and bowing.

Howard arrived later than expected and I was getting into a frantic state knowing we had a deadline for the coach tour and his 'sliced beef' - with accoutrements had arrived. When he appeared, it was to say that the coach tour had been called off as so many roads in Hong Kong were closed because of the royal visit. We were no longer in a rush and we had the afternoon to ourselves.

We took the opportunity to visit the Space Museum and the Planetarium. It wasn't *quite* like the Washington DC version - no space capsules, space suits, space men - just lots of space - and illustrations. We had tickets for the Space Theatre Show so our hopes were raised. They were soon to be dashed, for, after five minutes of neck-aching expositions of Zodiac signs (we've never understood how four stars can be joined up to look like a water-carrier - let alone a lion!), we had a thirty-five minute film about beavers. This latter was projected onto an overhead spherical wrap-around screen and, as some was filmed underwater, we had the distinct impression of drowning. Still, we'd paid for it so we were determined to get as many distinct impressions as possible. We learned that beavers were 'in there' at the beginning of time, building away at their dams, before Quasars or Black Holes were ever thought of!

The other attraction we'd promised ourselves this afternoon was a visit to the Opal House, to see the opals being fashioned by skilled craftsmen and to 'share the Opal Experience'. It wasn't quite like that. It was just a small shop with opals round the walls. They cost *lots* of money - but of the 'skilled craftsmen' there was no sign.

On the way back to the hotel, we visited a mosque where, leaving our footwear behind, a very welcoming member of staff gave us a guided tour and explanations of the Muslim tradition. As we left, he presented us with a booklet about Islam, the five-times daily timetable for prayer and another booklet entitled *The Ideal Muslim Husband*. There was a score sheet on the final page - marks were out of forty-nine. Forty-nine was 'A Pious Muslim', nil for wealth but fifteen marks for 'Ability to be contented with one wife'.

Later came the first of the three Bach Choir concerts. There was very tight security because of the presence of TRHs so the Choir was 'bussed in'. I walked there, bearing my gold-crested invitation - but no one was remotely interested in it and I was not asked to produce it. The only thing that aroused interest was the actual ticket. The new circular concert hall was impressive with a very large organ (any specifications for Charles Proctor?). The instrument had horizontal pipes in addition to the vertical ones - similar to those on the Notre Dame organ in Paris. As soon as the concert got under way, I felt we could have been in any concert hall in the world - except that there was something rather odd about hearing the words of the *Te Deum* some 8,000 miles from home. In Walton's *Belshazzar's Feast*, when the choir sang "How shall we sing the Lord's song in a strange land?", that somehow summed it up. The concert was well received by the audience which was made up of not only TRHs but all the glitterati of Hong Kong - and me.

Thursday 9th

The Hong Kong Standard reported the opening of the Cultural Centre on its front page. Thirty-five lines were given over to details of the clothes worn by not only the Princess of Wales but the Governor's wife and the other important notables. The 'world famous Bach Choir' got six lines and the report also recorded that 'the show (?) featured music by Handel, Vaughan Williams and Walton'. (That said *something* about where their priorities lay.)

We took the Star Ferry to Hong Kong Island where we were to visit the Man Mo Temple. (Literally 'Man' meant 'Civil' and 'Mo', Mortal. The Man Mo Temple itself was dedicated to two gods - King-Emperor Man and the Holy King-Emperor Kwan, 'who were believed to have the purview of protecting the well-being of man and were thus worshipped as thus'.) This was an extraordinary place to Western eyes - and noses! Never had we smelled so much incense. We tried to work out what the worshippers were doing. It seemed they purchased the incense sticks (rather like candles in Western churches) except that they purchased a sheaf of them, then they placed them in front of whichever god took their fancy - and there were many from which to choose. When praying to these gods, the people bowed very low to the deities, almost prostrating themselves in front of them. Then they stood up - and this was repeated a number of times. (Certainly they needed to be fit for this way of life!) The people brought gifts for the gods - fresh fruit, packets of things (we couldn't work out what the packets contained). One lady brought a cooked chicken! It was not very peaceful in the temple as everyone was milling about and talking so there was no feeling of reverence from that point of view. There was from the point of view of the incense and the intensity with which people seemed to be praying. We wondered what happened to the 'gifts', whether perhaps the monks would eat them We hoped so as it would have been very wasteful to ditch them!

From the Temple, we descended to the *Luk Yu Tea House* for a Dim Sum snack. It was packed with customers. There was nothing English on the menu; it was written completely in Chinese characters, so we were mystified. A 'pad' of menus was on the table - but that was also in Chinese - so we hadn't a ghost of an idea what anything was. Howard indicated to the waiter that we would like 'a beef thing, a prawn thing, a pork thing - and rice' and the waiter ticked some of the Chinese characters. (We realized how the eatery got its name. When our food hadn't arrived after some minutes, Howard said to the waiter "Look, you - where is our lunch?") Eventually our selection arrived and it was the sort of thing we were expecting. (More luck here than we had with the 'favourite sandwich selection'.) Meanwhile, a Chinese man seated at our table, was brought his tea. To our astonishment, the waiter poured the tea all over the cup, which was contained in a metal dish, before extracting the cup and filling it with tea. *Our* tea was delivered to us in the normal way and we couldn't work out why the Chinese man had had to go through this strange ritual. Another thing that struck us as odd was that a large number of people in the tea house were using mobile telephones. (Bear in mind this was many years before they were as commonplace as they are now.) We felt it was not much of a lunch break if they brought their work with them!

Howard had to go to his next rehearsal. (I couldn't help noticing that my clothes still smelled very strongly of incense.) When the rehearsal was over, we headed for Victoria Peak - 1,305 feet above sea level. From the top, there would be a 360-degree view of the whole territory. The ascent was either a three hour walk or an eight minute ride on the Peak Tram. No prizes for guessing which option we took.

Recently, the Peak Tram had undergone modernisation, making it one of the most advanced systems in the world - and the funicular railway had come from Switzerland. It was a thirty degree incline and it was a strange sensation to see all the buildings in Hong Kong suddenly adopt a 'Leaning Tower of Pisa' attitude. Though we knew it was *us* who were no longer parallel with *terra firma*, the human brain has the uncanny ability to convince its owner otherwise - that it was the rest of the world that had moved through thirty degrees. There was a lot of gravity about on this particular evening so our bodies felt heavy as they were pulled through such a steep angle. The guidebook said that 'the chairs were angled back as if for a moon shot'. (We felt this would stand us in good stead when we applied to join the first British space mission and had to state our 'previous relevant experience'.)

The view from the top was as spectacular as we had been led to believe. We had our first sighting of the Boat People, though from a great distance. We walked around Lugard Road - which encompassed the Peak - taking about an hour but affording wonderful views throughout. We returned to ground level by bus - a hair-raising journey which seemed to be a permanent Z-bend.

Back at the hotel, we collected our passports (which we had entrusted to the travel agent to obtain our visas for China) then made our way to the *Golden Island Bird's Nest* restaurant nearby. The assortment of small dishes of things which arrived (free) seemed to increase with each place we visited. Here we got six tiny bowls of tea, a dish of something that made chillis taste bland (!) and another dish of something which was a cross between gherkins and ginger. All this was preceded by the delivery, by tongs, of hot towels with which to wipe our travel-stained hands. We felt this was a very civilized idea that could well be exported to the UK. A large aquarium, full of wonderfully coloured fish, was adjacent to our table. Our concern was that they were not there for purely decorative purposes - but, happily, we were proved wrong. (One of them looked distinctly surly and we agreed that he/she was not unlike the photo of Sean Connery that had adorned the cover of the colour supplement which accompanied us from England. If we were to give marks out of ten for surliness, they would both have received at least eight.)

Friday 10th

We sought a laundry (of which the phone book listed a vast number) and entrusted some things to it so we would have clean attire for the forthcoming second leg of our trip. The contrast between the shopping arcade in which the Purity Laundry was located and the shopping arcade in which our hotel was located was striking - and only a narrow road divided the two. We were discovering that Hong Kong was a city of great contrasts. It was also a city where not one square inch was left unfilled. 'Seething with people' would be a fair description. There was no alleyway or doorway which didn't have a little stall or a café set up within it. Huge numbers of people were everywhere; so too were skyscrapers.

We went in search of Hong Lok Street and the Bird Market, a long narrow street full of birds and cages of all shapes and sizes. Some of the cages could have been much bigger to contain more comfortably the size of bird, so we hoped they would be sold quickly and removed to larger premises. There was much evidence of birds being taken for walks in their cages - something we had read about in the guidebook but little thought we would encounter. One man was holding his cage up to another containing a large number of similar birds, so we assumed he had brought *his* bird for a chat with its friends. Some stalls sold stick-insect-looking things (locusts?) and we presumed these were to feed to the birds. We weren't at all keen on the idea of that and wondered what might happen if, whilst carrying your live bird-food home on the tube, the plastic bag burst!

From the bird market, we took the same tube line for a few more stops to the Sung Dynasty Village - a re-creation of a 1,000 year-old Chinese village from the time of the Sung Dynasty (960-1,279 AD). We watched a traditional marriage ceremony and acquired some incense sticks and a couple of Chinese writings which we were assured meant Good Luck. Next was a visit to the Wax Museum, where were displayed wax models of famous people from China's history. What a bloodthirsty lot they were - the men, at least. Any women on display seemed to have been merely concubines of differing levels of importance. No wonder the Bach Choir chose to bring *Belshazzar's Feast* to Hong Kong! The men seemed to have been either assassins, torturers, livers of lustful and lascivious lives - or suicidal! (So ran the notes which accompanied the effigies.) We supposed it was all part of life's rich pattern - but we were glad we hadn't been around at that time. In Kennington, the nearest we got to Ghenghis Khan was the Spring Garden, our local Chinese takeaway.

The second concert was to take place this evening. The work was the *B Minor Mass* and it appeared that there were many more Western people in the audience. I sat idly wondering what the Chinese people in the audience thought of this piece. How many of the Chinese population were Christian? For those who weren't, it must have seemed a bit odd. At least the gods they worshipped were visible and they visited them regularly. What do they make of *our* God - who is invisible, who died and rose again but is still invisible, and about whom we sing - in Latin? It must have been quite puzzling for them. I mused on why it was that

137

Western music was played worldwide but, on the whole, Chinese music did not export. Were there any equivalent Chinese musical works written in praise of *their* gods? What a lot of things to ponder…

Saturday 11th

After breakfast, we changed some more travellers' cheques - but in the bank this time, rather than in the hotel - and we got a better rate. Then it was off to the boat trip which the sponsors of the Bach Choir Tour had organized. Hangers-on were included too so I went along. We were told there would be seven junks for people and two for food. (Jokes about junk food were immediately embargoed!) On arrival at the quay side, Mr Simon Murray greeted the party. He was a 'top dog' in Hutchison Whampoa, the sponsors. By way of a thank you, the Choir sang *Ding Dong merrily on high* to him - then it was into the seven boats. Each boat could hold twenty-eight passengers. They turned out to be motor boats, rather than junks - and very comfortable they were too. Hardly had we taken our seats than we were offered some white wine. The craft were pitching rather a lot but we observed it was because of the wash from other boats. We assumed that, once under way, it would be very smooth - which it was. We cruised around Hong Kong Island, via Aberdeen and the Jumbo Floating Restaurant, to Repulse Bay - in perfect weather. Here we dropped anchor and the nine boats were lashed together making it possible to walk the length of them. Never had we seen such a huge buffet. It contained every imaginable thing - both hot and cold - and yet more wine, which had been flowing non-stop during the voyage. Some people took the opportunity to swim off the boat - in the South China Sea. We didn't take that opportunity! After the really sumptuous meal, we cruised back to Hong Kong Island and headed off to Stanley Market where it was reported there were numerous bargains to be had. The report proved to be true.

This must have been where the American ladies we had met at breakfast had come for their bargains. ("Gee, only 250 dollars for some designer stuff which would be at least 400 dollars back home. But then my husband reminded me that it had cost 2,500 dollars to get here in the first place!") It didn't seem to concern them too much as they had recently visited London, the British Isles (spoken as though they were two separate places), Switzerland and Amsterdam. We were not remotely interested in clothes - designed or *un*designed - but we got some presents before heading off to the *Jumbo* restaurant at Aberdeen.

The *Jumbo* restaurant was billed as 'the largest and most luxurious floating restaurant in the world'. It was moored in the Harbour and was reached by free ferries which plied to and fro every couple of minutes. We accepted that it was probably the largest floating restaurant in the world - though, come to think of it, how many floating restaurants did we know? We queried the description 'luxurious'. It was very crowded and the decibel level was high. While we waited for our table, we ordered an orange juice. At £1-60 each, we were immediately curious to know how much wine would cost! When we discovered that the cheapest was £10 - for half a bottle, we realized just how fond we were of Chinese tea. The table numbers were announced over a microphone - but not always in English. As we did not know the Chinese for ninety-one (our table number), we waited longer than we needed as it had already been called! No matter - eventually we ordered Peking Duck and a very large quantity of it arrived. We knew that it was only the outside that was eaten and we wondered what happened to the rest of the meat. We ate our way through the outside (served on a bed of crackers) and, just as we thought we were coming to the end, another plateful of meat arrived. We suggested to the waiter than he had the wrong table but it transpired that this was the answer to our query about what happened to the rest of the duck. This was it! It was a formidable sight to which we couldn't do justice. (We had never known this to happen when we had had Peking Duck in England so we were rather taken aback.)

Throughout the meal, people were being photographed, seated on thrones and dressed as Emperors and Empresses. The photos were developed immediately - and no doubt cost a fortune. All this happened to the accompaniment of two female instrumentalists; one played a thing which could have been a lute (though it was so quiet as to be inaudible over the high-decibel count occasioned by the conversation). Her partner played a machine that would have become a 'cello when it grew up. At that moment, it was a pentatonic 'would-be' 'cello which was thrilling its listeners with droning 'every-piece-sounds-the-same-as-every-other-piece' offerings. My question of the previous evening was answered here. This was why Chinese music did not export - its hearers would die of boredom. Indeed, the two exponents looked as though that fate had already befallen them. (From now until December 16th, we had to take malaria tablets to ward off the disease - we wondered if there were equivalent tablets to ward off pentatonic music.) We couldn't help but be reminded of the balalaika players in the Monty Python Cheese Shop sketch.

Sunday 12th

This was Remembrance Sunday but we had seen very few people wearing poppies during the week. Would they have a service as we did? There was a Cenotaph on the Island, which was a copy of the one in Whitehall - so perhaps they would.

We took breakfast at the YMCA - a tip from one of the Choir - followed by a visit to the OmniPrince Hotel, to which we would return for the night of Saturday

November 18th, before flying back to Gatwick on November 19th. We were relieved to find that they had our reservation and that we could leave some luggage there to save carting it with us to China.

In the afternoon we took the deferred coach trip, then back to the Hyatt Regency through the Park - where there was a man taking his birds for a walk. It really *did* happen!

This evening was the final concert of the Tour - a repeat of the first concert except that *Hymn of Jesus* replaced *Serenade to Music*. Before leaving the hotel, I watched an episode of *Ever Decreasing Circles* - with Chinese sub-titles! After the concert, we took our bag of things we didn't need for China and left it at the OmniPrince Hotel to await our return.

Monday 13th

The morning paper confirmed that there had been a service at the Cenotaph on the previous day and Prince Charles had laid a wreath. He had stayed on in Hong Kong for a few days though Princess Diana had returned to England.

Today we were off to Peking (Beijing). We were booked onto the 1015 CAAC (Civil Aviation Administration of China) flight from Hong Kong. It would take three hours to fly to Peking. The security people confiscated our glass cleaning fluid which was in our hand luggage. It was not allowed on the plane because it was in a pressurized container so we were given a receipt for it and had to collect it on our return to Hong Kong at the end of the week. (I wondered about things like my deodorant which were also in pressurized containers but were in our suitcase.)

During the flight we were given three forms to complete for Immigration. There were so many questions: "Please mark a tick before the symptoms if any now - Fever, Rash, Cough, Lymph-gland swelling. Have you any of the following: Biologicals(?), Blood Products, Second hand Clothes?" (What an odd combination!) Then we had to list items we had on entry: "Gold and Silver Ornaments, Camera (with make), Tape Recorder, Video and Movie Camera. Other articles due to Custom procedures - Goods and samples, Recorded Video Tape, Printed Matter, Antiques." This was a two-part form on NCR paper, with a further column for items we would have on Exit - presumably so they could check we hadn't sold any of our items in the country. (?) We wondered how much of this would be checked on arrival and/or departure. We didn't have to wait long to discover that none of it was checked - but then it *might* have been - and we didn't want to find ourselves in a Chinese jail!

Baggage Reclaim and Customs didn't take long so we went in search of our Speedtravel representative. The first big surprise was that no one was displaying a Speedtravel board - but a diminutive oriental lady was bearing a sign reading "Mr and Mrs Spurr". The second big surprise was that, not only were we the only two people doing this tour, but the diminutive lady (Jenny) would accompany us throughout, together with Mr Zhong, the taxi driver. We were to be driven by taxi to all the places we would visit! Our first taxi ride took half an hour and took us to our hotel, the Holiday Inn Lido. It was miles from anywhere on the edge of a forest but was very comfortable with all the mod. cons. you could imagine. Our suggestion that we might take a walk around outside was not welcomed by Jenny and we had the distinct impression that we had been accommodated in this rather distant location for a reason. The authorities did not want us 'looking around'. However, a Holiday Inn is a Holiday Inn, no matter where in the world you might be. Little did I know it at the time but this was to become a source of great comfort to me during our stay.

There was just time to check in and leave our luggage before meeting up with Jenny to go to the Temple of Heaven. We changed a travellers' cheque into Chinese money - of which there were two kinds. One currency was for the tourists and one was for the local population, though they were of equal value. The ordinary currency was the Renminbi and this was divided into Yuan, Jiao and Fen. 100 Fen = 1 Yuan, 10 Fen = 1 Jiao and 10 Jiao = 1 Yuan. The tourist currency was called the Foreign Exchange Certificate (FEC). We had to keep a receipt for the money we changed as we would need to show it when we changed it back again on leaving the country. We were advised not to accumulate Renminbi as they could not be changed back and it was illegal to take them out of China. If you think that all sounded complicated, it was! (I wonder if all this still applies in the twenty-first century.)

We set off for the Temple of Heaven and immediately we were struck by the difference in temperature. Indeed, Jenny was 'muffled up' against the cold. Our problem was that we had no warm clothing whatsoever! Hong Kong had been warm the whole time and we had not realised that the temperature would be very different in China. I shivered because I did not have nearly enough garments to protect me from the cold. In particular I had no gloves and my hands suffered.

The Temple of Heaven was some 500 years old and very ornate. It was where the Emperor went to worship the god of Heaven and to pray for good harvest. He would bring gifts like silk and roasted ox. I enquired what happened to the roasted ox when the Emperor had left it on the altar. Jenny's English was good but she didn't always understand our questions. This was a case in point because her answer to my query was that the Emperor only went there twice a year! (Howard thought that what would have happened would have been that one of the priests would ask the Emperor to close his eyes in prayer. When he opened them, the goodies would have disappeared and the priests would be able to assure the Emperor that the appropriate god had taken the offerings. In reality, the priests would have stashed the goodies behind a pillar and, as soon as His Imperial Highness was on his way back to his concubines, the less religiously inclined would have had a good tuck-in!)

Our 'religious observances' done, we were driven to the Guangming Hotel, a block of service apartments containing, on the twelfth floor, a restaurant. Since all meals were included in our trip, this was not going to cost us anything. The restaurant wasn't open but Jenny pointed out to the management that 'there are foreign visitors who need to be served' so, with a clap of hands, we were admitted and served with an excellent Chinese meal. But what a meal it turned out to be.

We were to discover, with each Chinese meal we consumed, that rice was not usually served, though soup was - as the final course. Despite the fact that it *was* the final course, it was brought to the table at the beginning of the meal so, by the end, it was not as hot as it might have been. During this particular meal, one or two things conspired to make us slightly anxious. The first thing was that a few dishes of food were delivered to us, and, just as we began to make inroads into them, another dish arrived. This was repeated until there were about twelve dishes of things on the table. We wondered how many more would arrive and should we have left room for extra food. There was absolutely no way of knowing and, since we hadn't ordered the meal (it had been pre-ordered for us), we couldn't even hazard a guess. The next thing that made us slightly anxious was that the waiters (who seemed to be 'legion' - just for the two of us) came and stood around our table staring at us - and watching us eat. As soon as we took a sip of tea or wine, one of them was at our side refilling the partly-emptied vessel. It was a very disconcerting feeling and, at its height, there were four 'starers' and a Suzie Wong type in a full-length red silk dress. It got to the point where we wished they would all go away and stare at someone else (except there was no one else in the restaurant but Jenny and Mr Zhong - who had seated themselves at a separate table, though we had asked them to join us). The 'starers' seemed to be closing in by the mouthful and we felt we should invite them to sit down and join us - to save standing all that time! Two of them spoke a little English and we wondered if they wanted to practise it on us - which we were more than happy for them to do. The final curiosity came when the Suzie Wong look-alike told us (in rather fractured English) she was going to give us a present. It turned out to be a mini-questionnaire - containing just two questions. "(1) Please write

142

down the attendant's name service number who satisfies you with good service (2) Please write down the attendant's name whose smile leaves on you a favourable impression." Hardly had we read the questions when one of the 'starers' produced a pen for our use. I got a mini fit of hysterics; it seemed we were in another Monty Python sketch. The point was that the 'starers' had done nothing *but* stand and smile (except when they were rushing to top up our drinks when we had consumed the merest drop of anything). They had all left 'a favourable impression' so we noted their names and numbers on our forms - adding a rider that all the staff had been very friendly.

Tuesday 14th

The weather in Peking was like a very cold, frosty, autumnal English day, so before setting out, we devised different combinations of garments that we could wear in order to counter the effects of the cold. Everywhere people rode bicycles - a car was an unusual sight. Jenny told us that there were eleven million people in Peking and seven million of them rode bicycles. It felt like being at the start of the Tour de France race - permanently - and the riders seemed to observe few, in any, traffic regulations. To get across a busy four lane highway, they pointed their bikes and went - four wheeled traffic avoided them if possible. Crossing the road involved a similar operation. There seemed to be no obligation on the part of the cyclists to cross at a particular spot; zebra crossings seemed to have no significance whatsoever. Nevertheless, braving the cold and the cyclists, we met up with Jenny and Mr Zhong (who spoke absolutely no English) at 0900. My piano socks did sterling work and another pair were converted into gloves. Two vests provided extra warmth and a multiplicity of other garments completed the ensemble. The same went for Howard - except his socks didn't have any piano keys on them.

Surprisingly, our first visit was to Tiananmen Square. We had wondered if we would not be shown this in view of the events of June 4th that year. It was a huge square (four times as big as Grosvenor Square in London), bounded on one side by the Great Hall of the People (their 'sort of' Houses of Parliament) and on another by the Museum of Chinese History. There were impressive gates at the ends. However, the Square was completely cordoned off and could be entered at only one place. It was guarded by a combination of police and military and we were told that the security of the Square was in the process of being handed over to the police from the military. No one was allowed to take any bags into the Square, so not only did we have to leave our shopping bag in the taxi but I had to leave my handbag! I was never separated from my handbag - especially at this particular time when it contained all documents vital to our health, safety and transport! I was more than reluctant to leave it but was assured that Mr Zhong would remain in the taxi throughout. We had to take our passports to gain admission to the Square and, to our surprise, we were allowed to take cameras. There was a large memorial to those who died in the Chinese Revolution and we were just in time to witness a visit to it by some high-powered military people. We couldn't help but wonder how many lives came to an end on June 4th, on the very spot where we were standing. What was that about 'man's inhumanity to man'? Once inside the Square, we paid a visit to Chairman Mao's Mausoleum where his embalmed body was lying in state. We filed past in a very orderly procession - in pairs.

Our next stop was The Forbidden City, which we had seen very recently in the film *The Last Emperor*. Its proper name was the Imperial Palace or the Palace Museum and it most certainly came up to expectations, making us realize that the film had been very true to life. Jenny gave us lots of information about the Emperors of the past. Their names all sounded somewhat similar - Wang, Chang, Deng etc. It was hard to remember who was who, once Jenny got into her stride - but it seemed that they all had armfuls of concubines. One, who bore the Emperor a son, was promoted to Empress! (How to succeed in business without really trying?) Jenny told us that the Emperor never walked anywhere but was carried by minions, whilst he was seated in a sedan chair. The Forbidden City was very extensive, containing over 900 rooms. What an odd life it must have been, living there at the time it was a Palace. Now, in its museum format, there was much jewellery on display and a hall full of ornate clocks, brought as presents for the Emperors from around the world - many from England. We realized what it was that was forbidden in this city - it was heating. It was very cold throughout and few of the rooms had any heating at all. Just before we left, I headed for what was ironically called the 'public conveniences' - and soon wished I hadn't. A Kennington friend, Claire, had warned us about this before we came but I had forgotten. However, following Claire's advice, I headed for 'the end one' - where at least no one would pass by! That was an important consideration as there were no doors! A veil must be drawn over the remainder of this episode. (I would have been quite happy to draw a veil over where the door might have been…)

The two long visits we had made had certainly given us an appetite for lunch, which was taken at a restaurant in a public park. We had another very good Chinese meal, most of the constituent parts of which we did not recognize. Again we invited Jenny and Mr Zhong to join us but they declined. Jenny said, in a rather conspiratorial way, "different prices" - and she and Mr Zhong retired to another section of the restaurant - behind screens!

The Friendship Store was our next port of call and here we purchased many presents, including ones *to* ourselves *from* ourselves. On to the British Embassy where Howard wanted to look up some former colleagues. Unfortunately one was off for the day, taking an exam and the other was on holiday. A very pleasant member of the Press Department greeted us and we had an extremely interesting chat with him, learning amongst other things what *really* happened on the night of June 4th. He had been there.

The Lama Temple contained no four-legged ones. The reason was that Lamas (thus spelled) were Buddhist monks and there was a smattering of them around. This particular temple turned out to be a series of temples, each containing different combinations of different Buddhas. (Heaven, Earth, Longevity, Health, Past, Present, Future...you name it, they had a Buddha for it. They seemed to share a motto with the Boy Scouts - Be Prepared!) There was much incense around, so we felt quite at home, but there the similarity with St Peter's, Vauxhall ended.

After our religious 'instruction', we were taken to a nearby restaurant for supper. Though it was only 1700, we didn't mind as we were already looking forward to our evening in the hotel - the postcard and diary-writing - and the rest. The fresh air, change of climate and environment and assimilation of so much knowledge was a tiring combination. On our return to the hotel, we learned that our flight to Shanghai on Thursday would leave at 0835 and we would be collected at 0700. That gave us more reason to make the most of our rest evening.

Wednesday 15th

Our itinerary today included the Great Wall and the Ming Tombs. (We doubted we would be able to walk the full 4,000 miles of the Great Wall as we would be somewhat pushed for time.) Jenny had warned us that it would be somewhat colder at the Great Wall (it was a two-hour drive away) so we donned even more layers of clothing. We felt like astronauts about to board a spacecraft - so bulky was our apparel.

The Ming Tombs were first. There were thirteen of them in a huge valley, but only one had been excavated up to that time, since it was an extremely costly business. That was the tomb of Ding Ling Ming (yes, that really *was* his name!). He was around sometime in the sixteenth century. Though the tomb was built into the hillside it was nevertheless some distance underground. We tried to imagine what it must have been like for the people who discovered it originally. It was an enormous place and we stopped to marvel at how it had been built all those years ago, without the aid of modern technology and with minimal light - indeed, they would have had just candlelight by which to work. The building involved tons of stone which had been brought from many miles away, and heavy marble doors which were closed permanently once the dead Emperor had been placed within - along with his dead Empresses. Some of the doors weighed four tons each and the experts did not know how they were closed. The reason for this was that on the 'wrong side' of each door was a huge stone lock and no one (up to that time) had worked out how these were fixed into position from the other side. (I wonder if science has yet come up with an answer to this puzzle.) We saw copies of the coffins of the Emperor and his two Empresses (one of whom was the promoted concubine) as the originals had decayed by the time the tomb had been excavated in 1956. There were twenty-six boxes containing things that had been buried with them - jewellery, cooking utensils, chopsticks, coins - in fact everything they would have needed in the afterlife. These items were on display in the little museum attached to the tombs and in the Museum of Chinese History in the centre of Peking. It was breathtaking to consider the work that must have been involved in making these tombs - and even more breathtaking to think that the Emperors had a hand in the preparation of them. They would oversee the work throughout their lifetime and Jenny told us that, sometimes, on seeing the almost completed tomb, they would decide it just wasn't big enough so the lads would have to start again - building another, bigger and better, version!

The thought of all the work involved made us very hungry so we were glad when it was time for lunch. Another delicious Chinese pot-pourri arrived, not all of which we recognized but all of which we ate. Then it was time to approach the Great Wall.

This had to be one of the highlights of the trip - and it was. Words could not describe what it was like - or the dimensions of it. We recalled that, on television, we had seen the Queen on the Wall the previous year but, until we were actually there, it was difficult to comprehend the scale of it. It was, in fact, two walls and a space in between, where six horses could walk abreast. It was very undulating as it followed the contours of the mountain. We walked along it for perhaps half a mile and most of the time we walked up an incline of about forty-five degrees, either on very sloping pavement or up very high steps. I took some photos in an attempt to capture the height of the steps and the incline but, when developed, they showed neither! (Rethink the evening classes in photography?) As Jenny had warned us, it was very cold. By now, I had two pairs of socks on my hands and one pair on my feet. The sheer effort required for the steep ascent made us very warm indeed. Looking both backwards and forwards, we saw the Wall extending as far as the eye could see. To think that the construction of the Wall was started in 2,000 BC left us speechless and we could see why it was classified as one of the wonders of the ancient world. Even if had been built in the twentieth century, with modern technology, it would still be a wonder of the world. The descent was as hard as the ascent, but this time we were hampered by the snow which lay on parts of the pathway. We were pleased to return to the warmth and comfort of the car.

It was a two hour drive back to Peking where we were to eat a Peking Duck Banquet at another restaurant. Just before this, we visited a department store. It wasn't *quite* John Lewis' but we did make an attempt to obtain a stopwatch for Eric James (my boss). He needed this for timing things like his contribution to *Thought for the Day* which he used to broadcast on the radio. The only kind that were available looked rather odd, with three knobs and digital figures that seemed to flash on and off at random. We couldn't understand how they worked and we knew that Eric would have even *less* understanding of it. Howard tried to explain to the inscrutable assistant that we didn't want to purchase it because it would be too complicated for our friend "who was a very simple man".

Back at the restaurant, Jenny and Mr Zhong were allowed to join us this time. (We never did discover why they were allowed to do this in some places and not allowed to do it in others.) The restaurant was divided into a number of separate rooms, each containing varying numbers of tables. We had another excellent meal which included local fungi. The meal ended with the Peking Duck - well, *almost* ended with it, because there was still the duck soup, made from the bones - and the water melon - and 'cookies'. We felt sorry for Mr Zhong because he could not participate in the conversation as he spoke only Chinese. Our Chinese was non-existent. We passed things to him with much smiling and nodding and he seemed to be quite happy - in his oriental world.

Over the meal, we heard about Jenny's wedding and we exchanged information about our different lifestyles. We told Jenny about our visits to the opera back in London and this prompted her to relate a rather long-winded tale which was the basis for a Chinese piece of music - not, as far as we could understand, an opera. The finale of the story provided us with one of the most (unintentionally) hysterical moments of the trip so far. It went something like this. The lovelorn maiden, on her way to her arranged marriage, passed by the tomb of her late *real* love. She stopped - and, as she did so, the tomb opened and she jumped in - and out jumped two fly-buttons! Further questioning elicited the fact that it was two *butterflies* that jumped out - but it was too late! Never will we forget the scene!

It was a perfect end to the day - which had been rather dominated by tombs. We returned to the hotel to pack because we had an early start the next day for Shanghai.

At this juncture, I must record how very homesick I was in Peking. I had never felt this before when I was away from home. I am not an avid watcher of television but we were able to get CNN in our room - and I watched it, avidly. It was the only channel in English - all the other channels were in Chinese so we could not understand a word of them. When we switched on CNN, it was like a dream come true - just to hear English spoken - even *with* American accents! During the time we were in Peking, the Berlin Wall came down and we tuned into the news to see ecstatic scenes of people celebrating. I was glad we were in a western-style hotel - a Holiday Inn. I concluded that, to me, Peking was such an alien environment, peopled by human beings with whom I could not communicate in any way and full of signs (on buildings and shops) that I could not *begin* to understand. Furthermore, most of the population dressed in Chairman Mao-type clothing, such as we saw in caricatures of Chinese people, which reinforced the impression that 'all Chinese people looked the same'. Add to all that the inscrutability of them, as I mentioned much earlier, and maybe all this explained why it felt so alien. I longed for something 'western' - and CNN provided it - temporarily.

Thursday 16th

By 0730, we were at Peking airport. This had been 'done up' and was the best in China - though we found that hard to believe. It was very basic and our flight number was sellotaped to the 'departure lounge' - a somewhat grandiose term for what amounted to a scruffy room. Our flight was comfortable, though breakfast on board was a box of assorted sweets and biscuits with either orange juice or lemonade.

We arrived in Shanghai where the airport was quite stunning - stunningly tatty! It was nothing more than a few corrugated iron sheds. A hand-painted sign bade us "Welcome to Shanghai" and they *did* have a luggage conveyor belt - but that was it. We'd seen more impressive bus shelters. We were met by our Shanghai guide bearing a sign reading "Mr Spurr Howard David". The guide's name was Jane and she escorted us to our waiting car. No taxi this time, but a huge Chevrolet, with electrically operated windows (very unusual back in 1989) and a lady driver by the name of Mrs Fang. (Is this *another* Monty Python sketch?)

Our first stop was the Nikko Longbai Hotel, only five minutes' drive from the airport. This was a 'Joint Venture' hotel with the Japanese, though we learned that, in order to work in it, you had to be able to speak English. It was a very smart place with red-coated doormen who whisked up and extracted us from the Chevrolet. We checked in and left our luggage then returned to meet Jane and Mrs Fang for the drive to lunch.

The first thing we noticed driving into downtown Shanghai was how much more of a Western-style city it was than Peking. The most striking thing was the *colour*. Everyone's clothes were so colourful in comparison with those in Peking. That was not to say there was no variation in colour in Peking; there was dark brown, lighter brown, dark grey, not so dark grey - and two shades of black. In Shanghai, not only were the clothes the same colours as you would have seen in any London street, on the whole they were Western styles - as opposed to the Chairman Mao look-alike uniforms worn by almost everyone in Peking. The other thing that struck us was the relative absence of a police or military presence.

After lunch, we went to Yu Gardens. These had been built for someone's parents but, unfortunately, the parents had died before the gardens were finished. They were very attractive with lots of dragons and a little pond running throughout, which was full of goldfish. Next was a walk along by the harbour. Shanghai was a large and busy port, especially for container ships.

Howard phoned the British Consulate. The Consul, Iain Orr, a former colleague of Howard's from the Foreign Office, was very keen to see us, so we drove to the Consulate and spent half an hour with him and Mr Duncan Jackman, the Regional Director, British Council Consul (Cultural). Mr Orr was very complimentary about the visits organized by the Central Office of Information (for which Howard worked) for people from Shanghai and hoped that they would soon be resumed. Since June 4th, all that kind of activity had been put into abeyance but it was only a matter of time before visits would be resumed.

We visited the Arts and Crafts shop, which was just closing, but we were allowed to have a demonstration of paper cutting. It was fascinating and very skilful and we bought the little design that the lady made for us. We were told that she was famous for her craft and had been to a number of places in the world teaching people how to do it.

At supper, we were joined by Jane and Mrs Fang. Unfortunately, like Mr Zhong, Mrs Fang didn't speak any English but we tried our best to communicate with much passing round of plates of goodies. Just when we thought we couldn't squeeze another plate onto the table, a whole flat fish arrived. I was beaten but Howard made a sterling effort and Jane the guide and Mrs Fang joined him in making inroads into it.

Friday 17th

There was a little machine in our room which allowed us to make a cup of tea - bliss! By now, we were used to drinking tea without milk. With every meal we had in China we have been given Chinese tea. It was nothing like our usual

Typhoo. First it was served in tumblers and second, all the leaves were left in the container. Initially, all the leaves floated on top and it was not easy to hold a tumbler once it was filled with boiling water. Gradually, the leaves descended to the bottom and, when you had drained your glass, what looked like dark cabbage leaves remained - such was the size of each 'tea leaf'. Nevertheless, we found it a refreshing drink.

In the hotel restaurant, we indulged ourselves as American Breakfast was on the menu. This was our first Western food for almost a fortnight. Fried eggs and bacon had never tasted so good!

Our first stop in the Chevrolet was a Jade-carving factory. It was fascinating to see how the intricate jade ornaments were carved, using high speed machines, permanently cooled with water. They were operated very delicately by the craftsmen, who had to train for some time before they were allowed to start carving. An item could take about six months to carve, working on it every day; the more intricate ones took even longer. There was the inevitable shop attached to the factory where we bought a jade tortoise to add to our collection of little animals back home.

The next stop was a carpet factory where we saw the carpets being woven. The pattern was permanently displayed behind the loom and the weavers worked to that. When they were finished, the carpets went on to carpet engravers who chipped bits out so that the final result was three-dimensional. In the inevitable shop, inevitably we didn't buy any carpets!

The Jade Buddha Temple attracted us, the strong smell of incense luring us in from the pavement. The Temple contained a large jade Buddha brought to Shanghai from Burma some years previously. It must have been very slow progress as it was immensely heavy. Before we entered the room where it was kept, we had to remove our shoes and don the slippers which were provided. An old man helped us on and off with them using some pincers!

Lunch was taken at the Jiajang Hotel, which was where President Nixon had signed the trade agreement with China. We were becoming quite expert on Chinese food and the use of chopsticks.

After lunch, we visited the panda - a solitary figure similar to that in London zoo. He was in residence so we were lucky. He might have been snoozing in his private apartment within his cage, but he obliged us all by coming out and eating his huge bamboo shoots.

Next stop was the Silk factory, where we saw silk being screen-printed. We didn't buy anything in the shop but, we visited another section of the factory where we encountered a man making hand-painted handkerchiefs. As we watched him painting flowers onto hankies, the guide told us that, if we would like it, he would paint two hankies for us. What design would we like painted onto them? We suggested a blue bird for one and a dog for the other. The painter also added our names and the date. We were amazed at his skill and happily paid twenty Yuan for this very special souvenir!

At this point, we broke off for some reflections of our time in this very different land. How we would have liked to be free to just wander where we wanted to go. Though it was very comfortable being driven around in a huge car, it did mean that we saw the country from the perspective of a goldfish bowl. It was not a pleasant thought that there were we, receiving much attention, being fed wonderful meals and staying in huge plush hotels while most of the inhabitants of this poor country hadn't got 'two halfpennies to rub together'. It was not possible to reconcile the two things but it made us feel very guilty. No wonder the Chinese stared at us Westerners all the time - and stare they did! We were struck by the total lack of black people in China. We had not yet seen one. A really depressing statistic was that Chinese people were allowed to have only one child. If they found they were expecting another, they must have an abortion. Failure to do this resulted in a fine of some 1,000 Yuan - a fortune for a Chinese person. Nobody would have that kind of money. We dreaded to think what happened if you couldn't pay it. Enough reflecting for now - it was all too depressing.

We were off to the Children's Palace. This was a school which selected children attended after ordinary school had finished for the day. They were there from 1530 to 1715 doing many different activities. At the gate, we were met by an official of the school and some of the children who bowed and greeted us in English. I was led away by hand by one of our young guides, a little girl of about eight. Two other children followed Howard as we set off for a tour of the activities. The first room was called 'Folk Music' and it turned out to be a collection of fourteen children playing 'Pipas'. These were instruments rather like lutes but with a larger neck and played in the upright position. We were treated to a rather wailing pentatonic piece but, for an encore, they played *Jingle Bells* - chorus and verses! As we left each classroom, there was much bowing and some of the children shook our hands and asked "How are you?" in measured, well-rehearsed English. They were so sweet and their hands were so tiny. The next room was entitled 'Electronic Instruments' but it turned out to be an accordion band. Five little ones played tunes from *Some Like it Hot*, followed by the *Sabre Dance*. We were truly impressed by their abilities! The third room was 'Typing' and here a number of children were touch-typing - against the clock. The teacher stood with a stopwatch (we considered grabbing it and running - but thought better of it) and when we looked to see what the children were typing (in English), it turned out to be things about Silicon and Semi-Conductors! Room Four was a computer room, where they were learning basic computer language; room five was 'Ballet'. Room six was 'Chorus' and we were given a performance of *Silent Night* in two parts! Room seven was 'Violins', in which fourteen children of differing ages were playing the violin - some of them with quarter-sized violins. To our amazement, they rendered a Strauss waltz - one with lots of quick passages which they all executed with great dexterity, giving the impression that they had been doing this all their lives. (Perhaps they had?) Room eight was 'Calligraphy' where a number of children were laboriously copying complicated Chinese characters. We were shown a Chinese character dictionary and I vowed never to complain about the Oxford Dictionary again! Our tour was almost over but one last thing we were shown was the garden and - we should have guessed - the shop! We had to buy some little things as the profits went to the Children's Palace.

Our last Chinese meal was taken in a hotel near our own after which we returned to *our* hotel to pack for the return journey to the UK.

Saturday 18th

Shanghai International Departures was rather more sophisticated than the Domestic Arrivals had been. The Departure Lounge was a rather singular affair, with only two departure gates, compared with almost one hundred at Gatwick.

We were back in Hong Kong by lunchtime where we checked into the OmniPrince Hotel. It was very similar to the Hyatt Regency - all mirrors and brass fittings - and characterless. Once again, we could have been anywhere in the world. Our room was excellent, except for the fact that, when it flushed, the loo made a sound as of a werewolf. We were not *that* intimately acquainted with the sound of a werewolf but we thought that was what one *would* sound like. This little imperfection in the plumbing suddenly made us believe that the hotel was real, after all.

For our late lunch, we paid another visit to the *Golden Island Bird's Nest* restaurant. Having rested during the afternoon, our evening meal was a return to the Jade Garden before doing the final pack for our return home which would start next day. It was to be a very long day indeed - in fact it would be two 'tomorrows' rolled into one.

Sunday 19th

As our flight was not until later in the day, we went to Ocean Park in the morning. The Park occupied a whole hill and to reach the top we took 'the longest escalator in the world'. It was in four separate sections. Ocean Park certainly lived up to its reputation and the highlight was the Ocean Theatre at 1030, when the seals, dolphins and killer whale were put through their paces. They were all really sweet - even the killer whale - despite an impressive set of teeth. It was a female and she seemed to get on very well with her trainer who swam around with her and rode on her back. After the dolphins and friends, we headed for the bird theatre. It was mostly parrots and the odd parakeet who performed there and, when the show was over, we visited the aviary itself. The public was permitted to walk through the aviary. To get out of Ocean Park, we opted for the cable car and a ten minute journey, suspended in space.

We had another late lunch back in town before collecting our luggage which we had left in the care of the hotel. The moment we had been waiting for was here. A taxi took us to the airport and though eighteen hours separated us from Reedworth Street, every air mile would take us nearer to our destination.

The Captain informed us that we were travelling at almost 500 miles an hour and there were head winds of almost 100 miles an hour. (We didn't think it *could* be windy at 35,000 feet.) We approached Dubai where the local time was 0100. Our watches showed 0500 and GMT was 2100! (Which day? That was anyone's guess!) It was a very surreal experience to be wandering around Dubai airport in the middle of the night, surrounded by lots of gentlemen in sheets and wearing no shoes. Back on board, the Captain told us that one of the computers had 'gone down'. They could just "put it into redundant but the engineers were mending it". (That made us feel a whole lot safer!) Once the computer was fixed, we were told we were awaiting clearance for take-off - from *Iran*! Apparently the sky was quite crowded. The next piece of news was that conditions for the remainder of the journey were 'murky' and there was fog at Gatwick. The Captain assured us that he had "a nice lot of fuel in case we have to circle round for a bit and, if we couldn't land there, we would go somewhere else"! We were already crossing our fingers that we would be able to land at Gatwick. The cabin crew announced that, before take-off, regulations specified that they must spray the cabin with insecticide! (Whatever next?) The threatened delay proved to be very short and we were soon airborne once more. The Captain apologized for the noise of the plane which was due to the fact that we were only travelling at 26,000 feet. (Why should that make it noisy?) "As soon as all the aircraft go their separate ways, we shall be able to 'pop up' to 35,000 feet" he assured us. Two hours from Gatwick, breakfast was served. By now we had no idea what time it was in *any* time zone - but we were very tired. The Captain predicted an 'on schedule' landing at 0605. We were amazed to think we had been with this plane for eighteen hours, had travelled some 8,000 miles and yet we were about to land exactly on time.

We were back in Jennifer House by 0735 and in our very own bed within minutes. *That* feeling was one of the *wonders* of the modern world.

RETURN TO PARIS
March 1990

This trip to Paris was taken with our friend Janet, to celebrate (a little belatedly) her fiftieth birthday.

Friday 9th

We did not have to make an early start, so it was a quite civilized 0930 when we met up with Janet and made our way by taxi to Victoria station. At Gatwick airport, we headed for the Panorama restaurant where Howard had booked an early lunch for us at 1130. When we got to the restaurant, we found it had changed its name - it was now the *Bay Tree* restaurant. Its new identity had not adversely affected the quality of the food.

On the flight to Paris we were served a snackette which, having just consumed our good meal at the restaurant, we didn't really need. Somehow we managed to force it down and in no time at all (well, in forty minutes), we were landing at Charles de Gaulle where we were met by the Thomson representative and taken by coach to our hotel. We must have been very lucky in the past because our hotels always seemed to have been among the first to be reached. This time, ours was the penultimate one. After crawling through rush hour Paris traffic, we arrived at the Hotel Lorette, where we put our feet up for a little while before embarking on our evening meal. Once more, we went to the *Bistro de la Gare* (we enjoyed it so much on all previous visits) then turned in for an early night as we had a busy day ahead of us.

Saturday 10th

Saturday morning saw us buying the wherewithal for our lunch time picnic and booking a table in our favourite restaurant, the *Brasserie Flo*, for Sunday evening. We had told Janet about this so many times and we were anxious that she should see it for herself. Picnic bought and table booked, we set off for the *Bateau Mouche*, one of the many river boats that plied up and down the Seine. It was a wonderful way of seeing all the tourist sights of Paris from the river - in great comfort.

We took our picnic to the Tuileries Gardens - and shared it with the little birds. We did not have far to go to reach the Musée d'Orsay, where all the Impressionist paintings were to be found. We revelled in Impressionism for a while but, by the time we came out - and to our dismay - the bookshop had closed. This was a major disaster as we had hoped to buy our postcards there, so we vowed to return the next day for that purpose.

We rested in the hotel (big cities are so tiring) before going in search of another restaurant that Howard had found for us, a couple of blocks down the street. We were not disappointed. It had a big menu, including a *Prix Fixe* which, as its name suggests, was a fixed price, but within that, a goodly selection of dishes was on offer. The choice was the *Prix Fixe* menu or to eat *à la carte* - the latter was usually more expensive. We chose the *Prix Fixe* option. For the first course, both Howard and Janet had snails in garlic butter (very French!) and I had oysters. This was a 'first' for me - I felt very adventurous. History does not record what else we ate but the first course was too memorable to omit.

In the early hours of the next morning, we were awoken - very suddenly. Someone shouted *"Vous êtes un voleur"*, some thirty times in rapid succession. I suggested that the person being shouted at might be either an airline pilot or a thief - the general consensus of opinion was that he was almost certainly the latter. This episode had served to disturb our slumbers and, in our wakened state, we became aware that there was a disco going on in what appeared to be the adjacent premises. We couldn't hear the 'music' (euphemism) but could hear the continual thud, thud, thud of the drums. It was impossible to resume any kind of sleep.

Sunday 11th

Despite our interrupted night's sleep, we were all 'raring to go' to our first visit, the Basilique de Saint Denis on the outskirts of Paris, at the end of a métro line. As it was at the end of the line, we assumed it would be miles out - like Totteridge, or Morden, so we set off in good time. The Paris *Métro* system was much smaller than the London Underground network so we took just fifteen minutes to arrive at our destination. As a consequence, we were there much earlier than anticipated and a service was under way. We wandered around outside until 1100, looking at an archaeological site right next to the church. Many tombs and skeletons had been excavated and were lying around for all to see. On our return to the basilica at 1100, we were just in time to hear the outgoing voluntary. We didn't know what it was but it was very French, very loud and an excellent work to display the organist's undoubted capabilities. We wandered round the basilica and, by peering over some railings, we had minor sightings of the tombs of the kings. To have major sightings meant taking 'the tour' but, needless to say, that only happened at certain times of the day - and this was not one of them.

After all that culture, it was time to consider the inner man and woman, so we returned to central Paris for lunch, to *Chartier*, the truly enormous eatery which we tried to visit each time we were in Paris. After lunch, we took a little nap in the Tuileries before girding our loins to attempt a visit to the Louvre, via the new

Pyramid. The Louvre was an overwhelming place; its sheer size was rather forbidding. We vowed to concentrate on only one little gallery. ('Little'? There are no little galleries in the Louvre.) The *Wingèd Victory of Samathrace* was still there (in a headless sort of way) and we made our way to the *Mona Lisa*, passing by Veronese's *Wedding at Cana*. This was being 'done up' behind glass screens, scaffolding and impressive-looking special equipment for the restoring of such masterworks. As it was Sunday, there were no impressive-looking restorers doing the work. Finally, we headed back to the Musée d'Orsay to buy the postcards which we had been unable to buy the previous day.

Sunday evenings in Paris were always spent the same way. First stop, Notre Dame for the 1745 organ recital, then to the *Brasserie Flo*. Finally, Janet was able to see for herself the place we had raved about for so long. She was not disappointed. We ended the evening at the Sacré Coeur. We had told Janet how quiet and magical it would be. We were not prepared for the fact that there would be a Sung Mass in progress. The church was almost full and Confessions were being heard until 2300. Nevertheless it was very peaceful with lots of candles - and very dark. Our last stop was the artists' quarter, where there were not so many artists as usual - but then it was out of season.

Monday 12th

Though this was the day we left for home, there was still time to do one or two more Parisian things and the first was a visit to the Pompidou Centre and St Eustache Church. The organ in St Eustache had been renovated, the end of fifteen years of work. Sadly we didn't hear it but we were able to get a postcard of it for Charles Proctor.

Howard told me that he wanted to go off on his own to buy a secret present for Janet - and he had told Janet that he wanted to go off on his own to buy a secret present for me - so neither of us was suspicious when he said he wanted go off on his own! Janet and I went in search of Saint Chapelle, to see the wonderful stained glass. Imagine our disappointment when we arrived to find a sign indicating *Fermeture Exceptionelle!* Instead we sat in the sun on the river bank for an hour. It was very hot...

Our time in Paris was rapidly drawing to a close so we returned to the hotel to collect our luggage and joined the Thomson coach at the Rue de Tivoli. We sped along to Charles de Gaulle airport and were soon back in Gatwick, where we landed at 2000. As our luggage came off first and there were no problems with passports or customs, we boarded the waiting train to take us to Victoria station. We were back in Kennington by 2100 - wondering where we should go to celebrate Janet's sixtieth birthday!

"It's not quite the same as Sainsbury's calamari, is it?"

THREE CHOIRS FESTIVAL
August 1990

My boss, Canon Eric James, was to give the sermon at the opening service of the Three Choirs Festival. Howard and I decided to go to the Festival so we teamed up with Eric to travel to Worcester.

Saturday 18th

Eric lived just around the corner from us in Kennington so we collected him at 0930, in not very promising weather, for the drive to Worcester. We broke our journey not far from Moreton-in-the-Marsh where we had a good lunch of gammon and baked potatoes at *The Bell*. Thanks to Howard's superb journey planning, not to mention driving, we arrived absolutely on time at the Deanery in Worcester, where we met Bob and Ruth Jeffery, the Dean and his wife, with whom Eric was staying. We left Eric in their tender care and drove on to Trumps Hotel in Great Malvern where we had stayed in 1981 and I had stayed with our friend Janet in 1982 when Howard made his *first* visit to Hong Kong with the Bach Choir. As soon as we saw the pink spotted ducks in our rooms (ornamental - not live), we knew it was going to be as good as it had been all those years ago.

We discovered that Great Malvern boasted a Chinese restaurant so we thought that would deal with our supper. Though it looked promising, there was no indication of the opening times, so we changed our plan and decided to eat in Worcester. (We had to eat early as we were due to attend the performance of Mahler's *Eighth Symphony* that evening.) Our afternoon stroll did lead us into the Bluebell Tea Shop, where we had tea and toasted teacakes. We felt very rustic. At the end of the afternoon we put our noses into Malvern Priory with a promise of another visit later in the week.

Our evening meal was taken in *Rivels*, a little bistro in Worcester. Many of the eateries did not start serving until 1900 but this little bistro was in full swing. The people were very friendly but we could only give it two out of ten for 'ambience' as they started to clean the floor (with sweet-smelling disinfectant!) while we were finishing our meal. (To be fair, they did ask us if we minded...)

The Cathedral was packed and our seats were in a side aisle but the whole thing was relayed on a row of television sets, placed at strategic points along the side aisles. Before the main work, there was a 'Dedication' which included a performance of Ivor Atkins *Hymn of Faith*. It seemed he had taken all the Elgarian 'devices' and put them together - but the combination hadn't quite worked and we felt that climaxes were lacking. This particular work was being performed as 1990 was the centenary of Elgar's first meeting with Ivor Atkins and hence the beginning of one of music's great friendships. Mahler *Eight* was well worth the wait. It is rarely performed because of the vast forces required - and we hadn't heard it for ages. (It is not called the *Symphony of a Thousand* for nothing.) In the acoustics of the Cathedral, it was really 'quite something' - especially the final chords when everyone and everything was singing and playing *fiftissimo*! Just hearing a chord with that number of decibels (including full organ) is rather overwhelming - but at the end of that particular work, it was 'something else'.

Sunday 19th

From our bedroom window, we could see mist on the hills but an excellent full English breakfast helped to clear our minds. We discovered that the evening meal in the hotel was normally served at 1900 but the management were happy to serve us at 1830 if we would choose our main course in advance. It had rained in the night which pleased us as Malvern had been having the same hot weather as London. We strolled down to the paper shop, admiring the freshness of everything. There seemed to be many white doves everywhere - we never did find out why. We quickly discovered that everything was *uphill* in Malvern - and if it wasn't uphill, then it was *downhill* - the gradient being equally steep in both directions.

Worcester Cathedral was packed and Eric James was to preach the sermon at the opening Festival Eucharist. Ruth Jeffery had sent us a car parking permit allowing us to park in the Deanery Close - College Green, right outside the Deanery. In his opening remarks, Bob Jeffery gave a mention of Eric's book of sermons, *Judge Not: A Selection of Sermons preached in Gray's Inn Chapel 1978 - 1988*. The music for the Mass had been composed by Jonathan Willcocks, son of David Willcocks who was, at that time, the Musical Director of the Bach Choir. Mr Willcocks Junior proved he could juxtapose major and minor tonalities, but we didn't feel an immense urge to rush out and buy the LP. Eric was his usual brilliant self and, when the service was over, we were invited for drinks in the Deanery. Everyone was there - including David Willcocks and his wife and composer son and the Bishop of Worcester, who had been Chairman of the Development Affairs Committee of the Board for Social Responsibility when I had 'done my time' in Church House, Westminster. I met David Thomas, someone I had known when I first went to London. He was now a Canon of Worcester Cathedral! We also met Tom Holme, the present Precentor and a long-time friend of Eric's. The Deanery cat, Kitty, introduced herself. She was multi-coloured and very affectionate.

160

The Deanery was huge and, when all the drinks guests had dispersed, lunch was served. We had been invited to this so I was able to catch up with Ruth who I had known many moons before. She wasn't able to linger over lunch as she had to rehearse at 1430 for that evening's concert. The junior members of the Jeffery family did us proud - not to mention Dad. Ruth's brother and sister-in-law were also at lunch. It made for complications as their names were Ruth and Geoffrey! There were many lovely salads and puddings which meant all we could do afterwards was to return to Trumps and sleep until it was time for the evening concert.

The programme for the concert was Petrassi *Magnificat*, Respighi *Church Windows* and Verdi *Four Sacred Pieces*. We were apprehensive about the Petrassi *Magnificat* as the programme had warned us that 'his musical character had developed through phases - Neoclassicism, Serialism, Avant-Garde experimentation'. We feared the worst but it proved to be quite tonal and not peppered with 'silly effects for the sake of them', so we were pleasantly surprised. Respighi's *Church Windows* was very good. The titles had been added after the pieces were finished. (Wonder why?) Some of them were quite *tours de force* - the second ending with 'a triple fortissimo crash on the largest available tam-tam'. From what we could see, the percussionist had two 'largest available tam-tams'! They were very impressive. Verdi's *Four Sacred Pieces* we knew would be lovely - and they were.

Monday 20th

We drove into Worcester early to locate John Quill's house. John was Treasurer of Christian Action and he had said we could park in his car park. However, we decided it was too far from the Cathedral to park there regularly so we stopped in a pub car park instead. A notice told us it was 'for Patrons only'. We couldn't be Patrons at 0930 but decided to become Patrons after the organ recital for which we were headed. On the way to it, we took a look into the Royal Worcester Factory shop, which also sold Spode. Were they all one and the same firm?

Simon Preston was giving the organ recital at 1100. Our tickets said we were seats numbers 395 and 396. They also said 'unreserved'. We wondered how many more people we would find sitting on them. We enquired of a steward where our seats were and he assured us we could sit anywhere at all - 'the seat numbers were merely the computer record'. We found seats right opposite the console, in the Choir stalls. For the Mahler *Eight* concert and for the opening service, a computer organ had been used, the console being at the front with the choir and orchestra. (The front was, in effect, the back as the whole Cathedral furniture was reversed for the Festival and the platform was erected at the West

Door.) For Simon Preston's recital, he used the real Cathedral organ. His programme was: Elgar *Imperial March*, Dupré *Symphonie-Passion*, Elgar *Vesper Voluntaries* and Duruflé *Toccata*. The Cathedral was packed and we were equidistant from both sets of pipes so we got 'the full impact'. Simon Preston had no page-turner or anyone to help with the registration, so it was a very 'athletic' affair, all of which we could observe from where we were sitting.

We returned to the pub and, to confirm our status as 'Patrons', we had a swift drink before driving out to British Camp for a ploughman's lunch in the hotel there. (Ploughmen certainly had a rich and varied menu in these parts.) *En route*, we checked the location of the *Croque-en-Bouche* (the restaurant where we had planned to take Eric on Friday evening) and the church where Elgar was buried - St Wulstan's, only 500 yards away. We had patronized this restaurant when we were here in 1981. It was quite small and run by a husband and wife team - but it was very, very good and featured in many 'guides to eating places'. It had one *étoile* in the Michelin Guide making it one of only twenty-six restaurants in the whole of the UK to have that distinction.

After lunch, we made our first sortie into the Malvern hills with our trusty walking sticks. We had donned our lovely warm sweaters which Rosemary Proctor had knitted for us and they 'came into their own' in the course of the afternoon when the wind made its presence felt. We managed to find a sheltered spot to read our books. I was re-reading Rosa Burley's Record of a Friendship. Miss Burley struck me as rather a strange lady. If she really *was* so matey with Elgar, how come she didn't appear in the Enigma Variations and how come she was hardly mentioned in any of the other Elgar books?

When it got too blowy to stay on British Camp, we continued our reading back at Trumps. Our evening meal was taken at the Chinese restaurant which was as excellent as it appeared. An early night was the order of the day - after all our exertions climbing British Camp.

Tuesday 21st

At the suggestion of the Proctors, we went in search of Prinknash (annoyingly pronounced 'Prinnage') Abbey and the Pottery. The old house/Abbey was not available to be visited until the afternoon so we went in search of the more modern Abbey Church.

The monastery itself surprised us by its rather modern 'university hall of residence' look. It was not at all what we had expected - but then what *did* we expect? The Abbey Church was also something of a surprise. It was rather dark, though adorned by beautiful stained glass. No sooner had we arrived than a monk appeared and made preparations for the Eucharist. By the time the service started, there must have been about ten people in the congregation. It was of very short duration - not attended by the other monks - and even the server appeared not to be one of the brothers.

We arrived at the Pottery just in time for the guided tour. The guide was quite knowledgeable but not over-enthusiastic - though he did have a sense of humour. It transpired that the Pottery was merely a commercial enterprise, which happened to take place there. The monks no longer worked in it as there were only a few between the ages of fifty and sixty, the remainder being sixty and above. There was *some* financial gain for the Order but the involvement seemed to start and stop there. Through glass panels we were able to see each stage of the pottery-making 'as it happened'. Some of the ornate cups and goblets had twenty-four carat gold leaf insides. They were very beautiful but we had to ask ourselves what we would have done with them if we had owned them. They would be yet more dust-collectors - so we refrained from purchasing any in the shop at the end of the tour. Having seen all the processes involved in the making of the items, it was not hard to understand why they were so pricy! The Bookshop was rather disappointing, but we did meet a most friendly black dog outside, so all was not lost. We didn't see the incense-making place; we were told we would get very smoky. Perhaps, too, there wasn't a lot to see where incense-making was concerned? As we drove away, we had the feeling that the Pottery and adjoining shop could have been anywhere in the country as it seemed to have no connection whatsoever with Prinknash - apart from the place name appearing on the items. The Abbey was set in a beautiful spot, however, so we were envious of the monks' habitat.

We drove into Tewkesbury for lunch at the Royal Hop Pole Hotel. There were wonderful views from the flower-filled garden where we sat to eat our chicken and mushroom pie. Thus refreshed, we went on to Tewksbury Abbey, another place the Proctors had urged us to visit if at all possible. For the second time in one day, we arrived just as a guided tour was starting. This time the guide was 'exceeding enthusiastic'. The tour took seventy-five minutes - and it was fascinating. We would have missed so much had we not taken the tour. The guide told us that in days gone by, the residents hereabouts had been a gruesome lot. We were astonished when he showed us someone's tomb, bereft of the brass which had once covered it - an area of approximately five feet by three feet. He told us it had been stolen! A later, smaller brass was still *in situ* only because the thief was disturbed as he was trying to chisel it out of the ground! A real 'plus' for Tewkesbury Abbey was that there was a booklet about the organ. We wasted no time in buying one for Charles Proctor.

In the evening, we went to Worcester Cathedral once again for a performance of Beethoven's *Missa Solemnis*. We had a good pre-concert meal at another discovery - Heroes. On the way back to the Cathedral, we ran into Andrew Davies, a former student of Trinity College of Music. He was there to play in the *St John Passion* as a member of the Hanover Band. We were pleased to learn from him that Sam, his lovely black dog, was still fine. (Sam used to stay in our office at Trinity sometimes when Andrew was rehearsing.)

The Beethoven was quite superb - enhanced by the setting of the Cathedral. We mused over how the setting 'added to' works like this - though they didn't actually need any 'adding to'. It was one thing to hear them in the Festival Hall or similar but another thing completely to hear them in a Cathedral setting. Did not Eric talk, in his opening sermon, about 'the significance of place'?

Each time we had driven into Worcester, we had passed the sign to Powick Hospital - where 'Elgar's skills as an arranger were put to the test but not found wanting'. He used to arrange music for the band there, such as it was. Rosa Burley reminded us that Elgar had been appointed in 1879 to the Bandmastership of the Worcester 'lunatic asylum', where the 'orchestra' was made up of officials of the hospital - not the patients - but the combination of instruments available was something like: first and second violins, (no violas or celli), flute, oboe, clarinet, first and second cornet, euphonium, bombardon, double bass and piano.

Wednesday 22nd

Today we decided to climb the north face of the Malverns - to the Worcestershire Beacon, the highest point - 1,325 feet above sea level. I remembered that the first part, up to St Ann's Well, was by far the steepest. I was right - but once we had accomplished that initial climb, we were on the hills themselves and it was a much more gentle gradient; indeed, it was a very pleasant stroll. We met a group of five Americans, though we soon overtook them. We continued to wave to them to encourage them each time we came within sight of each other. Those times were intermittent because of the circuitous route taken by the pathway. We made it to the top and have photographic evidence - to this day - to prove it! Two things surprised us when we reached the Beacon. The first was that the café, which had been there for years, had gone. All that remained was the concrete base! It was as if something had come down from outer space and plucked it up into the stratosphere. We were told that it had been burned down and planning permission had not been forthcoming to build another one. The second surprising thing was that the circular brass plate on the actual Beacon, showing directions and distances for the surrounding area, had also gone. Had this been removed by the same person who had taken the brass from Tewkesbury

Abbey? Or had it been removed officially? If so, why? It had been a feature of great interest to walkers and we were sad to see that it was missing. We knew we *had* ascended 1,325 feet as that fact was chiselled into the stonework of the Beacon.

Feeling justifiably proud of ourselves and fully convinced of our unfitness, we descended the 1,325 feet - always a more difficult undertaking than the ascent, as our legs did not stop reminding us. On the way down, we encountered two men with a Land Rover, drawing a trailer full of rocks, which they were throwing up the hill! They told us they were filling in the holes in the hills to retard the rate of erosion. (Well, I never…)

When we reached the town, we made a nostalgic visit to the *Bluebell Inn* for lunch. This was the first place I had stayed in Malvern when, some years before, with my friend Doreen, we had set out for a holiday in Wales. We had broken our journey and stayed the night at the *Bluebell Inn* - and fallen in love with the Malverns. (We never did get to Wales!) After lunch we drove to Colwall, found a bench with a good view and returned to our books. I was surprised to read in the Rosa Burley book that, when one of the characters who appeared in the *Enigma Variations* asked her if she was a 'variation', she replied "No, I'm not a variation. I'm the *theme*." (She did go on to say "Edward was much amused when I told him of this." I *bet* he was!)

In the evening, we attended the *St John Passion*. It was sung in German and was conducted by Simon Preston - with his left hand! So everything was inside out! In the interval, some sad news cast a gloom on the proceedings. We met up with Eric who had returned to Worcester earlier that day to stay for the remainder of the Festival. He had been home in the meantime and, while he had been out for a meal with some friends, his house had been burgled. The thief had taken small silver items, many of which had been presents to Eric from people whose marriages he had conducted.

Thursday 23rd

We collected Eric from the Deanery to take him on the pilgrimage to Elgar's birthplace. Since we were last there, an addition to the collection had been a facsimile of the full score of *The Dream of Gerontius*, housed in the strongroom under special lights and temperatures. Charles Proctor had asked us to obtain a copy of *Pomp and Circumstance Number Four*, arranged for organ and we found one on sale at the Birthplace. We deemed it would be worth even *more* having been bought there. It was a beautiful day so we ended our visit sitting in the garden, in the warm sun, writing postcards and admiring the flowers, which were both plentiful and colourful.

Eric's friend, Tom Holme, came to meet us at noon as he and Eric were to lunch together. We had a drink together in *The Plough* - nearby the Birthplace - before going our separate ways. Thanks to Howard's excellent memory, we were able to find our way back to *The Talbot* at Martley, the hotel where lunch had been laid on by the Trinity College of Music Guild on the occasion of the Guild's visit to the Birthplace in 1989. We had one of the best Ploughman's lunches we had ever had, sitting in the sunshine. We resolved to change our jobs and become ploughmen.

We went back to Trumps to watch the Test Match (India v England) and to sleep/read/write before returning to *Heroes*, the eatery we'd discovered that met all our needs in terms of price, convenience and, indeed, food. Some Canadians who were staying at Trumps, had also eaten at *Heroes* so we suggested a joint meal before *Gerontius* on Saturday evening.

Tonight's concert was Elgar's *Second Symphony*, together with the JSB-Elgar *Fantasia and Fugue in C Minor*. We agreed that Alban Berg's *Violin Concerto* (also on the programme) was not going to be one of our Desert Island Discs, despite the diagram explaining the note row to us. (Was it really true that Berg's mother used to take in washing for Eric James' family in years gone by? That's what he (Eric) told us - and had he ever been known to tell anything but the absolute truth? When Tom Holme mentioned that Petrassi's mother used to do that part of the washing that Berg's mother couldn't manage, we did begin to smell a rat!) The *Second Symphony* was, as expected, marvellous. Mr Berg could have learned a thing or two about writing tunes by listening to this. The wonderful ending ('wrought flame in another man's heart') was a fitting conclusion to a lovely Elgar-filled day.

Friday 24th

The Canadians had liked the idea of joining up for supper before *Gerontius* so we agreed we would make the necessary arrangements. The day was spent very lazily. We drove to Upton-on-Severn to find a shady spot by the river where we could read and write. We succeeded - and spent a couple of hours thus occupied, interrupted only by the odd boat passing by or a swan coming to see what we were doing. No doubt he was hoping we would have some food, but we had to disappoint him. We had a light lunch at the *White Lion* in Upton-on-Severn then back to Trumps to watch cricket until it was time for Evensong in the Cathedral. We met up with Eric in the Cathedral and, when Evensong was over, we made our way to the *Croque-en-Bouche* restaurant in Little Malvern. On the way there, we found 86, Wells Road - Craeg Lea - where the Elgars had lived for a time. (Craeg Lea is an anagram of CAE and Elgar - CAE being the initials of Elgar's wife,

Caroline Alice.) Just before embarking on our gourmet meal, we took Eric to the other bit of the Elgar pilgrimage - the grave of both Elgar and his wife and that of their daughter, Carice, in St Wulstan's churchyard.

The *Croque-en-Bouche* did not disappoint. Though it had been nine years since we had been there before, they had not lost their touch. A truly memorable meal took the whole evening so it was quite late when we delivered Eric back to the Deanery and ourselves back to Trumps.

Saturday 25th

The highlight of the week was to be this evening - the performance of *The Dream of Gerontius* in the Cathedral. Prior to that, we attended *My Friends Pictured Within* - a dramatized reading, devised and presented by Zena Miller and John Crocke, in the Countess of Huntingdon's Hall. The event was described as "The characters of Elgar's *Enigma Variations* as seen not only by the composer but also by some of their friends and contemporaries". The Countess of Huntingdon's Hall was a very strange place with large box pews. From where we were sitting, it wasn't possible to see the performers at all! We were invited to move for the second half. The performance was 'interesting', with lots of quotations from all the well-known Elgar books (including some from Rosa Burley) but the actors *read* the whole script - not always accurately! All this was rendered to the accompaniment of some of the *Variations* on tape. It was a somewhat disappointing experience.

We were cheered by lunch at the pub, whose car park we had patronized earlier in the week, then home for cricket and to prepare ourselves for the evening's big event. Could the week be almost over? It didn't seem possible.

We met up with our Canadian friends, Donald Marjerison and Suzanne Wilson, in *Heroes*. Suzanne came from Ottawa and had known John Churchill some years ago, as she had sung in his choir. (John Churchill, an old friend of Howard's, used to be in charge of music at St Martin-in-the-Fields for some time.) What a small world! It was fun to share our final meal with the Canadians as they had been at the Festival all week and we had swapped thoughts about the previous night's performance each breakfast time. They were delightful people and loved all the olde-worlde things in Worcester and the surrounding area - as do all our transatlantic friends whose history only extends back a few years in comparison.

The Cathedral was packed once again for this final concert - a performance of *The Dream of Gerontius*. It was an odd feeling to think that Elgar himself had been in this very building with the very work we were about to hear. We almost felt we should knock on the door before entering. It was a most wonderful performance and there were no words to describe what it was like to hear *that* work in *that* place. It made a marvellous end to a marvellous week.

Sunday 26th

We collected Eric from the Deanery at 0930 and set off for London - and home. The Dean told us that his sermon, which he had prepared for the 1100 service, would remind his congregation of reality, after what had been an 'unreal' week. We had to face that same prospect but we were anxious to delay our return to real life for as long as possible. We had lunch in Henley, in the pub to which we repaired each year on the way home from our Summer Music School. There was little chance that she would be at home or free but we thought it worth calling on our friend Pat Hemphill. We were delighted to find that she was both free and able to join us for lunch. It made a little bonus to our day.

We were home by 1530 - back to reality - but the 'unreal' week would live on in our memories for many years to come.

MOOR TALES FROM THE ALHAMBRA (BUT DON'T T'EL CID)
January 1991

The start of this adventure was delayed by four days because I had a 'severe respiratory infection' which became 'more severe' according to what our GP put on the Insurance Claim form. We were to have spent a week as 'culture vultures' on a coach trip - taking in places like Cordoba, Seville and Granada - followed by a week in Torremolinos, lying in the sun. Because of my respiratory state, the first week was cancelled and the holiday was rearranged to be just ten days of lying in the sun - no culture! We hoped that when we were there, we might arrange day trips to places like Granada and Gibraltar, which were within reach of Torremolinos. (It is interesting reading this now and noting that 'lying in the sun' was something I liked to do. In more recent years, that has become something I can't bear to do and strong sunlight is something I have to avoid.)

Thursday 10th

The holiday started in style. A 'first' for us as a hired car took us from Jennifer House all the way to Gatwick. In view of my weakened state, Howard thought this would be much better than getting a taxi to Victoria station and then the Gatwick Express out to the airport. The car collected as at 0530 and sped us through the dark and rainy streets of South London, arriving at Gatwick at 0615. We had to collect our tickets from the Thomson desk as, because our plans had changed, there had been no time to post them to the travel agent. My 'doubting Thomas' (Thomson?) fears that the tickets would not be there were quickly dispelled. The tickets were waiting for us - but not so for another gent who was greeted with the sad news "I'm afraid I can find nothing in the computer" (!) Thank the stars the computer had got up early too and had had time to find *our* tickets!

Just after checking in, we ran into a colleague of Howard's from the COI - one of the escorts, Vernon and his wife Maggie. Together with two friends, they were heading for the same place as us, though to a different hotel, just 'up the road'. Another 'first' - we had never seen armed policemen at Gatwick - and they were armed with machine guns! (This was just before the Gulf War had started.)

We arrived at Malaga airport where the change in temperature was most marked. We couldn't wait to get into the coach to shed all our winter coats. The fifteen minute coach journey delivered us to our hotel, the *Pez Espada*, which Howard had discovered meant 'swordfish'. As if to leave us in no doubt, there were pictures of swordfish on the door handles. (We hoped there would not be pictures of door handles on the swordfish.) The *Pez Espada* was the oldest hotel in Torremolinos (then thirty years old) and had been the first to be built, long before the takeover of the coastline by the British tourist industry. We were impressed to see signed photographs of previous guests adorning the walls - Sean Connery, Mary Pickford, Edward (nearly the eighth) and Mrs Simpson…and even the then King of Spain. We rushed to our room to see if we had a photo of ourselves in our luggage as, obviously, the management would want to add this to their collection. Sadly, we had nothing suitable but we thought we could forward one to them on our return.

Dinner that evening gave us our first opportunity for 'people watching'. We recalled what our fellow guests had been like when we'd stayed in a similar Spanish resort at this time of year on previous occasions. The majority fell into the category of 'Young at Heart', for whom there were special brochures and special deals. To qualify for this, you had to be fifty-five or over - so we were *almost* 'Young at Heart', but not quite. Our observations led us to believe that most of our companions were well into that category - indeed some were *so* young at heart they were positively adolescent.

We noticed that some of our fellow diners wore quite extraordinary apparel which we were sure they wouldn't dream of wearing 'back home'. There was a proliferation of 'glittery bosoms' (amongst the ladies!) and sometimes matching glittery feet (also amongst the ladies). The gentlemen seemed not to enter into the spirit of the thing. There were interesting combinations of personnel. There was a father, mother and adult son. The latter seemed to say nothing at all, looked quite bemused when confronted by the buffet and generally seemed ill at ease. We wondered whether he might have been recovering from a nervous breakdown. The parental conversation consisted of a seemingly non-stop account of the father's medical condition, hospital appointments and medications. We concluded that, if the brow-beaten son lived with that all the time, it probably gave him a nervous breakdown! Poor chap - he certainly looked like a fish out of water.

Friday 11th

The original small village that was here before the British 'invasion' was still very picturesque and Howard had found a fish restaurant that we would try for lunch - *El Roqueo*. One entrance was in the street in the old town and the other entrance was on the seafront. We knew we would be able to identify it easily from the seafront because, even though there was a long line of restaurants, stretching the length of the beach, *El Roqueo* was the only one with a concrete mixer adjacent to it. Unfortunately, the concrete mixer was in full swing but, undeterred, we took up our eating stations on the patio, looking out to sea. We had a particular reason for wanting to try this restaurant as it had a very good write-up for its fish dishes, which are Howard's favourite food. We ordered what had the makings of an excellent repast and sat back, sipping our sherry (what else now we are in Spain?), serenaded by the concrete mixer. Our peace (?) was interrupted by a man insisting he should clean Howard's shoes. Howard was equally insistent that he should *not* clean them - and, eventually, he won the day. We didn't mind this touch of local colour; it helped to fill in the time while we awaited the arrival of our meal. What we had not bargained for were the other eight touches of local colour that were to follow, to aid our digestion.

The food arrived and so did a very, very old lady, selling national lottery tickets. The first course was *garni* by a second lady wanting to sell us lace tablecloths. The main course had musical accompaniment. (They think of everything, these Spaniards.) We had to admit that the music did leave a *little* to be desired. It was rendered by two very, very old gentlemen (possibly brothers of the very, very old national lottery-ticket-selling lady?) who tried their best to serenade us; one played a mandolin while the other strummed accompanying chords on a guitar. Their repertoire seemed limited to just one piece. They didn't seem particularly conversant with many chords; everything was restricted to the basic four - all, of course, in E minor. We were spared the rather wailing kind of singing that often went hand-in-hand with such music-making, though the duo did hum along some of the time - and there was the concrete mixer *obbligato*. Privately we decided they were bad enough to qualify for participation in the Royal Variety performance. They were no worse than some of the 'turns' that our poor long-suffering Royal Family have had to endure down the years. We were still eating our main course when the next touch of local colour arrived - to sell us bracelets and necklaces. We selected our pudding from a long list. One of the choices was 'strawberry and cream' but we felt that sounded rather singular so we opted instead for pineapple in kirsch. Before it had chance to arrive, another national lottery-ticket-seller did! We had just got stuck into our pineapple and kirsch when the penultimate touch of local colour made his appearance. It was difficult to describe his wares. Suffice it to say they were attached to his head, rather like antennae, and by blowing through a connecting length of hose, the antennae sprung into life. A 'must' for anyone of taste. It confirmed what we had always thought - we have no taste.

It was time to pay the bill but, even as we were doing the complicated maths of dividing the total by 175, a free gift was thrust at us - a card explaining deaf and dumb sign language. We wondered what else would have arrived had we stayed for coffee…

We returned to our hotel and sat in, and then out of, the sun. On a previous holiday, we had learned a painful lesson about staying in the sun for too long on the first day. At 1800 it was time to meet Mark, our Thomson representative. The 'welcome' was rather predictable; we were given slightly unpleasant sangria but we took the opportunity to book our trips to Granada and Gibraltar.

Dinner was Gala Night - which meant is was a huge buffet. All the ladies were given a carnation and all the gentlemen, a cigar (one each, that is, they didn't have to share the same one). Everyone, regardless of their sex, was given a glass of champagne. A guitar-playing trio serenaded us for a while. Unlike their compatriots from lunchtime, this group were very professional and very good at what they did. (At least they played in something other than E minor - they even ventured into major keys now and again. Just shows what joining the Common Market can do...)

After dinner, we thought we would take a walk up to the harbour at Benelmadina. Our route took us past Vernon's hotel. We looked in and they were just coming out of dinner so we joined them for a drink and a chat. By now, it was too late to go to the harbour so we made our way back to the hotel, along the beach. It was very dark and difficult to pick our way. Silly us - it would have been much more sensible to go back along the road, but we were just not that sensible.

Saturday 12th

We made our walk to the harbour at Benelmadina - and what a lovely picturesque place it was. We had never seen so many stray cats. They were very friendly and we were delighted to see someone walking the length of one of the walkways with food for them. This was dispensed at various strategic points where little groups of feline friends immediately forgathered. We admired all the very expensive-looking boats moored in the marina. Some were for sale but it was very difficult dividing by 175 all the time. We decided not to tax our brains to find out how much they were in sterling - but we did just one sum, just to get an idea. One little boat, that was really nothing special, cost in excess of £30,000! We decided against. How could we have got it home when we were weighed down with lace tablecloths, bracelets, necklaces, national lottery tickets and things to affix to our heads?

We gave lunch a miss and contented ourselves with some *tapas* - small dishes of things often found on bars. The rest of the day was spent quietly with our books.

Sunday 13th

We took the train to Malaga where we wanted to attend High Mass in the Cathedral. The time of the service was advertised at 0915 and, as it was then almost 1000, we thought we would just catch the last fifteen minutes. Imagine our surprise as we went in when the (very large and very ornate) organ started to play. This continued until the service began at 1000. (Note: Spanish notices are not all they seem.) The service was held in the choir stalls which were right at the West End of the Cathedral. It was not well attended. The congregational singing of the sung parts of the Mass was desultory (there was no choir) and the organ playing was very indifferent. We hoped there might have been some impressive organ music, in view of the size of the machine, but we were disappointed. We found we could understand some of what went on as the form of service was very like our own. Both spoken and written Spanish was very like Latin, so we were able to work out quite a bit for ourselves.

Howard had found a particularly attractive place for lunch - *Casa Pedro* on the *Paseo Maritime*. What the guidebook didn't make clear was that that it was about three miles up the road! "It's a long *Paseo* that has no turning", but we were determined as we had set our hearts on this place. We walked and walked...and walked - nearly all the way. A bus took us the last bit of the journey.

It was well worth the trek. It was a very popular place - and we had our first paella of the trip. It reminded us of French Sunday lunchtimes, in that the whole family turned out, from grandparents down to the little tiny ones. We were glad we had got there in good time as we were able to install ourselves in a little corner table from where we could watch the rest of the world.

We let another bus take us back into Malaga, where we walked up the walls of the castle to take advantage of the panoramic views. They were more panoramic than they might have been since we had our binoculars with us. It was a steep climb, but that was intentional as it was meant to deter marauding invaders. Our progress was so slow and geriatric that, on a scale of one to ten for 'marauding', we would have been at 'minus five'.

Monday 14th

We had a 0730 start for our trip to Granada and the Alhambra, which it is said would be the Eighth Wonder of the World, should the world chose to increase its wonders by one. The two-hour coach drive took us through the mountains and, though it was sunny, the temperature dropped considerably as Granada itself was many feet above sea level. We had not been warned about this when we booked our tickets so, though we had taken one extra jumper each (just in case it was 'cooler') we were by no means adequately kitted out for what seemed like sub-zero temperatures. This impression was reinforced when the local guide joined the coach and she was wearing an overcoat, scarf and gloves! Howard *did* have shoes and socks but I had sandals and nothing else on my delicate little feet.

No matter. We suffered for our art and surely the Alhambra must have been one of the most beautiful palaces we had ever seen. Everywhere the walls were covered in stucco work, giving the impression they were made of lace. Ceramic tiles covered the lower parts of the walls and the colours were still bright and alive even after all those years (600 or so?). Everywhere there were fountains, and the ceilings were lavishly decorated to resemble stalactites. All this was done to give the impression of coolness in the hot weather. It got *very* hot during the summer so they really needed all that 'air conditioning'. In the winter, they lived on the upper floors, which we didn't see. (We could *easily* see why they didn't live on the ground floor in the winter....) The history of some of it was rather bloodthirsty. Some high-powered chap invited twenty-eight chums around for a reception - and murdered them all. (Was it something they said?) And were the men jealous in those days! The musicians had to be blind people - so they couldn't see the women in the harem. It turned out that the Moorish princes were allowed four wives and a selection of concubines.

From the Alhambra, we walked up to the Generalife, via the spectacular terraced water gardens. It was only a stone's throw away but this was the Summer Palace of the Kings of Granada. (Obviously they weren't great ones for travel.) By now, the temperature was looking up. My feet had lost their blue colour and were gradually returning, through bring pink, to their more usual hue. We were taken on to the local restaurant (*Neptune*) passing the place where Manuel de Falla had once lived.

After lunch we were driven back to Torremolinos, leaving behind us the snow-covered mountains of the Sierra Nevada - and my frost-bitten feet.

Tuesday 15th

Saddam Hussein had just twenty-four hours left to leave Kuwait. Along with the rest of the world, we wondered... Even the weather was overcast and windy. We spent a day pottering - but what luxury to have *time* to potter. Our lunchtime pottering took us to the restaurant *Juan*, which was excellent. For once it was me who was really brave. I ordered swordfish and it was delicious. It has remained a favourite dish of mine from that day. The rest of the day was a continual potter, interspersed with sleeping and reading.

Wednesday 16th

Howard wanted to locate another street in the centre of Torremolinos, famous for its restaurants. He had read about it in the guidebook. We found it, but were rather disappointed. Perhaps they only operated in the height of the season? None could compare with the vast choice we had just two minutes from our hotel, in what remained of the old town. There was one more place to try - at thirty-seven *Calle Carmen*. We couldn't believe it - thirty-seven *Calle Carmen* no longer existed. It was a building site where the main attraction was a concrete mixer. Could it be the same concrete mixer that had serenaded us earlier in the week? Today is the concrete mixer's day off, so when we returned for lunch, it was to *El Roqueo*. This time, there were no elderly guitar or mandolin players, tablecloth vendors or similar - just a very good meal. The rest of the afternoon was spent sleeping and reading. After all, that was the main purpose of this holiday. This was certainly the life. We decided we were never going to return to the real world.

In the evening, we decided to watch the magician who was performing in our hotel. We were pleasantly surprised as, for some strange reason, we thought he might be less than convincing. Far from it! If Howard's predictions were correct as to where all the things disappeared (up his sleeve, in his pockets, down his shirt front), the man would have been ten feet wide with bulging arms and legs by the end of the evening. We had to admit we were foxed. Where *did* they go? Especially difficult to explain was the disappearance of two beautiful white doves.

Thursday 17th

Baghdad was bombed in the early hours of today. Mr Bush was on television but it was difficult to hear what he said as there were Spanish 'voice-overs'. We gleaned enough to know that it didn't look good!

At least the climate returned to what we expected of it - sunny and warm - so it was inevitable how the day was spent - more lounging around. Our relaxation was interrupted only by a picnic lunch on our balcony. We bought an English newspaper but they were always one day old so we could never get up-to-date news. Furthermore, the English newspapers were, understandably, exceptionally expensive!

Friday 18th

A pleasant coach drive of about eighty miles took us to Gibraltar. The route went along the coast, passing through places like Fuengirola and Marbella, the latter being where all the jet-setting rich people had their expensive residences. The ones we could see were huge and doubtless the most expensive of all would have been even bigger - and not visible from the road. The King of Saudi Arabia had a little place along here; Bjorn Borg owned one of the tennis clubs and Manuel Santana owned another. Some potentate or other rather fancied the White House so had a duplicate of it made in Marbella. (I expect we would have found duplicates of Jennifer House if we'd had more time.) This was not called the *Costa del Crime* for nothing. It seemed there was a preponderance of the more successful of Britain's criminal fraternity around these parts - living in some luxury on the proceeds of their criminal activities. There was something about the extradition treaty with Spain (like perhaps there isn't one?) that meant they were safe there.

We arrived at Gibraltar at 1000. We couldn't miss it on account of the rather large monolith which we glimpsed some miles before we got there. Because we were going out of Spain into Britain (!), we had to have our passports to hand. No one looked at them; the guide on the coach gave the customs officials a list of our names and confirmed that we were all *Inglese*. And now for something completely different, we approached the town of Gibraltar by way of the airport, driving right across the one and only runway! As luck would have it, no planes were landing at the time - but it was a weird sensation.

We left the coach and were decanted into a series of minibuses which took us on the tour of the Rock. (On the way there, the guide pointed out the garage where the IRA people had been shot by the SAS a couple of years before. A bullet hole in a petrol pump bore silent witness to the event.) As we ascended, there were spectacular views in all directions and, from the southernmost point of the Rock, we could see North Africa, only nine miles away. In another direction we had views of the harbour. There were three Dry Docks which were kept busy maintaining all the ships that stop here, including those which were based here belonging to the Navy. The current Army battalion was the Third Battalion of the Royal Greenjackets. We were told that each deployment is for about two years. To complete the trio, there was an RAF base. From another vantage point, we were able to observe military aircraft on an airfield (which was used for both military and civil aviation). The runway is but a mile and a quarter long and, because it was on the isthmus, both ends of it fall away into the sea. It didn't pay to make any mistakes when taking off or landing. We were rather glad that we flew in and out of Malaga airport.

The highlight of the tour of the Rock was the Barbary Apes. Though they were called apes, they were not a regular 'ape' size. They were more like monkeys and, consequently, very appealing. The driver told us that on no account should we stroke them as they might bite, but we could feed them - as long as we gave them only the prescribed foods - nuts, fresh fruit, fresh vegetables etc. (It was hard to believe but we had none of these about our person.) The driver also told us that they love chocolate, but they are not allowed to have it as it is bad for them. As soon as the minibus stopped, a couple of the apes jumped in through the driver's window, much to the astonishment of all the passengers. All the apes had names and the driver obviously knew them. He had a supply of nuts so was very popular. Some of them jumped on the roof of the bus, while others swung from the side mirrors and radio aerial! The legend goes that Britain will leave Gibraltar when there are no more apes on the Rock, so they are looked after - officially - by the servicemen. There are approximately eighty-six of them (apes - not servicemen) in two colonies. We saw the one colony; the other could not be seen by civilians as its residents inhabited an area nearer the top of the Rock that was restricted to military personnel. When the apes were born, not only were they given names but they got a birth certificate! That was how closely monitored they were. The guidebook told us they were fed twice a day - at 0800 and at 1600 - by a sergeant, officially known as the 'Officer Keeper of the Apes', and two soldiers.

We managed to tear ourselves away and proceeded to another vantage point where we had a panoramic view of everywhere, including an excellent view of the airstrip - from one side of the isthmus to the other. The next part of the tour took us into the Upper Galleries - tunnels inside the Rock, built at the end of the eighteenth century to protect the Rock at the time of the Great Siege. They were amazing by any standards but the more so because they were built 'by hand', using pick axes, with the help of some explosives. The driver, Robert, (a most enthusiastic and knowledgeable man) told us that there were some thirty miles of tunnels inside the Rock. (We wondered how it could continue to stand, riddled as it was with all those holes. Why didn't it implode?) Most of the tunnels were secret and therefore not accessible to the public, but they contained a cinema, food store and various other things which could supply the whole of Gibraltar for five years in the event of a present-day siege! (I wonder if that still applies in the early twenty-first century.)

The minibus returned us to the centre of town where the remaining time was occupied with lunch and shopping. Leaving Gibraltar, on our homeward journey, we had to get out of the coach with all our belongings - and passports - and go through customs. That was because we were now leaving Britain and re-entering Spain. (It *did* seem a silly arrangement!) Again, this procedure was a mere formality - but the Spanish authorities *did* have the right to detain anyone...The return journey to Torremolinos was even better than the outward journey because the setting sun added lustre to everything, especially the red-hot poker plants, of which they were many. What continually amazed us were the huge amount of properties (villas, apartments, hotels, restaurants) that were for sale and the equally huge amount of construction work that was taking place - speculatively we assumed. All the sites had advertisements exhorting the public to buy or rent the places when they were completed.

Saturday 19th

This was our penultimate day and rest and relaxation were planned for it. We bought two newspapers (in excess of £1 each) but we wanted to find out what was happening in the War. We lunch at *Juan's* once more then a long period of 'doing nothing' followed, interrupted only by supper.

Sunday 20th

The return journey to Kennington was imminent. Today would be a long day as we had to vacate our room by midday though the coach was not due to collect us until 2020, to take us to the airport for the 2220 flight. We calculated that we should be back at Gatwick by midnight, just in time to miss the 0015 train to London, so we would have to wait until 0100. After lunch we sat in the garden for a siesta as we would not be able to sleep again until much later.

When the coach arrived to take us to the airport, the Thomson representative warned us that there would be increased security at the airport because of the War. She said we shouldn't worry if, while waiting in the check-in queue, armed men with sniffer dogs were patrolling. All we had to do was cooperate with everything! We saw one armed man, but no canines. Two burly military gents were on duty at the security check. They were heavily armed and wore bullet-proof vests. It seemed like another world - a bit like being in a television play. We couldn't believe it was happening. Our flight was delayed by forty-five minutes, though no reason was given. When it was called, buses took us out to the plane, where we were amazed to find all the luggage laid out on the tarmac! Everyone had to identify their own pieces of luggage before they could be loaded onto the plane. All this after the luggage had been checked in and taken from us much earlier in the evening. Just to make the task more difficult, the identity parade happened in the dark. (It was nearly midnight by now.) There were some spotlights around the airport but the bus parked itself in such a way that it came between the luggage and the beams! We supposed it was the Spaniards idea of a bit of fun to fill in the time before take-off. There was a strange postscript to this. Once we were airborne, the Captain apologized for the delay, which had by now extended to two hours. His apology included the 'hunt the luggage' game and he reassured us all by saying "Don't worry if you couldn't find one of your pieces of luggage out there. All it means is that someone else had identified it so it will have got onto the plane anyway." The thought of 'someone else' identifying 'someone else's' luggage seemed to defeat the object of the exercise. Reassuring it was not!

We landed at Gatwick at 0145 and in a world record time we collected our cases, dashed through the customs at breakneck speed (the customs people must have thought our behaviour very odd but they did nothing about it) and caught the 0205 train back to London. Home seemed heaven-sent.

BRITTANY
May 1991

Thursday 23rd

0400 - a British Telecom alarm call…whose idea was this? Were we quite mad? We crept about in a sleepy state and at 0430, we were joined by Mary from upstairs. Our friend Janet arrived in her trusty Janet-mobile, to whisk us off to Portsmouth. There was not too much traffic about so we arrived at Portsmouth in good time for *le bateau* which would take us to *La Belle France*. We had yet to meet up with our other travelling companions, Pauline and her friend Freda. We wondered whether they were already on board or still in the queue to get onto the ferry. We didn't have to wonder for long as, no sooner were we on board than we ran into them - looking for us. Now our party was complete and we could all travel together. Pauline's car had to go up on one of the ramps and, though she was the second car to be loaded onto the ferry, the general feeling was that she would be one of the last to be unloaded at St Malo. The 'general feeling' proved right. The crossing on the *Remarque* (*Slogan:* Crossing becomes Cruising) was unbelievably smooth - and made a millpond look positively rough. An excellent meal whiled away some of the time - the rest was spent sleeping, catching up on that which we missed the previous night.

We arrived in St Malo at the time appointed and a short drive took us to Dinard, where we were to stay at the Hotel Balmoral. A teeny problem - despite the fact that we had requested one double room and two twin-bedded rooms, the hotel had allocated two double rooms and one twin-bedded room. We waved our computer print-out confirmations at the concierge - but to no avail. Eventually, and after some insistence, we got what we wanted - or so we thought - but, when we went to our rooms, Pauline and Freda still had a double room. Howard's brilliant French was summoned to sort out the situation. Pauline and Freda were moved - but it appeared they could only stay in their new location for three out of the four nights. The room would then be needed for a 'group'. We decided if they 'stayed put' on night four, there would be little they could do about it. All we wanted was sleep - but we thought perhaps we should have a tiny bite of something before turning in. We discovered a *crêperie* - which provided us with just what we needed - a not big meal, but something to keep the *loup* from the *porte*. Thus sustained, it was directly into the arms of Morpheus.

Friday 24th

A better way to get back to St Malo (better than driving round the headland via the barrage across the river Rance) was to take the ferry - a ten minute trip across the bay - so we did just that. St Malo is a walled town and it was possible to walk right around the ramparts. The centre of the city was called *Inter Muros* (wonder why?) and it was here that we bought all the ingredients for a very promising picnic. Before feeding time, we took the opportunity of looking into the local church. There was wonderful stained glass in abundance, much of which had been replaced in recent years. We wondered if the original had been destroyed in the war. The organ was playing a Lefébure-Wély type piece and we were astonished by how very cold it was in the church. When we went back outside, it was like going into an oven - the difference in temperature was so marked.

We went our separate ways and arranged to meet again at the church at 1315 to proceed to the beach for the picnic. When we got back to the church, the organ was in full flow and could be heard right across the square. It was an impressive sound - and even more impressive when we nipped back inside to hear it at close quarters. The organist had moved on to something more Mozartian.

The call of the sea was strong. We picked our way over slippery rocks, endeavouring not to break our collective ankles and we found a suitable spot. Not far out to sea and joined to the mainland by a narrow strip of pathway was an island on which the remains of Monsieur Chateaubriand were buried - yes, he of steak fame. As we sat and picnicked, the tide came in so we were not able to pay our respects to Monsieur Chateaubriand. Indeed, we had to remove ourselves rather smartly as the tide was coming to get us too.

Some spent a lazy afternoon, others were more active but we met up once more for a circumnavigation of the ramparts before returning to the little boat that took us back across to Dinard. Our pre-prandial drinks had been purchased in the duty-free shop on the ferry so there was just time to consume some of them before setting out for the fish restaurant which we had spied. The management must have been thrilled to see us because we were the only customers for quite some time. The waiter bore a distinct resemblance to Simon Rattle. We supposed he must do *something* to supplement his income from conducting. The meal came up to expectations - so, too, did our second night's sleep.

Saturday 25th

We set off to visit Dinan which, according to the guidebooks, was a not-to-be-missed place when in Brittany. It was another very old walled town. We purchased another picnic in *Monoprix* and headed for the *Jardin Anglais* to consume it. I was wandering around with stale bread from breakfast for our feathered friends. The only problem was they seemed to be out of town for the weekend as none was forthcoming to eat the ill-gotten gains. It was their loss. We made short work of our goodies (the *un*stale variety) and then went our separate ways to explore the town and the beach. There were large statues of people who had made it into the history books, but on the whole, they didn't sound like people we would chose to have for our favourite uncle. They were a bloodthirsty lot on the whole - and somewhat violent. An example was Monsieur Guesclin, who defeated Thomas of Canterbury in single combat to hold Dinan in 1359. I maintained it was an unfair contest as Thomas of Canterbury had only one arm, sight in only one eye and only one leg - and that was wooden!

We drove back to Dinard on the back roads, where we encountered minimal traffic but were rewarded with panoramic views. These were detailed in our trusty Michelin Guide - without which Howard went nowhere. One of the huge 'plusses' of our travels was that Howard had researched the whole trip carefully before we left England and had produced a detailed itinerary for all members of the party. Not only was this a great time-saver, it also ensured we did not miss anything of interest en route.

Back in Dinard, our evening meal was taken at the crêperie right next door to our hotel. We partook of the local cider, which was what you had to have with crêpes - apparently. The cider was drunk out of cups, which also seemed to be 'the thing to do'.

Sunday 26th

The destination today was Val André. On the way we passed through exotic-sounding places like Ploubalay, Matignon, Erquy (how do you pronounce that?) and Pleneuf. We arrived at yet another wonderful panoramic view, this time with a restaurant attached. We availed ourselves of some refreshment and discussed the possibility of having lunch here. However, Howard had found us what sounded like a marvellous eatery in the centre of town so we retraced our steps to find it. We concluded that we would have rather a long wait for our meal as the restaurant was closed until June 9th - so we hastened back to the first place.

Time was not on our side because Sunday lunch is a great institution in France and today was likely to be even busier than usual as it was the Fête des Mères - their version of Mothering Sunday. It was already very full, and there were six of us to be accommodated. It was our lucky day; the waitress asked a smaller party if they wouldn't mind moving to another table so that the six of us could be together. They agreed, and we were enormously grateful to them. They were moved to the next table so we had not deprived them of the lovely views. We had a real five-star meal and Howard was able to have his favourite assiette de fruits de mer. Not only that, but he had a delicious lobster too! The rest of us didn't do too badly. I was amazed when my first course arrived. It was about four feet high and consisted of lobster soup surmounted by a sort of 'turban' of frothy pastry. In true French style, the meal lasted well over two hours, after which the inviting sandy beach claimed us all.

We were tempted to dip our toes in the warm waters of *La Manche* (for that is what it was - the Atlantic Ocean was just around the corner). We paddled in the silky warmth of that particular bit of sea. On the way back to Dinard, we made a detour to the Cap Fréhel, another much-acclaimed panorama hereabouts - and we could easily see why. In every direction wonderful views abounded and there were steep drops to the sea a long way below. We didn't go too near the edge!

We returned on quiet back roads once again and for our final meal in Dinard, we paid another visit to the *crêperie* that we had sampled on arrival.

Monday 27th

Surely it couldn't be time to go home yet? There was still so much to see. That was a good reason to plan a return trip as soon as possible. At 0900 we were all ready to make the short drive to the ferry. While waiting to board, we marvelled at the skill of the people who load the boats. The weight distribution had to be just right. When we saw the huge container lorries being loaded, we were glad we were not in charge of the operation. There was much activity with mobile phones and much signalling to the numerous queues to get/stay in lane then, just as we thought we were at the head of the queue, our lane had to wait while the adjacent lane boarded. It was not 'goodbye' to Brittany, just *au revoir*.

The return trip on the Duchesse Anne (*Slogan*: Crossing becomes Cruising - where had we heard that before?) was as smooth as the outward journey. We were hard-put-to to know the boat was moving, thanks, presumably, to the excellent stabilizers on the Brittany Ferries.

Only one question remained. Where should we go the following weekend?

WHEN IN ROME...
June 1991

The day before we set off, I covered our suitcase in red and green spots (for ease of identification in transit) making it look as if it had multicoloured measles. We were flying to Rome on *Pilgrim* Air - the Church seemed to have this whole Rome operation buttoned up!

Thursday 13th

An early start meant we were at Gatwick in time for breakfast. The restaurant we had enjoyed so many times before had changed hands - yet again! Now it was called *Route 66*. The food was fine, but the Musak had to be heard to be believed - though, come to think of it, we *heard* it and *still* couldn't believe it. How can people be paid money to shout on a monotone, to the 'accompaniment' of a minimal selection of oft-repeated chords? Our request that it might be turned down (we didn't even try 'off') met with no success. We were told "It's on a fixed level. It's to give the place atmosphere." We couldn't argue with that - it gave it the atmosphere of Death Row. (The day cannot be far away when society will have to pay for silence.) The relative peace of the departure lounge was interrupted only by the repeated security announcements warning passengers not to leave luggage unattended as it would be removed and may be destroyed. We recalled seeing that happen the last time we were at Charles de Gaulle airport, when an unidentified piece of luggage became even *more* unidentifiable after it had been the object of a controlled explosion.

Flight BY570A to Rome Ciampino (lovely name) was gradually making its way up the departure screen. No sooner had we boarded than the Captain told us there would be a forty minute delay as we had 'lost our slot' due to a strike of French Air Traffic Controllers the previous day. (Hooray for the EEC!) The result of that was that all the planes were in the wrong places at the wrong times. Eventually, we were airborne and in what seemed like 'the twinkling of an eye', we were high over the Alps with Rome in our gunsights.

When we landed, the temperature was seventy five degrees and rising (we couldn't understand centigrade). The drive to drop everyone off at their hotels was tedious but it did include a sighting of the Castel Sant' Angelo, where Tosca met her sticky end. From the colour of the river Tiber, she would have died of typhoid anyway, even if the water *had* broken her fall...

The Hotel Canada was very comfortable - and a shower was very welcome. Then we were off to our first port of call - the Spanish Steps and the Church of *Trinità dei Monti*, in the *Piazza di Spagna*. (We were rather surprised that we had to

183

buy our *Metro* tickets in a café in the station.) The Spanish Steps and the Church were very reminiscent of the Sacré Coeur in Paris, but on a smaller scale. This was the first of many churches which we were to visit. There were over two hundred in this city. Next we went in search of the Trevi Fountain, immortalized in the film *Three Coins in a Fountain*. Could a fountain be closed? This one was! It was undergoing restoration and most of it was covered in tarpaulin. The idea was that tourists threw a coin into it to ensure they would return to Rome. It didn't seem quite the same, throwing a coin onto the tarpaulin. One little boy was supplementing his pocket money by trawling the dried-up pavement for the coins which had been left there.

The Church of Sant' Agnese in Agone was very firmly closed, but the Piazza Navona, with three enormous fountains, was very picturesque and 'worth the detour'. They certainly went in for fountains in a big way in this city. It seemed, if in doubt, build a fountain - or two. (Would Howard want to get busy with his DIY marble sculpture kit when we got back to Reedworth Street?) Howard had found us a super restaurant (*Il Giardino*) from one of his many books so we wrapped ourselves round a delicious *Scallopini al fungi*.

All the streets in Rome seemed to be cobbled. (It couldn't be good for the tyres.) The city was a strange mixture of modern shop fronts, appended to very old buildings and, at every turn, there was either another church, an obelisk (that was another thing they had lots of) or a fountain. The street names were carved into the walls. I suppose they had been there since J Caesar's time and they wouldn't have had blue street signs then, would they? Written on the bus stops was *Fermata* - as good an indication as any when I stopped to think about it. On all the manhole covers appeared SPQR - *Senatus Populusque Romanus* (The Senate and People of Rome). And then there was the traffic! We had been warned that this would be like nothing we had ever experienced before. How true that was. There didn't seem to be any rules. The only things anyone seemed to observe were the traffic lights. Everything else was 'up for grabs' and, without doubt, 'the weakest went to the wall'. As for pedestrians, they just mingled with the traffic. There was no such thing as waiting to cross the road - people merely walked out into the fast flowing traffic which weaved its way around them. We were recommended to cross the road with either a nun or a priest as they were generally spared. We were surprised how many police were in *evidence*... *Carabinieri*, traffic cops with clipboards, and female police - with rifles!

The next day would be 'the big one'. We were to see St Peter's and the Vatican Museum. Was the Pope ready for us? Time would tell. It seemed he would appear on the balcony at midday on Sunday.

Friday 14th

A coach picked us up ten minutes early (thank goodness we were up in good time) to take us to the Vatican Museum. We met up with a number of other coaches and we were divided according to our native tongue. We were with forty English-speaking people and four Germans, which meant everything had to be said twice. A guided tour was by far the best way to see the Vatican Museum and our guide was excellent and very knowledgeable. She had done an art degree, followed by a further three or four years training to be a guide.

We couldn't *believe* the numbers of people in the Museum. In each room or gallery, we ran into another party and another guide, with commentary in every language known to the civilized world. We moved from one amazing work of art to another until we got to the point where we would hardly take in another masterpiece. Everything led to the Sistine Chapel, which came up to all expectations that anyone could ever have of it. A Japanese company had donated millions of dollars for its cleaning and the famous ceiling was completed. Art boffins had been critical of Michelangelo for his lack of bright colours, but, since the restoration work had started, it was discovered that the ceiling was very brightly coloured indeed; over the years, the smoke from the candles had dulled the colours but now, thanks to the inscrutable orientals, all was revealed in its true glory. The only drawback to the ceiling was that it gave us a stiff neck. (Those 'in the know' were looking at it through mirrors.) Sadly *The Last Judgement* was closed (not even a *Penultimate Judgement* to make up for it). That was the section that was being renovated so, instead of the huge end wall being covered by another masterpiece, we had to content ourselves with a much reduced-in-size photo of what it looked like.

After a self-service snack, we were off to St Peter's itself - the other real highlight of this city. We were to run out of superlatives. The colonnaded approach to St Peter's was breathtaking; four rows of columns on either side, surmounted by statues of previous popes and theologians of note. Appropriate dress for entering the basilica was strictly enforced. There were four custodians at the entrance, solely for this purpose and they *did* turn people away who were not suitably attired. Everything about this building was huge. The guidebook said that the total area was 49,737 square metres; in comparison, St Paul's, London was 26,639 square metres. St Peter's was as long as a football pitch; the statues were about twice life-size. Michelangelo's *Pietà* was one of the first things we saw. It had been behind bullet-proof glass since someone attacked it with a hammer in 1972. Luckily a cast of it had been made, which still survives in the Treasury attached to the basilica, so the experts had been able to repair it faithfully. Despite its enormous size, apparently the number of faithful who attended on a regular basis was not large as there were but a couple of hundred chairs in evidence, right at the front. The rest of the space was left empty for tourists to perambulate. The Romans didn't seem too interested in the Pope and it appeared that those who go to the regular Sunday Papal Blessing were the tourists. Two days later, we were to be among those tourists who saw him when he came out onto a balcony at midday and gave a Papal Blessing.

We made our way to the Treasury which was filled with monstrances, bejewelled artefacts of all descriptions, illuminated musical manuscripts - and much more. Next we went up to the base of the cupola which was similar to the Whispering Gallery of St Paul's. We tried whispering but it didn't work. We wondered if it was because the walls were covered in mosaic. Outside on the terrace, high above the city of Rome, we had wonderful views of the city and, standing at the foot of the massive statues of Christ and the Apostles, we were quickly brought down to size - literally and metaphorically! Our final visit within the walls of the Vatican was to buy postcards and special Vatican stamps. We were assured we could use these stamps anywhere in Rome. We would not have to return to the Vatican to post our cards.

We took our evening meal at the *Trattoria da Nazzareno*, in the Via Magenta, very near our hotel. Our legs were pleased about that as, by now, they were letting us know that they were 'into injury time' after all the walking we had subjected them to earlier in the day. At the next table was an Italian, eating alone, but obviously well known to the management. In due course we struck up a *conversatione* with him, but it was not easy as he spoke no English and our Italian was (and still is) minimal, consisting mostly of musical terms. We tried French but without success. Nevertheless it was surprising what we learned about each other. He was fifty years old and had been retired for two years having been manager of a fishing business. He lived in Venice with his wife, Maria, two daughters and a cat. Much of our information was gleaned by way of mime. Monsieur Marceau would have been proud of us - or would he? We endeavoured to find out if he had a dog by doing a dog impersonation. The rest of the customers thought we had taken leave of our senses as we appeared to be barking at a perfectly innocent Italian man. We tried to explain to Domenico (for that was his name) that we were from London and had a little bird but, from his bemused expression, we thought he had interpreted our mime and attendant forays into the vernacular as meaning we were drug dealers with a pet albatross. The *conversatione* taxed our brains to the limit - and caused not a little mirth. Our new-found friend ordered a bottle of wine which he insisted we shared with him. How very hospitable were the Romans! No wonder J Caesar kept coming back.

WHEN IN ROME...

Saturday 15th

With great daring, we explored the buses. We worked out how to buy the tickets and even found the right bus to take us to the Galleria Borghese. For such a dodgy family, they certainly amassed a fine art collection. *Doloroso!* Only the ground floor was open - eight rooms of sculptures and mosaics. The remainder were being renovated, as was the whole of the Villa in which the galleries were housed. It was clad from top to bottom in scaffolding and polythene sheets. We couldn't complain though because the eight rooms we were able to see contained some of the finest works of Bernini and a few of his chums. The Borgias weren't content with ducks flying up the wall. For them it was *The Ten Labours of Hercules*. (Hercules completed them all - they didn't think he would. His prize? No, not two weeks in a timeshare - but immortality. Can't be bad...) It was good to think that Lucretia had time for the pursuit of art, in between poisoning people.

We had some time to spare so we wandered down to the zoo which formed part of the extensive grounds of the Villa Borghese. There wasn't time for a sighting of the zoo's inhabitants but we did glimpse some flamingos through the gate. The temperature continued to rise as we made our way back to the hotel to join the coach which was to take us on a tour of Ancient Rome - the Colosseum, the Forum *et al*.

The Forum was the first stop. The guide told us that it was the centre of religion, politics and commerce - generally the 'downtown' area of ancient Rome. Some of it had been there since 800BC. A lot of it still stood but the parts that didn't hadn't necessarily been worn away by the elements. As later generations wanted to build things in Rome, they merely came to the Forum and nicked bits, as it was disused. The saying went that what the Barbarians failed to spoil, the Barberini completed!

On to the Colosseum, which was the entertainment centre of Rome. It held 55,000 spectators and they could be admitted or cleared out in ten minutes! The audience sat in strict order of class, the Emperor and his cronies being nearest to the action. Then the vestal virgins came next (horrid things happened to *them* if they stepped out of line - including being buried alive!) and upwards and outwards until the very top, where sat the slaves and lesser mortals. There was even a canopy which could be stretched right over the top of the whole building. (I have always advocated such a thing for English cricket pitches - just to think these ancient people had already thought of it.) I suppose if your idea of a 'fun' night out was to watch gladiatorial combat with men v. men or men v. animals killing each other, then this was the place for you. In the case of men v. men, it seemed the Emperor had to decide whether the winner should kill his opponent or not (if he hadn't killed him accidentally during the combat!). But then, as Howard pointed out, in 1991 we still had bullfights and boxing matches so we hadn't come *that* far over the years.

St Paul's Outside the Walls, (which, as its name suggests, was outside the walls of Rome) was quite some way away which made us glad we were doing this tour by coach. The remains of St Paul were reputed to rest in this church. It was the second biggest church in Rome - almost as big as St Peter's - and the windows were made of alabaster, given by the Khedive of Egypt. They afforded a beautiful 'peaceful' light. Outside was a wonderful cloister, with mosaic columns.

We saw almost nothing of St Peter in Chains as the interior was being renovated, but we *did* see the Michelangelo *Moses*, which was very famous. Michelangelo had certainly been a busy little soul when he was in Rome.

We left the coach at the Basilica of Santa Maria Maggiore, which was alive with busy confessionals - it being Saturday night. The tomb of the Bernini family was in here. It was very plain and simple, the only thing in this church that was. The rest was very ornate indeed. The ceiling was covered in gold leaf made from the first gold that Columbus brought back from America.

In the evening, we ate again at the *Nazzareno*, but this time there was no sign of Domenico. An early night followed as the next day would be very long, ending with the return journey to London.

Sunday 16th

We made our way back to St Peter's for the big service of the day at 1030. Though we got there in what we thought was good time, all 200 seats were occupied and quite a number of people were standing at the back, where we joined them. Compared to the size of the church, the congregation was not large and we concluded that many of the people were tourists, like us. The procession of clergy (which included not a few cardinals) numbered about fifty. No Pope - perhaps he didn't go to St Peter's, even when he was in residence.

An introit was performed by a female choir with a female conductor. (Very broad-minded for such an institution!). We thought it was by Cherubini and it was very good - so we had high hopes for the music for the service. Our hopes were to be dashed. (The one disappointment of this trip was that we had been unable to find any organ postcards for Charles Proctor. One of the main reasons for this was that none of the churches seemed to have an organ - certainly no impressive-looking instruments over the West Door, such as we have found in France and other European countries. In the churches here in Rome, we were lucky if we found even an apology for an organ.) St Peter's *did* have an instrument though not a very large one considering the size of the church. The Cherubini-esque piece was the last piece of good music we were to hear. The setting of the service (though in Latin, which was good) was dreary in the extreme. This impression was not improved by the priest, who sang things a fifth lower than everything and everyone else. The organist saved the day on each occasion by playing the real note for the congregation and choir to join in, after the priest had gasped his last, out-of-tune one. The congregation and choir then joined together to sing a most desultory unison setting, which made Gregory Murray sound interesting. After one of the readings, the Choir sang an anthem from the *All in the April Evening* school. It was littered with diminished sevenths. The sermon was not long which pleased us as we were unable to understand a word of it. As soon as it had finished and *à propos* of nothing as far as we could see, a lady literally pushed her way through the crowd, taking a collection.

We left when communion started so that we would be in good time to see the Pope on the balcony at midday. As we were leaving, the choir sang a number of anthems, one of which was to the music of *Abide with Me* though we couldn't work out what words were being sung to it. Outside, the heat was overpowering and we had to stand in it for a short time awaiting the arrival of the Pope. On the dot of twelve, he appeared on a side balcony - not the big impressive one we had seen so many times on television on Easter Sunday. A carpet was hung from the window - we supposed it was to indicate which window was to be used - and, as soon as his Papal Blessing was over, it was hauled back in again. The Pope was greeted with cheers (a bit like a football team taking the pitch for a big match) and he spoke for about ten minutes. At the end of his speech, he mentioned certain groups of people who were in the square. We assumed he was giving them a special blessing as, at the mention of their names, more cheers erupted.

After St Peter's, and still in blazing heat, we returned by Metro to Flaminio and the *Capricianna* restaurant which Howard had researched for lunch. What a very good piece of research it proved to be as we were able to sit outside in the shade to eat our delicious meal, which was preceded by cold mineral water - never had anything tasted so good.

Back to another church, which would not open until 1600, so we took in a small Dali exhibition in an adjoining building. He must have been a *very* strange person…Our last port of call was Santa Maria del Populo which was very old and very historic but we didn't find it particularly riveting. Or were we suffering from culture overkill?

We went back to the hotel to collect our luggage and meet up with the coach which would take us to the airport. Some hours and miles yet separated us from Kennington but Big Ben struck midnight as we let ourselves into our flat. We scuttled in, before we turned into pumpkins - or white mice.

" the Sphere of Divine Self Begetting and a Creation ... you wanna matt or gloss?"

FLORIDA
March 1992

The Bach Choir was going to Florida for a series of concerts so we decided go a week early and have a holiday before Howard had to 'sing for his supper'. I came back at the end of the week as being a hanger-on was no fun at all.

Sunday 15th

I spent much of the previous night hours rehearsing in my mind all the things that needed to be done before we left. By 0600, when we were having our first cup of tea, we decided to note down the different feelings that overtook us when setting off for such a trip. First was the 'anxiety factor' that worked its magic throughout the night, making sure we would worry about everything that needed to be done. Then we slid into 'efficiency mode' - actually *doing* all those things over which we lost sleep. Closing up our home was done with mixed feelings. Part of us was excited and looking forward to the trip; another part was anxious to leave everything neat and tidy, ready for our return. Yet a third part of us wanted to stay at home and not go at all! We rationalized all these mixed feelings by telling ourselves that they were a reflection of how extraordinarily happy we were in our home. Finally, all checks done, the door was locked. We headed for the Kennington Road - and America.

Check-in at Gatwick was enlivened by a bomb scare. An announcement over the tannoy asked that that the owner of the Samsonite briefcase left unattended at the Virgin Atlantic check-in desk (Agh! - that was where we had to go!) should return to it immediately. The owner *didn't* return. The area was cleared and policemen with machine guns and sniffer dogs appeared as if from nowhere. The armed policemen cordoned off the area and then just *stood*, looking pretty menacing - but who could blame them? The speed, efficiency and lack of fuss of the whole operation was very impressive. There had been crowds of people at the check-in desk and all of them had had to be moved, with their luggage, trolleys, children etc. Further announcements were made appealing for the owner of the case and, after a time, we were allowed back. We never did hear the end of the saga. Check-in was enormously slow and we came to the conclusion that we would certainly not take off at 1115. We didn't.

When we boarded, we registered our next set of feelings. We resigned ourselves to nine hours of interrupted tedium, mostly spent 35,000 feet above *terra firma* - or not - as, in this particular instance, we assumed that most of the journey would be over the Atlantic Ocean. It was difficult to put into words our feelings being in the plane, because we were very much in a state of limbo. The airline did everything possible to make our flight comfortable. Virgin (on the ridiculous?) Atlantic had won a sheaf of awards for all their efforts on this front and we could see why. The lunch menu included a choice of five 'gourmet' main courses. A complimentary 'in-flight' pack arrived - containing a toothbrush, toothpaste, comb, eye shades, ear plugs, head set for the video and radio channels (ten of them!), socks...all of which we were encouraged to take away with us but, should we not want to, we were also assured that all would be recycled, as Virgin Atlantic had a 'green' policy. We were amazed at the sight of an actual *bar* in the first class compartment (Upper Class!), which we could see through a gap in a curtain. It was difficult to believe that we were 35,000 feet above the earth's surface, travelling in excess of 500 mph - and yet everything seemed to be so *normal!*

All 300 or so of us - and our luggage, landed at 1600 American time. We were amongst the first off the plane, which was to bode well for the Immigration queue. Our previous experience of US Immigration had been long and tedious and had involved 'waiting in line' (the word 'queue doesn't exist in America) for a very long time. We were through this one in *minutes*. The procedures were very efficient - no long-winded questions about where we were going, what we were doing, did we have any foodstuffs about our person etc. The Immigration officer set us on our way with our first 'enjoy' of this trip. We made up for our swift passage through Immigration as we had to wait an age for our luggage to arrive - only to be expected with 300 people travelling. Once we got our cases, we were through 'Nothing to Declare' in a flash, but not before having met a wonderful police dog, whose handler told us that he was there to sniff out food and narcotics - both of which were banned.

The Hertz Car Rental was quite an experience. We took a courtesy bus to the 'Renting Lot', some way out of the airport. Everything we had encountered today had been done on a computer - checking our luggage, printing out our duty-free shopping bill, checking us through Immigration and now, hiring the car. In a split second, there were Howard's details on *their* computer. They were amazed that we wanted a manual car. We were told that there were no manual cars in the entire State! Having 'filled out' the formalities, we were advised to feed into a computer right behind us our request for the best route to the Florida Turnpike - the huge road on which we would drive the 200 miles to our hotel. The computer produced it in about five seconds. (It seems odd to be so amazed at what the computers did but, remember, this was some while ago - 1992. Computers did not rule our lives to the extent they do today and we were not used to such a profusion of computer technology.) In a matter of seconds, brave Howard had given himself an instant lesson in driving an automatic gear change car. Our problem was how to operate the safety belts - two each! Little did we know that, when the starter was engaged, the clip (into which the safety belts hooked) shot round the window frame into its required place. Who'd ever have thought of *that*? A four-hour drive lay ahead of us, though sundry tolls and 'have a nice day's - even though it was 2000. We arrived at the Econolodge Maingate Hawaiian Resort, 7514 West 192 Bronson Memorial Highway, Orlando (what an address!) at 2215. That was 0315 the next day in English time. It had been a very long day.

Monday 16th

The Disney World complex was made up of the EPCOT Centre, Disney MGM Studios and the Magic Kingdom, plus a few other odds and ends which don't get a mention here. Today it was the turn of the EPCOT Centre (Experimental Prototype Community of Tomorrow) containing *World Showcase* and *Future World*. It was enormous - indeed, we were to find the use of the word 'enormous' becoming somewhat meaningless - the whole thing was vast and, in terms of size, difficult to describe.

World Showcase contained pavilions allocated to a number of countries to demonstrate what happened in those countries. The pavilions surrounded a large lake.

Norway provided us with a Maelstrom boat ride, together with a short film about the country, all to the accompaniment of the loudest music we had ever heard!

China had a film entitled *Wonders of China* which was shown on a 360 degree screen, made up of fifteen separate screens. The audience stood throughout, in the middle, the reason being that the action happened 'in the round' so if, for instance, you were in a train, you could see both ahead and behind 'at one and the same time'. It was very spectacular and impressive.

France also had a film - but only on five screens! It was as good, if not better, than the Chinese film. It contained super photos of châteaux, Mont St Michel and many other sights that were familiar to us. Was our judgement coloured by the fact that we love France so much and do not have a similar feeling for China?

Italy and **Morocco** got a cursory glance before a totally unmemorable burger lunch, shared with some of the local birds.

Spaceship Earth was an educational ride in the seventeen-storey Geosphere, tracing the history of communications from the dawn of civilisation to the present day - and on into the future. It was a masterpiece of construction.

To give our feet a rest, we took a ride on the monorail before sampling the **Living Seas**. Predictably there were lots and lots of fish to see and information about oceanography.

We felt we should be patriotic and see what the **United Kingdom** section had to offer. It had a strange street play, red phone boxes, a Rose and Crown pub, a thatched cottage - and the gift shop contained everything from English tea to Royal Doulton china. (We wondered if the other EPCOT visitors came away with the impression that we Britons sat about all day in thatched cottages, drinking English tea from expensive Doulton China cups.)

To **America**, where we were entertained by a vocal octet performing close harmony numbers. Not only were they excellent, but they performed everything from memory.

Back to **Norway** for an excellent supper. We had booked the meal using interactive television. (This really was something new to us - back in 1992.) We touched a screen, selecting our requirements, until, eventually, a real live person appeared and dealt with our request. I couldn't believe she was real so I asked her - and she confirmed she really was there. Using yet more computers, she could tell us the availability of reservations in *all* the restaurants in the EPCOT Centre. We decided on the Norwegian one and she booked us in for our meal. We found ourselves wondering what these computers *couldn't* do.

The evening was rounded off by a fantastic display of lasers, lights and fireworks in the central lake.

Back at our hotel, exhausted, we caught a glimpse of American wrestling on television - and we thought English wrestling was bad?

Tuesday 17th

Disney MGM Studios was our destination for today. All these places were about ten minutes drive from our hotel so we really *did* need a car. Though most hotels ran shuttle buses to and from the Disney places, they were very restricting and time available was dictated by the bus schedule. There was no way we could have walked from the hotel, though, from the literature, it appeared that would have been possible. We felt strongly that the literature should have been much more specific.

The car parks at the various Disney sites were gigantic - the size of between six and ten football pitches. That was an indication of the size of the actual site! In the car parks were parking attendants who indicated where we had to go. This saved lots of time which would have been taken up driving aimlessly around, looking for a parking place. We were issued with a card on which, when we had parked, we noted the aisle and the relevant number. It would have been impossible to remember where we had left the car without this *aide memoire*. Everything in Disney World was organized for speed and efficiency - and it worked. Disney got very good marks for cleanliness. There was not a scrap of litter to be seen anywhere. It really was spotless, which was quite something considering the quantity of 'trash' that resulted from all the fast food eateries, overflowing with paper cups, paper plates, serviettes and the like. Disney got more good marks for wheelchair access, which was available everywhere. Wheelchair guests were very well looked after and were taken into rides and exhibitions ahead of everyone else.

Our first visit in the MGM Studios was to the **Star Tours Ride**. We spent a few minutes in an out-of-control spaceship going to planet Endor. It proved that the eye really *does* deceive - especially in tandem with the other senses. Our brains convinced us that we were on a collision course to destruction. This was not for the faint-hearted. I was beginning to rethink my career as an astronaut.

The **Great Movie Ride** took us through various film sets, with some action-packed activity involving the guide and a bank robberess - yes, this was the land of Equal Opportunities.

Backstage Studio Tour took us by bus around the sets and into a canyon which filled with water, near to an exploding petrol lorry which was set on fire. It was very realistic and we were shown how these effects were created. Driving round the back of the 'canyon', we were able to see how umpteen tons of water were stored and then released under great pressure, to produce a real cascade - or flood.

Indiana Jones Epic Stunt Spectacular was another amazing display by both stunt men *and* women, including a fire, a small plane, and an exploding jeep. I decided that was the second career option I needed to rethink.

Animations showed us just how Disney cartoons were drawn. We were able to see the animators in action and the actual cartoons being drawn. It made us realize just how expensive it must be to make a cartoon film. We would look at Mickey Mouse with different eyes!

We were saturated with new experiences so we returned to our hotel for our first session of sun worship and time in the hotel pool. The temperature was in the seventies (permanently) so the pool was most welcome.

Our evening meal was taken at the Hilton next door. It was not *quite* like its Park Lane equivalent. Our waiter, Tim, went out of his way to be helpful and must have asked us a dozen times if there was anything else he could get for us. In the end, we felt like requesting something really idiotic, like a couple of tame flamingos, but we restrained ourselves. We came to the conclusion that even politeness can be overdone.

Wednesday 18th

The **Magic Kingdom** was today's destination. That was made up of *Fantasyland, Tomorrowland, Adventureland, Frontierland, Liberty Square, Mickey's Starland* and *Main Street, USA*. There was the usual gigantic car park from which we were collected by the courtesy bus - it was *that* big! The courtesy bus only took us part of the way, the remaining one and a half miles of the trip to the actual gate was done by monorail.

We followed the recommended route as detailed in the guidebook that Howard had acquired. We started on the **Jungle Cruise** in *Adventureland*. This took the form of a boat trip through jungle terrain, with audio-animatronic (very life-like 'robots') scenery. Next to *Fantasyland*, **It's a Small World**. This was another boat ride, through dolls of all nations. We thought this was one of the best things we'd yet seen for the little ones as there was nothing frightening in it. On second thoughts, we concluded that perhaps we were the ones who scared easily; the children didn't seem to mind anything! To *Frontierland* for the **Big Thunder Mountain Railroad**. The guidebook described it as 'a tame roller coaster'. It was a gold mining train that was out of control. If that was a tame one, we had no wish to see a wild one! We were so *brave!* We didn't know we could scream so loudly......**Country Bear Jamboree** was a 'hoe-down' performed by audio-animatronic bears. It was 'OK if you liked that sort of thing'.

After lunch, we took a leisurely ride on the stately Paddle Steamer before going into the **Hall of Presidents** in *Liberty Square*. A very cleverly put together film of 'stills' on a wide screen traced the history of the USA and ended with more audio-animatronic figures, representing the forty presidents of the USA - up to and including George Bush (Senior) and ending with a final speech by Abraham Lincoln. The characters were so real that we had to pinch ourselves to remind us that they were only working models! The **Magic Journey** in *Fantasyland* was a 3-D Fantasy film for which we were issued with 3-D spectacles, the like of which sometimes came with comics when we were children. It was a very clever and beautiful film but the 3-D effects were lost on me because of my eye condition (I am unable to see in 3-D.) Howard assured me it was very dramatic. We took a ride on the old steam train whose track encircled the **Magic Kingdom**, before returning to *Adventureland* and the **Pirates of the Caribbean**. This was a boat trip through some unsalubrious pirate-infested waters - with remarkable special effects.

It was time to go back to our hotel so we retraced our steps; first the ferry across the lake to the car park entrance, next the courtesy bus to our section of the car park and finally to the Car Center to fill up with 'gas'. (You can see we were getting very Americanized by now.) We discovered the petrol cap *and* how to work the petrol pump!

A *Quality Inn* provided us with an indifferent supper but it filled a gap and we were content. On return to our hotel, we saw the menu for the restaurant and realized we would have done much better here. We made a note to try it the following evening.

Thursday 19th

Today was one of the highlights of the trip - to the JF Kennedy Space Center - known as 'Spaceport USA' - at Cape Canaveral. It was a seventy mile drive but on the excellent American roads, we were there in no time. Retrospectively, we appreciated the Disney efficiency when we found that the Kennedy Car Park had *no* attendants. Much time was wasted on fruitless meanderings in an endeavour to find a parking place. Once inside the Center, we joined long and slow-moving 'lines' (note: no queues) to get our bus tour tickets.

Our first stop was the Imax Theatre to see the film *The Dream is Alive* - on a five and a half storey-high screen. (Remember we said everything on this trip was *big*!) Astronauts had said of this film "it's as close as you'll get to space without riding the Space Shuttle". It was a wonderful film; we felt we were in the spaceship with the astronauts. There was film of the earth as seen from the Shuttle in space, shots of the astronauts inside the Shuttle carrying out their tasks and doing things like having their meals in their weightless state. All five of them went to sleep, strapped in, standing up - except there was no such thing as 'up' in the weightless state. Finally we saw the Shuttle landing at Edwards Air Force Base in California, after its three and a half million mile trip! This was filmed from the cockpit so we saw it just as the Captain would have seen it.

The two-hour bus trip was next. The first stop was the place where all the Apollo astronauts trained - including the three who did the very first moon landing - Aldrin, Armstrong, and Collins. We were shown a video of the last few minutes of a countdown, followed by a sighting of the lunar module, complete with gold foil round its base, and the command section of the rocket. The 'gold foil' discovery was put to practical use in premature baby units to maintain babies' temperatures.

On to the Vehicle Assembly Building (VAB) which was one of the world's largest buildings. Inside, the Shuttle and its rockets were assembled, in a vertical position, hence the immense height of the building. From here, the completed scapecraft was loaded onto the Crawler Transporter which carried the whole thing the three and a half miles to the launch pad. 'Crawler' was a very appropriate name for this piece of equipment because it moved at only half a mile an hour - or was it a *day*? It was a gigantic structure, whose dimensions were staggering - so staggering it was difficult to take them in. The whole thing weighed six million pounds! The Crawler made its way along a specially constructed track, the width of an eight-lane highway. To make this track, deep holes were dug and filled with concrete and other durable material which would bear the weight of the Crawler *and* its load. We were not allowed to go any further as, on the following Monday, there was to be a launch of the Shuttle *Atlantis*. Even though we were three miles away, we could see *Atlantis* sitting on its launch pad ready for its long journey. That was rather breathtaking.

The bus took us back to Spaceport USA, passing by a real Saturn V rocket, which had been laid on its side so it could be viewed. The whole rocket was longer than a football field and we felt very insignificant standing next to it. We always wonder how fully loaded planes ever get off the ground - but at least they 'have a run at it' and ascend at an angle. The Saturn V preferred the Vertical Take-Off option and, once again, there were un-take-in-able statistics about how many tons of this and pressures of that were used to effect its launch.

At the end of the bus tour, we looked in at the Gallery of Spaceflight which was reminiscent of the Air and Space Museum in Washington DC. Here, too, they had a piece of moon rock. The Astronaut Memorial was a sad sight, especially the names of the seven who died in the horrific catastrophe in 1988. On the way back to the car park, we photographed a Challenger Shuttle in the Rocket Garden - an area full of rockets, this time pointing in the right direction - up. The Challenger Shuttle turned out to be a full-size model. We had to stand further and further away to get it into our viewfinders.

Back at the hotel we engaged in some extra vehicular activity in the swimming pool before having supper in our own hotel. What a good decision!

Friday 20th

We drove just a few miles to *Sea World* which was much smaller than the Disney sites. We were issued with a plan of the park - nothing unusual in that - except that it was a computerized print-out indicating the time we could go to each event, starting from the time we arrived. We realized that everyone was given a personalized time-table - and that computers *were* beginning to rule the world.

The first stop was the **Stingray Lagoon** where the sign posted over their little home encouraged us to touch the fish as they were very friendly - so we did! Because they were so friendly, they didn't sting us. On to the **Whale and Dolphin Stadium** where they were put through their paces. We were not in the 'splash' area so did not get soaked in cold water, but many others did - and they really *were* soaked to the skin. We took enough photos to ensure that our friends would be bored silly when we got home. Next to **Seaworld Theatre**, a multi-media presentation looking at marine life and preceded by a beautiful coloured fountain display. The big attraction was **Shamu the Killer Whale - and friends**. Indeed he (she?) was featured on all the advertisements for *Sea World* nationwide. Six killer whales had been born in various Sea Worlds and we saw a film of the birth of the latest arrival.. Shamu and Friends was another marvellous display by both the humans and the Killer Whales. They looked so harmless that it was hard to believe they would kill so much as a stick insect, let alone a human being. We realized what an incredible relationship existed between these creatures and the humans when we saw the whales following the trainers around and having their fish lunch put between their formidable-looking teeth.

After lunch, shared with some little birds, we visited the **Penguin Encounter**. The penguins were behind glass in a special, very spacious, home. These were amongst some of the most delightful creatures we were to see. There were two ladies in their home, cleaning the glass but their progress was impeded by the penguins who continually distracted them and wanted to be cuddled! They succeeded in their distraction techniques. (My third career option might be a Penguin Keeperess.) Another aquatic adventure was the **Sea Lion and Otter Stadium**. Their display was put together as a comic routine and it included a warm-up artist who successfully organized audience participation in a *very* clever way. The most amazing member of the cast was the little otter whose job it was to clear up 'garbage' left by the 'baddie'. It was easy to take the sea lions for granted - and they were marvellous too - but the diminutive otter was a 'star'. The last attraction was **Terrors of the Deep**, which included an educational presentation (with 'stills' and a video) and sightings of real live menacing members of the ocean fraternity - eels, venomous and poisonous fish, barracudas and quite an assortment of sharks. The Puffin fish was particularly unattractive; it injected a sting which paralysed the nervous system instantly and, as yet, there was no known cure! We made a mental note not to have any for supper.

To maintain our piscine theme, supper was at the *Red Lobster*, about seven miles away - but that's just around the corner to an American. Howard had lobster, I had salmon. The portions were enormous and I was easily beaten.

Saturday 21st

Together with a fellow Bach Choir member, Sarah Bronzite, Howard was to drive from Miami to Tampa when the other half of the Choir arrived in America, as there were not enough places on the Choir coach. We drove to Tampa to check on the location of the Ramada Hotel and the Hertz car-hire place where the car would be left. It was a pleasant enough sixty-five mile drive but two things were rather distracting. The first was that our eyes were never still. When they were not reading road signs (very important), they were bombarded by roadside advertisements for everything under the sun - hotels, food, golf courses, factory outlets and, to our amazement, the local Memorial Park. As if *that* wasn't amazing enough, the billboards quoted prices for cremations, burials and shipping! Now we really *had* seen it all...The second distraction was the road surface. At one point we drove off onto a side road to check our tyres as we thought there was something wrong with them. They were fine - it turned out to be the less than ideal road surface.

In Tampa, we checked with the Hertz people to find out what Howard had to do with the car and asked about signing in Sarah Bronzite authorizing her to drive. On to the Ramada Hotel where we were relieved to see some members of the Bach Choir in the lobby. Howard checked with Basil, the organizer, to see if anyone had dropped out, thereby allowing him and Sarah to join the coach and avoid the long drive from Miami to Tampa. Unfortunately no one had dropped out.

We took ourselves off to St Petersburg (not the one in Russia) and its Beach. It was not *just* a beach, but a large conurbation. We paddled for a few minutes in the Gulf of Mexico. A most considerate beach attendant not only let us use the beach chairs free for twenty minutes, but also recommended the *Hurricane* restaurant, just up the coast. His recommendation was good and we had lunch overlooking the Gulf of Mexico.

We returned to the Econolodge for a final swim, a Jacuzzi and a pool-side beer - covered in sun-tan oil. (We were covered in the sun-tan oil, not the pool-side beer.) We had supper in our hotel (preceded by a Harvey Wallbanger!) before packing and dealing with the necessary paperwork ready for the parting of our ways the next day.

Sunday March 22nd

We made an early start for our four-hour drive to Miami, where we took ourselves down to the beach for lunch, leaving the car in a very odd car park. I was convinced we would not see the vehicle again - neither would we see our luggage which was in the boot. Luckily I was wrong, but lunch was in a weird uncomfortable-feeling area. (Perhaps this was where they filmed *Miami Vice?*) My tomato and cheese omelette was fine, except it had everything in it *but* tomato or cheese. We cast the swiftest of glances at the Atlantic ocean then were relieved to find the car where we had left it.

We were at the airport in good time for me to check in. The computer had 'gone down' while checking in the person ahead of me. The operator told us that the computer 'was run from Los Angeles' (!) and assured us it would come back to life very soon - which it did. We made our way to Arrivals to meet the remaining members of the Bach Choir. Howard found Stuart, the person in charge of the incoming group. Stuart told us that everything was in chaos. Some people he was expecting to be on the plane weren't - and *vice versa.* Howard asked Stuart if he would look out for Sarah Bronzite as we were not air-side and could not look for her ourselves. Another Bach Choir member asked Howard if he would mind taking Pippa as she was 'not good on coach journeys'. Howard agreed and we waited for the two ladies to arrive. After a long wait, there was still no sign of them - and suddenly the Choir party moved off, headed by Stuart. Howard asked again about the whereabouts of his two passengers. Stuart's response was that he didn't know - and off he went, leaving Howard high and dry. We were not impressed by this lack of efficiency, especially since Howard was doing the Choir a huge favour by undertaking the car journey. Out of nowhere, Pippa appeared, as did Sarah, at one of the Hertz desks.

Next came the moment to which neither of us had been looking forward, the actual parting of our ways. I felt very brave, flying alone across the Atlantic - well, not quite alone as there were another 300 or so people with me, but Howard was not one of them and I had never done anything like that before without him. I went to Gate B11 where the jumbo jet stood waiting. Boarding was by rows and as I was almost the last row to board, it gave me the opportunity to continue standing for a while longer, before being consigned to eight and a half hours *sitting.*

I managed to sleep for four hours in the plane. There's always something good about arriving back in England. After a very swift exit from the airport, I was soon in a taxi taking me from Victoria to Kennington. On the taxi-driver's wireless, I heard that "the launch of the Shuttle *Atlantis* in Florida has been postponed indefinitely due to a fuel leak". I told the (very unimpressed) taxi driver that I had seen that very Shuttle just days before. I went into our empty flat - to await the return of Howard in a week's time.

""This is Houston - sorry there's no one to take your message at the moment.""

MONET'S GARDEN
June 1992

Thursday 18th

After work, we drove down to Portsmouth where we arrived around 2100. Our travelling companions were Janet and her mother, Dorothy. When Howard had made the ferry reservations, all the cabins had been fully booked, but he had managed to book two reclining seats for the overnight crossing. Janet and her mother had to occupy these - Janet because she was driving and Dorothy by virtue of her seniority. However, we had not been on board very long when, over the tannoy came a message "Would Mr. Spurr go to Information". Mr. Spurr *went* to Information and learned that a cabin had become available.

Friday 19th

All had a good night's sleep and were ready for disembarkation at 0600. There was a general craving for that first cup of tea and we felt we couldn't wait until Pont Audemer - a pretty little town where we had planned to have breakfast - because it was thirty minutes away. We found a little café in Le Havre and satisfied our tea craving. We drove on to Pont Audemer, where it was market day. All of us loved markets, of any size, shape and description, but particularly markets in foreign countries where we didn't necessarily recognize all the goods. We spent an educational time trying to identify certain things, easily identifying others and purchasing the wherewithal for our picnic lunch later that day. The saddest sight was the dear little rabbits. They were not being sold as pets - but as *dinner*. The thought of them ending up in a stew was just too horrible. They looked so sweet - and they had no idea why they were there, thank goodness. We found a little café in which to have breakfast of croissants and 'all that goes with' - and it was clear that it doubled as the betting shop.

We drove on to Vernon, where we were to stay for two nights. Vernon was about two miles from Giverny where the Monet house and garden were to be found. We left our luggage at the hotel and set off for Giverny as we were to visit the Monet house that very afternoon. On the way, we called at *Les Jardins de Giverny* to book a table for our meal in the evening.

Howard had found us a vista-filled spot in which to eat our picnic; on a vista-scale of one to ten, we gave it ten. We unpacked the picnic, our very colourful picnic set, a rug and all the goodies. Janet remarked that 'it did look somewhat rainy over yonder'. Hardly had the words fallen from her lips when 'over yonder' became the spot where we were sitting. Within seconds, torrential rain was seriously hampering our picnic. With a certain degree of urgency, we gathered up all the things we had barely unpacked and poured ourselves back into the car. The picnic was eaten *en voiture*, but was none the worse for that. A pre-prandial sherry, which Dorothy had bought in the duty-free shop on the boat, got us off to a fine start and the very good bottle of French wine soon ensured that we were no longer worrying about the weather. The food wasn't bad either!

The *Maison et Jardin Monet* awaited us. It was just four years ago that Howard and I had made our first visit to this magical place but Janet and Dorothy had never seen it, so it was a 'first' for them. The weather was not too good but it didn't stop us taking far too many photographs. Because it was not the weekend and because the weather was not ideal, it was not nearly as crowded as when Howard and I had been there in 1988. This time, we were able to see everything at our leisure.

In the evening, we returned to *Les Jardins de Giverny*. We had an excellent meal and the restaurant was very pleasant but, with the exception of two ladies at the adjacent table, we were the only patrons that evening. The management must have been thrilled to see us. We concluded that it was probably due to the recession. (Typing this in 2009, it's clear that nothing changes.)

Saturday 20th

The weather had deteriorated even further. On the way to the supermarket, we looked into the local church, to find a baptism in progress. While the baptism party signed seemingly endless official documents, the organist gave a very indifferent (indeed, inaccurate) rendition of the Bach *G Minor Flute Siciliano*. However, when all the signing was complete, the instrument (and presumably the player?) burst into life with an impressive (but unidentified) outgoing voluntary.

A large part of the morning was spent in the supermarket and it was fair to say that we bought lots more things than we needed. It was all *such* a temptation and we were so weak-willed. Having indulged in what we would now call retail therapy, we wondered how we would get it all back to the hotel. Howard suggested we took it in the supermarket trolley. I thought we would be arrested - but I was overruled. We *weren't* arrested and it proved to be by far the best way to get everything back to the car, which we had left in the hotel car park. Howard returned the trolley to the supermarket and reclaimed his ten franc coin while the rest of us prepared for our next picnic, the ingredients for which we had purchased in the supermarket.

By now the weather was dreadful so we drove out into the country, parked in a forest and picnicked *en voiture* once again. We decided it was rather fun - after all it wasn't something any of us did every day. We wrote messages on the steamed-up car windows.

On to the Château de Bizy, a sensible-sized chateau, in which we were given a guided tour. As it was in French, the only person who understood it was Howard. I tried very hard to follow the explanations but I had a problem. As soon as the guide mentioned a date (*mille huit cents, soixante-douze*), I wanted to work out what that was in English. Apart from the fact that it mattered not at all, it meant that I'd missed the next two minutes' worth of commentary - so I was lost, again.

We had supper in a little bistro in Vernon which was near the hotel so we were able to walk to it. The bistro itself was fine, so too was the food - when it arrived. The service was lamentably slow and some of the dishes arrived only after Howard reminded the young lady more than once that we hadn't yet received certain parts of the meal. Another 'minus' was that we were the only table at which no one was smoking. In some cases, people were smoking both between courses and *during* them. We couldn't believe our eyes. We *could*, however, believe our noses!

Sunday 21st

It was time to start our return journey but we did a number of things *en route*. The first thing we did was to regret buying the cheese as it was almost walking out of Janet's car. None of us thought we had bought any strong-smelling cheeses, but our noses told us the opposite. The weather had improved considerably so we sped along the long straight French roads with the windows open so the local populace could share the odours of the fermented curds.

We stopped at the Château Gaillard, a very old ruin (?eleventh century) in a strategic spot, high on the banks of the Seine. The peace and quiet was broken only by motorcyclists taking part in a motor-cross competition on the opposite hillside. A large coach disgorged a quantity of inscrutable Japanese tourists who seemed to be taking innumerable photos of each other in various groups, rather than the ruin itself.

We headed for L'Abbaye de Jumièges, which we had visited in 1986, just as it was closing. This time, we were able to see the whole thing. It was quite marvellous - and so peaceful. By now the weather looked as if it was closing in once more. No one else was venturing into the Abbey, so we had the place to ourselves. It was reminiscent of Greyfriars in Winchelsea - but there was much more of it.

Time was not on our side but we had spotted a good restaurant across the road from the Abbey. We had a good lunch though we were not able to dally as we had to keep an eye on the time if we were not to miss our ferry. We made it back to Le Havre in good time. The ferry Captain told us that the weather in England was very good, and so it proved as we sailed nearer and nearer to our 'green and pleasant land'.

"We're thinking about the Holy Land next. Glorious things of it are spoken."

BOULOGNE
November 1992

Friday 20th

We had decided to 'pack up all our cares and woe' (as the songwriter has it) and head for Boulogne-sur-Mer. In particular we were headed for the Metropole Hotel as it was very comfortable, convenient for the port and the town and generally very welcoming. We knew this because we had stayed there on previous occasions.

We caught the 1015 ferry from Dover and it arrived in Boulogne fifteen minutes early, though we had to put our watches *on* an hour, as it was that time of the year when they were ahead of us. We checked into the Hotel Metropole and set off for the *Bar Hamiot*, just across the road, for lunch. Suitably refreshed, in body mind and spirit, we headed for the *Auchan* supermarket which was three miles out of town. We caught one of the many local buses that did the journey to this 'temple' for British visitors. *Auchan* was quite enormous but this was not our first visit to it and, by now, we were seasoned shoppers in this particular *hypermarché*. In no time at all we had made all our purchases and were 'dug into' the long and tedious check-out queue. I noticed a much shorter queue so we manoeuvred our overflowing trolley in its direction and gloated that we had saved ourselves a long wait...until Howard (older and wiser) observed that we were in a queue for 'ten items or less'. We could hardly throw out the majority of our purchases to bring ourselves down to the legal limit. We took the only course open to us. We slunk - yes *slunk* - back to one of the other long queues. Silly me...that should teach me a lesson! What was that about 'the first shall be last'?

We returned to the Metropole where we stored all our purchases in newspapers and plastic bags and stashed them in the cupboard. We were having a little rest before pre-prandial time when our peace was interrupted by loud and continuous banging on an adjacent door. My fertile mind pictured a corpse behind the door being banged upon, but we were not to know. We found that we could get two English channels on the television, from one of which we learned about the Windsor Castle fire disaster. What sadness - for everyone.

We set out for our evening meal at *Le Doyen*, a restaurant which we had patronized on previous visits. (As we left our room, a couple of ladies were pushing a note under the door which we assumed was that on which we had heard banging. How would the corpse be able to read the note? was my question.) On previous visits to *Le Doyen*, the menu had been hand-written in children's exercise books, but we were to find that things had changed somewhat.

Our biggest surprise was yet to come. The *patrone* (yes, it was a lady) was not the most welcoming person we'd ever met. We thought she was trying very hard to force a smile to her lips, but she was not succeeding. We were shown to a table and we handed our coats to her - it seemed to be that sort of a place. Imagine our surprise when the cheerless one threw them in a corner! (We always knew the French were not as sophisticated as us but that seemed to be going a bit far - even for them.) The meal made up for everything - though we did notice that all the other customers had left their coats over the back of their chairs...

Saturday 21st

Breakfast was something of a revelation. The two ladies we had observed putting the note under the door, appeared and started their breakfast. Eventually, they were joined by two men. All four were English and we couldn't work out the relationships. Of the ladies, one was 'older', the other 'younger'; the men fell into similar categories. The younger man - a callow youth - was unshaven and his older companion revealed that this was because he had forgotten to pack his razor. We wondered if the two men had indulged in quite a large amount of alcoholic libations the previous evening - and, perhaps, the previous afternoon too, which is why the ladies got no reply to their banging on the door. The older lady was rather posh and the older man rather uncouth. He did not endear himself to us (or to the ladies) as he lit up a cigarette the minute he sat down - filling the breakfast room with acrid smoke. The younger one displayed no obvious signs of 'couthness' so we really couldn't fathom out the situation.

Howard removed the bread which we had not eaten for breakfast so we could feed it to the seagulls later. The birds seemed grateful to us for our thoughtfulness. We had a look round the fish market on the quay-side (some of them were still alive!) then went to the market in the central square. Like the market in Pont Audemer, everything under the sun was for sale - including, once again, live rabbits and birds. (I am a hypocrite really because I eat meat but I can't bear the thought of those cute little animals becoming a meal.)

We went right to the top of the town and had a little potter round the Cathedral. It was impressive in size but we were not greatly enamoured of it. It had an 'uncared for' feeling about it. We had a favourite restaurant up in the old town so we lunched there. The proprietor's son recognized Howard from previous visits. We thought it was because, though we were English, we were quiet and we understood the menu. We did not emulate our fellow countrymen whom (to our embarrassment) we had witnessed on more than one occasion giggling over an incomprehensible selection of food and (deliberately?) mispronouncing everything - like juvenile first year 'O' level students.

In the evening, we eschewed a rather grand restaurant which we had patronized on previous visits as we felt we wouldn't do justice to another large meal. Instead we thought we would find anything that took our fancy in the centre of town. There was a most unpromising-sounding place called *The Welsh Pub*. Wild horses would not have dragged us into it, except that the guidebook said it was good and a couple of our friends had recommended it. It had as much in common with a Welsh pub as the *Ritz* did with a *Wimpy Bar*. It turned out to be a very good French restaurant and, when we enquired why it was called *The Welsh Pub*, we were told that it was because it served Welsh Rarebit. That was the only concession to 'things Welsh'.

Sunday 22nd

Sunday did not find us in church as the Cathedral didn't seem very inviting, nor did the Parish Church. We went in search of the *Calvaire des Marins*, at the top of the hill, overlooking both the town and the sea. It was a sad little memorial to people 'missing at sea' in various marine tragedies.

Back at the quay, we discovered the *Fête des Harengs* was being celebrated. From the 'blurb' which was posted up on the stalls, we thought it was some kind of demonstration against the government to do with fishing restrictions or new EEC rules and regulations. It turned out to be nothing of the kind; merely publicity for the start of the herring season (we didn't know there was a time when herrings were not in season) and the arrival of the Beaujolais Nouveau. For a few francs, we were given a *dégustation* of a cooked herring and some Nouveau Beaujolais. It was all very tasty, especially in the open air. While we were sampling the food and drink, a very voluble French lady explained to us what it was all about. Unfortunately, she spoke so quickly that even Howard didn't understand it! I thought I had understood one word - *automne* (rough translation: autumn) but, alongside three minutes of quick-fire French, I could not weave that solitary word into a lucid explanation.

By now, it was nearing time to contemplate lunch at *Nausicaä*, but not before we watched the Sea-Cat leaving the port, heading for England. (The Sea-Cat was a catamaran-ized version of a hovercraft.) *Nausicaä* was a brand-new complex made up of everything to do with the sea: a museum of the sea, demonstrations, lots of fish to be viewed - and some to be touched in a special tactile-sensation tank. Before that, there was lunch. We had booked ourselves a table (looking out to sea) the day before, knowing what Sunday lunch in France was like. Our meal was excellent and afterwards we were just able to muster enough energy for an exploration of the sea centre, which included two films.

It was time to collect our voluminous and heavy luggage from the hotel. The volume was mostly wine and cheese so we were not complaining but we knew we had to allow lots of time to trundle our way to the ferry terminal, negotiating the bag-on-wheels up and down kerbs and staircases. We were soon on board The Pride of Canterbury and though our crossing was quite rough, the ferry was so well-stabilized that it caused us no problem.

We arrived at Dover Station five minutes after the train had left for London, and fifty-five minutes before the next one was due to leave. There was another train we could have taken but it involved changing three times - one of those changes being on to a bus. With our very heavy luggage, that possibility did not commend itself to us so we whiled away the time in the buffet, sampling one of British Rail's offerings, a brunch-burger(?). It was so cleverly constructed that we couldn't tell the difference between the taste of the brunch-burger and the serviette in which we held it. Clever old British Rail - they think of everything, don't they.

MEDITERRANEAN MEDITATIONS
FROM VAUXHALL TO VALLETTA
January 1993

We had had some advance intelligence about our trip from a television programme shown on the previous Sunday. Also two friends had visited Malta the previous year and they told us we mustn't miss a ride on the local buses; they were boneshakers and the drivers sat in a little shrine, surrounded by religious artefacts. When we saw the way they drove, we would understand why.

Tuesday 12th

We took the Gatwick Express to the airport. British Rail had devised a new intelligence test to make sure its passengers would not be bored on their journey. How do you consume a cup of coffee, served to you with a lid firmly affixed, a carton of milk (lid similar) and a packet of sugar? We found we didn't have enough hands. It was not easy to do without spilling it on oneself - or a fellow passenger. We chose a fellow passenger. (The young Canadian gentleman was very good about it - hooray for the *entente cordiale*.) We were in good time for our flight so we used the time profitably discovering how many words can be made out of MALTA. Depressingly few, if any, was our conclusion. (Should anyone know the meaning of ATLAM, TALMA or LAMAT, we'd be pleased to hear from you.) It was times like this we wished we'd gone to Fuerteventura; much more scope there for our spellcheck-oriented minds.

The flight might have been boring were it not for a fellow passenger, George - of Irish extraction. He vowed never to travel by Britannia Airways again, as the in-flight drinks were not complimentary. He was rather strange (?understatement) and, towards the end of the flight, specifically requested that Jill (one of the stewardesses - or 'flight facilitators' as we were urged call them) brought him some oxygen. We weren't totally convinced of his need for this as, when offered assistance by a *male* flight attendant, George stressed that 'Jill' be asked to attend to him - which, in the end, she did.

Passport Control at Malta took forever. We resigned ourselves to the fact that our week's holiday would be spent standing in this queue. "It'll be OK as long as they bring us food and the sun shines through the big glass panels" Howard concluded, in his usual optimistic fashion. I did not share his optimism.

We made it to the Mellieha Bay Hotel just in time for dinner - and an early night. It had been a long day.

Wednesday 13th

The Thomson Welcome Party was very informative. We spent the rest of the day getting our bearings and walking (what turned out to be) quite a long way to the other side of the bay to investigate the church. (It didn't *look* far from our hotel window.) The second half of the walk was up a very steep hill. The interior of the church was a bit of a disappointment, after its impressive exterior. We were not *too* upset as there were another 364 churches to see. We took our first trip on a boneshaker bus to St Paul's Bay, where an omelette filled a certain gap in the inner man and woman. We located the statue of St Paul - said to mark the spot where he came ashore, though the fountain mentioned in the guidebook turned out to be a stagnant pond. We thought we had the wrong place but the restaurateur assured us 'this was it'. St Paul's Bay was deathly quiet, except for twelve cats being fed by a local and one welcoming little dog and owner. We retraced the path of our morning walk - downhill this time - then rested our weary legs until supper time.

Thursday 14th

This was the day of the hired car and the picnic provided by the hotel as we were to spend the day out and would therefore miss our lunch. The Hertz Car Hire man delivered our car early so we were able to make the short drive to the Gozo ferry and catch one half an hour earlier than we'd planned.

Gozo was one of the five islands that made up the little group of which Malta was the largest, though *that* was only the size of the Isle of Wight. Malta, Gozo and Comino are inhabited, the remaining two are not. The ferry to Gozo took a mere thirty minutes. Our first visit was to the Citadel and the Cathedral. The latter oozed marble and had a *trompe l'oeil* dome. They went in for domes in a big way in these parts and, if you hadn't really got one, you did the next best thing - painted one. Just as we arrived at the church of St George, a service started, so we beat a hasty retreat. Giving culture a miss, we made our way to Ramla Bay to consume the picnic which the hotel had provided. It was excellent and plentiful. We sat on a wonderful sandy beach pondering the question how many grains of sand were there in the world - and, when counting them, did we include those contained in egg timers? Was it any wonder that we had not been awarded the Nobel Prize for Original Thought?

After lunch, we went to the Megalithic Temples of Ggantija, constructed some 3,500 to 4,000 years BC - the Copper Age. How? - we asked ourselves. Many other - and much brighter - souls had asked this question before us, without coming up with an answer. The gigantic rocks weighed several tons, those of the outer wall reaching as high as six metres. It is still a mystery how the people of those early days were able to move these enormous rocks with only the primitive tools of the period. According to an old myth, a female giant named Sunsuna carried the rocks on her head. (Why should this be a myth?)

On to the church in Xewkija which was built between 1952 and 1982 and contained the third largest dome in the world - a real one this time, not painted on! It was a magnificent achievement, both 'on site' and in the distance.

Friday 15th

Today we took a guided tour of places of interest on the island of Malta itself - starting at Mosta and the famous domed church - another one, but rather a special one this time. This dome was one of the largest in the world, larger in diameter than St Paul's Cathedral, and was built without scaffolding. (No, we don't know how, either.) On April 9th 1942, a bomb came through the roof, slid across the church where 300 people were attending a service, but did not explode. A replica of the bomb remains in the Sacristy. It was a remarkable building with so much gold leaf everywhere that we began to think we were imagining it.

The next stop was the little fishing village of Marsaxlokk. (We couldn't pronounce it either - it seemed there were a lot of 'x's and 'k's in the Maltese language.) The harbour was full of the brightly painted fishing fleet, some of which were being brightly painted as we watched. All the boats had little eyes at the front to ward off evil spirits. There was a fascinating market, full of tablecloths, leather goods, lace work and the like. Best of all, we met a tiny Labrador puppy (real) who was keen to have a chat. He was chained to his owner's stall and looked very bored, except when besotted tourists broke up his day!

We were taken for a twenty-five minute boat trip in the Blue Grotto in a little outboard motorboat, through crystal clear water, to the natural limestone and granite caves. The light slanted into the caves and reflected off the sheer white sand at the bottom. Lots of jelly fish were in evidence. I've never been very keen on them but I've only seen them lying dead on beaches. Live and swimming about, they were rather elegant.

Next we went to the Craft Village at Ta 'Qali, a converted airfield. We were taken into the filigree workshop, which, not surprisingly, had a huge selection of wonderful filigree things which we resisted the temptation to buy. After lunch, we visited the glass-blowing factory, though we didn't see anyone actually blowing glass. There were a number of craftsmen fashioning things from molten glass, some of which we couldn't resist buying.

On to Mdina which was the capital city of Malta in the year dot. The Romans called it Melita until they discovered that was the name of a food-processor. The Saracens renamed it Mdina in the ninth century, just to ensure that English people wouldn't be able to pronounce it. It was a walled city, entered through Howard's Garden. Mdina was known as the Silent City as there was hardly any transport within it. There was the odd horse-drawn cart (the horses enjoyed the polo mints that I fed them) but cars and motor vehicles were few and far between, the reason being the streets were much too narrow to allow them access. The whole place seemed deserted and the only people we met were one or two other tourist groups with their guides. This was certainly a 'well worth the detour' place, if only for the peace and quiet. The Cathedral of St Peter and St Paul (seat of the bishopric and Co-Cathedral with St John's in Valletta) was not nearly as large as we had imagined, but, once again, it was full of amazing works of art and marble mosaic floors covered the tombs of bishops. Most of the walls were covered in damask, not yet removed since Christmas. A short walking tour with our guide concluded the visit. It was encouraging to think there were still some peaceful places in the world.

Saturday 16th

We took the trip to Valletta 'under our own steam', on one of the boneshaker buses. It really was ancient and we were surprised it could move. The driver climbed over the gearbox to get to his seat. Fares were collected in a battered old Quality Street tin. There was a reassuring sticker on the front window which proclaimed 'Jesus loves me', so we supposed we would be safe....time alone would tell. The door of the bus was not closed throughout the journey (round hairpin bends, up and down steep hills). After a while, we realized this was because there was no door. We entered and left the bus through a gap in the side. It was certainly 'different'...

We went straight to St John's Co-Cathedral where hardly an inch of wall or floor was not highly decorated. The walls were carved and the floors were covered in ornate tombs of the Knights of St John. The ceiling was completely covered in paintings and carving - a mini Sistine Chapel. In one of the side chapels (each one dedicated to an *auberge* of the Knights of St John) was one of the two Caravaggio paintings that they possessed. This one, St Jerome, had been stolen from the Museum in 1984 but recovered and returned to the Cathedral in 1986. The biggest attraction was the same artist's *Beheading of the Baptist*. This was kept in the Oratory and, in the way of such things, we had to pay to see it. We were lucky that a group of Japanese tourists were being shown this great work, so we were able to eavesdrop on (the English part of) the guide's commentary. We eavesdropped on the Japanese part too, but couldn't quite follow it. The 'Beheading' was a rather horrific and bloodthirsty painting. The authorities had only recently realized it was by Caravaggio when his signature was discovered beneath the drops of blood in the painting. Apparently Caravaggio was a rather violent and unpleasant character and had been thrown out of Malta for picking a fight with an important personage, almost killing him. He had already been thrown out of other places for misdemeanours. He sounded a 'nasty piece of work' all round, but redeemed by the fact that he was an 'ace' painter.

St Paul's Shipwreck Church was next on our itinerary. We arrived not a moment too soon as it closed at noon and didn't open again until 1600. Though it was almost noon, the kind custodians not only let us in but spent a little time telling us about the church. We were able to buy some cards so we counted ourselves lucky. Five minutes later and we would have missed it altogether.

On to the Armoury in the Grand Masters' Palace, a collection of armour and other 'militaria' going back to the sixteenth century. We would not have enjoyed being encased in that all that metal for too long. It looked very uncomfortable and we couldn't imagine what it must have been like in the hot weather. We would not have been able to *walk* in it - let alone run and/or fight - so perhaps it was as well that we weren't around in those times. And whatever happened if the joints of the armour went rusty? They must have been incarcerated in it for ever…come to think of it, we fancied that we saw some people blinking behind the visors…

We took our picnic lunch (again provided by the hotel) and shared it with some birds in a little garden overlooking part of the harbour. To conclude our Valletta visit, we walked right round the perimeter wall of the city, stopping only to look in their War Museum. It was almost all Second World War exhibits and, because it was so small, we were able to see the whole of it. The island of Malta had been awarded the George Cross for communal gallantry during the Second World War. The statistics of the bombardment of Malta made sad reading and it was amazing to think that the islanders survived. We learned that more bombs fell on Malta than on the whole of Coventry. The George Cross was well-deserved and it was displayed in the Museum, together with the letter from George VI which accompanied it.

Our return journey to Mellieha Bay was on a much superior vehicle that not only had a door but air conditioning too!

In the evening, we decided to treat ourselves to a meal at *The Arches*. It looked good from the outside - so, too, did the menu. The lady in our hotel shop told us that 'it was very posh' - so we wondered what to expect! It turned out to be really delightful. The restaurant itself was a sea of pink tablecloths, candles, mirrors and clever lighting. It would have been lovely just to *sit* there - without eating a thing. We *did* eat things - and very good they were too. A different person brought each item of cutlery, glass, food and drink. When the main course arrived, it was delivered by no less than four waitresses who all appeared in a formation - rather like a troupe of dancers. (We observed the same troupe taking up another formation to move back the chairs for incoming guests, so that they were able to sit down at the same moment.) The staff were very solicitous and enquired on a number of occasions if everything was to our satisfaction. This was most definitely a place where we didn't pour out the wine for ourselves. The wine waiter made repeated visits to our table to ensure that we didn't have to undertake this arduous task. It was an excellent meal in all respects and we learned later that it was the most famous restaurant on the island! We walked back to our hotel. It would have been an insult to such a gourmet meal to have done anything else.

Sunday 17th

Our first visit was to a Flea Market. We did this as part of an organized coach tour. We decided it was far better to do these excursions that way because we were collected at our hotel and returned to it at the end and the bookings for everything were done by Thomsons. We merely followed the guide into each place without a care in the world. We did wonder why an hour had been allocated for the visit to the Flea market, but when we saw the size of it, we understood why. It was enormous - and very crowded - a pickpocket's paradise. There was nothing that could not be purchased in this market - *except* fleas. There were birds of all descriptions, fish, puppies (so tiny they sat in the palm of our hand), food, leather goods, plastic religious artefacts by the van-load, clothes, electrical things - to list but a few. When we'd exhausted all the possibilities, we took photos of the Triton Fountain and the Independence Statue.

The coach took us on to Sliema, where a Captain Morgan cruise ship awaited us. To our great joy, we were able to buy some English Sunday newspapers. Howard was keen to find out about the rugby - and was not disappointed. The cruise round the huge harbour area was as interesting as it was picturesque, and was enhanced by a lively commentary. We were offered coffee or Maltese hot chocolate, which bore not a little resemblance to English hot chocolate. Payment for the drinks was again collected in a battered Quality Street tin. (Did the Captain have a bus-driver brother?) It could not have been better weather for the seventy-five minute trip and it was one of the highlights of our week.

Back at the quayside, our coach was waiting to take us back to our hotel where we spent the rest of the day with the ninety-six pages of each of the Sunday papers.

Monday 18th

Our penultimate day began with breakfast (which was brought to our room) shared with the tiny birds who had no qualms about sitting on our balcony to help us out with the bread. They were quite blatant and, for their size, they seemed quite fearless. We wouldn't have been surprised if they had flown in and snatched the food from our fingers - but they seemed to draw the line at that.

Having ensured our little feathered friends were adequately fed, we took a local bus to Mellieha Village. This time the fares were collected in the bottom of a plastic mineral water bottle. We couldn't decide whether this was a step *up* or *down* from the battered Quality Street tin. We went straight to a grotto in Mellieha Village since others had recommended it. It was down a long staircase whose walls were covered with baby clothes which, it transpired, were thank offerings for the birth of children. We sought out the crypt of the local church where was housed a painting of the Madonna and Child 'attributed to St Luke'. As we entered the crypt, a diminutive nun invited us to join her and one or two other English visitors for a small guided tour. She was a sweet little person, and obviously very enthusiastic about her church. She was a Sister of the Order of the Sacred Heart which had only 200 Sisters now on the island - though there were large numbers of them in Africa and India!

By the time we'd strolled along the beach back to the hotel, it was lunchtime. The afternoon was spent in slumbering pursuits. At 1800, the Farewell meeting with the Thomson representative filled us in with the details of the homeward journey the next day.

Tuesday 19th

We made the most of the last morning by walking along the coast in the opposite direction to that which we'd taken hitherto. Unlike the seven cats who lived in the gardens just below our room (but who were rather timid), we were joined by a little kitten who insisted on coming along. It walked with us for quite a way but we became worried that it would either not find its way back or would follow us all the way and be exhausted, though we could have carried it back as a last resort. Eventually, discretion became the better part of valour and it returned from whence it came. We returned from whence we came to pack and consider the most propitious method of ensuring the safety in our luggage of the glass things we had bought.

We took a final pre-prandial drink on the balcony (the birds even ate the peanuts!) then, at midday, apart from changing into white mice on the stroke of noon, we had to vacate our room. Our final lunch and subsequent siesta set us wondering what the temperature would be back in SE11 and how good it would be to fall into our very own bed. On arrival at the airport, we learned that that pleasure was to be deferred for a further two hours - the length of time our flight was delayed. Since we were already at the airport one and a half hours before the anticipated departure time, we realized we were in for a long wait. We realized also that the plane was *only* just taking off from Gatwick. Nothing for it but to get stuck into our newspapers and books.

It was 0045 when we arrived back at Jennifer House. There could have been no better sight.

PARIS - ENCORE UNE FOIS
May 1993

Friday 28th

Today was the day when we might have gone to Paris - or, if BA carried out its threatened strike, we might have spent the weekend in Gatwick airport. Howard had made all possible enquiries from his desk in the corridors of power but, to be on the safe side, we left somewhat earlier than planned, in case we had to recycle ourselves onto another airline - or even find our way to Heathrow.

Our journey on the Gatwick Express was enlivened by a strange couple sitting opposite us. They had just become engaged - but we wondered whether they would ever get as far as the altar! Most of the conversation was about the quantity, type and cost of the jewellery that the bride-to-be had, might have, or was, was not wearing. It appeared that her mother designed it. We gathered there were already 'in-law' problems, and they weren't even married yet! The bride-to-be was a rather terrifying person, with steely eyes and a very domineering manner (not to put too find a point on it). What a sad situation it seemed to be.

We had a bite of breakfast in the North Terminal before heading for the duty-free shop to buy our pre-prandial bottle of Dubonnet. A perfume assistant pounced on us to demonstrate a new Dior fragrance. Her sales chat sounded like a long-playing record but then, poor thing, she had to say the same thing over and over again, day in, day out. Either the fragrance was called *Peace, Calm and Serenity* or that was how you felt when wearing it. It did mean that I could write up this diary in total peace, calm and serenity, making a change from my usual frenetic life.

We fell to wondering where all our fellow travellers were going. Were there *really* planes waiting on the other side of the windows, ready to transport huge numbers of humanity to far-flung destinations? Somehow it didn't seem possible - but we knew that was exactly what *would* happen. It all seemed rather unreal. Suddenly we discovered that we would have to wait another half hour in Gatwick before we were whisked away. Our flight was delayed. We assumed it was because of 'works on the line' - after all, that's the reason that's usually given.

In the end, our flight was ninety minutes late leaving. We had time to be amazed at the ingenuity of man to design space-saving, recyclable things, such as we were served for the mini-breakfast provided by British Airways. We were even more amazed by the even greater, but unfathomable, ingenuity that goes into packaging them in sellophane to ensure that we would never be able get into them. All part of life's rich pattern...

Having settled into our hotel and had a quick omelette across the street, we headed for the *Marmotton* Museum, just ten minutes' walk away. In this Museum was a collection of Monet paintings which we'd never seen. There were water lilies in abundance and the famous *Soleil Levant*, which Howard said was the start of the Impressionist movement. They were displayed to great advantage in a basement gallery. In one of the water lily paintings, we could have *sworn* we saw a goldfish plop up out of the water to get some air - then plop back down again. And we could definitely smell the steam trains in the *Gare St Lazare*. We found it odd to see the *gardiens* sitting around, chatting to each other, seemingly disinterested in the great works of art which surrounded them. We couldn't understand why they were not staring in rapturous amazement. (It was a bit like reading a book through a Beethoven Quartet.) Then again, they saw them every day, so we supposed familiarity bred...not contempt but...well...familiarity.

Saturday 29th

First thing this morning saw us off to the Strasbourg St Denis market to buy our picnic for lunch and to book the *Brasserie Flo* for Sunday evening's supper. Then we went to the Thomson office to validate our tickets for the *Bateaux Mouches* and to buy our coach tickets for the return journey to the airport on Monday. On the *Métro*, a young woman suddenly hung up a curtain between two upright poles and, with the aid of a tape recorder, proceeded to entertain the carriage with a puppet show - a rabbit and a crow singing *What a wonderful world*. It was quite amazing and rather pleasant. How hard she must have worked. We didn't begrudge her some money.

Our picnic in the Tuileries was a great success, a notion seconded by the sparrows and pigeons. Some of the tiniest birds actually sat on the bread roll to have their lunch - we didn't blame them. After all it was much more hygienic than eating off the dusty floor. We really had overdone the strawberries for pudding so we earmarked the remainder for a midnight feast.

The Titian Exhibition at the Grand Palais was our next stop. It turned out to be Titian 'and chums' and the works of art had been collected from all over the world. Some had come from the National Gallery and the Queen's collection at Windsor. (Amazing how we could hardly see the scorch marks!) There was so much to see and we were reminded of our friend Geoff's comment after his visit to the Louvre: "Once you've seen one Rembrandt, you've seen them all". He was joking (we hope!) but with so many great works of art, it was easy to get visual indigestion very swiftly.

In the evening we ate at *La Fermette Marbeuf*, sitting outside watching the world go by.

Sunday 30th

Another of life's intriguing mysteries to start the day. Why is that that some showers (type 'A') seem to have little or no variation in water temperature - despite one's best efforts - while others (type 'B') can change from liquefied icebergs to boiling geysers with but a mere millimetre's turn of the tap. In the Hotel *Hameau de Passy*, we had type 'B'. The burn marks took a while to wear off. Perhaps one day we will be able to solve this enduring mystery.

To the Madeleine where we hoped for goodly organ playing and choral music. Last time we were here, and much to our amazement, there was a Sullivan hymn tune - *Lux Eoi. (Alleluya! Alleluya! Hearts to heaven and voices raise.)* Our hopes were realized, especially the two improvised pieces that the organist played for *L'Offertoire* and *Sortie*. They were 'really quite something' - the *Sortie* being improvisations on *Veni Creator* and *Credo in Unum Deum*. We could hardly believe our ears when some people started conversations during the *Sortie*, though how they could hear each other was a mystery, because Monsieur Houbart certainly 'let rip' and the decibel count rose somewhat. The Choir sang a Gounod Mass but the loud sections of it were all but drowned by Monsieur Houbart. In the case of the tenors, this was probably the best thing! Choirs in French churches are nothing like those in English churches. They are not robed and, here in the Madeleine, all appeared to be very informal. Indeed, the 'team' were a very disparate lot. It was said that they had come from the chorus of the Paris *Opéra*, but some of them looked a bit 'long in the tooth' for that. Perhaps when they reached a certain age, they were allowed to play pillars or trees or other bits of scenery, as and when required. The congregational responses were 'conducted' - I use that word rather loosely - by a Dennis Thatcher look-alike - after he'd had a few tinctures, we fancied. There was no point in him being there as the congregational singing was extremely nondescript. It made a run-of-the-mill C of E congregation sound like the Huddersfield Choral Society. The congregation wandered into the church at all sorts of times. There didn't seem to be much interest in the 1100 starting time. Still, it was full choral Latin Mass - and we didn't come across *that* too often. So, despite all the little quirks, we enjoyed it, especially the organ music and the organ itself. It whetted our appetite for the recital in the evening.

To *Chartier* for a swift lunch then on to our *Bateau Mouche* trip, which was included in the cost of our weekend. I slept until Notre Dame, but woke in time for the Eiffel Tower.

From the *Bateau Mouche*, we went straight to Notre Dame for the organ recital. We had been reliably informed that the organ was working again, having been out of action for renovation. Our spies were right but what we didn't know was that the recital started at 1730 instead of 1745. The consequence was that there was absolutely nowhere to sit. Eventually, we lit upon the base of a pillar, where we installed ourselves. We were seated facing the outside wall of the Cathedral, opposite two confessionals in side chapels. The first side chapel was occupied by a young couple who, we assumed, were having some kind of marriage preparation. How they could hear the priest, or each other, when the organ reached a fortissimo, we could not understand. The recital was being given by Olivier Latry, one of the four *Organistes Titulaires* of Notre Dame. His programme included César Franck, Louis Vierne, Maurice Duruflé and Jean Guillou. Another extraordinary aspect of these recitals is that people walk round the Cathedral throughout! It can only be compared to a very busy railway station in the height of the rush hour. We found ourselves in a rather surreal situation, seated in relative discomfort, watching the world go by in large quantities, very quickly, and, at the same time, watching a microcosm of the world going to Confession. The hordes of people who passed by didn't seem to be the remotest bit interested in the Cathedral - indeed, we thought some of them had come in out of the rain. There was something rather sad about it all.

The *Brasserie Flo* was up to its usual high standard. Half way through our meal, a party of sixteen Germans arrived. The poor waiter trying to take the orders was not helped by the fact that the only one of the party who appeared to speak French asked if they could pay 'individually in pairs'. This seemed to be an impossible request but, bearing in mind the great differences in prices of the items on the menu, it was the only fair way. The waiter waited, while the interpreter translated the menu into German for the assembled company. The request to pay 'individually in pairs' would not have seemed quite so difficult if the diners had been sitting in the pairs in which they intended to pay. They weren't! The resourceful waiter made a sterling effort to cope - by drawing out a large chart, with arrows, indicating who was with whom and who would pay for what. Imagine his consternation when he returned with the aperitifs, to find that some of them had moved - we think in an attempt to be helpful - so they were sitting near to or opposite the person with whom they were to pay the bill. We were mightily relieved that the resolution of this problem was not our responsibility.

We returned to our hotel for an early and relaxed evening and watched an extraordinary circus on television.

Monday 31st

Because we were getting old, we didn't go to the Sacré Coeur after our meal the previous evening. We left the visit until this morning. It was so different in the daytime. Though there were signs everywhere requesting SILENCE (in umpteen languages), it was clear that the majority of the human race could not read. It was rather reminiscent of the Notre Dame 'railway station' crowds of the previous evening. It made us realize how lovely it was to go to the Sacré Coeur at 2200 (which we usually did) when it was really quiet and quite beautiful. Why must people be so noisy?

To the Salvador Dali exhibition off the Place des Tertres. There was a large collection of things we'd not seen before. What a strange man S Dali must have been. How did his wife put up with him? Everything was so weird that the *Melting Watch* (of which there were many examples) is now 'old hat'. *Real* melting watches - that worked! - were on sale in the gallery shop.

Our time was drawing to a close so we went off to Les Halles for lunch at *Les Deux Saules*. We sat outside and had an excellent meal. We watched the strange passers-by, not to mention the couple who occupied the table next to us. Howard did not immediately understand my mime which was meant to indicate all the kilos of jewellery with which Madame was adorned - not to mention the bracelets and headgear. Perhaps she was an 'extra' in *Aida*?

A final visit to the birds in the nearby park to give them the remains of our breakfast bread, then it was time to return to Charles de Gaulle airport for our return flight. This time it was not delayed. They must have got the 'works on the line' sorted out over the weekend.

"I'm impressed - we don't go on holiday till tomorrow!"

ON THE LOOSE IN ANDALUCIA
January 1994

Sunday 16th

We flew to Malaga, where the time was one hour ahead of the UK. On arrival at our hotel in Benalmadena, we had time for a stroll before supper. (Benalmadena is the 'not quite so lager-louty' end of Torremolinos and, luckily, this was not the season for lager-louts. They crawled out of the woodwork in the heat of the summer.) Benalmadena was a picturesque and romantic spot, which we had visited before, so we knew all about the Marina. Once again we decided *against* buying a yacht.

Our search for an eatery drew a blank; that wasn't to say there weren't any, but any that there were, were deserted. The Spanish don't eat until much later and, as it was only 1900, it was much too early for a sighting of the natives, so we returned to the Hotel Riviera and ate there. To our great delight, it transpired that dinner was included in our trip, so we ate at no extra cost. We couldn't grumble at that and, furthermore, we reduced the average age of the diners quite considerably. The Hotel Riviera was certainly full of 'Young at Heart' people, but it was obvious that their hearts were the only bit of their anatomy to which that adjective applied. We were somewhat concerned as the information about the Cities of Andalucia Tour had indicated that 'This type of tour is not suitable for the less mobile'. We searched in vain for people who might be our travelling companions during the forthcoming week but it was clear that the assembled company would definitely fall into the category of the 'less mobile'. We supposed all would be made clear in due course so we put ourselves to bed to recover from the long journey and prepare ourselves for the days ahead - and all that culture we were going to soak up...

Monday 17th

Breakfast was at 0730 as we had a long journey ahead, including a stop in Gibraltar, before arriving at Seville later that day. We assumed, therefore, that our fellow breakfasters would be our fellow travellers - and that proved to be so. We watched each person come into breakfast. Certainly their average age was about the same as ours so we felt they could be described as 'more mobile' and therefore could qualify for the Cities of Andalucia Tour. When we finally assembled, we numbered only twelve though we had a full-sized coach with seating for about forty. Space and comfort were not going to present a problem, and there was plenty of room to swing the proverbial cat.

Our guide for the week was Antonio (Tony) and the Thomson representative who accompanied the tour was Patricia. Both seemed very pleasant - and so it proved. We were not quite certain what Patricia's role would be. We were no more certain by the end of the trip. Tony, on the other hand, was a mine of information, a marvellous guide and a lovely person who went out of his way to make sure we were all content. Not the slightest detail did he overlook. Indeed, some of the details we thought should have been dealt with by the Thomson representative, but all seemed to fall to the lot of Tony.

We set off to drive to Gibraltar and, as with the trip we did three years before, the drive took us through Marbella - home of film stars, tennis players, bank robbers (as we noted in 1991, they don't call this part of the world the *Costa del Crime* for nothing) and sundry other rich people. On to Gibraltar and this time the driver *didn't* point out where the famous IRA shooting had taken place.

We decanted ourselves into a mini-coach for the tour of the Rock, including another close encounter with the Barbary Apes. One of them leapt up to one of our companions, snatched the whole plastic bag full of peanuts which she had just bought to feed to them, opened it and scoffed the lot. Prior to this meeting with our ancestors, we had visited St Michael's Cave, a prehistoric area full of stalagmites and stalactites. It was a most evocative place, well lit with coloured lights and, of course, the inevitable background music. It was the Albinoni *Adagio* and I have to admit it sounded rather splendid in this setting - but why must we have sound at all? Why can't the human race appreciate silence, especially in such a place?

After a swift lunch back in town (omelette and *crêpe*), it was on to Seville via *Alcala de los Gazules*, where we partook of some *tapas* that Tony had recommended. We sat outside among the *real* orange trees. The Hotel *Porta Coeli* in Seville (though perhaps 'Gate of Heaven' was a *slight* exaggeration) was very comfortable but our attempts to use the electronic security box in our room were thwarted. Despite following each instruction to the letter, we failed to make it work. We merely succeeded in locking the key *inside* it. Nothing we could do would persuade it to *unlock*. We got a green light, followed by a red light which, according to the instructions, meant that we had to wait for twenty minutes until we could try again. Undeterred we went along to meet Patricia to arrange for the optional tours that we wanted to do during the week. Then it was time for supper where we met our travelling companions at close quarters. With only twelve of us on the tour, we reckoned that we should get to know each other - which would be good.

Tuesday 18th

A guided tour of Seville was on the programme for today, partly by coach then on foot. We had the services of an excellent local guide, Mario, who was a walking encyclopaedia about the city. We were taken to see the sight of EXPO 1992, a huge area just outside the town on which were constructed numerous buildings for all the countries taking part in EXPO. The statistics of the numbers of people who flooded into Seville for the six months of EXPO were staggering - much too staggering for us. It was clear that it had been 'a good thing' for the city. One of the people who had flooded in was a colleague of Howard's who had spent some time there working at EXPO. She had given us some good tips for eateries in Seville. There had been a similar EXPO-type thing in the city in 1929 and a number of very elaborate buildings had been erected but these were dotted all over the city, rather than being concentrated on one site. A most interesting place for us was the cigarette factory where Carmen was reputed to have worked - before she became entangled with the bullfighter. There was no Government Health Warning on the exterior, though maybe that was because the factory was now part of the University of Seville.

The walking part of the tour took us past the monument to Christopher Columbus, through Santa Cruz, the old Jewish Quarter (at least, it *had* been Jewish until the Christians had forcibly removed them), past a statue of Don Giovanni (or rather the gent on whom the Don Giovanni character was modelled) and on to the Cathedral. As Mario said "Christianism (sic) had a lot to answer for at one time" - but the Cathedral made up for lots of things. It was the third largest in the world, the first two being St Peter's in Rome and our own St Paul's in London. Seville Cathedral was rectangular rather than cruciform so we were fooled into thinking it was not as long as it might be. But it was - and was huge by any standards. The altarpiece went right up to the ceiling. It had more than 1,000 figures on it, painted in gold leaf, and the higher up the figures were, the larger they were. That was done so that all the figures looked the same size. Apparently the highest ones were life-size. Mr Columbus was entombed there, on a raised dais - at least we *hoped* it was Mr C. There was some argument whether it was Mr C or his son. Mr C's mortal remains had been moved four times before finally ending up here but historians and experts think that, at some point, Christopher's remains got mixed up with his son's - how careless some people can be!

The Cathedral was the end of the guided tour so we made our way back to the Santa Cruz quarter and found ourselves some lunch. We ordered just in time because a party of twenty-eight Japanese tourists descended on the restaurant. We wondered how long it would take for them to order, but it was obvious that the meal had been pre-ordered for them so they were able to get on with it in their inscrutable way. We more scrutable souls, refreshed by our lunch (which had included one of our all-time favourites, *gazpacho*) made our way to the Alcazar - a mini-Alhambra - but no less ornamental, and mosaiced at every turn - walls, floors and ceilings.

In the evening we went to a flamenco show, which was one of the Thomson optional excursions. *What* a sight! It made our legs feel exhausted just watching them! The performers were excellent and, in the way of flamenco dancers, they spent most of the time looking either haughty or upset or as though they had an unpleasant smell under their noses. Some of the time they were accompanied by recorded music, inevitably including gems from *Carmen*. The remainder of the time the accompaniment was two guitars and two 'singers' - though singing is perhaps too exact a word to describe what they did. It was more 'wailing' in a rather tuneless quarter-tone way. Only one of the two singers sang at a time. Meanwhile his colleague looked on, clapping, in a rather desultory manner. At a certain point, they swapped roles. Though the guitarists were very skilful, the harmonic interest could have been more adventurous. There was a preponderance of tonic and dominant - mainly dominant - with everything ending on the dominant chord, in the way of Spanish guitar-type things. What the music lacked in harmonic interest was more than made up for by their skilful and highly decorated treatment of the material. And let it be appreciated, it is not easy to harmonize in quarter-tones on the guitar. This was real Spanish guitar playing *par excellence* Some of the younger male dancers performed in such a dervish-like fashion that we imagined they were driving themselves into a frenzy. It was a good evening and restored our faith in flamenco dancing. Our previous experience of such was on our honeymoon in 1980 when, after much *sangria* and a rather long flamenco-only show (undiluted by any other form of entertainment), the particular art form had begun to pall.

Wednesday 19th

To Cordoba today, arriving at 1130 with time for a guided tour of the Cathedral and their Jewish quarter, though, once again, no Jews lived there any more. The Cathedral was, first of all, a Mosque, started in the eighth century, but when the Moslems were thrown out, the Christians built a church *inside* the existing mosque. It was one of the most enormous buildings we had ever seen, bigger (we thought) than St Peter's, Rome, St Paul's, London or Seville Cathedral - but perhaps they didn't count this one as it was not built originally as a Cathedral. With hundreds of pillars (literally) inside its walls, we assumed it must qualify for some world record or other. The Christian part of it, which only occupied a section of the original mosque, was also huge. It contained a Choir with 106 seats in carved mahogany. There were many more mind-blowing facts to take in from our local guide Christopher. He spoke so slowly and in a most peculiar English accent that we had to concentrate very hard to follow what he was telling us. We never *did* catch the names of the caliphs and other Eastern potentates. It was obvious that he had invested in a new set of false teeth for the purpose of pronouncing all the names.

In the afternoon, we were taken to the remains of a palace, the Madinat Al-Zahra, which had been built originally around 900AD. After thirty years of construction, others came along to whose taste it was not, so they spoiled it, plundering much of the decoration (marble, pillars etc.) for themselves. It had been buried over the years until quite recent times, when it had been excavated. The work was still ongoing; it was an enormous task and a remarkable archaeological undertaking. The experts had unearthed, and, in many cases, pieced together and reconstructed, what was now on view. Tony, the guide who took us on this trip, was a mine of information about the whole place.

Just outside the archaeological site were a couple of fields of fighting bulls. They were grazing when we saw them - must have been their lunch hour. Tony told us that they belonged to El Cordobes, one of Spain's most famous bullfighters, who had been retired for about fifteen years. The weather had warmed up to 12C so we saw everything under ideal conditions. Tony said it would not be possible to bring people here at the height of the summer as the temperature would be about 45C - *in the shade* - and people tended to collapse in the heat. Converting 45C into Fahrenheit was not our strong point - but we did know it was *very* hot!

The best dinner of the tour so far happened in the hotel that night. All twelve of us sat together and tables had been reserved just for our party. We needn't have worried because there were no other diners except we twelve, our guide, driver and Thomson representative.

Thursday 20th

Granada was our destination for today. (We didn't know Granada meant 'pomegranate' until we got there. Might be a useful piece of information for quizzes in the future.) The drive took us through a mountain area where every hillside was covered in olive trees. Tony, the guide, told us there were 3,485,002 trees. He assured us that this was correct because he had counted them! We were not sure whether to believe him; by the same token, had he *really* been a basketball player and a bullfighter? The explanation of how the olives were collected and how the olive oil was subsequently produced made us realize why it is such an expensive commodity.

In Granada, we stayed at the Hotel Los Angeles, a relatively small hotel in comparison with those we'd so far sampled. This one was run by a family rather than being part of a hotel chain. There was a swimming pool, at the bottom of which was the Olympic symbol, but with only three rings instead of five. Howard concluded that they had held three fifths of the Olympic swimming championships there. We had lunch in the hotel, where a sign on the window of the restaurant indicated that it seated 400 people. With bated breath, we awaited the arrival of the other 398. After a while, Arthur and Barbara from our party joined us after one course. The other 396 never *did* arrive.

In the afternoon, we had a tour of the old Arabian quarter, where we encountered a large number of four-footed friends. Then it was off to the Carthusian Monastery. This was no longer occupied and was, in effect, a museum. We were told that it had been home to a very strict silent order. The cells in which the monks lived had long since been destroyed but the small cloister, sacristy, chapel and the refectory survived. Men of the town were allowed to attend services in a very restricted area of the chapel. Women were not allowed anywhere near as the monks were not allowed to see women! Considering it was such a strict order, it was a most elaborately decorated place with fantastic carvings, paintings and gold-leaf-covered 'everythings' everywhere. The sacristy was a work of art in itself - and then, in a chapel behind the High Altar, was the *most* decorated part, which was only entered by the Prior. The other members of the Community received communion through little holes in the wall - so they never saw the most wonderful part of the whole building. It struck us as amazing, and not a little sad, that all this existed but was unseen to all except a strict order of monks. The gift shop was full of some of the most trashy plastic *religioso*-type things we'd ever seen.

On to the Royal Chapel in Granada where were buried King Ferdinand and Queen Isabella, King Philip the Good-looking (yes, he really *was* thus known!), Queen Joanna the Mad and Prince Michael, who died aged only five. Apparently King Philip the Good-looking spent his time chasing other women, which is why Joanna went mad. Who could blame her? Ferdinand and Isabella had requested that they be buried very simply. According to all accounts, they were modest folk, considering their time and position. Their coffins were in a small crypt in the Chapel. The rest of the place, built by Charles V, was a sumptuous place, full of the most amazing effigies, paintings, sculptures and religious paraphernalia of all descriptions.

Friday 21st

0900 saw us at the gates of the Alhambra. Remembering our visit three years previously, this time we were much better prepared. We had donned lots of extra layers, two pairs of gloves and I had my coloured socks with eyes, which were much admired by the rest of the party. They all agreed that, should an avalanche cover me in the Sierra Nevada, all I would need to do would be to put a coloured sock on a stick and the St Bernard dog, complete with brandy, would have no difficulty in locating me.

The Alhambra tour was slightly different from the one we had done before and we saw some parts that we had not seen previously. We had the services of an excellent local guide who told us that we would never see any red paint in the palace, the reason being that it was very difficult to put red onto ceramics. We learned that when the last Arabian ruler left the Alhambra (he and his people were starved out so, eventually, they surrendered to King Ferdinand and Queen Isabella), as he was riding away from it, he turned round to have one last look - and he cried. His mother said "Now you cry like a woman because you did not defend like a man". (With friends like her, who needs enemies?) The guide went on to say if that's what his *mother* said, what would his mother-*in-law* have said? We wondered if the guide had mother-in-law problems because he also said that, though the Arabian kings had 300 wives in the harem, they did *not* have 300 mothers-in-law!

After the tour of the palace, we moved into the Generalife Gardens. This was the horticultural equivalent of the palace, and the guide was anxious to point out that it was not pronounced 'General Life' (like some kind of insurance company) but 'Henairaleefay'.

Back at our hotel, we had a Lumumba - brandy in hot chocolate - to which Tony had introduced us on a previous refreshment stop. It was a wonderful antidote to the cold weather! As it was almost lunchtime, we found a secluded little place for lunch then did some shopping before returning to the hotel for a much needed siesta. We were not really interested in supper, having had such a large lunch, so we whiled away the time watching Torvill and Dean win yet another skating competition.

Saturday 22nd

Today was our last day together as a group. We had been very lucky with our travelling companions; we could not have wished for a better crowd. The drive back from Granada to Malaga took us through Nerja (pronounced 'Nairheear') which was known as 'The Balcony of Europe'. Tony took us to the very large balcony overlooking the Mediterranean, from which we could see how it got its name.

On to Benalmadena where we were to stay, once again at the Hotel Riviera, for our last night. One other couple were returning to Gatwick at the same time as us but the remaining eight were staying on for a week in the sun. At dinner we said our final goodbyes to our new-found friends before an early night to prepare for our return to the UK next day. We hoped to be home by 2030 but as travelling was always tiring, a good deal of advance rest was a sensible precaution.

Sunday 23rd

We had a late breakfast which gave us time to read a day-old English newspaper on our balcony before setting off for the restaurant which we had found three years ago, El Roqueo, back in Torremolinos. On the way, we ran into John and Beryl, two of our travelling companions from the week. We took a stroll in the sun along to El Roqueo where we arrived an hour too early, so we spent some time with John and Beryl over a pre-prandial drink. (It was strange to think we shall not see any of these people again after today.)

Our meal at El Roqueo did not disappoint. The waiters remembered that we had to catch a plane (we had mentioned this when we called in to book the table) and the meal was served promptly, much to my delight as I find it difficult to 'eat against the clock'.

At 2030, it was a great pleasure to be back home and to make a *real* cup of tea, before turning in for a night's sleep in our very own bed.

D-DAY LANDING
April-May 1994

This year marked the fiftieth anniversary of D-Day (June 6th 1944) and many events were organized on both sides of the Channel. We took this trip with our friend Janet and her mother, Dorothy. Janet, Howard and I were ashamed of our lack of knowledge of the details of D-Day, Mulberry Harbour, Pegasus Bridge etc. We had a vague idea what it was all about and we knew it was an extremely important event in the history of the Second World War but we had much to learn. Dorothy, however, was truly a *vétérane de la Deuxième Guerre Mondiale* and was much more knowledgeable.

Thursday April 28th

After work and a potato Bolognese (yes, it does exist!) at our flat, we drove to Portsmouth to catch an overnight crossing to France. Sailing was at 2330 and we thought it was smooth and uneventful. We could not be certain because we were dead to the world for the duration.

Friday April 29th

After disembarking at Ouistreham, the port for Caen, we found our way to the *Bar des Fleurs*, where we had our first authentic French breakfast of bread and various jams. We were thrilled to see that our paper placemats were emblazoned with 'Welcome to our Liberators'! We were to see many such notices during our stay but, this being the first, our little British hearts swelled with pride, even though most of us were not of an age to liberate anyone in June 1944; indeed, I was not even a speck on the horizon. An English family came into the café. They were travelling in a real 'old crock', such as would have done the London to Brighton race proud. At our last sighting of it, however, it was being towed off the ferry, so we were rather surprised to see it looking hale and hearty.

We couldn't get into our hotel until midday so we had planned to go straight to the beach at Arromanches to see the remains of the Mulberry Harbour. We asked ourselves what the men must have felt like, leaping off their boats into waist-high, cold water. We encountered a real live D-Day veteran, making his first return to the beach since the day he landed there in 1944. Needless to say, he was a mine of information. He told us that he and his comrades had been imprisoned in their transit camps for three weeks before D-Day, such was the secrecy that surrounded it. He said the 'powers that be' had declared that they were prepared to lose one million men to achieve this landing. It was *that* important - as we were to appreciate many times during the course of the weekend. Inevitably, many thousands were lost - on both sides. One of our guidebooks told us that both the Allies and the Germans lost 10,000 men each on D-Day alone. There was still much to be seen of the remains of the Mulberry Harbour - and we assumed this would be the case for many years to come. A most interesting visit to the Arromanches D-Day Museum followed - where our education about D-Day began in earnest. It was all so sad.

We learned immediately that there were five main beaches: Utah and Omaha Beaches (American), Gold and Sword Beaches (British) and Juno Beach (Canadian). Our first picnic lunch was taken in a park quite near to the Omaha American cemetery. In the park were two memorials, both large, but a third, a very small cross, was most moving. That was for a platoon of German soldiers, also killed at this spot. So many young men ended up as names on a memorial. Was there *really* any sense in all this - especially after the First World War must have been equally (if not more) horrific?

Eventually, we made our way to the hotel for a well-earned rest (especially for Janet who had done all the driving) before setting out for a buffet supper at *Le Chantegrill.*

Saturday April 30th

We noticed that already many coaches were disgorging veterans and families into hotels all round the area. We could only imagine what it would be like on June 6th itself. There wouldn't be an inch of space between the visitors. Perhaps some would come in time for June 5th, the original date for D-Day. It had to be postponed due to adverse weather conditions, though, from what we had learned, the conditions on the day they *did* do it were atrocious and many of the troops were in various stages of queasiness when they landed.

We made our way to the Abbaye aux Hommes (Eglise Saint-Etienne) in Caen to see, amongst other things, the tomb of William the Conqueror. We were led to believe that the only 'remain' that remained was a femur, the rest of him having been scattered to the four winds when the church was desecrated during the French Revolution. We had hoped for a guided tour but it wasn't possible as there were numerous weddings in the Town Hall, which formed part of the church 'complex'. We had hoped to see a painting of William the Conqueror dressed up as Henry VIII, but it was not at home. It was on loan to an exhibition in Rome. They had a postcard of it - but somehow it wasn't quite the same.

We took our picnic to a grassy glade below the walls of the Château which had been built by William the Conqueror. Suitably refreshed we felt able to storm the ramparts. We stormed them as far as we could but there were building works happening…made us feel quite at home.

In the evening we tried out *Le Boeuf Ferré,* which Howard had found for us.

Sunday May 1st

This morning we went to the 'Memorial', a very modern museum, cleverly devised and constructed to show the history of what *led up* to the War, what happened *in* the War and what had happened *since* the War. The films (of which there were three) were particularly impressive. There was wonderful old black and white film of the battles - heart-rendingly sad - but very clear. We were used to films of that era being a dark, flickery difficult-to-follow representation of events, but it was clear that the experts had been able to enhance these to a high degree. It was quite unforgettable. On a split screen, we watched the Allies invading the beaches (on the left hand screen) and the Germans defending them (on the right). We thought it might be too muddly, having two screens happening simultaneously, but once we got accustomed to what was going on, it was quite marvellous. Museums, however interesting, are so tiring so, after a while, we refreshed the inner man and woman at the little cafeteria within the site. The ladies of our party were given *muguet* (lily of the valley) at the check-out, as it was May 1st. Howard explained that it was traditional to do this on May 1st.

Our final visit was to Les Floralies de la Paix, the Peace Garden, officially opened only the previous day. There was a rose garden which would, one day, have a wonderful display of roses, but as this was only Day Two, there were no roses to be seen. There were plenty of other *floribunda,* however, so we were not disappointed. To familiarize ourselves with the terrain, we took a little trip on a train which travelled round the gardens. The weather couldn't have been kinder, and we felt bold enough to investigate the Maze. As the Maze was only two days old also, the hedges were only twelve inches high so it was not difficult to look over them to find our way.

Dorothy treated us all to supper back at the *Le Chantegrill* before we retired for an early night. We had a long day ahead of us and the combination of fresh sea air and sun had a soporific effect - not to mention the goodly food and *boissons* of which we had partaken.

Monday May 2nd

Our first stop today was the famous Pegasus Bridge, the first thing to be taken by the Allies during the night of 5th/6th June 1944. We could see how it was absolutely essential to capture, but not destroy, this bridge over the Caen canal. On this date, paratroopers were dropped into the area to carry out this dangerous mission. Later that morning, 135,000 men and 20,000 vehicles were brought in by sea onto the five landing beaches. The organisation of the whole enterprise must have been mind-boggling, to say the least. The original Pegasus Bridge had recently been removed, much to the annoyance of the veterans, and its replacement was still under construction. Perhaps it would have been better to have deferred this construction until after June 6th, but it was not to be. The official opening was due to take place in two weeks. We visited the world famous Pegasus Bridge Café and their D-Day Museum.

We bought our final picnic and took it along to a beach. Lunch was taken looking out over the English Channel. England was too far away to be seen, but we were convinced it was over there - somewhere. We enjoyed our sand-filled French bread - there really is nothing quite like it. It was rather a fine picnic, though we said it ourselves.

We caught the 1630 ferry back to England and, after the long drive back from Portsmouth, we were back home by 2330. All that remained was to thank Janet so very much for being our chauffeur.

PARIS FOR *LE WEEKEND*
May 1994

Thursday 26th

We had arranged to start this weekend with our favourite aunt Lorraine in Redhill so that we would be much nearer to Gatwick for our 0730 (!) flight. Not only was that a good idea from a practical point of view, but there could be no better way to start *any* weekend.

Friday 27th

0600 saw us creeping out of 12, Ridgeway Road. We caught the 0622 train to Gatwick where we arrived at 0635. We had thought that would allow plenty of time to check in for the 0730 flight. What we had *not* bargained for was the fact that we had to join a very long queue - in Zone F - made up of everyone who was taking a British Airways flight to anywhere in Europe! There was no separate check-in desk for Paris, or for any other destination. It was 'every European for himself'. We made it to the head of the queue by 0715. The plane was due to leave in fifteen minutes! Predictably Gate sixty-three, where our flight was waiting, was just about the furthest gate from where we were. An Olympic sprint, taking in passports and security (Howard was detained because of his keys) meant we got there by the skin of our teeth!

Charles de Gaulle Luggage Reclaim got only two out of ten. We found ourselves on the perimeter of the large circular Arrivals building, but there was no central information point to indicate the whereabouts of luggage by flight numbers. The result was a huge number of people milling about asking each other if they knew where luggage from any particular flight might be! *Surely* this could be improved? (A word with that nice Mr Mitterand when we see him.) When we *did* track down the relevant carousel, our brightly spotted case was the first one to appear. What joy! Did it mean that, because our case must have been the last on to the plane, it was therefore the first off? We always wondered about that and never found the answer. Presumably the luggage had to be stored in some sort of scientific way, rather than randomly 'flinging it all in'?

We took the train into Paris then the *Métro* to our hotel, Arcade Bastille, just five minutes walk from the Opéra Bastille. *Tosca* was on, but all the performances were *complet*, so we were not able to see Mr Domingo. In any event, the tickets would have been astronomically expensive. We had lunch at a little eatery a few streets behind the Place de la Bastille after which our next quest was for a bank. We had 'come by' two American $100 notes and we wanted to change them into French currency. (I am fascinated to know how we 'came by' them - the passage of time does not permit my memory bank to download the answer.) The exchange facility was closed at the first bank we tried. Access to it was through two locked doors through which customers were admitted by the staff. The French seemed much more security conscious than us. The *Banque de France* was across the road. Once again, locked doors were opened to admit us. The first thing we saw was a large sign indicating that American $100 dollar notes could not be changed as, apparently, there had been a large number of forged ones in circulation. The sign went on to say that the only place in Paris which *would* change them was the *Banque de France* at the Palais Royal. We got there *just* before it closed (1600) and we realized this was the equivalent of our Bank of England! There was airport-style security here; our bags had to go through an X-ray machine and we had to go through a metal detector. The banking hall was huge with a large number of *guichets* and an enormous marble table in the centre, at which we sat to divide the proceeds of the $200, now changed into francs. This was a precaution we took so that, in the event of either of us being robbed, we would not lose all our money.

Our next quest was to find the *Brasserie Bofinger* where we made a reservation for our evening meal.

Back at our hotel, over our pre-prandial drink, we came across an interesting article in the Evening Standard entitled 'US copies Britain over forgers'. It went on to say 'The US may introduce dollar bills with a metal strip, like those in English notes, to counter a flood of forgeries from Iran.' No wonder the banks were unwilling to change ours.

The *Brasserie Bofinger* was very old, and very 'mirrored', so we were able to observe our fellow diners without seeming to be so doing. As in the *Brasserie Flo*, the waiters rushed about, sliding on the highly polished floor. They rushed even when there was hardly anyone in the restaurant. Our meal was excellent.

The next adventure was how to use the telephone using a credit card. It wasn't quite as simple as we thought, because the instructions (in four languages) did not mention that certain digits had to be omitted! How were we supposed to know that? We didn't, of course, but a very helpful passer-by explained it to us.

Saturday 28th

Breakfast in the large Ibis hotel was buffet-style, much to our delight. Some facets of it caused us problems; how to use the fruit juice machine and how to make tea and coffee without ending up with a large proportion of it all over our shoes. The array of equipment was rather daunting.

We set off for the *Galeries Lafayette*, Paris's equivalent of Selfridges. Here we were successful in purchasing two birthday presents and using the discount card provided for us by the Thomson office, so ten per cent was deducted from our bill. We learned the word for an apron - *tablier* - after endeavouring to describe it in mime to an assistant. We went to the food department to buy the wherewithal for our picnic lunch. On the way to the Tuileries gardens to picnic, we called into the Madeleine to check on the time of the service on Sunday and to find out what music was to be performed.

The one thing we lacked were plastic cups for our wine. A brilliant thought crossed our minds: whenever we went to the Thomson office to enquire about anything Parisian, the first thing they did was to offer as a glass of wine - in a plastic glass! We thought of a question: what time was the organ recital at Notre Dame on Sunday? It worked; we were given our plastic glass of wine. We had not realized that it had been a wise question as we were told there would not *be* a recital, as the organ was under repair. We chalked up our strategy as a two-fold success; not only did we have the receptacles for our picnic but we saved ourselves from making a wasted journey on Sunday. We would go to the recital at St Eustache instead.

The picnic in the *Tuileries* was the usual success - for us and the birds. Next stop was the *Bateau Mouche* trip on the Seine. (Though we had done this on a number of occasions, as the ticket was part of the weekend, we didn't see any reason not to do it again. After all, it is a painless way of seeing Paris.) On the way to the *bateau*, we ran into Ernest and Celia Yeo, friends of Howard from the Bach Choir. They were in Paris for a week and we agreed that we might all meet up at the St Eustache organ recital. It was always rather tiresome having to listen to the commentary on the boat in a number of languages, and we thought they had increased the number since we last visited. There seemed to be *seven* of them now! Luckily English was the second one so when the commentator said "Coming up on the left...", it really *was*. For those in language number seven, the *bateau* would have long since passed the relevant monument or sight.

Back to the hotel where we had a less than impressive supper in the restaurant. Never mind - a performance on television of *The Marriage of Figaro*, 'live' from the new Glyndebourne, occupied our evening to advantage. During the long interval there was a programme about the Second World War, showing archive film put out by the Germans. It showed things from the German viewpoint, or, at least, from the viewpoint from which they *wanted* it to be seen. It occurred to us that we had seen hardly anything in this city about D-Day; just one or two posters mentioning it. Perhaps there would be much more about the Liberation of Paris in August.

Sunday 29th

Today was the French equivalent of Mothering Sunday and they were just as commercially-minded about it was we were in England. In every shop, by every article, signs indicated how thrilled Mamam would be to be given this on the *Fête des Mères*. We couldn't think of any *mère* who would be thrilled to receive a vacuum cleaner as a *cadeau*, but then, perhaps the French *mères* had different tastes?

We went along to the Madeleine for High Mass. As we were early, we walked round the block, taking in the British and American embassies and a cluster of very expensive shops, selling perfumes and other extravagant things. So many shops didn't display any prices - always a sign that we couldn't afford anything in the window. (I remember my mother saying 'If you have to ask how much something is, you can't afford it". She was right.) Some prices we did see, in what were (obviously) the cheaper shops. Some men's shoes were advertised at £200 (yes, pounds - we did the conversion) so we were forced to admit that we couldn't afford the 'cheaper' shops either!

Outside the Elysée Palace, a *gendarme* told us that the nice Mr Mitterand was at home, but was still asleep, though it was now 1015. Howard mused that Mr M might have had an exhausting time the previous night, interviewing the prospective lady Prime Ministers!

Back at the Madeleine, we awaited the start of High Mass at 1100. What a shambles it turned out to be at the start. People 'came and went' until about 1115, making no attempt to enter or leave quietly. Everyone chatted away to their friends, quite regardless of the fact that the service was in progress. People took flash photographs throughout. Immediately in front of us were three children who were not well behaved (understatement?). Why the parents had not brought some books for them to read, we couldn't imagine. Instead, two of them ran about, climbed on and off the free-standing chairs and, despite threats/entreaties from the father, continued in like manner for the whole of the service. Mother seemed to disown them! We were anxious in case the chairs fell backwards, depositing *les petits* on the floor, when 'all hell would have broken loose'. It was rather unconducive to worship. The choir singing was rather raucous, as we had found on previous visits. As the Choir was made up of singers from the Paris *Opéra*, Howard suggested that perhaps it was time for re-auditions! The organist was excellent and made up for all the other deficiencies.

We headed to *Chartier* for lunch. The size of it always took our breath away and the speed of the service likewise. The waiter wrote down our order on the paper tablecloth - rather than on a pad - so, presumably he had to remember what had been ordered and by whom. When it was time to pay, he added up the total on the paper tablecloth and then threw the cloth away - *after* we'd paid.

In the evening, we went to the organ recital in St Eustache. We concluded that organists were ignored here just as they are in England. We could find no signs or leaflets to tell us who was playing or what was to be played. The titles of the pieces were announced through a 'whispery-voiced' microphone, from which we caught only scant details. Not surprisingly, there was a very small audience indeed, certainly compared to Notre Dame where 2,000 people packed the Cathedral for the Sunday evening free recital. No sign of the Yeos so we went off for our meal at the *Brasserie Flo*, which was excellent, as usual.

Monday 30th

Our last morning had arrived so we took the opportunity of going to the Louvre to see the newly opened Salle Richelieu. What a place! After ninety minutes in there, not only were we culture-saturated but our feet just didn't belong to us any more. The new Salle Richelieu was laid out wonderfully and was very light and airy. Many of the exhibits that previously had not been displayed due to lack of space, now had an outing. It was a 'well worth the detour' type place.

Our reward for such intense mental activity was lunch at the *Repaire de Cartouche*, a former hideout of the French equivalent of Robin Hood.

Back at Charles de Gaulle, I fell off the top of an escalator as I was not paying attention to where I was going. The result was that the tray, so carefully selected for a friend's birthday and carried as hand luggage so it would not get broken in the suitcase, got broken! *C'est la vie…*

Back home by 2115 to be greeted by new curtains and a new sofa bed, which had arrived on Saturday. It made coming home even *more* pleasurable.

e-Mahler

TREASURES AND LANDSCAPES OF CENTRAL EUROPE
or
SIZZLING IN SWITZERLAND AND SAXONY
July 1994

The Jules Verne brochure advertised this holiday as *Treasures and Landscapes of Central Europe*; the subtitle was ours. We took this holiday with our friend Hazel.

Saturday 23rd

We let the Piccadilly Line take us to Heathrow Terminal 2. When we joined her in the queue, Hazel had already met up with the Jules Verne representative. In spite of the French air traffic controllers' strike, boarding was not delayed, though take-off was, as there was such a vast amount of traffic this weekend, the first weekend of the annual holiday for many.

Our flight to Zurich took just seventy-five minutes and by the time we disembarked, Hazel had met two Glaswegians, Frances and June, who were on our tour. The coach transfer to Lucerne was efficiently handled which meant we didn't have to handle our luggage - a real bonus. Very soon we had our first sighting of Mount Pilatus, which we hoped to ascend the following day - probably not on foot, though it was only 7,000 feet. The Hotel Drei Könige was just what was needed, so after a good omelette and some excellent Lucerne wine (the waitress insisted, in what seemed like four languages at once, that it would be so good for us), we turned in to prepare ourselves for the lake and mountain adventure. Our party numbered twenty-seven and we wondered what our travelling companions would be like. Time would tell.

Sunday 24th

Christine, our guide, met up with us all at 0900 and briefed us about the week. The lecturer, Jaroslav Hanus, gave a much *less* brief 'briefing' about the history of the country. He was to prove very knowledgeable throughout and an extremely pleasant man - another bonus. The local Swiss guide, with the improbable name of Rita, had met us at the airport the previous evening and had shown us the remarkable Lion statue in the centre of Lucerne. We were intrigued to see that the ground floor in the lift was marked 'E'. Howard, being clever, pointed out that it stood for *erde* - as in *Das Lied von der Erde* of Mr Mahler. Why didn't I think of that? Our combined knowledge of German was minimal but, because of our musical connections, we discovered that our vocabulary was slightly larger than we thought.

Briefing over, we headed for the boat which was to take us for a two-hour trip on Lake Lucerne. The weather was perfect for such a trip and we had a front seat - in the back of the boat - from where we had unimpeded views of mountains, birds and cuckoo-clock houses. At Alpnachstad we disembarked and took a thirty-minute ride on 'the steepest rack railway in the world' to the summit of Mount Pilatus. The railway admitted to forty-eight degrees but some of the gradient signs that we passed indicated one in thirty-six. We marvelled at the feat of engineering that had constructed this. It took us to a height of 7,000 feet, which, vertically, is approximately one and a third miles. As we went along at varying angles, we estimated that *our* journey must have been between two and three miles. We overtook many intrepid walks, heading for the same place - but the hard way. The summit of Mount Pilatus was shrouded in cloud from time to time but the cloud was so fast-moving that, after hovering for a time, it was replaced by brilliant sunshine. I was happy as I had been wanting to reach 'cloud level' all morning.

At the summit, we had an excellent lunch which included *Ferment* wine, (which Hazel knew), and large ice creams to give us strength for the final assault. The restaurants were located at what turned out to be 'base camp'. We left Hazel at base camp and Howard and I made the final assault. We all emerged from cloud and so were able to wave to her from the top - to prove we had made it.

The descent from Mount Pilatus was taken in two cable cars, the first very large, holding about thirty standing people as it was a relatively short journey. The second stage was in individual cars, holding only four people - much more 'James Bond'-like. It was a very long way down and we sighted many more walkers from our glass-covered eyrie.

In the evening, we walked across the famous old *Kapellbrüche* in search of somewhere for supper. There was a vast choice of eateries, all of which were in full swing. We had another lovely *al fresco* meal, in front of a highly decorated house. The restaurant, too, was decorated but in more garish colours. The Panoramic Train awaited us the next day.

Monday 25th

First we had a coach ride back to Zurich. We joined the train at the station (where else?) and what huge long trains they had in this part of the world. But then, they had to cover huge long distances so we presumed this was the reason. Our Panorama Coach was ushered in, like a film star, and attached to the front of the train. It had been the *back* of the train, but, as it was a terminus station, that end suddenly became the front. Is that what the Theory of Relativity is all about?

Our group had the whole Panorama Coach to itself. There was also a lower deck in which some of our number chose to travel from time to time. The coach had its own bar and a steward who would travel with us all the way. It was all very comfortable - and air-conditioned. 'Air conditioning' was to be the mantra for the whole of the trip because the temperature was well into the 90's so it became the very essence of our existence. Lunch was taken in the restaurant car. It was a very long way back (we thought we were walking back to Zurich) and we appreciated our air conditioning even more when it became clear that most of the other carriages didn't have it. (Phew!) We were joined by Malcolm who turned out to be a very pleasant young man, very knowledgeable, with a sense of humour as silly as ours - well, *mine* anyway. Mild panic ensued when Malcolm got off the train from time to time to take photos. Admittedly he only got off at a station but we had visions of the train pulling out, leaving Malcolm snapping away, oblivious of the long walk that lay ahead of him. Lunch could be paid for in any of four currencies - what a task for the waiter! Needless to say, he had a calculator but, as far as we could tell, it wasn't *air* conditioned! We hoped the excessive heat wouldn't cause it to malfunction.

Christine announced a competition. The person who could remember all twenty-seven names by the evening would win a bar of Toblerone. Much silliness set in with people giving false names - people we would have least expected. It helped to break the ice in the party. Indeed, after an hour of asking people their names then trying to remember them, the ice had fairly melted. It was not too difficult as long as people remained in their seats - but some of them got up and moved around. (There must be something in the rules about that?) Christine wondered if we should re-enact *Murder on the Orient Express*. There weren't many volunteers to be the corpse, but rather an alarming number to be the murderer! (Were we wise to come on this trip? False names? Would-be murderers? It all helped pass the time.)

We arrived at a border where the train was boarded by armed German border guards. (We hoped they would have had Border Terriers with them but they didn't - an obvious oversight on the part of the German authorities. We made a note to mention it to that nice Mr Kohl when we next meet.) At the Czech border, some few miles further on, they wanted to see our passports but they didn't want to stamp them. All of us *wanted* them stamped so we could prove we had been to the Czech Republic - so they obliged. We had to wait fifteen minutes at the Czechpoint (spot the deliberate mistake) where several men had a wash at an old-fashioned water pump. One of them was our driver. Others washed their feet - then their socks!

In the evening, as we neared Prague, Jaroslav told us lots of information about the Czech Republic, previously part of Czechoslovakia. It was clear we were *never* going to be able to pronounce the place names, or things on menus, or *anything*, come to that! We concluded that the main problem with the Czech language was its lack of vowels. Perhaps we could find another country with a surfeit of vowels and, through the good offices of the EEC, the Czech Republic could import some - or swap some for consonants. The written language has peculiar accents on odd letters - not at all like French. One of them is a little 'v' - but then we were used to that, being intimately acquainted with Mr Dvorák - who should have a little 'v' over the 'r' but, would you believe it, my computer won't let me do it! Dvorák and Smetana are their heroes in these parts - which was super as musicians are mostly ignored, the preference being to name streets or buildings after politicians and military people. Jaroslav even mentioned where Dvorák and Smetana were buried - they really *have* made it to the 'big time' - almost as noteworthy as footballers.

After supper on the train, we arrived at Prague at 2115 and found, to our delight, that the Forum Hotel had air conditioning. Jaroslav was keen to give us a talk about the city at 2145 so we rushed up to our room to settle in before drinking in the culture. We failed to find the secret of the computerized room key, even though we had just shown Hazel how to do hers! We had to summon the help of a hotel employee. The secret seemed to be the speed at which you inserted and extracted the card. We learned something new every day. After a very swift turn around, we went down for the talk but the meeting room had to be vacated sooner than we thought. Jaroslav compressed 2,000 years of Czech history into fifteen minutes - no mean feat!

Tuesday 26th

Today we had a coach trip with the local guide, Helen. Her English was very good (especially compared to our Czech) but, inevitably, there were one or two amusing words which cropped up from time to time. For instance, in the Natural History Museum, she told us there were some 'dinner-soars'. Originally the plan was that we would not return to our hotel until 2300, after our evening meal. Our combined hearts sank because we really needed an early evening shower and rest, and never more so than now since the heat was in the upper nineties. We were amongst the youngest members of our party and we wondered how our older companions would cope. To everyone's delight the plan was revised to *include* an early evening return to the hotel.

The walking tour, led by Helen, was very interesting and she was exceedingly knowledgeable and enthusiastic about her city. She stopped at every possible place to point out things. We wished she had chosen *shady* 'possible places' to do the pointing out - but the blistering heat didn't seem to deter her at all - and it really *was* blistering. We visited so many churches, monuments and buildings of one sort or another that is would not be possible to list them all. We have the guidebooks and memorabilia of the city to remind us. We did not see Wenceslas Square, much to Jaroslav's dismay. Jaroslav was a native of Prague though he had lived in England for twenty-six years, but when the local guide was 'in charge', he could not interfere.

Back at the hotel we discovered that *everyone* had run into problems with their computerized room keys. That made us feel *much* better. Our next initiative test was how to get into the mini-bar - not that we wanted to use any of its contents, but we wanted to put *our* drinks inside. We had tips from our fellow travellers and, in a trice, we had cracked the secret of Hazel's safe. In our room, there was no problem as the key was already in the mini-bar door. Life felt infinitely better, having showered, rested and changed.

The International Hotel was previously a Russian hotel and very grim-looking on the outside. The evening was a success, though gastronomically, we didn't rate it very highly. The musical accompaniment was a little quartet of two violins, double bass and a zither-like machine - plus the odd singers and dancers. When the wine had flowed freely for a while, some of our party took to the floor.

We were back at the hotel by 2300 to find it operating on an emergency generator - and there were no lights in our rooms. There was a power cut throughout the city. We couldn't pack, which we'd hoped to do as it was an 0545 start the next day. Instead we cleaned our teeth by the light of my torch - and the silvery moon.

Wednesday 27th

No one had told the restaurant that our breakfast must start at 0615 instead of 0630. The natives were getting restless and attempts to gain access to the room were fruitless. Eventually, we *were* fed and watered and left for Dresden at 0715.

The first stop was the Castle of Karlstein, one of the 'not to be missed' sights of Prague. It was about twenty miles out of the city and, having left the coach in the car park, we had to undertake an ascent on foot to the reach it. It dated from the fourteenth century and was founded by the famous Emperor Charles IV. Much of it was closed to the public but the very informative castle guide knew his stuff and we were shown some wonderful fourteenth century frescoes and altar pieces. The part that *was* open to the public was very well maintained. Before the long descent back to the coach, we were allowed a 'drinks break'.

How welcome that was! The temperature when we left our hotel at 0715 was very pleasant. It lulled us into a false sense of coolness. By the time we rejoined the coach, it was back into the nineties and was only going to go up.

For part of the journey to Dresden, we went back to the Panorama Train. Our carriage steward, Walter, was the most patient of men because everyone was pressing him for cold drinks before the poor chap had got himself organized for the next leg of our journey. The carriage was very hot as it had been standing in the heat for the previous two days, since disgorging us at Prague. And it had a glass roof…Because of the different electrical systems on the main train and in our special carriage, it was not possible to produce enough power to work the air conditioning until the train got under way. We took it in turns to fan ourselves with the Jules Verne tour sign from the front of the coach. Lunch was in the train again, this time with Malcolm and Dorothy. The ordering of the meal seemed non-existent; we presumed it had been pre-ordered - until half way through, when a menu was produced(?). The air conditioning in the restaurant car was achieved by tying the windows in the open position with the ingenious use of belts from the gentlemen's trousers, and, on one occasion, Hazel's belt too. Failure to secure the windows in this way meant that they snapped shut again. But it added to the excitement of lunch and helped to pass the time.

We arrived at Rathen around 1500 to join a cruise ship on the river Elbe, to take us on the final leg of our journey to Dresden. The temperature was now in the high nineties. (Looking back on it from this distance of time, I think this was where my loathing of extreme heat started.) The boat was late. We stood under the shade of a tree where the temperature was only in the *middle* nineties; ice cream and cold drinks did nothing to cool us. Eventually, when the boat arrived, it wasn't the one that was expected but a much smaller vessel and, consequently, already very overcrowded. The one we *should* have had could not function as the level of the river was much too low. There had been no rain in these parts for many a long week. We had no idea how long this trip was to last; two to two and a half hours seemed to be the consensus of opinion. It turned out to be *four hours* - very hot, very crowded and with scores of children running around. It was amongst the worst four hours of our lives. All members of the group had only one thought in mind - a shower.

When we reached the Hotel Am Terrassenufer, it was a very new four-star edifice. We were unprepared for the fact that there would be no air conditioning in the rooms! It looked as if the management might have a riot on their hands as some members of the group were exceedingly vocal in their complaints. (Readers might find our insistence on air conditioning slightly trying. Rest assured that the lack of it made living *very* trying indeed. We were totally unused to such extreme temperatures and they were taking their toll.). The night was *very* hot and very uncomfortable.

Thursday 28th

During breakfast, two of our company were robbed of their holdalls which contained their passports and air tickets. Their day was spent at the police station, endeavouring to get their tickets re-issued.

Our local guide was Hannelore who took us on a coach tour of the city. The guidebook said 'Dresden is the most famous building site in Europe' and we could see why. Everywhere we looked rebuilding was happening. It was so sad to think that this city, like some English cities, was almost destroyed in the War. Where was the sense? The amount of rebuilding that had already been completed was phenomenal. As well as rebuilding of new things, much reconstruction of original buildings had taken place, using old photographs and very skilled craftsmen. When we compared what we saw with the photographs of what it looked like the day after the bombing, it made us realize just how skilled were the people who carried out this work.

At the end of the coach tour, Hannelore took us to the Zwinger, a sort of palace complex of art galleries and orangeries of Augustus the Strong from the early eighteenth century. (Was there an Augustus the Weak?) Hannelore was very thoughtful and moved from one shady spot to another to give us information. Inside the Zwinger, we had a 'Cook's Tour' of some of the most important paintings including the one that Charles Proctor had mentioned to us, Raphael's *Sistine Madonna*. We saw what was unusual about the clouds - they turned into cherubs! What a collection of masterpieces, under one roof!

Our next stop was Meissen where we were to see the famous Porcelain factory but before that, lunch had been pre-arranged and, much to everyone's delight, was included. What a complicated meal it turned out to be! Hannelore didn't have a very loud voice so when she gave out instructions, we couldn't always hear or understand them. It was not clear immediately that it was a set meal, so many of the group were consulting the menu, much to the consternation of the waitresses who were wondering what they would do with twenty-seven set meals if we all chose different things. When the situation was clarified, the contents of the set menu were disclosed. There was much putting up of hands if we did/did not want the soup, beef etc. This was further complicated as Hannelore referred to each course as a 'meal' - so there was a notion that *two* meals were on offer. There was more to come. Our party occupied five tables, three of which had large jugs of iced water. Howard and Hazel were at one such table. I was with Dorothy, Jaroslav and Melody - at a jug-*less* table. Our request for a jug of iced water could not be fulfilled. The waitress vouchsafed that the restaurant only *possessed* three jugs, so we couldn't have one! We tried to obtain iced water in other large containers, indicating Jaroslav's beer glass and suggesting that water in such a glass would be most acceptable. Four bottles of mineral water arrived, and, as swiftly, were removed. Much more shaking of the head and reiterating that there were only three jugs. Eventually we ended up with four beer glasses filled with sparkling mineral water. The meal was hot potato soup (just the thing for a hot a day!), sour beef, sauerkraut and dumplings followed by an ice cream confection. We thought our troubles were over but worse was yet to come. Perhaps the next bit is not for the faint-hearted...

After lunch, there was an optional visit to the Albrechtsburg Castle and thirteenth century Cathedral. Hannelore pointed out that it was all uphill, much of it in the sun (the temperature was still in the upper nineties) so only those who wanted to go should go - it would not be compulsory. (It was not a little unsettling when the guide told us that on a previous occasion when she had done this walk, she had blacked out!) The party split into two - the Castle and Cathedral viewers and 'The Others'. Howard was in the first group, Hazel and I took the easier option. At this point the story divides.

Hazel and I looked into a church, mainly to escape the beating sun. Back outside, we decided that, instead of retracing our steps, we knew we could find our way back to the coach by taking the parallel road and cutting through at a lower level. We bought some water and fruit drinks and set off to join the coach. At this point, we realized we were well and truly lost - and the coach was due to leave in five minutes. We asked directions twice, but our lack of German and their lack of English meant they were not the most productive conversations. Up and down, round and about we wandered, eventually returning to the church and the restaurant from whence we had come. I was convinced we could find the way from there, by retracing our steps. We were now well 'into injury time' for the coach leaving. With an uncertain degree of confidence, I led the way - and luckily it turned out to be right. (Phew!) At the last corner, John (one of our party) appeared, having taken upon himself the mantle of a search party. It was a classic 'maidens in distress saved by knight in shining armour' situation. We were embarrassed about being seven minutes late and apologized profusely to our companions. Little did we know...

At this point, there were only ten of us in the party as the plan was that the coach would drive to an agreed location to collect those who had gone to the Castle and the Cathedral. We were somewhat mystified, therefore, when the coach drove quite a way out into the countryside. We couldn't quite reconcile this with the fact that our friends were going to walk up a steep hill for twenty minutes. By now, the coach had run out of steep hills, but we assumed the driver knew what he was doing. That was a false assumption. Quite suddenly, we ran out of road, so we had to reverse about a mile up a hill, with quite steep sides. (All part of life's rich tapestry, we told ourselves.) Hazel and I were feeling less guilty by the second as our seven minute penalty clause faded into oblivion with this latest turn of events. Back we went into town and, by now, Geoff (one of our number) was helping the driver with the map reading. Eventually we arrived at the end of a road, thought to be the right one, but we could go no further because of road works! A second search party set out, in a variety of directions, with instructions to return in ten minutes, with or without the others. All did - except Geoff who was 'missing presumed still searching'. Geoff's wife was convinced he would have gone right to the top of the hill. (In *this* heat?) It is important to remember that of the ten of us in the coach, not one of us spoke German and the driver spoke no English. The resulting 'conversations' were memorable. How we wished we had had a tape recorder. Margaret had a German dictionary so with a combination of pointing, miming and searching in the dictionary for the odd word, we managed to work out what to do. Our attempts to communicate with the driver were somewhat less than useful. He replied with very very long sentences in German, not one word of which any of us could understand.

Time was passing. The next step was that Geoff's wife would wait at the foot of the hill for the return of Geoff. The remaining eight of us would be driven to the Meissen factory (we had no idea how far away it was) and the coach would return for Geoff and his wife. We noticed that the driver had a conversation with his office on his mobile phone. The content of it was a mystery to us, of course, as we could not understand what he said and he could not explain it to us, save for much mention of '*deutsche Damen*' (ie our German guide). In the nick of time, Geoff reappeared. Off we went to the Meissen factory where we met up with the other members of our party.

Their story. They had *discovered* that the road was blocked at what was to have been the meeting point. Having walked all the way *up*, to see the Castle and Cathedral, they had then walked all the way *down* to meet us. They walked all the way back to the top (not quite sure why) at which point Hannelore had said she felt ill! (The poor thing had either a heart complaint or was a diabetic - or perhaps both.) Suggestions of buses into town, taxis, phoning the coach driver all came to naught. Furthermore Hannelore did not have the coach driver's mobile telephone number! In the end, the group had walked all the way to the

Meissen factory. As it turned out, it was not very far out of town but it seemed a long way because they had already gone up and down to the Castle *twice*, followed by the additional walk - all in the blazing heat. They arrived in time to see the demonstration of the porcelain making, but it was *only* a demonstration. We didn't see the actual items being made in the factory. The shop closed at 1700 and it was now 1635 and many of our group wanted to make purchases. Melody got very angry! That made the guide feel even more ill!

Back at the hotel, there was much discussion about the events of the day. It reminded Dorothy of her trip to Albania some years previously. At the border, the border guards had shone torches into their faces to see if they were spies. (We couldn't quite see how this would have worked - unless they had had 'I am a spy' tattooed on their foreheads.) The food had been meat which was unrecognisable, the only alternative being cabbage with a fried egg on the top. The oddest thing was that there was an enormous statue of Stalin and, at the liberation, instead of demolishing it (as most other places had done), they merely crossed out his name at the bottom of the plinth! We wondered if they had put another name in its place. Dorothy turned out to be a well-travelled lady.

We had our evening meal in the hotel with Steve and Vera, an astro-physicist and mathematician respectively.

Friday 29th

Today was the only late start of the trip. We didn't meet up until 0945. We went to the Albertinum in the Zwinger to see the Green Vault and the Porcelain collection. This was preceded by a walk along the Balcony of Europe - so called because of the sweeping views along and across the Elbe. In the Green Vault were priceless gems and jewellery of every description. A coffee set was made of gold and inlaid with precious stones, some parts being covered in enamel as well - just to add that *je ne sais quoi* (?). (Our Nescafé would have tasted entirely different in this.) Then there were sets of jewellery worn by Augustus the Strong. He had one set for receiving dignitaries and a separate set for watching fireworks! The sets were something to behold, all real and astronomically expensive. (It gave me the idea of encrusting my socks with semi-precious stones on my return to London.)

Our next destination was Berlin where a drama unfolded on our arrival at the thirty-seven storey Hotel Forum. The temperature was still in the high nineties. Not only was there no air conditioning in the rooms (so they were literally oven-like), it was not possible to open the windows because of fixed double glazing. Christine, the guide, had a major revolt on her hands; a deputation asked if we could move to another hotel. That proved to be impossible. We were told that there were only two hotels in Berlin with air conditioning and, in one of those, the system had broken down - due to the intense heat! (It turned out that there were only two in the former *East* Berlin. In the former *West* Berlin there were lots of hotel with AC.) A few of us changed our rooms, but it made no difference. Suddenly, out of the blue, we had a phone call to say we could have fan! Why we had been selected for this great honour, we never found out. I asked if all our party would be getting fans. The answer was 'no' as there was only one fan in the hotel! (One fan in a thirty-seven storey hotel?) When the fan did arrive, however, the fan bearer had another two with her. (We never *did* find out who were the lucky recipients of those.) It did make a tremendous difference, so we gave it to Dorothy for the second night.

Howard had found us a wonderful restaurant, only a short taxi ride away so we sat outside in the (relative) cool of the evening and chewed over not only our supper but also the events of the never-to-be-forgotten day.

Saturday 30th

In the morning, a coach tour of Berlin was scheduled, including a visit to the Charlottenburg Castle and the Egyptian Museum. The first stop was the Brandenburg Gate. It was impossible to imagine what it must have been like when the Wall was there. At the Reichstag (their former parliament building and soon to return to being just that), there were some crosses attached to a fence, in memory of some of those who lost their lives trying to escape. (What right had any human being to imprison other human beings like that? It was all so angry-making - and sad.) A piece of the Berlin Wall had been kept intact so we were able to see it in the distance. As we walked up the steps of the Reichstag, we remembered that Hitler had trodden these very same steps some decades before. It was an odd feeling and it surely tested the Christian idea of forgiveness to the absolute limits.

We had lunch in the centre of town, not far from the Zoo. Considering it was a very busy shop-filled city, there was a distinct lack of restaurants. All the shops shut at 1400 on a Saturday and did not open again until Monday morning. The only exceptions were bakeries and florists. Apparently shops were fined very heavily if they flouted this rule.

Our way back to the hotel took us via the Olympic Stadium, built in 1936, and we were reminded that Mr Hitler refused to present a gold medal to Jessie Owen because he was black. Words failed! We three and Dorothy decided not to join the group for a meal on this final evening as Howard had his eye on a lovely restaurant where we felt it would be much more relaxed and quiet - and we would have better food. A telephone call told us that it was closed for the summer holidays, so we went to the thirty-seventh floor of our hotel where we had a wonderful meal with an equally wonderful view of Berlin by night.

Sunday 31st

The end of our holiday had come round far too soon. The one thing we would *not* miss was the heat, but we *would* miss the company of our group, who had been lots of fun. Along with Dorothy, we took a boat ride on the river. An air-conditioned cabin and cold *Apfelsaft* added to the pleasure! On the way to the boat, we had put our noses into the Cathedral. It was very big with a very big and impressive-looking organ, but sadly no postcards of it.

We had a salad lunch at a nearby café. We wanted to have it in the hotel because the Room Guide had indicated that the hotel café was open at 12 noon every day of the week. There must have been something special about July 31st 1994 because it didn't open! Reception said they would 'make a note of it, so it could be amended'. (So *what* could be amended?) That, along with the air conditioning problems and the lack of trays at breakfast did not endear us one little bit to the Hotel Forum Berlin.

We were at Tegel airport in plenty of time for our flight. We found the duty-free shop didn't open until half an hour before the plane was due to leave. When it did, it was little more than a shack behind a metal roller blind, which, when lifted, revealed its sparse contents.

We were back at Heathrow at 1815 and Hazel had laid on a car to meet us - with a chauffeur and darkened windows! It dropped us in Kennington then took Hazel to West Hampstead. It had been a super holiday but, at times, for me the heat had been unbearable. We vowed *never* to go to a hot place again.

A SUBTERRANEAN SAFARI - COURTESY OF EUROSTAR
November 1994

Monday November 28th 1994 saw the intrepid Spurrs taking their first *TransManche* trip - *sous-manche*. We had planned to go with the Franco-British Society but the dates they had chosen happened to be before the train service was operating, so that posed a minor problem. We revised our plans and travelled with our friends Rosie and John Searle, Rosie's sister Debbie and their mother, Cynthia, for whom this trip was a surprise birthday present. Eurostar was a very new thing indeed.

We had hit our first snag when trying to book the tickets a few weeks previously. I suppose we should have smelled a rat because the leaflet was entitled 'Eurostar Discovery Service'. The first thing to discover was how to buy a ticket. On October 24th, the day the booking opened, at the instant it opened, 0700, Howard telephoned the number advertised in the literature. He was still trying to telephone it thirty minutes later. A recorded voice kept telling him "The other line has cleared now...the other line has cleared now..." *ad infinitum*. (No, we didn't know what it meant either, except it certainly meant he couldn't get through to anyone, anywhere, to ask anything.) Research, via the operator and then via the engineers, confirmed that the message "the other line has cleared now" is code for "There is a fault on the line". Eurostar had been swift to learn from their colleagues at British Rail what to do to frustrate its passengers (customers?) without even trying. (It was rumoured that British Rail was running courses in this, so great is the 'frustrate-ability factor of the travelling public.) Undeterred by these telephonic impediments to progress, Howard *went* to Waterloo station that same morning, arriving soon after 0800, and purchased the tickets.

The day of our adventure dawned. Our four travelling companions had to get to Waterloo from Hampton Court but we strolled the short distance from Kennington in just over ten minutes, leaving home at 0730. Our tickets had to be fed into horrible automatic gates before going through the security check. There were steel archways, as in airports, but we were told to go *round the side of them* and therefore were not security checked. Why was this? We still don't know - but it was not very good from the point of view of security, especially as we had a kitchen knife in our luggage. This was purely for use with our picnic but the powers-that-be weren't to know that.

In the departure lounge, we met up with our friends and heard details of how Cynthia had found out about her surprise journey. She had thought it might be Eurostar - or Concorde - but she wasn't disappointed when it turned out to be the former. She had not been told the identity of the two other travellers, however - just that they were people she hadn't seen since 1976. Cynthia thought that if they were people she hadn't seen for so long, she was either out of touch with them altogether - or they were dead. We did our best to do a convincing impersonation of being alive, but it was not easy at that time of the morning. The Departure Lounge was also very airport-like - comfortable and quite spacious - though whether we would be saying that if it was a completely packed train in the height of the summer holidays was a matter for conjecture.

Time to board the 'iron horse'. Our seats were in carriage number two of eighteen and the train was about nine yards short of a quarter of a mile long. Access to the platform was via a series of escalators which were positioned to coincide with specific carriages. All the seats were numbered and reserved at the time of booking so we knew in advance where we would be sitting. There followed much taking of photographs. John had a video which also had audio things on it so posterity would be able to hear our inane comments like "Isn't it long", "Are you sure you can get us all in?". There was nothing quite so memorable as "This is one small step for mankind..." but then none of us knew that we were to be stars of the silver screen.

It occurred to us that Paris was only a quarter of a mile away, since, from the moment of boarding we would be in a 'time-and-distance-warp' and, when our feet next stepped outside the train, we would be in Paris. Furthermore we would put our watches *on* one hour when we arrived in France and put them *back* one hour on the return journey. Time would tell whether we would suffer from train-lag.

The train was very comfortable with ample leg room (even for tall people), a table which folded down as in aircraft and a personal litter-bin at the side of the seat. The lighting was excellent and when the train started to move, we realized there was hardly any sound. Indeed, our voices were rather penetrating so we found ourselves talking in hushed whispers. The loos got 'ten out of ten' but it took us time to fathom out the instructions for the operation of the various impedimenta.

The photos in the brochure showed smooth, smiling, contented passengers standing around very clean tables in the buffet car. We bought some goodies and stood around doing a fair impression of smooth, smiling contented passengers, the only difference being we were about thirty years older than our counterparts in the brochure. The buffet car attendant hadn't quite got the hang of the calculator which he used to work out the prices of purchases. To be fair, payment could be made in either English, French or Dutch currency (maybe more - we weren't sure), so there was that added complication, but he seemed rather perplexed by the whole thing. We were allowed (even encouraged!) to put our noses into the First Class compartment, where complimentary meals were served at Pullman tables. The First Class fare was almost £200 return. We had paid £95 return in our Standard Class compartment, though, of course, such mundane terminology was no longer a feature of this high-tech transport. The return ticket prices were 'Discovery Gold' £195, 'Discovery' £155, or 'Discovery Special' £95. The difference between 'Discovery' and 'Discovery Special' was that for the latter you had to book at least fourteen days in advance. With the 'Discovery' ticket, passengers could turn up 'on the day', while running the risk of the train being fully booked.

We returned to our carriage to discover what we thought was the greatest weakness of this enterprise. This was the refreshment trolley which operated (seemingly) one to each carriage. Whilst that would seem to be a good idea, the problem was that the trolley completely blocked the gangway so passengers wishing to walk through the carriage while the service was being offered had to wait patiently (or not!) for a considerable time while the refreshments were distributed, or the trolley attendant had to move the trolley to the end of the carriage to let people pass. It was a very tedious business. (We thought it was ironic that the Safety Instructions in the on-board leaflet requested that 'Passengers should ensure that no items block the aisles or entrance gangways' - unless that 'item' was a refreshment trolley - we presumed!) Our solution: either make the trolleys half as wide and twice as long or station the trolley permanently in the large area at the end of each carriage

An announcement told us that we were just about to enter the tunnel. We might have worked it out for ourselves as, a moment or two later, the scenery went rather black. The journey through the tunnel took twenty minutes, then another announcement told us that we were in France. That was an exciting moment. We had come through the tunnel unscathed and with no wet feet and it was now time to start on our picnic which we had brought with us. (With only a maximum of five hours in Paris, we realized there would be no time to eat or, if we *did* allow time for that, there would be very little time for sightseeing.) By now the speed of the train had increased to 186mph, a speed which had not been possible on the tracks in England. The people pulling the scenery past the windows must have been running very, very quickly as it was flashing by...

Three hours after leaving Waterloo, we pulled into the Gare du Nord, in the heart of Paris. We went to the *Métro* station and bought three *carnets* of tickets. Our first visit was to the church of St Eustache, but we only had a swift look inside as there was much ground to cover in the five hours at our disposal. On to the Louvre to see the new Pyramid (from the outside) and a short walk in the Tuileries gardens, with a sighting of the Musée d'Orsay in the distance. Another *Métro* journey took us to the *Bateau Mouche*, on which we enjoyed a seventy-five minute river cruise on the Seine. The advantage of this was that we were able to see all the sights from the comfort (and warmth) of the boat. We had to endure the commentary in seven languages, but we coped. At the end of the river cruise, we caught a bus which took us all the way back to the Gare du Nord.

Check-in was again very simple and there seemed to be many more people boarding the train. The train had been by no means full on the outward journey. Despite the seemingly large numbers of people at the check-in, there were a number of unoccupied seats for the return journey. We assumed this was because it was only week three of the whole operation and it was still a very new toy.

Our return journey was as pleasant as our outward journey. There was a slight hitch in the buffet car. We were some of the first in the queue to purchase a snack and Rosie and Debbie were just behind us. When they got to the head of the queue, some of the items on offer were already sold out! (It was that British Rail training again. We assumed that when Eurostar really got into its stride, they, too, would make sure that they had run out of *everything* five minutes into the journey.) Once again, entry into the tunnel was announced and, on leaving it, we were told we were in England. It was a comforting thought, and set our minds at rest; after all, you never know... We had left Paris at 1709 (local time) and we were back at Waterloo by 1910 - the change of hour explained the apparent shortness of the journey. It really *did* take three hours. We were home just twelve hours and ten minutes from the time we had set off that morning.

PARIS IN THE THE SPRING
May 1995

The sharpest eyed readers will have noticed what they will think is a mistake in the title. I have always longed to write that. Years ago, there used to be an advertisement for a certain method which would improve reading skills. It was headed *Paris in the the Spring*, in an attempt to catch everyone's eye - though I often wondered whether it succeeded. Suffice it to say, it caught mine!

Friday 26th

As a result of certain 'local difficulties', our tickets on the Eurostar train were upgraded to First Class, provided we were happy to travel one hour earlier, at 0723. (Happy? We were ecstatic!) The tickets were in the name of Mr and Mrs Farringdon - our first identity crisis of the weekend. At the check-in, there was no difficulty about our changed identity because the computer ticket thing only recognized little metal strips. It couldn't tell the difference between a Farringdon and a Spurr at twenty paces. This was our second trip on this 'state of the art iron horse' and on both occasions, no one had shown the remotest interest in making us go through the security check. We felt we must drop a line to Mr Eurostar on our return.

Our journey in the First Class compartment was splendid. No sooner had the train left Waterloo station than fruit juice was dispensed, closely followed by the menu from which we could select breakfast. It *had* to be traditional English breakfast. Next to arrive was some fresh grapefruit and orange segments, rolls and croissants, followed, at a discreet distance, by the traditional English breakfast. We were not disappointed. There was tea and coffee in abundance. There had been a slight anxiety in our minds prior to the trip. Supposing we arrived at the mid-point in the tunnel while we were still eating our bacon and egg, would we have to put it to one side and take up our croissants? As we had both, no such difficulty arose. Indeed, we had finished our not-so-*petit déjeuner* before we entered the tunnel.

We arrived in Paris at 1123 (one hour ahead of British time - *and* they drove on the wrong side of the road!). We took a taxi to our hotel which was quite close to the Gare du Nord and, even though it was before midday, we were able to check in straight away and leave our luggage. The first eatery we saw, *Les Deux Frères*, provided us with a good salad. Another customer seemed eager to engage us in conversation. He was an elderly man and it transpired that he lived in Albert Square in Kennington. We learned that he had been in London for sixty years, had been to school in Dulwich and was proposing to return to France. He told us he was a Baron who had a large property in the north of Paris. (We didn't know whether to believe this - but who knows?) He also told us that his wife had been 'assassinated by burglars' a few years before (?). He seemed to be a very lonely person.

During the afternoon, we did odd bits of shopping before returning to our hotel for a rest and to watch World Cup rugby.

Dinner was at *Au Petit Riche*, a restaurant which held happy memories for us.

Saturday 27th

A buffet breakfast set us up for the day then it was off to the market at Strasbourg Saint-Denis to buy our lunch time picnic, making sure we had enough to share with the birds. We included two slices of smoked salmon, none of which would be shared with the birds.

We took a trip on a *Bateau Parisien*. This was included as part of the Thomson package but, until now, these trips had been on the rival boats, the *Bateaux Mouches*. For some reason, Thomsons had changed and we thought it was a distinct improvement. It was all on one level, loading and unloading was much quicker and the commentary was done by a real person (rather than recordings) in only three languages (French, English and Spanish) rather than the seven which became rather tedious. At the place where we disembarked, there were numerous little eating places, such as were conspicuous by their absence at the *Bateaux Mouches* terminus. The weather was perfect so we had an excellent trip.

Our picnic was taken in the gardens of the Palais de Chaillot. We were not alone for more than ten seconds when we were joined by a host of feathered friends. At least this time, they waited to be offered things, but they didn't have to wait for long. They had a bonus of bread left over from the Eurostar train and the remains of my breakfast roll.

We thought we would investigate the numerous museums at the Palais de Chaillot. We selected the Museum of Monuments. In it were full-size (!) copies of church portals, tombs and similar edifices. It was *huge* and *very* tiring. There was a special exhibition on the first floor but to get to it we had to ascend so many stairs, we thought we would end up in the clouds! History does not record whether or not we did thus ascend.

Dinner was at *Le Charlot* whose extraordinary décor included mirrors, brown tiles and velvet wallpaper. We had a wonderful meal; Howard had a whole lobster (dead). We went back to our hotel by way of Pigalle. (We lamented that there are some nauseating bits in *any* big city.)

Sunday 28th

It was Mothering Sunday in France and we wondered what manifestations of this there might be in the Madeleine where we were headed. Perhaps the Madeleine was too posh for things like that? The magazine in our room at the hotel had a whole article on suggestions for presents for Mothering Sunday. They included a Cartier brooch (a cheetah in diamonds, emeralds and onyx, resting on a coral branch) or a 'quartz watch Steel d'Acier in mother-of-pearl, covered in hearts in a silver background. In the daytime it is worn with a sharkskin bracelet for a dip in the pool while for cocktails it becomes a sophisticated jewel with its pearl or satin bracelet.'

The Madeleine did not disappoint us. Monsieur Houbart played some very powerful Dupré as a postlude and an impressive and long improvisation during the offertory. The first hymn was 'Praise my soul the king of heaven' tune and, to our utter astonishment, the anthem was *Ave Maris Stella* by none other than our own Elgar! (Never did we expect to hear Elgar in a French church.)

After the Madeleine, we walked along to *Chartier* where we had the usual very good and inexpensive lunch. When we got back to the hotel, we noticed there was a wedding taking place in the synagogue right across the street. As we were peering through the doors, an official invited us to go inside. He gave Howard a head covering (obligatory for men) and we went in through separate doors and sat on separate sides of the synagogue - women on one side, men on the other. A rather strangulated tenor sang (from a balcony) something that might have been by Mozart, accompanied by a small orchestra.

The hotel had telephoned Notre Dame for us and had discovered there were no organ recitals there until October so we had decided to patronize Monsieur Jean Guillou at St Eustache where we were treated to some Bach and César Franck. This time there was a very good audience for his recital. Perhaps everyone from Notre Dame had gravitated here until October.

We were going to stroll to the *Brasserie Flo* for our dinner but a fierce thunderstorm forced us to shelter opposite a sleazy film emporium. Eventually, the rain abated so we made our way to our restaurant. We had an excellent meal which began with *Gazpacho* and included 'sole swimming in little vegetables'.

At the end of the evening, we eschewed a visit to the Sacré Coeur as my legs were making me feel my half century. Instead we went back to the hotel for an early night and a Monty Python film (not previously seen) on television.

Monday 29th

The morning was set aside for a visit to the Château de Malmaison, in the suburbs of Paris, a little place where Josephine lived for a while. Whether it was where Napoleon uttered his deathless phrase "Not tonight, Josephine", we knew not, but it was fun to think it *might* have been...We wondered why it was called *Malmaison*. For obvious reasons, it didn't seem the most suitable name for a *château* of any description. The leaflet we were given told us 'The etymology of the name is obvious (bad house) but the origin of this derogatory nomenclature is not precisely known.' Howard said that Josephine was 'quite a gal' - but I think we could say that Napoleon was the male equivalent. He didn't seem to think twice before jumping into bed with anyone and everyone. But, when all was said and done, it was a lovely place to visit, because it was very small and easily manageable. Our visit was made more interesting as we latched onto a school party, being told all there was to know by their teacher, who didn't mind us joining them. My 'A' Level (failed) French stood up to the test - mostly. The folk from those bygone days sounded an odd lot, but then, there was no television... (lucky them!)

Transport back to the centre of Paris proved to be a bit of an IQ test, but we managed and ended up at the Grande Arche de la Défense - Monsieur Mitterand's legacy to the nation. (You could tell he was a quiet, humble man.) The arch is large enough to enclose the whole of the width and height of Notre Dame. The Défense Centre was the largest shopping mall (!) in Europe, which is great if shopping malls are your thing - they are certainly not ours! We had to admit it was very clean and user-friendly but these places leave us cold. Bring back the nineteenth century is what I say. It was not all bad as the Défense Centre provided us with an excellent lunch.

We had purchased the wherewithal for our train picnic in the mall so, having collected our luggage from the hotel, we set off for the Gare du Nord in plenty of time for our train which left at 1818. Again no security checks! (We wrote a letter of complaint on our return to London.) The train was thirty minutes late arriving in Waterloo. Whilst we didn't mind, we felt sorry for those who had to catch connecting trains or coaches. Even as we were disembarking, we heard an announcement that the 1929 from Brussels had just arrived. By now, it was 2029, so we considered ourselves lucky that we had been a mere thirty minutes late.

It had been another lovely weekend in Paris, thanks to Howard's impeccable planning.

WARSAW WALKABOUT
June 1995

Our friends Jean-Marie and Mirjam Fèvre, whose wedding we had attended in August 1987, were living in Warsaw. Jean-Marie was in the employ of the French Government and, at that time, he was part of the Ministry of Foreign Affairs, which meant that they moved around Europe more than most. By now they had two delightful children - Victor (6) and Nicole (3). We thought we would take advantage of the fact that they were in Warsaw and pay a visit to that city.

Friday 9th

0800 was the starting time for our groundbreaking journey to Warsaw. (Yes, it really *was* Warsaw, not *Walsall*, as some people thought.) Check-in at Heathrow was slow as a new computer system had come on line that very day and the British Airways operator was not yet fully *au fait*. (*Now* we understood why they wanted us to be there two hours before the flight.) In the bar, it was the barman's first day too. He didn't seem to know which drinks were which so Howard indicated the relevant bottles...We hoped it would not be the pilot's first day as Howard would have felt slightly challenged if he had to point out various dials to him...

We arrived in Poland at 1500. (They, too, were one hour ahead of London time.) Our first encounter with the Polish tongue had been on the plane when some of the announcements had been in both English and Polish. There seemed to be a lot of 'z's in this language and everything seemed to end in 'a' or 'i'. (It put us in mind of the Czech Republic and their lack of vowels.) We wondered if we would see lots of the natives doing polonaises or mazurkas. The word was that they drank lots of neat vodka in Poland; perhaps they wouldn't be up to dancing after a few of those (?). Jean-Marie was waiting at the airport to meet us. So too, was the Sovereign Holidays representative who looked somewhat crestfallen when we explained that we wouldn't need her services or her car. It turned out that we were the only people she was meeting. Warsaw hadn't yet made it into the top ten holiday resorts in Europe. The representative did give us an envelope full of information, including a ticket for a City Sightseeing Tour the next day.

Jean-Marie drove us to our hotel. Driving in Warsaw was quite an experience. They didn't seem to be hampered by too many rules and regulations, or, put another way, they paid scant attention to whatever rules and regulations might exist. When we arrived at the large, modern Holiday Inn, Jean-Marie not only explained the currency to us but advanced us some so that we didn't have to pay commission at a money exchange office (*Kantor*). The currency had changed very recently - in a fairly dramatic way. In order to translate amounts into the new currency, it was necessary to delete four '0's, Jean-Marie gave us 5,000,000 (yes, five *million*!) zlotys but this was now a mere 500. He went on to say that one zloty equalled two French francs, so, after a while, and some heavy maths, we concluded that one zloty was approximately twenty-five pence. To make it even easier for visitors, both sorts of currency were still in operation for a period of two years while the changeover happened. Old bank notes (incorporating all the extra '0's) and new ones were both legal tender and prices in shops might be advertised in either or both forms. Now we really *were* confused!

After checking in and leaving our luggage in the hotel, Jean-Marie drove us to their house at ul. Poprzeczna 20A, PL-04-614 Warsaw, about twenty minutes drive from the centre. A warm welcome awaited us from Mirjam, Victor and Nicole and the lovely supper which Mirjam had prepared. We had made it! So many times had we said "We must come and visit you in Warsaw" that it was hard to believe we were actually *there*. The children were very excited to see us and were anxious to show us their toys. We were pleased when Jean-Marie and Mirjam told us that Victor and Nicole had been thrilled with the presents we had sent them from Canterbury Cathedral and the Imperial War Museum. Each time Nicole drew with her pencils from the War Museum, her activity was preceded by 'Howard and Jane'. We were to witness this for ourselves. We didn't think she had made the connection that we were the people she had seen last November in London. It was a while ago, for a small child, but she certainly knew our names. Victor was very interested in knights, castles and heraldry so the Canterbury Cathedral things had gone down very well.

Their house was almost in a forest. There were a number of houses nearby but they were all set in woodland and subject to possible (and actual) burglaries. There were quite a number of criminals round about and, indeed, their next-door neighbours 'did things with cars', the provenance of which was uncertain. It didn't pay to ask too many questions! Jean-Marie cautioned us against taking a stroll near our hotel. He told us that the area round about was dangerous. I needed no second warning, after my experience earlier in the year when I had been mugged in Camberwell. Jean-Marie said it was obvious that we were not Slavs and we would 'stick out like sore thumbs' to potential attackers. We were worried!

Warsaw had been completely destroyed in World War Two. Because they had an uprising, which was put down by the Germans, Hitler ordered the city to be destroyed as a punishment. Eighty-five per cent of the city was razed to the ground, the remaining fifteen per cent was used by the Gestapo, so that part had survived. The former Gestapo HQ was then the Ministry of Education. There seemed to be a great deal of poverty in Poland; things were not yet a lot better since Communism. Much of this could be put down to the usual human condition of greed - wanting everything at once - not being prepared to wait for things or save or manage money sensibly. There were very few people with lots of money, and it might have been interesting to find out how they came by it. Many people had hardly anything. Their infrastructure left a lot to the imagination. The buses looked old and battered but Jean-Marie told us they were *not* old. They looked battered because they were not properly maintained. The roads needed attention and the hospital (which Mirjam's mother had had cause to visit in January when she broke her foot while staying with them) was in a very poor state. Warsaw seemed, as yet, a sad place and buildings like our Holiday Inn and the adjacent enormous Marriott Hotel seemed out of place in the city.

We were opposite the Palace of Culture. The Poles didn't like it. It was built by the Russians (the Poles' most unfavourite people) and named after Stalin, though that had now changed. It was a really ugly building (better at night when illuminated). There was a wonderful view from the top and the locals said the view was all the more wonderful because it was the only place in Warsaw from which you *couldn't* see the Palace of Culture. A few other skyscrapers were being built, including the offices of LOT, the Polish national airline. It wasn't advisable to drink the water in the hotel so we bought a bottle of mineral water from the mini-bar. The cost was three zlotys (or 30,000 until a few months ago!) - seventy-five pence to us.

Saturday 10th

The City Sightseeing Tour was this morning. The excellent guide on the coach was Anna and, though there were ten nationalities represented, to our delight, the commentary was in English.

Our first stop was the Old Town of Warsaw. We had to keep reminding ourselves that everything we were seeing had been built since 1945. The town had been reconstructed as faithfully as possible, using old records and photographs. From that aspect, it was an impressive sight. It was very attractive and, because the Poles didn't seem too hot on maintenance of their buildings or roads (or *anything*), we could have been forgiven for thinking the buildings were old. It was just that they were ageing before their time.

We met an interesting Indian lady who was living in Poznan for a year, teaching English in the University. She told us that her impression of the Polish people was that they were rather apathetic and resigned to their lot. She went on to say that since Communism, though in some quarters there was lots of money, the average Pole earned an exceedingly poor salary - so they lived very sparsely and, in many ways, their lives were no better than they had been in the days of Communism. The saddest thing was that all the young people wanted to leave Poland as quickly as possible so they were learning another language in order to do that. The Indian lady wished they would stay or, she said, there didn't seem much future for the country.

The buildings in Warsaw, built by the Russians, were mostly very gloomy. Blocks of flats looked like prisons and the large official buildings were amongst the most unattractive we had seen anywhere. Considering Russia had produced some of the world's most beautiful things in other art forms (music, painting, literature), their architects had a long way to go to catch up! It all added to the general gloomy appearance of the city. Things were 'tatty' - the only word that really described them. Bus shelters and other street furniture needed a lick of paint at the very least and preferably renewing altogether. Grass grew between the concrete in the pavements. In the Old Town, at least we had some idea of what Poland was like - once. We were going to add 'before their troubles' but this is a country which had had so many troubles for so long that it was difficult to think back to a time when things were anywhere near 'normal'.

The Guided Tour took us to the Opera House which we would see at close quarters the following evening as Jean-Marie and Mirjam were taking us to see an opera there. We went on to the Cathedral, the birthplace of Marie Curie (née Marie Sklodowska), the monument to the 1944 uprising and the monument to the Jewish Ghetto. (It was impossible to think that one set of people could have done what *was* done to another set of people. Words just failed.) We saw the President's Palace (where Lech Walesa then functioned) and a large monument (though, come to think of it, *all* the monuments were large) to Cardinal Wyszynski and one to the poet Adam Mickiewicz. They had their own Tomb of the Unknown Warrior which was guarded round the clock by soldiers.

Next stop was Wilanów, the baroque residence of King Jan III Sobieski, famous conqueror of the Turks at the Battle of Vienna in 1693. It was quite large but the guide provided by the palace made it most 'user-friendly'. Instead of *walking* round its interior, we *slid*, as we had to wear specially provided overshoes to protect the parquet floors. We had a whistle-stop sighting of the large collection of paintings. Most impressive was the guide's pronunciation of the long and complicated names of all the 'glitterati' whose pictures had found their way here. No name had less than four syllables and *all* sounded, looked and were complicated. Yes, the Polish language could benefit from a lot more vowels. It became clear to us that we needed two sets of teeth - one for ordinary conversation and one for pronouncing Polish names.

The coach delivered us back to our hotel at 1415, seventy-five minutes later than planned. We were anxious as Jean-Marie was to meet us at 1400. He was there, unconcerned; as he said "This is Poland" - with a shrug of his shoulders. Our second guided tour was led by Jean-Marie. He drove us to see the other monument to the Jewish Ghetto, very different to the one we'd seen in the morning. This one was plain and unadorned. We went on to the church where Fr Popielusko had been the priest and which is now almost a shrine to him. He was murdered by the Communists. Popielusko's tomb was an impressive sight. A number of large boulders circled the grave, joined by a chain, so that the grave was encircled by a rosary. In the tree immediately above the grave was a very large crucifix. On we went to the Chopin monument - a huge bust of Chopin by a pond. Next to the park was the building where President Jaruselski lived.

We had to collect Mirjam and the children from a puppet theatre performance. Two very excited children met us and we drove back to their home for another delicious supper. This time, Mirjam, had prepared for us the national dish of Poland - Borsch - a kind of stew made from red beet, sauerkraut, potatoes, carrots, celery, onions, leeks and beef. Mirjam said she didn't prepare this dish very often as it took a long time. It used to be the staple diet of the Polish people as it was not expensive to make, and now it had become a recognized dish on menus in all restaurants - even the most expensive. We could see why; it was *formidable* and, if any more proof were needed, the empty dish said it all. Victor was very pleased when he learned we were drinking Armangnac as the hero in one of his story books drank this and it seemed to help him defeat the Black Prince. Victor watched us carefully as we drank it, to see what effect it would have on us. We counted ourselves so lucky to have our very own personal hosts in this country.

Sunday 11th

Jean-Marie took us to Chopin's birthplace at Zelazowa Wola, about 40 kilometres outside Warsaw. Each Sunday there were two piano recitals, one at 1100, the other at 1500. The recital room seated only fourteen people and the remaining audience sat in the garden. Through the kind offices of Jean-Marie, not only had we had been lucky enough to get seats in the room but they were in the front row! Before the recital started, there was time for a wander round the garden. It reminded us of Monet's Garden at Giverny because of the water lilies and the bridge, though the plant life was very different. The recital by Anna Jastrzebska-Quinn was superb. (She taught at the Warsaw Conservatoire.) Naturally it was an all Chopin programme which included some of his greatest hits - the *Fantasie-Impromptu* and the *Andante Spianato* and *Polonaise*. Everything was sheer delight from beginning to end.

Back to the Fèvre home for another lovely lunch. Mirjam is a wonderful cook! Jean-Marie introduced us to *Pineau de Charentes*, an aperitif made of cognac and grape juice. After lunch we went for a walk in the forest.

In the evening, we were guests of Jean-Marie and Mirjam at the Warsaw Opera for a performance of Moniuszko's *Straszny Dwór* (*The Haunted House*). Moniuszko was Poland's great opera composer, who lived in the nineteenth century and was the first Director of the Warsaw Opera House. It was a splendid building but, again, as it had been destroyed in the War, what we saw was the rebuilt version. The stage of the opera house was the largest in Europe. Mirjam told us that what we would see of the stage would be only one quarter of it! The chorus numbered 120. Our conclusions about the difficulty of Polish names (and the necessity for different sets of teeth to pronounce them) were justified when we saw the cast list. It included:

Wlodzimierz Zalewski
Krystyna Szostek-Radkowa
Wanda Bargielowska-Bargeyllo

(They played havoc with the spellcheck!)

It was quite a treat for us to watch a genuine Polish opera in the main Polish opera house. To our shame, we had not heard of Mr Moniuszko but we made a mental inventory of the Polish musicians we did know: Wieniawski, Szymanowski, Penderecki, Stanislaw Skrowaczewski, Lutoslawski, Wanda Wilkomirska, Wanda Jeziorska - not forgetting my late piano teacher, Julius Lepiankiewicz. We were very glad we had abandoned the idea of eating *after* the opera as it didn't end until 2150 but that was not the end of the evening by any means. Kazimierz Pustelak, one of the soloists, was celebrating forty years of working in the opera house and he received lots of flowers. Indeed, lots of flowers were given to lots of people and Mirjam told us that the public can give flowers to anyone, through the proper channels. It might well be the case that a chorus member received more flowers than a soloist! Jean-Marie thought there would be speeches to the fortieth anniversary man following the floral presentations so we crept out before they started. Jean-Marie had to drive Mirjam home, having dropped us at our hotel, drive their babysitter back to central Warsaw and then drive himself home again. The following day at work would be very long as it was his last before a ten-day visit to Paris to undertake some important examinations.

Monday 12th

We went to the Palace of Culture, to see the view from the thirty-third floor. A taxi took us to Old Town Square where we had good wine and beer in the

Arkadia. We had managed to find six Polo mints to feed to three horses who pulled the tourist carriages through the Old Town. Polos certainly seem to be international horse fodder. (Perhaps they were invented in Poland - hence the name?) We had time for a more leisurely visit to the Cathedral where we heard the organ, but it was very *pianissimo*. Perhaps someone was practising very discreetly?

There was a twenty-minute film about the history of Warsaw 1939-1945. The door keeper did not want to admit us and insisted there was 'no film today'. Half an hour earlier, however, we had met a party of Americans leaving the room, who told us they had just seen the film. The Polish door keeper agreed we could have a 'special viewing' ('for two persons only') at 12 noon. To fill in the time, we inspected the *Basilisk* restaurant at the other side of the square. A very bossy lady told us in no uncertain terms that it didn't open until 12 noon but a much more pleasant colleague gave us a menu so we could see what was on offer. We agreed to return in half an hour (after the film) and made a reservation. The film didn't tell us anything we didn't know already but it showed photographs taken by and for the Gestapo to show Hitler to prove how Warsaw had been destroyed in accordance with his orders. We paid 300,000 zlotys to see the film. Howard paid with a million zloty note and got 700,000 in change.

Back at the *Basilisk*, we were to be the only customers! I had my first taste of native vodka. It could not have been a more perfect location because we were able to sit overlooking the Old Town Square. Some of the items on the menu intrigued us:

> Clamps with Black Caviar
> Smoked Eal
> Roast Piglet Krakow Style
> Deer in Beer Sauce

The menu indicated that some of these dishes were 'served at table'. We wondered where the rest were served. We gave them all a wide berth and had a light snack, as we were eating in the evening with Jean-Marie and Mirjam.

We walked half way back to our hotel then took a taxi in order to avoid the less desirable areas about which we had been warned.

Jean-Marie and Mirjam joined us for supper at the Holiday Inn *Brasserie* Restaurant and, with some difficulty, we managed to insist that we should treat *them* for once. During the meal, a thunderstorm shattered the peace. Jean-Marie and Mirjam left at 2200 as Jean-Marie had another three-way drive with the babysitter.

Tuesday 13th

We had to go back to London today but, before our journey, we had a last meal with the Fèvre family. We sorted out the money we had spent and exchanged it with Jean-Marie for English currency, returning our unused zlotys to him. We watched with great delight as the children were thrilled to bits with the little bag of English coins which we gave them. They each had a money box or purse and they saved all such coins for future use. We weren't *entirely* sure what shop would accept such a conglomeration of different foreign currencies, but the children didn't know that. They were in their own little world...Oh to be that age again... no responsibilities...

We travelled to the airport with Jean-Marie and Mirjam as he was catching a flight to Paris one hour before our flight to London. Finally it was time for the parting of the ways - Jean-Marie to Paris, us to London and Mirjam back to their house and thence to the Embassy for a special function.

What a trip it had been but we were convinced that it would not have been nearly so enjoyable if it had not been for the wonderful generosity of our dear friends, the Fèvre family, to whom we owed a great debt of gratitude. When we got home, we needed no reminding of how very lucky we were to live *where* we lived and in the *way* that we lived. Seeing Poland really was seeing 'how the other half lived'.

FROM THE PLEASURES OF PROVENCE
TO THE BEAUTIES OF BURGUNDY
July 1995

Saturday 22nd

We met up with our friend Hazel at Heathrow for our flight to Nice, which was uneventful. Always a good start. We soon made up for that at Nice airport where no coach was waiting to take us to Avignon. Nor was there a suspicion of a representative from the 'Transfer Agent', Treasure Tours. (Perhaps they didn't exist?) There *was* a coach representative waiting for six people from our flight who were taking the same journey to join the same river boat. He had a fifty-seater vehicle for their use, which we felt was slightly excessive, but who were we to complain? After much negotiation with Monsieur Frederic Blanc, the coach representative, phone calls to Cannes (the HQ of Treasure Tours - as well as film festivals) and by dint of Howard's excellent French and Foreign Office-type organisational expertise, it was agreed that we could go in the fifty-seater coach with Monsieur Blanc. He was pleased as his six people never did arrive! When he checked with the airline, they had never boarded the plane in London. (All very odd we thought…)

During our three-hour coach trip from Nice to Avignon, we made a short stop for refreshments and we heard *cigales* for the first time. The only thing we knew about *cigales* was the Chabrier song. But it turned out they weren't *cigales* after all, but *cicadas* - 'a large broad insect, most common in warm regions: the males produce a high-pitched drone' - so tell us something new. They sounded like grasshoppers on a day out in a corn field, such was the noise they made.

On arrival in Avignon, we boarded the M/S Arlène and, moored right next to it was a boat called Cigale. (We never did discover whether the Captain was called Monsieur Chabrier.) We found ourselves in the middle of a *mistral*. Our guidebook told us: "Mistral was the Provencal word for Master Wind - a strong, dry wind which sweeps down when the pressure is high over the mountains, from the Massif Central to the Mediterranean, funnelling through the Rhône Valley. The violent blast of air clears the sky of cloud and purifies the soil. When the mistral rages, a storm-like atmosphere reigns. The Rhône makes waves and just moving about is difficult." We *did* find moving around on the upper deck was difficult; we found we were proceeding at forty-five degrees to the perpendicular.

Sunday 23rd

Each day, we were to have a comfortable coach provided by the firm, Philibert. By far its best feature was its air conditioning, without which life would have been intolerable. All the guides we had were to prove excellent as was their command of England. But each of the guides had one or two words which were endearingly incorrect.

Today's guide was Madame Benoit and she took us on a conducted tour of Arles, Van Gogh territory. Madame Benoit told us (many times) how important was the particular light, especially after the *mistral*. We could see her point and presumed that was why so many artists had flocked there. (Madame Benoit's *bête noire* was 'civilation' for 'civilisation'. These observations were not meant unkindly and were not criticisms; they were just that - merely observations. As we said, if our French was a quarter as good as Madame Benoit's English, we would be very happy. Somehow it was very endearing to hear French people make these errors.)

The temperature would have been unbearable had it not been for the *mistral*, which was still with us. I would have given up long since. The temperature we had left in England had reduced me to a shred. I could no longer cope with the sun or even mild heat.

Arles appealed to us immediately. We made a mental note to go there for a longer visit in the future - and at a cooler time of the year. It was a very ancient Roman place and, in the foyer of a hotel, we were allowed a glimpse of some ancient Roman remains which had been preserved under glass. Gingerly we walked round the side of the glass, endeavouring not to put so much as a toe on it. To our astonishment, a waiter walked right across it, without a care in the world. That's when we realized it must have been strengthened glass.

The *Café de la Nuit*, immortalized in Van Gogh's paintings, is now called the *Café Van Gogh*, and, outside, was a vase of sunflowers! There were postcards of Van Gogh in the shops but we didn't suffer from Van Gogh 'overkill'. The guide pointed out an art gallery in the town, Fondation Van Gogh, but it contained only things people had written about him and paintings by others. To our surprise, there were no original Van Gogh paintings in Arles. (*Quel dommage!*)

The Cathedral had an impressive portico which had been restored in recent times. It had been covered in sheeting, rather like the Reichstag in Berlin. (Would that people would cover *our* Houses of Parliament in sheeting. *News at Ten* would be so much shorter!) The portico was covered in carvings, depicting the life of Christ. Van Gogh wrote to his brother that when he (Vincent) was not feeling

well, he couldn't look at this portico as it was so strong. (Bit like listening to the *Ninth Symphony* when you've got the flu. Vincent didn't say that - I did.) The Cathedral Cloisters were very beautiful and they, too, were adorned with twelfth century carvings. We were to see so many twelfth, thirteenth and fourteenth century things that we became rather blasé about it all.

On to the first century Amphitheatre, which was like the Coliseum in Rome, only much more of this one survived. We were taken inside, where the arena was being prepared for bullfighting. Madame Benoit gave us information about it, standing in the baking hot sun. She told us that a week before, it had been ten degrees hotter - without the *mistral*! (I mentally passed out and prayed for winter.) How could the audience sit in that heat? How could the bullfighters and the bulls run around in it? Worse than Centre Court on Men's Finals day. Our minds raced - 'Advantage Bull' - or, perhaps, 'Disadvantage El Cordobes'.

We went back to the Arlène for lunch, the second in a string of incredible meals. Normally, we would have eaten like this once in a blue moon. This week, there were to be fourteen blue moons - an astronomer's dream. We must include a note about the 'on board food'. It was in three languages and we were reminded of an article we'd read by Keith Waterhouse in the plane's 'in-flight' magazine, on the subject of 'the language of menus'. He pointed out that everything nowadays was either 'in' something or 'on' something or 'with' something. For example: "Aromatic duck on olive oil mash and lentils. Roast loin of lamb wrapped in a potato galette with an aubergine and courgette timbale. Chicken sausages on spinach with a tarragon cream sauce. Daily I expect to see my favourite dish described as fish on a bed of chips." It made my baked beans on toast look a little sick...but thank you Mr Waterhouse for paving the way for our menus. We wondered if his meals were copyright...

While we were looking round Arles, the Arlène had sailed from Avignon to meet us. Lunch was taken in the company of our new-found friends Jim and Yvonne and Barry and Mary - Hazel, Howard and I making up the party. We hoped they would not get too bored with us too quickly as there didn't seem to be scope for changing tables.

The afternoon was taken up with a trip (in our two super-comfy Philibert coaches) to the Camargue, a nature reserve full of so many interesting things, notably flamingos, bulls, and wild white horses. (The white horses were quite even-tempered until they saw our two Philibert coaches approaching.) The tour details had sounded a note of caution about the flamingos which was that we might not see them. That *would* be bad news. In the event, we didn't need to worry; it was not flamingo early-closing day so we saw many of these fragile-looking creatures. Why didn't they overbalance? Their bodies were much too big for their spindly legs - and whatever happened if they got cramp? Perhaps that explained why they stood on one leg for such a long time. After a suitable pause for refreshment, we paddled in the Mediterranean Sea. (We must have had 'English Tourist' written all over us.) We were amazed at the number of ladies wearing rather minimalist garments. So that really *did* happen in the South of France…we supposed they were auditioning for a part in a Philip Glass opera.

Back at the Arlène, there was time for a refreshing shower and pre-prandial drinks before dinner. We eschewed the Happy Hour Tequila Sunrises, on offer in the bar. It was not so happy that it was free - but everyone smiled broadly while they signed the bill.

Monday 24th

There was a morning tour of Avignon with Madame Benoit, who was so very good and knowledgeable. There was not a stone or a view about which she didn't have a comment. All those dates, all those Popes and kings - how did she remember it all? The Papal Palace lived up to expectations. Those popes certainly had a chequered history.

Avignon was in the middle of a theatre festival and every nook and cranny was a site for a theatrical production - very reminiscent of the Edinburgh Festival. Everywhere we looked was a stage of bigger or smaller proportions. Some productions were under way, though it was only 1000. (We heard some blood-curdling screams from behind a wall and *assumed* it was a theatrical production…) In the Great Hall of the Papal Palace (or 'Popal' Palace as our guide had it) was an exhibition of Picasso paintings, starting with early works and moving on to his later offerings. It was clear he had had a bit too much cointreau before he started on the later ones. From the ramparts of the Papal Palace and the Cathedral, we had one of the best views of the famous Pont d'Avignon. *On n'y danse pas*…ah well, we couldn't have everything. There were only a few arches left of this pont and it stopped half way across the river, which led us to think that as bridges go, this was not one of the most successful. But others had been built since so it was possible to cross the river in safety, without having to swim the second half, which always played havoc with the shopping. (Those engineers thought of everything.) Madame Benoit told us that, in its time, the river had been 'over-floating' right up into the town.

On the way back to the boat, we took a short cut through the Hôtel de Ville where Madame Benoit showed us a list names inscribed on a huge panel. They were people who had lost their lives in the Second World War. Among them were three of her father-in-law's brothers.

After lunch, we set sail for Viviers. The instruction sheet advertised 'Streaching with Régine at 1600'. (Streaching?) Régine was our tour leader on the boat and she was a lovely person. We divided our forces. The sun was far too hot for me so I retired to the comfort of our air-conditioned cabin for sleep and reading. Howard slept for a while then went to observe the others doing the 'Streaching'. Hazel stayed on deck throughout, observing the 'Streachers' through the reflection in the Captain's turret.

After the next wonderful dinner, we took a stroll in the ancient medieval town of Viviers which was enchanting by night.

Tuesday 25th

We were to see Viviers by day as a morning walk was scheduled. It was very steep and cobbled but it was so small and quiet that it seemed like a ghost town, except for the market at river level. We looked into the Cathedral, much of which had been destroyed in various conflicts and rebuilt a number of times in a number of different styles. The Choir had survived and was original twelfth century.

The coach took us to the Château La Croix Chabrière, one of the many vineyards in the area (or 'Wineyards' as Régine had it). The owner, Monsieur Daniel, a man of few words but good miming technique, accompanied us, while our guide, Sara, told us all about the many processes involved in wine production. No wonder it is an expensive pastime. Things we take for granted, like the corks and the barrels, all had to be made, and made in a certain specified way. We had seen similar demonstrations before, but it was always fascinating and we learned something new each time. We were invited to go inside for a wine tasting. This was done by Monsieur Daniel Junior, whose new baby, Monsieur Daniel Junior Junior, joined us, but didn't participate in the tasting. We tasted white, rosé and finally a red which was older but, we were told, should really be kept until it was much older.

Our way back to the boat for lunch took us through miles of vine-growing countryside. If a piece of land wasn't covered in vines, it was covered in sunflowers. (Van Gogh did for sunflowers what Vera Lynn did for the *Entente Cordiale* - except Ms Lynn hadn't fetched quite so much in Sotheby's. There was still time...)

We docked for the night at Tournon. This evening, we *did* join the Happy Hour on the sun deck, where we had some rather appetising Bacardis and orange juice. After dinner was *Le Cabaret*. Our new-found friends, Jim, Yvonne, Barry and Mary, had reserved places for us in the salon - and ordered champagne! What a treat!

275

I bailed out after a while but I was quickly replaced by Hazel who had been having a little siesta on the sun deck, though the sun had long since set - but we didn't like to tell her.

Wednesday 26th

We took an excursion on a steam railway - twenty miles, uphill all the way - to the Mastrou District. It was a turn of the century train with wooden carriages which were very rattly and bumpy. There was much opening and closing of the windows because of the smoke and soot that came in, especially in the tunnels. (It took us back to our childhood.) Half way along there was a fifteen minute stop for the train to take on water and for our group to take on drinks, laid on for us at the side of the tracks. There was no shortage of them (drinks, not tracks, though, come to think of it, there was no shortage of those either) and the coach driver made a number of sorties, topping us up with Kir. The terminus was Lamastre, at the top of the hill (1,000 feet) and Hazel pointed out *L'Hôtel du Midi* where the cook, Elizabeth David, had operated at one time. We couldn't linger in Lamastre as we had to return to the boat by 1300 to set sail for Lyon. It was very important that the boat kept strictly to the sailing times because of the (huge) locks which had to be negotiated in the course of the trip. Our only previous experience of locks had been on canals in Britain - but these were very very deep.

Lunch was a little late today, because of our late return, then we fell to sleeping until the next wonderful meal. (Howard interspersed the wonderful meals with tea and cakes on offer at tea time.)

Thursday 27th

This morning was set for a guided tour of Lyon, France's second largest city (originally called *Lugdunum*) which went back some 2,000 years. There were umpteen Roman remains here and an excellent Gallo-Roman museum. The Basilique de Fourvière had been built in the nineteenth century. It was so clean on the outside that it looked like a theatre set. We couldn't believe it was real. Inside, it was very highly decorated, with six huge mosaics made of glass on the walls and more usual mosaics of stone in the floor. For all it's 'overdone-ness', we quite liked it as it reminded us of the Sacré Coeur in Paris. We went to the really old part of the town and suddenly our guide, Nadia, disappeared into a dark doorway. We followed, and discovered dark walkways which linked the houses. The dwellings were on four or five storeys, access being by way of a spiral staircase. Imagine having to carry the weekly shopping up all those stairs! There was neither time nor opportunity for Howard to look up his friends in the British

Consulate but, when Hazel saw us dash off from the group, she thought that was where we had gone. In fact, we had sighted a twelfth century shop wherein we could replenish our stocks of tonic water for our duty-free pre-prandials.

After lunch back on the boat, we took a trip to the Beaujolais country. The statistics which the guide provided boggled our minds - how many hectare-litres per owner, how many bottles were produced, how long the vines have to be left... We promised to test Yvonne that evening to make sure she had taken in all the details. We stopped at Salles where there was the remains of a cloister (only one side left) of a convent. The church was still there; it had a very ancient door and a very simple interior. The next stop was Vaux, which was also called Clochemerle - after that book. The story went that a local resident, having read the book, recognized the fictitious Clochemerle as his home, Vaux. The authorities got permission to add Clochemerle to the title of the village. We sighted the 'offending' public convenience before tasting some Beaujolais. We bought a bottle to take home.

Friday 28th

En route for Brancion, we stopped at the Romanesque church at Chapaize. Brancion was a tiny hilltop town, miles from anywhere, with a very ancient church, where a film was being shot. We couldn't decide whether the monk was real or an actor. We all agreed that two weeks here would be idyllic. It was so quiet and peaceful and the auberge looked very comfortable. Quite a few English cars came and went so we wondered if it had found its way into guidebooks; we hoped not, or it would be spoiled. Brancion also boasted a castle which was privately owned.

On to Tournus and the eleventh century Abbey of St Philibert - obviously named after the coach company. This was one of Burgundy's most famous and best-kept churches - so the details told us. It was very very big, with a narthex. It was also the first church we had seen with an organ and we managed to get a postcard of it for Charles Proctor. In fact there were two organs and a Steinway grand piano. The Verdi Requiem had been performed there the week before, so that gave an idea of the size of the place. Recorded music was being played which, to our surprise and delight, added to the atmosphere very well.

Lunch was back on the boat after which we sailed to our last mooring at St Jean de Losne. In the evening was the Captain's Dinner - five courses - how would we manage? It gave us an opportunity to express our thanks to all the crew who had been absolutely delightful. They couldn't have done more to make us contented.

Saturday 29th

After breakfast we disembarked and drove to Beaune. This was the worst day of the year for driving in France as everyone took to the roads at the start of the holiday season. Luckily we encountered a truck driver who had a mobile phone and he was able to warn our coach driver of motorways blocked by traffic jams and an accident. We had to take a very circuitous route to avoid all the problems. Beaune provided our first - and only - opportunity for shopping so we stocked up with some cheese, which was to make its presence felt for the remainder of the journey.

We stopped at Macon where lunch had been pre-booked for our group at the *Lamartine* restaurant - opposite the statue of Monsieur Lamartine.

As we approached Lyon airport, we felt we were really on the way home. Our flight was delayed but no one told us. The information screen seemed to have but one message in its repertoire, the number and time of our flight. It never changed. Long after is should have left, it was still advertising it! Eventually it left one hour late - it could have been much worse. We spent the time profitably as Howard met a very old friend, Michael Berman, so they caught up on news of mutual friends.

We said goodbye to Hazel and, when we were back in Kennington, we agreed that, wonderful as it had been - and it certainly *had* been a wonderful trip - there was nothing quite like a cup of *real* English tea.

YOUNG AT HEART IN THE ALGARVE
January 1996

Now that Howard had reached the ripe old age of fifty-five, he qualified for the 'Young at Heart' option in the Thomson holiday brochures. He was allowed to take a partner or friend - even *wife* - and that person didn't have to be the 'ripe old age'. As I had clocked up a mere half century the previous year (better than most of the English cricket team), that was just as well. How would our lives be changed by being 'Young at Heart' we mused?

Sunday 7th

We must have been amongst the first people to check in at Gatwick and we were asked if we had any illnesses or disabilities. We guessed why this was. We were reminded of a conversation with our Canadian friend Murray who used to work for an airline. Apparently, what are considered to be 'able bodied passengers' are selected (unknown to them but known to the cabin crew) to assist in the event of an emergency. Were we to be those people on this trip? We had visions of assisting with the evacuation of the plane, helping people into the emergency chutes and probably Howard being forced to fly the plane the last few miles when it was discovered that the pilot had ejected. (Oddly enough it was the most uneventful flight we'd ever taken.) A new feature of the Royal Britannia Service (Britannia Airways was the sister company of Thomson) was the 'Airborne Flightmaster', a moving map which kept us informed of the exact location of the plane in relation to both Gatwick and our destination, in this case Faro, Portugal. Every so often, this information was replaced by the altitude and the speed of the plane, together with the local time and how much of the flight remained. By the time we'd watched the safety film, had the 'in flight' meal and worked out how to pronounce some of the duty-free perfume and after shave (OK, *you* try pronouncing YSATIS), we'd arrived at Faro airport.

The coach transfer to the Hotel Jupiter in Praia da Rocha took fifty minutes so we arrived in time for dinner. At the next table was a classic Alan Bennett couple. She: "I don't know what you think, but seventy pence to go that short distance is ridiculous." "That lottery prize money really is too much now. What would the likes of us do with all that money? I agree with that Vicar." *He* said very little - there wasn't much need...

Our room on the fifth floor was very comfortable, with a highly polished floor and two small mats which enabled us to move from one side of the room to the other at an incredible speed, quite unpredictably. We would have to be very careful if we were to avoid a selection of broken or strained limbs. Howard tethered his mat underneath a coat hanging contraption. I just took risks.

Monday 8th

(Today would have been the birthday of my father - and Elvis Presley!) The Thomson Welcome Meeting was waiting to tell us about the 'Young at Heart Special Extras'. We feared it would be tea dances, bingo and library books with very big printing. We had noticed the previous evening that we were almost the youngest people here. The Inaugural Address was as predicted but Gavin and Angie, the Thomson representatives, were very much more informative than some of their colleagues we had met on previous trips. Much to our delight, their discourse was not punctuated with liberal doses of "Er" and "y'know", which seemed to be an obligatory part of speech - from politicians right up to football stars. (It has only got worse since 1996.) Gavin and Angie took us for a short walk round the town and they pointed out all the important local places we might need - the Post Office, chemist etc. Then we called into a local wine shop to buy our supplies of mineral water, tonic and fruit juice, though the mini-bar in our room was the cheapest we had encountered. Equipped with this survival kit, we were able to have our own pre-prandials, sitting on our balcony, contemplating the angry-looking Atlantic ocean. The sun had not yet ventured out and the orientation walk had been taken in raincoats and *gloves*.

For lunch we thought we would try the Hotel Algarve, right opposite. Our friends Robert and Susan had stayed there and given it a good report. We could see why, but it was *deathly* quiet; there was only one other person in the coffee room where we thought we might have a snack lunch. We changed our minds and decided to take our custom to a little bar just up the road, where we were one of only four pairs of people - but at least it was a *few* more. It was very very quiet here at the moment as it was out of season; indeed, many places were closed completely, but that suited us 'down to the ground'.

The afternoon was spent in slumber land then after dinner (beware the red wine - we *did* beware it after a couple of sips!), we had an early night as an all-day excursion to Monchique (in the mountains) was on the cards for the following day.

Just before retiring, we perused the 'Golden Book of the Algarve', provided by the hotel management. It appeared that some of it had been translated, word for word from the Portuguese, by what we thought was a novice translator. What were we to make of the following at the conclusion of an advertisement for a jeweller's shop: "Where the Rolex side by side to the Chopard confirms its sumpuosity, Where the jewel of that unparalleled and afar off distance, a mixture of matter and dream, still overwhelms us"? It was certainly food for Thought for the Night.

Tuesday 9th

Under the expert guidance of Marguerite, the local Portuguese guide, we set off for the mountains and Monchique. Marguerite's précis of Portugal's weather was not designed to give would-be visitors a great incentive to visit. Because of the strange climate of the preceding years, they had had five very dry years, followed by far too much rain (*this* year!) so that "the river is coming out of its banks". Lisbon had had "no electricity and no communication recently due to the flooding".

Our first stop was Silves, to see the castle and the Cathedral. When the coach stopped at the bottom of the hill (it was not allowed to go further), the precipitation, which had not stopped since we left, became a downpour. We were trapped in our coach by torrential rain, which showed no signs of abating during the forty-five minutes we were to spend here. Nevertheless, some of the more intrepid amongst us decided to make the ascent. As luck would have it, my emergency plastic bag supply did excellent service as impromptu head covering. We couldn't dignify them with the name of 'hats' but the National Trust and Rymans did add a certain *nous ne savons quoi* to our ensemble. Sadly, our raincoats and plastic headgear were no match for this downpour and we got soaked, right through to our clothes. (This would do wonders for my cold which I had brought with me from England.) After all this effort, we were not able to see the castle because of the inclement weather but we did have a peer into the Cathedral which, by now, fully qualified for the title *La Cathédrale engloutie*.

On to a restaurant where lunch had been pre-booked for us. We shared a table with members of a dance team who were staying in a nearby hotel.

Now for the highlight of the trip - the spectacular view from the highest point of the mountains, Foia - 3,000 feet above sea level. Sadly the only spectacular view we had was of dense cloud; visibility was restricted to a few yards beyond the end of our noses. On the way back down, we stopped at the Monchique spa, to try the waters. We had been told that, drinking the water from one of the wells would make us look and feel ten years younger. It didn't - but it did taste of hard-boiled eggs as it was extremely sulphurous. Back to the coach for the long descent to sea level, where the sun was putting in its first appearance. The strain was too much for it - it didn't last.

Wednesday 10th

This was the day of the Mystery Tour, one of the 'Young at Heart Special Extras'. It turned out to be a full morning coach trip along the western side of the province of the Algarve to the border with the adjacent province of Alentejo. The front half of the coach actually set foot (wheel?) in Alentejo when the driver was reversing to negotiate a tricky bend. The weather was much better today - only *light* rain and no wind.

The first stop was Odiaxere, a village with little to commend it as far as we could see. Probably it had been chosen for a 'comfort stop' - as our American chums would have it. We had a good cup of coffee and admired the orange tiled roofs and white painted buildings that made up the village. We headed up into the mountains. It was a very steep ascent and, once or twice, we wondered if we would have to get out of the coach and walk behind it until it reached the brow of the hill. All proved to be well and we had lots of sightings of orange and lemon groves, mimosa, olive trees - even *white* heather. Our guide (Marguerite again) was very proud of the white heather, which was rare in Portugal, though she acknowledged that we had it in England. On to Marmelete, where Marguerite particularly recommended the smoked ham sandwiches. We didn't want to eat so early so we didn't avail ourselves of them. When we returned to the coach, many of our fellow passengers were disappointed as they hadn't managed to have the ham sandwiches. It turned out that there had been a language problem; the sandwiches had been there but our friends couldn't make their requests understood. (Whatever happened to pointing?) Back at Praia da Rocha we had a good soup and omelette snack.

The afternoon was taken up with a trip into Portimão, the nearest shopping centre which was two miles away. We took the local bus as the rain was becoming heavier by the minute. With the help of a local policeman, we located the Centro Mondelo with its huge supermarket where we stocked up on essentials. We took a taxi back to the hotel as the rain was, once more, torrential.

Thursday 11th

The Atlantic Ocean, which we could see from our window, was as busy as ever. Howard said that the tide didn't come in and go out at night. It is switched off and only switched on again at first light. That seemed sensible - to preserve the energy - with all that global warming, the world can't be too careful. There was no danger of that at the moment. Global drowning was more likely to be on the agenda here in Portugal.

Our first port of call this morning was the Post Office, to mail our cards. There was a distinct smell of incense in the Post Office. (We assumed the staff were very religious.) Ron, my successor at Christian Action, had warned us that Portuguese stamps had no adhesive on them and they had to be glued onto the cards, using glue found in the Post Office. Either he was kidding or he had been to a very primitive part of Portugal. (Come to think of it, we thought he said he'd been to Lisbon. Perhaps he had been there in a power cut or flood, which might have affected the stamps.) We were beginning to get the hang of the money at last. There were approximately 223 Escudos to our pound (a simple number for calculations!). We thought of 1,000 of them being just under a fiver and it was not too difficult. At least it was much easier than the money in Warsaw - not nearly so many noughts.

We set off to walk to Alvor, about three miles round the bay. As luck would have it, we hadn't gone far when we realized we'd left something behind in the hotel so we returned to collect it. As we did so, the weather, which had looked somewhat dubious from the outset, took a distinct turn for the worse, so we aborted our plan. It was, indeed, a stroke of luck because, had we not had to return to the hotel, we would have been down on the beach, halfway between the two resorts and would have had our second soaking in as many days.

We made a virtue out of a necessity and went in search of lunch, this time to the other end of the resort. We found a very good place (in which, once again, we were the only customers) and at last Howard was able to have genuine Portuguese sardines. We ordered a bottle of really dry white wine and we were just a teensy bit anxious when we noticed it was called BSE! The waiter explained that this stood for *Branca Seco Especial* - white, dry, special. What could we do but believe him. After all, if we listened to what we're told back at home, pretty well every other thing we eat will give us Mad Cow Disease and it would be much more fun to catch it from a bottle of wine!

The rest of the day was spent quietly reading - except at 1800 when the sun shone. We were so taken aback that we had to go for a stroll. The only thing we lacked was thunder, but, during the night, we lacked it no longer. Weren't we lucky folk - to have seen all the world's climate in one week.

Friday 12th

We went into Portimão once again in an endeavour to have the sole of my shoe reunited with the rest of it. The shoe repairer in the Centro Mondelo vowed it couldn't be done until it was completely dry but, thanks to a shoe shop assistant in the town, we tracked down a real 'olde worlde' shoe repairer, operating in a little shop set into the wall. We didn't know what this shoe repairer did to my shoe, or how he did it, but when we returned at noon, there was my shoe once more in mint condition - and all for about eighty pence! While we waited for the shoe, we put our noses into the local, very ornate church, then pottered into the harbour quarter where, if we had come on a market day, we would have seen a huge fresh fish market in full swing. Today it was very quiet but we found a place that sold us some sandwiches for the picnic lunch we'd planned to have on our balcony.

In the afternoon, we took our final coach trip, this time to Sagres and the Cape of St Vincent, known locally as 'The End of the World' as it was the most south-westerly tip of Europe. There was nothing between there and America. The guide hoped we would visit *inside* the lighthouse but the lighthouse keeper wouldn't allow this - something to do with the condensation from our breath affecting some copper and the mirrors. The guidebook read: "The cliffs of Cabo de São Vicente signal journey's end, and to ancient mariners, it was more besides - *o fim do mundo* ('The end of the world'). This intensely bleak spot was the last sight of Europe for those explorers setting forth on marathon voyages into the unknown. Looking down from the cliff, even on the calmest of days, you can see the cataclysmic force stored in the Atlantic. The lighthouse, built in 1846, is visible up to sixty miles away." The other 'star attraction' at this spot was the Rose Compass. This was nothing like any of us had imagined. User friendly it was *not* as it was set into the ground and was 130 feet in diameter. It was a legacy of Henry the Navigator who had a Navigation School hereabouts. He wasn't a terribly good example to his students as he himself didn't do any navigating. According to the history books, he made just one trip! The views from this spot were wonderful. I had an additional close-up view of the ground when I fell over and cut my knee. My new pair of tights was completely ruined and my knee was not a pretty sight but, as we always carried plasters with us, an emergency operation was done *in situ*.

The coffee stop at Sagres, on the way back, overlooked the picturesque harbour, full of multi-coloured boats. We were home in comfortable time for supper at 1900.

Saturday 13th

For the first time in our stay, the sun appeared this morning. We had to make the most of it so we walked right down to the shore and along the coast as far as we were able, until the road blocked our way. We continued our walk on the higher level for quite a distance, then retraced our steps and purchased the wherewithal for another balcony picnic. At 1700, the Farewell Meeting with the Thomson representatives was due to happen. As well as telling us about the return travel arrangements, Angie set us a quiz from which we learned that the hotel had ten floors (everyone, including us, forgot to count the ground floor!), it was built in 1968, had eighty people working in it - and lots more. We should have known the maximum kilograms the lift would take. We knew it was seven persons but quite often, when we got in it, the alarm sounded, indicating that we had exceeded the maximum kilogram limit. This was the first time we had ever encountered an alarm in a lift. We had often wondered (in lifts in the underground for instance) how the total weight of the passengers was calculated.

We had our final dinner in the hotel before turning in for a good night's sleep ready for our long day tomorrow. We hoped to be back in Kennington by 2130. Our slumbers were disturbed by a huge amount of shouting and noise. At first we thought it was merely drunken people, but the noise became more and more aggressive and we feared the worst. It went on for four hours - so much for our early night!

Sunday 14th

The Thomson representatives told us that the 'off-stage' noises the previous night were just the local Portuguese youth. "It's always like that on a Saturday night" they said. If that was what happened in the 'off' season, what would it be like in the high season, when English lager-louts would be added to the mixture? Under no circumstances would we ever contemplate a visit to a resort like this in the summer.

There were just a few hours before we left and the weather had turned to very heavy rain again. Wasn't that where we came in?

It wasn't raining in Kennington. What a change for the better!

"*Let's get moving. I am beginning to feel
like an advert for a pension fund.*"

PARIS IN (WHAT PASSES FOR) THE SPRING
May 1996

Friday 24th

Once again, we took the Eurostar train to Paris. This was luxury for us living, as we did, only ten minutes walk away from Waterloo. For some reason, First Class travel was included in our package for this weekend. We were not complaining. We made our way to our compartment to await the arrival of lunch (also free). Relatively speaking, we crawled through south-east England, not stopping at Ashford. The announcement that we are just about to enter the tunnel came after seventy-five minutes. By far the longest part of the journey lay ahead but there was less than half the time in which to do it. Once we got into France, the train picked up speed and we were bowling along at 186 mph.

What happened next was rather strange. I wandered off to the buffet car in search of pre-prandial drinks. I was accosted on the way by a burly lady employee of the train company who indicated that I was not allowed to go to the buffet car! She explained that, because there were so many people on board, the lunch service would be somewhat slower than usual; but she would get the pre-prandial drinks *for* me. (At least, that's what I *thought* she said but none of it made much sense.) I was despatched back to my seat and, in a trice, this same Eurostar person appeared with the drinks - and would accept no money for them. In a subsequent trice, another Eurostar employee appeared, bearing complimentary glasses of champagne! I was extremely embarrassed. Had I known about the free champagne, I would *never* have ordered the other drinks. (I felt that they would think I was taking advantage of the system.) There had been no indication on the menu that champagne was included. That apart, the meal was very good indeed, eaten with real knives and forks - no plastic airline equivalents here.

The meal filled in the journey time nicely and no sooner had we had our last mouthful than we were pulling into the Gare du Nord, where we ran into a colleague of Howard's who was also in Paris for the weekend. *Métro* tickets left over from a previous visit allowed us to make a swift journey to our hotel near the Rue du Faubourg Montmartre. It was a Best Western hotel and was, therefore, efficient and clean. We took a short walk to obtain our own pre-prandial drinks and then had an evening meal of an omelette.

Saturday 25th

The morning was spent buying our picnic lunch and booking ourselves into the *Brasserie Flo* for Sunday evening. The weather 'turned nasty' so we had to retreat into a local bar, where we met Max, the resident Alsatian and were able to purchase stamps for our postcards. (We were a little previous as we hadn't yet bought the postcards.) The weather threatened to remain inclement so we retreated even further, back to our hotel room, where we demolished the picnic. It was not quite as exciting as the Tuileries gardens but it was much easier to cope with - and there was the luxury of being able to wash our hands at the end of our meal.

After lunch, we followed the walk described in a recent Evening Standard article by Giles Milton. Without this article, we would have never discovered it. It was the site of an old railway line, now disused and turned into a Promenade Plantée, for approximate three miles. It was a most interesting and pleasant walk and we had great admiration for the 'powers-that-be' that had had the foresight to do this. We ended up at the Bois de Vincennes where we fed the remaining picnic bread to the ducks on the lake.

We went back to the hotel for a rest before setting out for supper at Chez Jean, a restaurant that Howard had found in a Time Out supplement about Paris. We had a very good meal, but Monsieur le Patron was not the most welcoming soul we had ever met. He seemed not at all interested when we told him we had come to his restaurant on the strength of an article in an English magazine. That apart, it was near our hotel and the food was good so we had no complaints.

Sunday 26th - Whit Sunday

The Madeleine was our church of choice for this special day. We hoped to hear some good music. There was a light dusting of Gregorian chant and the Mass setting was by A Lesbordes, of whom we had never heard, but would like to hear again. (We looked him up in our reference books on our return to London but we could not find him.) The high point was César Franck's Third Chorale in A Minor. That really shook the Madeleine's rafters! As for the service itself, it was dominated by the recent murder of seven Trappist monks. As usual, the congregation wandered in (and out) for the first twenty minutes of the service, after which they 'settled down'. There was quite a sprinkling of young people in the congregation, which was good to see.

Chartier provided our very good and very reasonable Sunday lunch. An elderly Frenchman shared our table so we made sure we had a conversation with him. Howard's French can be understood by everyone but my 'A' Level (failed) version is not always so easily assimilated - but I love to try.

At 1730 we went to an organ recital in St Clothilde, given by two very young organists. The first played some Dupré - a Prelude and Fugue, followed by Trois Esquisses, the second of which (in E minor) made us think this was a new musical instrument that we'd never heard before, such was its originality and beauty. The second organist played Jean Langlais' *First Symphony*, written during the War. On our hotel door was a sign which read "Please do not derange this room". We felt there should have been a sign in St Clothilde reading "Please do not derange our eardrums". Monsieur Langlais' piece was 'quite something'. I fell to musing about sound in general and, in particular, about the sounds we were hearing from this great organ (where César Franck had once operated) which were a miracle of both science and the compositional and technical skills of the musicians. There were very bright lights shining in the church. As the light outside faded, they were a distraction, and we wondered why they weren't extinguished altogether. There was little to see and certainly the organists were invisible, so it would have been much better to listen to the music in darkness. Furthermore, three people in the seats right in front of us were clad in red (father) lime green/blue/purple (son) and red (mother), a visually most distracting combination. Mother's garb had what looked like a bar code attached to it. The temptation to run a lighted pen along it was great. That was even more reason for the church to be in darkness.

The *Brasserie Flo* concluded our evening. To my delight, they allowed me to have French Onion Soup as a main course, while Howard had poached salmon. The size of the French Onion Soup that they served had to be seen to be believed. I can't eat vast amounts of food so to have that as a main dish was ideal for me. We both had a good pudding to wind up the evening.

Monday 27th

This morning we went along to the Champs Elysées to look at the free outdoor sculpture exhibition which was there for only two months. There were works by Picasso, Henry Moore, Barbara Hepworth, Rodin, Miro and many more. Much of it was 'a bit on the weird side'. I was even more convinced that I didn't understand the twentieth century. (I can't *begin* to understand the twenty-first century!) We had lunch in the Beaubourg Centre at *Aux Deux Saules*, where we had eaten on a previous stay in Paris.

Our next visit was to the Musée Grevin - the Paris equivalent of Madame Tussaud's. There was a most unique sound and light show in a hall of mirrors. This has been produced originally in 1900, when it must have been nothing short of spectacular, especially as electricity was quite a new thing. In a theatre in the *Musée*, we watched a short conjuring show. We wondered whether the conjuror might be a wax work - but he wasn't.

It was time to return to the Gare du Nord for our 1747 Eurostar train back to London. In the queue we met Arthur and Diane Newman; Arthur was a long-standing singing friend of Howard's. Another excellent meal was served to us on the train, again preceded by champagne, and, this time, I resisted the temptation to order pre-prandial drinks. At 1943 we rolled into Waterloo station.

'*Vive L'entente cordiale*' was our closing Thought for the Weekend.

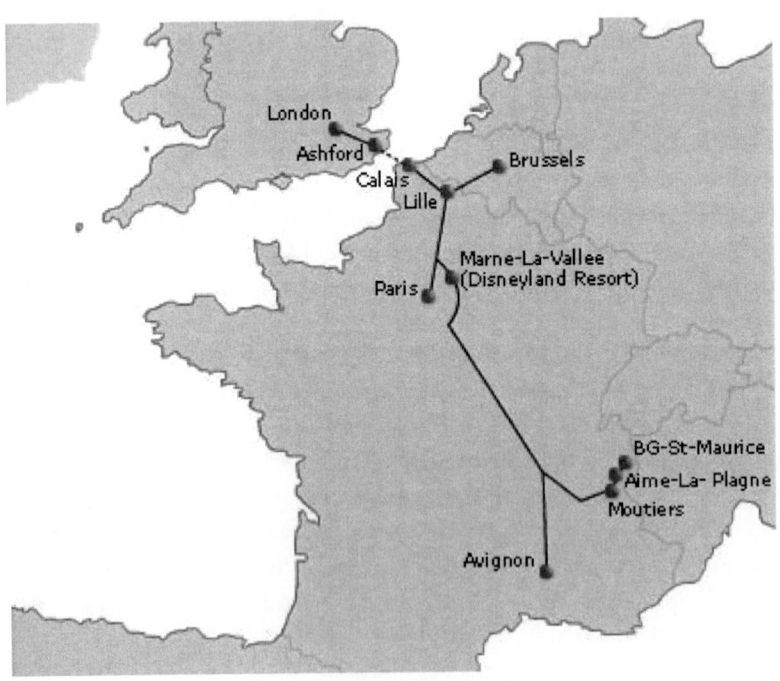

THE LAKE DISTRICT
July 1996

There were two reasons for the choice of the Lake District for this holiday. First, the pace of life being what it was, especially in Howard's job, we decided it would be no bad thing to 'step off the escalator of life' for a week and take time out doing nothing. Secondly, neither of us had been to the Lake District but we'd heard wonderful reports of it, so it sounded an ideal spot for our purposes. It turned out to be one of the best holidays we had ever taken.

Saturday 6th

We decided that the holiday should start in the style in which we hoped to become accustomed. We were much looking forward to meals being put in front of us without the necessity of buying the ingredients, cooking them and, of course, washing up afterwards. (How very lazy we intended to be!) I had enquired, when booking the railway tickets, if the 1230 to Windermere conveyed a restaurant car and was assured it did. The British Rail representative even went so far as to apologize for the fact that he was unable to make reservations for lunch but pointed out that we could do that as soon as we boarded the train. (My faith in any aspect of British Rail, on a scale of one to ten, is *nought*. They didn't let us down!) At Euston station we walked the length of the train - and didn't spot a restaurant car.

We settled ourselves into our reserved seats and Howard went 'in search'. He tracked down a buffet car where the attendant confirmed there was no restaurant car on this train. He went on to say "there never is at the weekend"! Knowing how quickly buffet cars can run out of stocks on long journeys, we knew we couldn't take that risk so as soon as the train tentatively dragged itself away from platform fifteen, we set off in search of something 'to keep the wolf from the door'. We were not a moment too soon. The service was extremely slow. Had we left it any later, we would have spent the entire journey in the queue. We equipped ourselves with the wherewithal for our improvised lunch and, fighting back our disappointment, retreated to Carriage J and made the most of it. (Little did we know that, before the day was out, we would be *grateful* to British Rail!)

We changed at Lancaster and boarded the little local train for Windermere. 'Little' was no exaggeration - it was only two coaches long, and we had reserved seats on it! A tongue-in-cheek muse as to whether *this* train conveyed a restaurant car almost had us eating our words. To our astonishment, along came a refreshment trolley! (It didn't take it long to work its way through the two carriages.) The scenery was becoming more and more enticing.

The taxi was there to meet us at Windermere station and the drive to Ambleside, along the side of Lake Windermere, confirmed that this was, truly, a beautiful part of the world. The Wateredge Hotel seemed like a dream, situated, as it was, at the side of the Lake. (Could this be how it got its name?)

A posse of ducks, swans and other assorted birds was waiting to greet us. We realized why - we had found this hotel from an advertisement in the RSPB magazine, so our wingèd chums would have felt it incumbent upon them to provide a welcome party. (As Howard remarked: "one good tern deserves another".) That was just the beginning of everything marvellous that we were to encounter at the Wateredge Hotel. It was one of the best hotels in which we'd ever stayed; our room had a view of the lake, *en suite* facilities (naturally), tea and coffee making things and, on this particular occasion, half a bottle of champage which I had requested as a belated celebration of Howard's birthday, which had been on the previous day. The information we had been sent about the hotel warned us about the six-course dinners. Our first encounter with them was sheer delight. The food, the service, the ambience (yes, even the ambience), on a scale of one to ten, we had to rate at twelve - at least!

We returned to our lovely room sixteen, very very satisfied. We had to admit that, had British Rail been true to its word and *had* a restaurant car, we would never have been able to do justice to dinner at Wateredge. We retired for the night, truly in another world. Would we wake up next morning and realize it was all a dream?

Sunday 7th

No, it wasn't a dream. We really *were* there and it was as beautiful as it had been the day before. Tea in bed - and everything looked as if it had been bought yesterday - the crockery, the trays, the gold bathroom accessories - it was all so perfect.

A full English breakfast set us up for the walk to Ambleside church for 1045 Holy Communion. We were in good time so we pottered around, looking for a suitable venue for a light lunch after church. The 1045 service had been moved to 1100 so we occupied the time reading the gravestones and musing on the inhabitants. The service was exactly as we liked it. The only blot on the landscape was that the fourth hymn threatened to be *Sing Hosanna*. The gods - or even God himself - were smiling on us. It didn't happen. We went straight from hymn number three to hymn number five - *Praise my soul the King of heaven*.

The pub lunch was just what we needed and we met Casey, a white golden retriever, and Fudge, a cute cross between a labrador and an alsatian. Home for the Men's Finals of Wimbledon.

Monday 8th

We decided to follow a recommended walk to Wansfell and Troutbeck so, armed with our guidebook and map, we set off at 0930. The book described the walk as being in three distinct sections: quite steep, steep and, finally, very steep. Had we been the book's authors, we would have written: very steep, even steeper and 'can we really do this?'. We were very proud when we made it to the top of Wansfell (1,581 feet) - even higher that the Worcestershire Beacon which we'd climbed in a previous incarnation, a mere 1,325 feet. The views on the way up became more and more breathtaking and, at the top, as the guidebook promised, they went off the scale of superlatives. Every so often, the peace and quiet was shattered by the terrifying sound of military aircraft practising low-flying techniques in the hills. The local bus timetable (?) warned us of this, pointing out that is was not only the British forces that carry out these flights. "Our NATO allies sometimes low-fly in the UK, but this has to be matched by a similar number of sorties by our aircraft, down to the same level, in the guest nation's own airspace." - so wrote Mr A L Parrini, the RAF Regional Community Relations Officer. The reason for these exercises was to practise flying out of sight of enemy-held radar for as long as possible. All that made us feel part of the real world again, which we don't want to be for seven days. We put it out of our minds as soon as silence returned and the wasp-like planes had vanished as quickly as they had come.

The descent was easier, though still quite exhausting for we inexperienced walkers. The local beer and sandwich at *The Mortal Man* pub at Troutbeck was more than welcome. We realized only too well how very mortal we were when we stood up after our lunch. It wasn't the effects of the beer, but the shock to the system of climbing to 1,581 feet. Were we in an ambulatory-challenged situation? It was then that we realized we were only half way through the seven mile walk. We thought the return would be a piece of cake but it, too, had its challenges and, by the time we neared the Wateredge hotel, our legs were *really* complaining. A two-hour rest, tennis mixed doubles and the bliss of a foamy bath, with the prospect of one of Wateredge's dinners, could not be bad. A toast to our trusty walking sticks, bought in Malvern in 1982 and which have been such a boon to us ever since - never more so than on this particular walk.

Tuesday 9th

It was clear to us that our legs were suffering from 'post walking distress disorder'. It was also clear that we were becoming very red; our arms were quite sore. We had caught the sun much more than we had realized.

It would soon be time for the ritual duck and swan feeding, with the left-over breakfast toast. We were very popular with our feathered chums, who wandered up and took the food from our hands, or, in the case of the swans, tried to snatch it from us in a most thoughtless and rude manner. Did their mummies never tell them? Not so the smaller fry who were consistently well-behaved. If the swans didn't mend their ways, they would not get their photos in future RSPB magazines. We pointed this out to them - adding how ill-manned it was to make that hissing noise...

The rest of the day was spent in sheer idleness. The weather didn't look too promising so we sat in the lounge and wrote our postcards and letters. A very good light lunch on the patio was followed by an afternoon sitting by the lake with the feathered chums, until we thought we might be getting burned. At that point we retreated to our room and learned to pronounce some of the food that we had had - and were about to have. The restaurant in this hotel was Egon Ronay recommended, as well as having four crowns of recommendation from the English Tourist Board. We were making the most of things like 'fanned galia melon, coulis of *fraise de liqueur* and fresh berries' and *would* make the most of '*clafoutis* with cherries' and 'sabayon sauce' when we found out what they were. At the other end of the scale, something else we were making the most of was a portable loo-roll holder. Never had we encountered such a thing before. We were so taken with this that we got one for ourselves on our return. (Hooray for the *Innovations* catalogue - that now seems to have 'died the death'.)

Wednesday 10th

Today we took a scenic bus ride to Kendal - home of the famous 'mint cake'. The scenic bus ride was to be recommended, Kendal not so. What a shock to our systems - all that noisy, fume-making traffic. As soon as we stepped off our Stagecoach bus, we were longing for 1430 when we could step on the return one! It was a busy town whose one-way system enabled solid masses of traffic to jam the main street. It was market day, but we found the market rather disappointing. Could anything good come out of Kendal? Yes - we found an optician who fixed Howard's glasses.

There was a small art gallery which had an exhibition of Lucien Freud. What a shame the models couldn't afford some clothes. They wouldn't have looked *quite* so ugly. My feeling was that perhaps Mr Freud should have stuck to cooking. (An elderly lady we were to encounter later in Kendal church told us she was 'most uncertain' about Mr Freud's work and was relieved that, when she had seen it, she 'had not been in the company of any of her gentleman friends'.) After Mr Freud's masterpieces, we looked into a small museum of traditional Lake District life, before patronising *The Ring o' Bells* for a sandwich and a beer. Always the traffic noise invaded our peace. There was just time to peer into the very large church (which was where we encountered the lady who was dubious about Mr F) and to hear the organ being played, by a young man who was practising. This was one of the most efficiently organized churches we had encountered - leaflets about itself in *seven* languages, and even a leaflet about the organ. (Charles Proctor would be pleased.)

We were mightily relieved to return to the peace and quiet of Wateredge and tea-time with the birds, for whom we had bought some rolls. A lovely surprise awaited us when we went to get our key. Our friend Theo had left a message, so we called him and arranged to meet the next day.

Thursday 11th

I made a determined effort to read our friend Jean-Marie Fèvre's book, which he had recently sent us. It was all about his connections with Poland and the Polish, leading up to his recent posting there with his wife Mirjam and their family, which now included *three* children, Eric being the latest addition. The book was called *Rencontre avec l'Aigle Blanc* (*Meeting with the White Eagle*), the White Eagle being the symbol of Poland, which appeared on their stamps. The snag was that the book was in French but I was determined to read it. While I didn't understand every word, I was well able to follow the narrative - and discovered lots of things we didn't know about our friend Jean-Marie.

A boat trip on Lake Windermere was planned and we arranged to meet Theo, co-owner with Elizabeth of a cottage in Kirby Lonsdale. We bought a round-trip boat ticket which enabled us to get on and off the boats at will. We spent part of the trip with a couple who were staying in our hotel. He turned out to be a retired headmaster and his wife told me about celluloid legs, so I became anxious in case mine turned out to be celluloid and melted in the hot sun. (Who cares? Life's too short to worry about trivialities like melting legs...) We broke our journey at Bowness and spent an hour pottering about there. The church was open and a team of parish ladies was giving it its weekly spring clean. Everything gleamed and sparkled - a tribute to their labours.

We met up with Theo and Elizabeth at Lakeside, the southernmost point of the Lake, after an idyllic boat ride. They were waiting on the quayside and they whisked us off to Newby Bridge, to a hostelry known to them. We were treated to a good lunch at *The Swan*, followed by a whistle-stop tour of the environs of Kirby Lonsdale, taking in the cottage about which we had heard so much over the years. Kirby Lonsdale seemed a delightful place, but much bigger than we'd imagined. There was time for a river bank walk before driving back to Newby Bridge to get the 'steam train' back to Lakeside. The first rain of our stay - but it mattered not as we were safely ensconced in our very comfortable boat, with padded seats, and carpeted floor - and not too many passengers, which made the trip even more agreeable. The feathered fraternity missed out on their food as it was pouring with rain by the time we got back to Wateredge, Their turn would come the following morning.

Friday 12th

We took an open-topped bus part of the way to Grasmere; we were going to do the Wordsworth Pilgrimage. It was rather blowy but we didn't mind the discomfort. Wordsworth's Dove Cottage and Museum were 'well worth the detour'. We had the services of an excellent guide who filled us in on Wordsworth and his contemporaries. What an odd lot they were! Both Samuel Taylor Coleridge and Thomas de Quincey were addicted to opium. (There's nothing new, is there?) Wordsworth seemed to be the only normal one amongst them, except even he had a garden door put into his house so he could nip into his study, avoiding the kitchen - his excuse being that he "felt a poem coming on". (Or might it have been that he was trying to avoid any domestic duties?) There was much 'daffodilia' everywhere, especially on trays, tea towels and mats. Lots of tourists were wandering about 'as lonely as a cloud mass before a thunderstorm'. The visit was very reminiscent of our tour of Anne Hathaway's cottage the previous year at Stratford-on-Avon.

The first half of our walk took us through perfect, picturesque scenery 'below the steep forbidding crags of Nab Scar'. We never did find out what they were forbidden to do. There were lots of lovely flora and fauna to arrest our attention, including a preponderance of foxgloves. I mused that I had never seen foxes wearing gloves until Howard pointed out that I had not seen *that* many foxes. Then we realized that the word is a literal translation of the medieval words *foufs*, meaning 'purple' and *glovis*, meaning 'bell' - hence the name which described perfectly their appearance. ("If you believe that, you'll believe anything" - Ed. - Shorter Oxford Dictionary.) A baked potato, a ploughman's lunch and some local brew went down a treat.

Thus fortified, we continued our walk which, though long, was not taxing, not after Monday's marathon. We were getting blasé about hills, gradients and hanging valleys by now. Eat your heart out, Chris Bonnington! Walking in the hills gave much time for musing and generally reflecting. At the Wordsworth Museum we had spied many an original manuscript of William and his literary chums. We wondered whether, in years to come, the manuscript of this diary would be unearthed and whether scientists would carbon date the paper to discover where we wrote it and what we had for lunch on the day - fragments of which had found their way onto the notebook.

Back at the hotel, we had our final six-course dinner - "for a while anyway" Howard said, "until we come back again". We could not believe our stay was almost over. It had been as perfect a time as anyone could have wished. "The best things in life are free" came to mind, and we had to admit it was absolutely true. While the hotel was anything *but* free, the Lake District itself certainly was, and must rank alongside others of God's greatest creations. It was not only all the things of nature, which were in abundance, but the peace, the quiet, the pace of life, the stillness - all of which passed us by in everyday life, all of which we craved and all of which we ignored at our peril. How different we felt on our return - like springs that have been completely uncoiled and the metal was once more 'malleable and ductile'.

We knew we would miss this place more than we could say, but we had the memories of it and the benefit of our visit would stay with us for a long time. Like Sorrento, it was definitely 'a place to go back to' - as it had been one of the most wonderful holidays we had every taken.

COPENHAGEN - EUROPEAN CITY OF CULTURE 1996
August 1996

Tuesday 27th

On the day of leaving for a holiday, the time between waking and leaving our flat was never my favourite. There was still the 'countdown to departure'. (How those astronauts ever get off, we'll never know.) Though we were going to be away for only four days, there were the same safety checks to be carried out as if we were going away for four weeks. At least they were now programmed into the Spurr memory bank, except they were not on a floppy disc, merely on a piece of cardboard pinned to the back of the door. "Gas out, plugs out, rubbish out". Then confirmation that the tickets and passports really *were* in the depths of my interactive handbag, to save the embarrassment of wishing we had brought the piano with us - "because the tickets were on top of it". ("But I thought you said *you'd* picked them up".) Even after this little ritual, I could never resist another ferret through the handbag as soon as we were in the taxi - just to check the passports were in date!

The tube ride to Heathrow Terminal Three was long and, on arrival, our luggage was searched. But we had been clever...they didn't find anything. That could be explained by the fact that we didn't have anything illegal to find. We were flying SAS, which I thought was unnecessarily secretive. Did we *really* need the protection of those leather-clad men in dark glasses, even though Howard was in the employ of the FCO. (Howard was bound by the Official Secrets Act so was unable to tell us what FCO stood for.)

The in-flight magazine was a disappointment. At least it was in English; we feared it might be in a Scandinavian tongue with 'O's crossed out or perched over the top of other letters in the manner of an *umlaut*. We were not let off the hook entirely as the very first article, all about the Baltic Sea, was by Måns Lönnroth. The second article was about some pop groups, followed by a full page telling us all we needed to know about gout. Usually the in-flight magazines had articles about well known people, shedding light on a part of their life little known to the general public. (Did you know that Petula Clark collected button hooks?) As if to make up for this, the 'Safety on Board' leaflet did us proud. Not only were there the usual diagrams of people doing right things (✔) and wrong things (**X**), but there were illustrations headed 'Arctic Survival'. Mercifully we did not have cause to refer to this excellent manual. We could never work out how to deal with the *ordinary* life jackets. The 'Arctic Survival' garb was much more extensive - and complicated. It looked like the equivalent of donning a tent. The drawing of the little group of ex-passengers, huddled together in a life raft in the snow, portrayed them as a happy enough bunch, especially as they were accompanied by a yeti-like crew member with a mobile phone. (It actually looked like a black blob but we could tell it was a mobile phone by the excited little concentric circles being emitted from it.) Of course, he might have been phoning to say "I'm going out and I may be some time". (To sow his wild Oates?) Our reveries were interrupted by the Scandinavian air hostess telling us that we were landing. As we seemed to be over the sea, we were somewhat uneasy about that idea. Perhaps she had made an air hostess equivalent of a typographical error - or maybe we were in a seaplane?

When we landed, there was an SAS bus waiting to ferry us into Copenhagen. In the bus were more pictures crossed out, indicating three things we must not do. The first was simple enough; it was a bottle. The second appeared to be two bananas. We thought that was a bit odd. Why pick on bananas? Oranges were a much more anti-social fruit when eaten in a public place. The third icon had us totally baffled. It was a fish slice. Since there was no possibility that we would be preparing any fish whilst on the bus, we weren't too concerned.

A phone message awaited our arrival at the Imperial Hotel. That was the good news. Howard phoned to find that tickets for the Royal Theatre had been organized for us for Prokofiev's ballet *Romeo and Juliet*. Furthermore, the tickets were being sent round to the hotel by the Danish Minister of Justice's chauffeur! The bad news was that the chauffeur would collect from us the 600 Danish Kroner. The exchange rate was 8.67 kroner to the pound. The shock to our systems, when we worked out the cost of the tickets, was almost life-threatening. It made a *huge* dent in our spending money. There was nothing for it but to grin - and pay up! When the tickets arrived, the instructions were in Danish - so too was the title which had become *Romeo and Julie*. Prokofiev's masterpiece suddenly had a ring of Essex Girl about it.

Howard had found us a restaurant for an early supper, just five minutes walk from our hotel, along the *Strøget*, a pedestrian precinct all the way. It was littered with street performers of every conceivable type, including an excellent violinist giving her all in Monti's *Czardas*. Then there was the odd Spanish guitarist. The secret of that is to learn a few simple chords, strum them very quickly, accompany them with wailing singing and look very intense and bad-tempered throughout. If standing up, a few stamped feet always perks up a performance. This particular performer was sitting down, so we had to forgo the stamping feet. The restaurant that Howard had chosen, *Kokken og Havfruen* (*The Chef and Mermaid*) was excellent. The waitress sounded so English. It was hard to believe that she wasn't.

She told us we had spent four years at Edinburgh University studying Art History.

The ballet was marvellous and we enjoyed every minute of it. Prokofiev's music was a knockout. Before this evening, we only knew the famous bit. (We were surprised to find that some gems from his *Classical Symphony* had found their way into the score.) We couldn't help thinking that ballet dancers are 'a breed apart'. Peter Gellhorn's description of them said it all: "They walk about on their toes, with a permanently disdainful look, as if the earth isn't quite good enough for them to walk on." He was absolutely right. We wondered if they walked like that in the supermarket. And how could they do all that dancing (almost three hours) without getting cramp? I wondered if their legs made clicking noises like mine, first thing in the morning.

Wednesday 28th

It was a perfect day for our boat trip on the canals. The open-topped boat wafted us around the Copenhagen waterways with commentary in three languages - English, German and Danish. There were two ocean-going ships in the harbour - the Princess of Scandinavia and her much bigger sister ship, the Queen of Scandinavia. Were these anything like the boat that would take us back to Harwich?

Back on *terra firma*, we set off in search of Ida Davidson's - a place famous for its open sandwiches, of which there would be about seventy from which to choose. On the way there, we stopped off in Nyhaven, the old sailors' quarter. We didn't see any old sailors, mainly because the area is now a collection of eating places of all sorts and descriptions. There were many adverts for Hereford steak, but we assumed they wouldn't be happening just now due to Britain's little 'local difficulties' in the area of meat. We played safe and had two glasses of BSE-free Tuborg lager - the local product. We passed a tatooist's shop. Howard said that where there were sailors, there was bound to be a tatooist. Though we had seen no old sailors, we assumed there must be some young ones in the town to crew things like the Princess and Queen of Scandinavia. (Or was it all done by computers these days? Could you tatoo a computer?) Another find - we stumbled across the Changing of the Guard at the Royal Residences. (There seemed to be four of them surrounding a square.) The Danish version of Changing the Guard was on a much smaller scale to the Buckingham Palace equivalent. No band and just two platoons with twelve soldiers in each. They really *did* look as if they had not yet left school. The Danish army must have been cradle-snatchers.

At Ida Davidsen's, there *were* about seventy choices of open sandwiches - not to mention additional hot dishes. The very attentive waitress (was she Ida herself?) explained what we had to do. When it came to the question of drinks, we put ourselves in her hands. She told us the usual thing was to have beer along with *Aquavit*. Always ready for a new experience, we took her at her word. She explained that we must have a sip of *Aquavit*, followed by a swig of beer. What sort of *Aquavit* did we want? As we'd never heard of it until that minute, we had no idea of the 'sorts', so, again, we left it to her. She recommended the sort that was celebrating its 150th birthday. It was *very* strong. *More* than a sip at a time and we'd have been under the table. (We suspect they also used it for paint stripper.) Both the food and the drinks were superb and we were really glad we had tracked down this place. We had our only sighting of Danny Kaye here, in a photograph with Ida herself. Considering what he had done for Copenhagen, we expected to see him all over the town - but it was not to be.

We floated back to the Imperial Hotel and rested for a while to work up our strength for the remainder of the day which was to be spent in the Tivoli Gardens, just across the road. On our previous visit to Copenhagen in 1982, the Tivoli Gardens had been closed as it was out of season. Inside there were all sorts of things to do, many of which frightened the life out of us - and that was just watching others doing them. The days were long since past when we would venture onto anything as daring as a roller coaster, let alone an out-of-control railway train or the Flying Carpet. We could hardly bear to watch. There was a choice of thirty eateries in the Gardens, ranging from the very expensive (thirty pounds for a main course) to the much more reasonable. No prizes for guessing where we ate. We watched a mimed play in an open-air theatre then made a final circuit of the Gardens, now illuminated by all the coloured lights. It really was 'fairy tale' like but somewhat noisy as, by now, some of the vocalists were getting into their stride and the more scary rides were always accompanied by screaming.

Thursday 29th

We started our return journey which was to take twenty-eight hours. We caught the 1252 train to take us to Esjberg, on the west coast of Denmark. The train journey was mostly by train, though one part of it, across the *Store Baelt,* would be on a ferry. But it was to be painless. The train drove onto the ferry. Passengers could stay on the train in the ferry but as the crossing took an hour, we opted to go into the boat and take a turn round the deck. We saw the bridge which was under construction to link the two pieces of land. A friendly native explained that the first part of the bridge was almost complete, the one which will take the railway. Trains will go from the West to the island in the middle, where they will descend into a tunnel for the remainder of the journey. The road traffic, however, would go the whole way over the bridge - the middle section of which had yet to be completed and it would be a suspension bridge. What a feat of engineering! It was hoped that the railway section would open in 1997 and the road part in 1998.

The MS Dana Anglia was awaiting the arrival of our train. It was indeed a large ship and it would carry us over the North Sea back to England's 'green and pleasant'. The Captain told us that the weather conditions were 'Force five to six' for the trip. Our first call was to make reservations for the smorgasbord supper at 1845. It was a really delicious buffet-style Danish meal so we could have as little or as much as we wanted. We took a quick turn around the deck (to check on the Force five or six-ness of things) before retiring to our cabin for the night. Howard, being the more scientifically minded of us, worked out how to detach the bunks from their moorings. The rhythm of the ship had settled into a comfortable 6/8 - very reminiscent of Edward McDowell's *AD MDCXX* from his *Sea Pieces*. We suspected that this was about the same amount of movement as we all experienced for the first nine months of our existence. It was a rather restful, reassuring feeling.

Friday 30th

A good night's sleep had given us the necessary energy to cope with the intricacies of the shower. (We would welcome international legislation requiring showers world-wide to behave in the same way. They are all so very different - the consequence being that, whilst trying to fathom them out, invariably we pulled, turned or pushed the very thing that released a torrent of water. This was always a shock to the system as the torrent was either very hot or very cold. Initial investigation *never* revealed the mixing apparatus.) This particular shower wasn't too bad, once we had got used to standing at forty-five degrees to the horizontal. A buffet breakfast whiled away the first half hour of the day. We were now four hours from docking at 1330, which would become 1230 on arrival in Harwich.

The remainder of the journey was without incident and we docked exactly on time. A train journey took us back to Liverpool Street and, in no time at all, the taxi was depositing us at the gates of Jennifer House. Another successful expedition and another host of good reasons why it was so good to get back to our very own permanent cabin.

*"Poor Yorick. No, Inspector, I didn't know
him well at all!."*

FOREIGN AND COMMONWEALTH OFFICE CHOIR TRIP
TO PARIS
October 1996

The Foreign Office Choir, of which Howard was a member, had been invited to give two concerts in Paris - one in the Ambassador's Residence and the other in the Scots Kirk. Some 'extras' were drafted in, of whom I was one.

Friday 18th

We caught the 1023 Eurostar train to Paris, due to arrive at the Gare du Nord at 1427. Now that Eurostar had been running for almost two years, and shared its 'berths' with British Rail, it had picked up British Rail's bad habits. It was fifty minutes late leaving. We were told that there were mechanical faults in the carriages, but that 'they had been fixed'. We thought they were *never* fixed as, when we made our way to the platform indicated, an empty train pulled out, and we were directed to the adjacent platform. We suspected that, during the fifty minutes, all the food and other refreshments had had to be moved from one train to the other.

Howard visited the buffet car as soon as the train was under way. He waited about twenty-five minutes as everyone in front of him was served individually and some wanted hot food, which had to be put in a microwave. The buffet car attendant waited for the food to be heated, received the payment and issued the receipt - all before moving on to the next customer, some of whom only wanted drinks and could have been served while the food was heating. Paying was quite a performance because of the possibility of payment being made in any of four currencies. When Howard made it to the front of the queue, he noticed another Choir member about fifteen people behind him. We could only assume that he would not have been served until the train was pulling into Paris.

As we approached the Gare du Nord, an announcement told us that, as compensation for our late arrival, we would be issued with a document that could be exchanged for a *free* single ticket on Eurostar. There were numerous Eurostar-uniformed ladies handing out the documents as we disembarked. As they were glossy printed things, we could only conclude that such late arrivals were by no means isolated incidents!

We took a *Métro* to the hotel where Howard had made reservations for quite a number of the choir to stay. Having assured himself that all was well, we had planned to go on to where we were staying, right opposite the Eiffel Tower. Julia and Richard Codrington and their two five-and-a-half year old twins, Nicholas and Thomas, had very kindly agreed to put us up for the weekend. Both of them worked in the British Embassy in Paris. Because the train had been late, there was no time to do that, so we made our way to the Ambassador's Residence where the first of our two concerts was to be given, in the Ballroom. (The Residence was right next door to the British Embassy, just a stone's throw from the Madeleine.) Two rooms in the Residence had been set aside for changing so that's just what we did before finding our way to the Ballroom for the rehearsal.

The time came for the concert. A veil is best drawn over it! At the end of the concert, the Choir Chairman made a short but fulsome speech of thanks to the conductor - whose last concert it was. (A new conductor was due to start that week.) A presentation was made to the retiring conductor and all agreed how wonderful it had been under his direction.

A reception followed, during which we chatted to the Ambassador, Michael Jay, who had been in the job for only four months. The Residence was amazing. There was gold leaf everywhere and olde-worlde furniture from 'Louis the this and that'. There was a throne that no one had sat on except Queen Victoria. (No prizes for guessing who *else* had now sat on it!) Our hostess, Julia Codrington, was singing in the choir for this concert, the music having been sent out to her in Paris 'about ten seconds beforehand'.

After the reception, she drove us back to their apartment near the Eiffel Tower. There we met husband who had been babysitting as they were 'between nannies'. We were invited to share some excellent wine and cheese with them. We learned that Julia was the First Secretary Political at the Embassy and Richard was the Commercial Counsellor. They were both very, *very* high-powered and at the top of their respective trees. Julia spent much time taking French politicians out to lunch to find out what was going on in French political circles. She sent some of the information back to the Foreign and Commonwealth Office in London and filed other information away for future reference. They lived in some state as they were expected to entertain at a high level, so they needed a large apartment - but it was paid for by the Embassy. They told us that the Ambassador and his wife had been to them for a meal the previous evening. They told us also that they had not gone to bed until 0130 for the past three weeks. (Phew! Rather them than me...)

Saturday 19th

When I woke, it dawned on me that I did not have my skirt and sweater that I had worn the previous day, I realized that, having changed into my concert clothes at the Residence, I had not changed back at the end of the evening, so my skirt and jumper would be there. Julia rang the Residence to ask about the possibility of our popping back to collect them. The Ambassador's wife suggested that we went along after breakfast, which we did. Though we looked in the relevant room in the Residence, there was no sign of my lost clothing so we concluded that another Choir member had found it and taken it along to return to us later in the day. (This proved to be the case.) However, an umbrella and a comb had also been left behind, so we were able to repay the compliment by taking those with us and returning *them* to their rightful owners. There was heavy security at the gates of the Residence. A massive wooden gate was opened by a security man but there was a safety chain on it so no one could have 'rushed' the gate, in the manner of a Bastille-type invasion.

We took ourselves along to the Rue de Rivoli as we wanted to get a present for someone. We were successful in our quest so we headed off to the Musée d'Orsay. Having spent a happy time with the Impressionists, we had a snack lunch in the café. We walked all the way back to the Eiffel Tower, at the end of which our legs felt as if they didn't belong to us.

There was just time for a ten minute break (literally) before we had to change into our concert gear once again and head for the Scots Kirk where we were to give the second concert. The rehearsal was at 1530, the concert was due to start at 1700. When we got there, the soprano soloist was still rehearsing with her pianist - and continued to rehearse until almost 1600. It didn't matter as many of the Choir did not arrive until almost 1600! We had a swift run-through and there was much panic as the men still could not manage one of the more difficult bits in the Bizet *Te Deum*. We were still rehearsing when the audience arrived, but they were restrained behind closed doors! The rehearsal finished about 1645 and the men were summoned to a sectional rehearsal (fifteen minutes before the performance!) which took place, unaccompanied, in the room where others were changing and some members of the audience were assembling. To our surprise, Mr and Mrs Ambassador turned up again - they were gluttons for punishment! The concert happened; there were sighs of relief all round.

Howard had researched a good restaurant and four of the Choir joined us. Our four friends were as impressed by the restaurant as we were. (We were very pleased because it is so easy to enthuse about somewhere then for others to find it not to their taste.) We returned to our host and hostess where, after a brief chat, we made our excuses and retired. They didn't mind in the least as it gave them the chance to have a relatively early night.

Sunday 20th

After breakfast, we volunteered to purchase tarts for pudding at Sunday lunch, to which our hosts had kindly invited us. We took their two little boys with us to show us the way and to help choose the tarts, which they *much* enjoyed doing. We dropped off the tarts and the little boys back at the flat and headed for the Madeleine for the 1100 Sung Eucharist. The incoming and outgoing organ music was some of the finest we had ever heard - and probably some of the loudest too. It was quite remarkable. According to the information board, they were improvisations, which made them all the more remarkable. The setting was a Mozart Mass and the anthem was also by Mozart, so we enjoyed a feast of music in that wonderful building.

We returned to the flat for lunch after which we went with Julia and the boys to a nearby park. We left them there while we took a pleasant walk by the river, returning in time to collect our luggage, say our farewells and make our way back to the Gare du Nord for our return train to London. It left ten minutes late but was half an hour late by the time we got to Waterloo. We were not offered any free tickets so, obviously, 'injury time' had to exceed thirty minutes to qualify for them. On the journey we had learned that one Choir member was going out to be our Ambassador in Senegal the following April and another was going to be 'Number Two' in Tunis! Never let it be said that we didn't 'mingle with the mighty', or, come to that, that the mighty didn't mingle with us!

FROM HARWICH TO THE FREE AND HANSEATIC CITY
OF HAMBURG
August 1997

Our friends the Fèvres had been posted to Hamburg as Jean-Marie had a job at the *Institut Français*, so we decided to visit them there and take the opportunity of seeing Hamburg, a city we had not visited.

Friday 15th

We made our way to Liverpool Street station where we were to catch a non-stop train to Harwich. The heat was rather dreadful - reminiscent of summer 1976 - and of all the available coaches on the train, we managed to select the one where the air conditioning had broken down! We assumed the whole train was affected but we heard some Americans talking about the air conditioning and how it was working in just a few carriages. Very quickly, we moved!

After Passport Control at Harwich, it was a long walk to the Prince of Scandinavia, which would take us to Hamburg. It was a very impressive vessel, nine storeys high - with lifts! - like a sailing hotel. It even had its own hospital on board. It was very well maintained, spotlessly clean, carpeted throughout and our cabin was larger than some hotel rooms we had occupied. The crossing was the smoothest we had ever encountered. The water was like a mirror and it was almost impossible to spot a wave; there were no sea horses.

Supper was spent in the company of two German ladies, returning to Hamburg after a week's trip round England. They apologized for their English. We assured them that it was very good and apologized for our lack of knowledge of German. (That was not strictly true - I had my four sentences [see *Austria - In Search of the Sound of Music*] but they don't get me far in most conversations.)

Saturday 16th

After a very comfortable night (with our own *en suite* facilities), we woke to a perfect morning, a huge buffet breakfast and nothing to do for four hours except lounge about in ideal temperatures. These final four hours were spent cruising up the River Elbe as Hamburg is about sixty miles along the river. We feared it would be hot in Hamburg, but, for now, we made the most of the sea breezes. (This is the life!) There was time to read the voluminous booklet detailing all the duty-free things; that was an education in itself. Whilst we'd heard of the more run-of-the-mill things like *Eternity, Obsession, Escape* (from what?) and even *Opium*, we were left wondering about *Time Zone for Eyes, Advanced Night Repair, Resilience Refirming Creme* and, weirdest of all, *Thigh Body Zone Streamlining Complex!* We knew we were out of touch with reality most of the time, but we didn't realize just *how* out of touch we were...

A minibus was waiting at the dock to take us to the Hotel SAS Radisson. (Would we encounter more leather-clad men in dark glasses?) There were twenty-seven floors of it and we were on the fourth floor, our room overlooking the famous gardens, Planten und Blumen, which was one of the 'things to see' in Hamburg. We telephoned our friends and very soon Jean-Marie arrived with two of his three children - Victor (now eight) and Nicole (now five). Like their parents, the children spoke an assortment of languages (including Polish since their time in Warsaw), but English was not one of them. They spoke French, of course, so we were able to get along in that tongue.

The Fèvre's house was very spacious, with an equally spacious garden. We could easily understand why they were so happy here. Now we were to meet Eric for the first time. He was almost two years old, very like his father - only with more hair! - and he was a bundle of joy. There was a lovely safe area where the children could play in the garden, with swings, a tent and a separate wigwam! Much time was spent catching up with news since we last met in Warsaw in 1995. They had been living in Hamburg for one year and they had some 300 empty packing cases in their attic, ready for their next move. Jean-Marie's present job would last either two or four years, after which he would be posted somewhere else, probably back to France and it might even have been to Paris.

We had taken some 'painting by numbers' things for Victor and Nicole and they rushed off to experiment with them. For Eric, we had brought a scrapbook as we thought he would be starting to draw very soon. For Jean-Marie and Mirjam we had taken some Mint Sauce - as they had asked us to do! They had come across it in Hong Kong (of all places) and had really liked it, but it seemed not to exist in Germany. We took the liberty of taking a bottle of malt vinegar too, as we didn't know whether they knew about adding vinegar to it. They were delighted and we explained how they could make it for themselves from the profusion of mint in their garden - if they had the time and patience to chop it into tiny pieces. They had a lovely surprise for us - a cake which had been made entirely by Victor and Nicole. Not only that but Victor had made a very good drawing of the Union Jack for us to take home.

In the evening, we wanted to take Jean-Marie and Mirjam for a meal so Jean-Marie had booked a delightful restaurant nearby called the *Alster Park*, which he had sampled but Mirjam had not yet seen. It was a super choice; we sat outside by the river Alster, being observed by the local ducks and, intermittently, we observed the passing canoeists. It was so peaceful and, during the six-course meal, (which was excellent and accompanied by wonderful wine), we caught up with even *more* news. Jean-Marie kindly drove us back to our hotel by midnight (just in time - before we turned into white mice) and we were asleep in minutes.

Sunday 17th

On waking, our first sight was the box containing six litres of wine - a present from Jean-Marie and Mirjam. We looked forward to drinking their health - but that would not be until our return to London. At 1000 Jean-Marie arrived to give us our own personal guided tour of Hamburg. It was hard to believe that it had been almost destroyed by fire 100 years ago, rebuilt, then flattened again - by *us* - in the Second World War. The first place we visited was the Rathaus. We didn't like the sound of that but we needn't have worried as '*Rat*' in German means 'council'. Their Council House was more like a Cathedral. It was very ornate and its restoration had been completed that very week to celebrate its 100th birthday. There was a picture of Herr Voscherau, the Mayor of Hamburg, for whom Howard had arranged a Foreign Office visit recently. In his pocket Howard had the tie which Herr Voscherau had given him - just in case we went anywhere requiring a tie! Jean-Marie gave us a whistle-stop tour of the city, pointing out places of interest, including the Consulates, and his own office at the *Institut Français*. Our next stop was the harbour area which was enormous. A large section was cordoned off with barbed wire as part of the port of Hamburg was a tax free area where tax doesn't have to be paid to the EC. Goods were imported, processed in the dock area then loaded onto other ships for onward transmission to their destination countries. Goods that were imported into Hamburg had to pay EC taxes. We had never seen so many containers and this explained why we had seen so many container ships on the river Elbe as we sailed into Hamburg. (We wondered how many men must be out of work as a result of containerisation.) The scale of the harbour, which covered many square miles of both land and water, was mind-boggling. Even *more* mind-boggling was the thought of the organisation required to run it - who brought what, when, how...

After our extensive tour, we returned to the Fèvre's for a barbecue lunch, preceded by champagne (!) and followed by a special pudding which, once again, had been made by Victor and Nicole. These two young people were 'ace' chefs and we could see that in just a year or two, Jean-Marie and Mirjam would be able to relax while the children prepared the meals.

In the afternoon, we had a ride on the Underground to the Planten und Blumen park, which was next door to our hotel. The children were very keen to see our hotel room (we couldn't think why!) so we popped in to satisfy their curiosity. Mirjam was keen to see the view from the top of the hotel (twenty-seventh floor) but the view could be seen only from the Night Club on the twenty-sixth floor. As we were six hours too early for the Night Club, we had to disappoint her. Never mind - the gardens awaited. Mirjam and the children headed for the children's play area while Jean-Marie took us to the rose garden. It was very hot again so we used that as an excuse to have a cold beer - our first beer in Germany on this trip. We met up with Mirjam and the children once again and headed back to the Fèvre house for some supper, accompanied by some *Entre Deux Mers*. They were anxious to give us more wine to take home but we had to decline as we would not be able to carry it in our luggage.

The time had come to say not goodbye, but *au revoir*. We looked forward to seeing them again very soon, maybe in London.

Monday 18th

First thing on the agenda for today was a boat trip round the harbour. The commentary was in German so we didn't understand most (any?) of it. I didn't hear any of the four sentences that I knew, so we were completely 'at sea' - or perhaps 'at harbour'...Most things were quite obvious and it was a very interesting trip round the docks, especially sightings of dry docks where enormous ships were being refitted. The scale of the operation was quite unbelievable.

At the end of the seventy-five minute trip, we returned to the booking place to claim our free drinks. We opted for two tins of cold beer and sat on the jetty to enjoy them. (Some wasps were keen to share our enjoyment but they didn't seem to realize that they were having the opposite effect.) On the same seat was an elderly English couple, who were spending four weeks in Hamburg with their son. They had not had much contact with other English people during their stay and they were keen to have a chat.

We took the underground to the Art gallery - only to find it was closed on Mondays. We did find a suitable lunch place where we had a good cheese and tomato salad and ice cream. The local sparrows shared our bread.

Back at our hotel, we were allowed to stay in our room until 1500, rather than the usual 1100. It was now 1400 so we had the ultimate luxury of having a shower before setting off on the longest leg of our journey, the trip back to England.

The minibus arrived to collect us at 1600 and the laid-back driver told us he had to meet seven people. After twenty minutes, there was still no sign of the other five people. The laid-back driver made some mobile phone calls, which we couldn't understand, but we *could* understand that he was getting less laid-back by the second. Finally we left, just the two of us, and arrived at the ship at 1630.

Checking-in and boarding were much quicker than at Harwich and there was a much shorter walk to the ship.

We installed ourselves in our four-berth cabin (which we didn't have to share with others) and made for the deck to watch departure. The moment it left, we headed for the shop, which didn't open until the ship left port. We hoped to buy a Sunday newspaper, of which we knew there would be only a few, if any. We were successful in finding two - not necessarily those of our choosing - but we filled in the time until supper catching up with that poor Lady Di and all her 'romantic' difficulties and that poor Prince Charles (ditto); likewise various film stars and footballers. (Who *reads* this stuff week by week?) Supper was another excellent culinary affair and the rest of the evening was spent with the papers and our books. When we woke the next morning, we would be within sight of Britain. We would have to sail parallel to the English coast for quite a way, and the final leg - into the river and up the estuary - would be slow, as was the Elbe section.

Tuesday 19th

The English coast was out there somewhere, but fog had descended so we could see nothing - except fog. It cleared only as we entered the estuary but the journey has been extremely comfortable so we had no complaints.

Safely home after trip number thirty-seven, we set about unpacking - and wondering where our travels would take us next.

"It's been a picture-book romance, Gianpedro, but I must go back to the library..."

A WINTER'S TALE

(Found in a cave in Nerja, Spain, in January 1998, proving it was not written by W Shakespeare after all.)

We had had short breaks after Christmas in previous years, and had found it to be 'a good thing', not least to help us recover from the Yuletide Season which was always a difficult time. But in 1998, we needed to recover from the whole of 1997. What a year it had been. We had had to cope with bereavements, illness of friends and 'problems' generally. We were still mourning the death of Charles Proctor when Howard's wonderful Aunt Lorraine died. To have the two most important people in our lives removed in a matter of two months was hard to bear. At the end of the year, our downstairs neighbour, Bernard, left Jennifer House to move north, closely followed by our other neighbours, Alison, Patrick and Isobel Casey (now just two years old). Isobel was the nearest we got to a little one of our own and their move was a real wrench, as we knew it would be. We consoled ourselves with the thought that we had been so lucky to have had the friendship and love of both Bernard and the Casey family for so long and we knew that all good things must come to an end. So we were trying to be brave - with a distinct lack of success.

We knew we must face up to 1998, knowing that our bereavements would work themselves out - eventually. To help us, American Express, (through whose offices we had booked our trip and who could never be accused of efficiency), sent us a card which we received that morning - January 3rd. It read: "Welcome Home. We hope you have enjoyed your trip and arrived back feeling relaxed and refreshed." As we didn't leave until January 4th, we felt is was somewhat previous...

Sunday 4th

We were leaving England in the grip of strong winds and gales. Our good friend Tom Johns had offered to drive us to Gatwick, so we arrived in style. He needed to track down a Centre for Immigration as he had to go there two days hence for a meeting. Immediately we found that our flight was delayed by one hour so we installed ourselves in *Garfunkels* for lunch. English was not the first language of the waiter. Indeed, we wondered if he spoke it at all as we failed to understand most of what he said to us and he looked distinctly puzzled by everything *we* said to *him*. He was very charming, nonetheless, and even mimed "hope you are enjoying your meal". I replied in similar mimed vein. Howard pointed out that he might have been miming something extremely unsavoury, to which I had just agreed! There was nothing I could say...

Because the weather we were leaving behind was so inclement, the flight was rather bumpy on the way up but, as soon as we were above the clouds, it was plain sailing (flying?) to Malaga. The temperature on the outside of the plane was minus sixty degrees centigrade. We wondered how the illegal immigrants, about whom we had read recently, survived in the hold of a plane at that temperature.

Malaga airport had a thing or two to learn about organisation. Howard went to get a trolley and it was almost a fight to the death - a scene reminiscent of Ghengis Khan on a training weekend. We waited an age for our luggage to arrive; we were beginning to think they had sent it back to Gatwick. While we waited, we noticed advertisements for Versace. I had only just learned how to pronounce his name when he was assassinated. (People with strange names - beware!) We were both wondering how to pronounce the place where we were to spend the coming week - Nerja. It is very difficult to explain it in writing. The nearest we could get was *Nairtha* - said whilst clearing your throat. Others had given up the unequal struggle and called in *Nerger* (as in verger) or *Nerka* (as in Ghurka) - neither of which we could believe was correct.

A one-hour drive from Malaga brought us to the hotel - Hotel Monica - by 2300. Never had bed been more welcome. It had been a very long day.

Monday 5th

The view of the Mediterranean from our balcony was good, but there was also a view of the building site next door. We had offstage pneumatic drilling, but perhaps it would not continue for long? At the travel agent's suggestion, we had changed our hotel as we had been told that there was some 'building work' going on at the Balcony of Europe Hotel - our first choice. We were to discover that 'building work' was no understatement. The letter from the travel agent had warned us that "they are rebuilding and renovating the restaurant (involving on-site JCB diggers), installing a new swimming pool (generating noise from time to time) and there are works to install an extra lift and new fire doors. Though this work involves cosmetic tools (?), it may generate minimal dust levels." That was *really* welcoming!

Breakfast was a feast and set us up for the Thomson Welcome Party at 1000. The representative was very informative but spoke in a quiet monotone throughout. We wondered if most of the audience would have heard what she said. We were definitely among the youngest guests in the hotel, but the brochure did advertize "more mature couples come here". It didn't mention the vintage of the single people who might have visited!

We made our way into Nerja itself, about half a mile. It was a small but busy town, with construction work round every corner. Now we were here, we could understand why the travel agent had dissuaded us from staying at the Balcony of Europe Hotel. However, we did have a very good light lunch there - gazpacho and avocado salad, sitting in exactly the same spot where we had sat four years ago, on our first visit to the Balcony of Europe. After lunch we went shopping for the castanets that we had promised to get for Tom Johns and Howard tried on a matador's hat. He decided against - red really *isn't* his colour!

Back at the Hotel Monica, two things took us by surprise. The first was a very, very loud noise, as of birds, but many, many birds, in an enclosed space. And that's exactly what it was. We were on the sixth floor and in the well of the hotel building, there were lots of trees and even *more* birds, who had chosen that location for their bedroom. We were very happy about that and, by the time we returned after dinner, a great silence had descended. The second surprise was the sunset. We watched as a complete orange circle descended below the horizon in the space of 120 seconds. It was something to marvel at..."The sun goeth down, Thou makest darkness and it is night" sprang to mind and made us just a tiny bit homesick. To be honest, we did not "commune with our own hearts and mediate on Thee"; in fact, we realized it was supper time and headed for the restaurant.

Tuesday 6th - Epiphany

It was the Festival of the Kings which, in Spain, was their Christmas Day, when the children got their presents. The Thomson representative told us that, these days, the children got *some* presents on December 25th and the remainder on January 6th because, if they didn't, they would go through the whole of the school holidays without any presents. We were warned that all the shops would be closed today, though restaurants would be open and the hotel was functioning as normal. We were greeted by the avian heavy-metal dawn chorus, such were the decibels produced by the enormous numbers of our little feathered friends below.

We took the beach walk to the Burriana Beach as we wanted to go in search of the Parador Hotel, said to be the finest in this part of the world. Before the steep ascent from the beach to the Parador, we fortified ourselves with a couple of Lumumbas - the hot chocolate and brandy drinks that we first encountered four years ago. That day, when we were en route to the Alhambra, it had been very cold. Today, though the temperature was beginning to creep up again, we still had the hot version of the drink.

We could see why the Parador was the finest hotel around. It was splendidly quiet, much smaller than the surrounding hotels and built in the Spanish style, round an almost 'cloistered garden'. It had only sixty rooms (as opposed to the 200 in the larger hotels) and the whole ambience was so different to all the other hotels we had frequented. Perhaps if we ever did a return trip to this part of the world, we would stay there.

We walked back along to the beach to Nerja for a sandwich lunch in the main square. While we didn't mind the intermittent church bells (summoning the faithful to worship on Epiphany day), the loud pop music played to us over loudspeakers all over the square was not to our liking. It was Spanish folksy-type - and put us in mind of the balalaika music in the Python Cheese Shop sketch. Like banging your head against a wall, it was lovely when it stopped. ("Go placidly amid the noise and haste and remember what peace there may be in silence" was not something that intruded too often into the late twentieth century way of life.)

Back at the hotel, Howard braved the sun for a while (suitably covered in sun-tan oil) but I remained in the shade, unable to cope with strong sun. Gradually, we were beginning to feel that the contents of our minds were being downloaded into the Mediterranean Sea. A good thing - and we had brought with us minimal reading material with the intention of having an uncluttered mental canvas on which to paint our new thoughts. Everyday worries of life were in meltdown. On a more serious note, we were so happy about the coat hangers. For once, they were the old-fashioned sort - not the types for which we needed at least an 'O' level in physics (and good eyesight) to enable us to hang up our clothes.

Wednesday 7th

We had an early start (0800) for the three-hour drive to Ronda, along the coast for the first two hours, and through Marbella where the rich and famous lived (not to mention the odd criminal). The guide seemed to have a 'thing' about Sean Connery. She wondered whether we would see him. (If we were honest, we could live without such a sighting.) A previous Thomson guest had told the guide that Mr Connery used to be his milkman many years ago - presumably before Drama School. The last hour of the drive to Ronda (in the middle of the mountains) was very scenic. Ronda was the original home of 'modern day' bullfighting and the rules of it were drawn up here in the eighteenth century.

The guide gave us some advice for possible lunch places so we went to the *tapas* bar she had recommended. She was right that the owner knew some words of English, but the ones he knew were very few and far between. We both had the famous *tapas* plate; Howard had fish and I had meat. The man carved my portions from enormous sides of ham, sharpening his knives in time to the 'fast bit' of the Rodrigo *Guitar Concerto*, which was playing over the loud-speaker system. A few of our fellow coach passengers drifted in and had some sherry. We wondered what they would make of the *tapas* selection; the meat plate was very strong-tasting and a bit on the chewy side.

The next thing was the guided walk round the old town. We stepped over the bridge spanning a gorge (120 metres deep). The first bridge they had put there in the sixteenth century had taken eight weeks to build and it collapsed within the year! Not surprising when we learned that it was made of cork! The second attempt took forty-one years to build and was still standing. Hence the old Spanish proverb "Those who build a bridge of cork, on it shall they seldom walk". (It loses something in the translation.)

Our next stop was a private house which, when the owners had died childless, was left for the use of retired Silesian priests. It was a beautiful house and garden, with a frog-lined fountain and spectacular views over the gorge and into the surrounding countryside. (We went in search of an application form for the Silesian priesthood.)

Next, to the Bandit Museum - the guide said one of them looked like Sean Connery. To us they *all* looked rather sinister - S Connery on an off day? Into the church which had been a mosque. The guardian was burning incense at the door, which put us in a suitably *religioso* frame of mind. It was a very ornate place, dripping in gold leaf. Diego, our guide, told us all about the 'retable' and many other features of the church. As we came out, the atmosphere was somewhat shattered as the guardian was playing rather raucous Spanish folk music on a tape machine. From the sublime to the ridiculous.

Our last stop was the bullring - the oldest in Spain, but seating only 5,000, whereas Seville holds 16,000 and Madrid 30,000. It was an odd feeling to stand in the very place where the bulls met their end. It was a strange pastime but part of the life and culture of Spain. We supposed that Spanish people might look on Morris Dancing with the same degree of curiosity - except there are far fewer deaths in Morris Dancing - maybe the odd broken leg or torn ribbon.....We put our noses into the small museum of bullfighting which was within the bullring complex. Diego refused to call it 'bullfighting' because, as he rightly said, in a fight, at least the opponent stands a chance of winning. So the events were more 'spectacles' or, as he said, 'tragedies', played out in such a dramatic way.

A three-hour coach ride took us back to Nerja. During the first hour, thick cloud engulfed the hills so we saw nothing of the wonderful views. We were glad we'd seen them on the way up. Back at sea level, the cloud dispersed and we passed what we thought *might* be Mr Connery's house, though we could see no sign of a milk float so perhaps we'd got the wrong place after all - unless, of course, by some strange chance, he had given up the milk round. The possibility had to be considered.

Thursday 8th

A half-day coach trip took us to see the famous Caves of Nerja, apparently the third most popular tourist attraction in Spain. When we went back to our room after breakfast, the *fortissimo* dawn chorus was in full swing and there *was* a building site *ripieno*.

Ann-Marie, from Blackpool, was our guide for today. The first stop was the Marina d'Este, a very exclusive spot. Ann-Marie told us that it was built with Mafia money. The *Cosa Nostra* certainly seemed to have good taste! But it was a ghost town - absolutely no one was around. There were some very expensive yachts in evidence but, presumably, the owners were in the city. We were told that the wealthy migrated here during the summer, when it became intolerably hot in the cities. Property was very costly - £75,000 for a miniscule apartment.

On to the famous Caves of Nerja. Ann-Marie told us that they were the second biggest tourist attraction in Spain, the first being the Alhambra. (We thought that was odd as they had been the *third* biggest attraction the other day.) I donned another layer of clothes. Our experience of caves was that they were always cold and damp. Surprise, surprise, these were dry and warm; they seemed to be air-conditioned. (Adverts in the local estate agents probably read: 'Des. Res. Caves for Rent'.) They were immensely impressive; people first lived in them from 20,000 years ago (the remote Paleolithic Age) up until 4,000 years ago (the Bronze Age). We supposed that, after that, they all moved into Timeshares (in the Tupperwaric - often confused with Teflonic - age?) The caves also contained archaeological remains, cave drawings and utensils from the different ages. They must be an archaeologist's paradise. What we saw was only one third of the caves; the rest were still not open to the public. They were discovered quite by accident by three boys in 1959 and they are now one of the 'most important historical monuments of the world'. We could see why. One of the guides who worked at the caves was one of the boys who discovered them. Another ran a paella restaurant at Burriana Beach. (We didn't know what happened to number three.)

The last part of our trip was to the Andalucian village of Frigiliana, a picturesque, white-painted sight, nestling on the hillside of the Sierra Almijara. All the white paint, without exception, looked as if it had been done that very morning. The village was from the fifteenth century, having been taken back from the Moors in

320

the latter part of that century. The streets were very narrow, though vehicles used them, much to the displeasure of the pedestrians. The church was rather unattractive and, when we finally tracked down the eatery recommended to us by the guide, it turned out to be closed. An Alsatian dog led us to another eatery which provided what we wanted. *Gazpacho* was 'off' but I had some vegetable soup and Howard, some healthy-looking fish soup. (Were all the ingredients *really* dead?) We each had a 'just the right size' Spanish omelette, which came with some green toothpaste-like accompaniment, which turned out to be rather good garlic sauce. We eschewed the local *Vino del Terreno* as we'd heard that it was very sweet - rather like Muscatel. Two of our coach party joined us but when one of them ordered the fish soup, that, too, had run out!

There was just time to look into the ceramic shop - a veritable treasure trove of all things ceramic. Thank goodness we had to be conscious of the weight of our luggage or we would have come away laden with too many goodies. We did treat ourselves to a bowl and bought another for a friend whose birthday was the day after we got back.

Then there was Ruth. After the first evening, we had shared supper with another guest, Ruth. Ruth decided that I needed tips in assertiveness and she promised to bring them the next evening - on 'one side of A4'.

Friday 9th

We went in search of W H Smiffs (really!) where we bought a book detailing local walks. Our minds were now in complete meltdown and had slowed to a record-breaking 0 mph; if they slowed down any more, we would be asleep. How good it was to wake up and not go immediately into 'activity overdrive'. A New Year's resolution - not to let that happen ever again. Sadly, we knew that it was a resolution that would be impossible to keep.

Our first assignation was to find a place for a paella Sunday lunch. It had to be the Burriana Beach, where it was cooked freshly while we waited. We bought some *turon* (nougat) for our respective places of work. I managed to find one decorated with a dog, though later, I discovered it wasn't a dog after all, but a dinosaur. (That'll teach me to buy things without putting on my reading glasses.)

From the book we bought at W H Smiffs, we selected a walk that took us along the beach to Punta Lara. This involved crossing 'the mighty Rio Seco river', which we did by walking on some old drainpipes. Perhaps 'mighty' was a slight exaggeration - but that was what the book said! The walk continued after Punta Lara - but we didn't. We stopped at the *Meson Castillo* where we had a light lunch of melon, prawns, cheese and fruit salad. When the bill came, so too did two complimentary glasses of *Frigiliana* wine.

The temperature had dropped to sixty-two degrees so we shivered our way back to the hotel, though our faces bore witness to the health-giving effects of the sun and sea breezes. The rest of the day was sheer idleness until supper, when Ruth, true to her word, turned up with the 'one side of A4' tips on assertiveness. She was very serious about it and ran courses in it as part of her job. Amongst others, some of her clients were GPs.

Saturday 10th

There were no fixed plans for today so we strolled around parts of Nerja that we had not yet explored. We found another church - the Eremita. It was very small but had an immense altarpiece which not only seemed too big for the size of the church but was all rather garish. There was a strange Madonna with a crown perched on her head at a very uncomfortable angle. She was surrounded by plastic flowers in great profusion. Another rather sad sign of the times which we'd noticed in other churches were the electric candles! They had an in-built flicker mechanism to make them appear real at a distance. To 'buy' a candle, you merely flicked a switch. It felt a bit like 'rent-a-prayer' - and what happened if there was a power cut?

We bought an English newspaper as the headlines were all about Howard's boss, Robin Cook, and his tangled love-life. There was even a snippet about S Connery, telling that his personal wealth was in excess of fifty million pounds. (We thought it was even *more* odd that he still did the milk round.) The paper also recorded the death of Michael Tippett - another 'Child of our Time' was no more. It had been marvellous to be away from the real world's happenings for a week but we would slowly return to them during the next forty-eight hours.

We had a light lunch in the hotel at the *Terrace Bar*, overlooking the sea, which was quite rough. We had quite a wait for our lunch because Howard ordered the fish plate which was obviously freshly made. When it arrived, it was still bubbling fiercely but it was 'very good indeed'. My tomato-avocado-tuna salad was equally good.

The rest of the day was spent reading and sleeping until the Farewell Party at 1700. Only twelve people turned up, out of a possible thirty. The Thomson representative was not surprised. Our final dinner was by candlelight and there was the usual enormous choice of food from the buffet.

Sunday 11th

Our last treat was to be the paella on Burriana Beach. We had no difficulty locating the restaurant (*La Parrala*), which was run by one of the original cave discoverers, as the paella was made on the beach in the open air, in a huge dish (a metre in diameter) over an open fire. The smell itself was worth the money we paid for the food! We were not disappointed but we were glad we hadn't watched the preparation of it *too* carefully before we ate it. Hygiene did not seem to be the watchword - but perhaps that's what made it all the more tasty?

There was a delay of only ten minutes on our return journey and we were back in Reedworth Street in good time to make a cup of real English tea - with *boiling* water. We opened our Latin Calendar Christmas present at May 23rd where we read: "*Dum vigilans sperat, per somnum cernit id ipsum*" which, we were reliably informed, meant "Sleep sees the day's hopes come true". That explained why we'd slept so much on this trip. We made a note to get a Latin spellcheck...Real life was just around the corner.

WADHURST 2009

The thirty-ninth step brought us to Wadhurst in East Sussex on March 29th 1999, our nineteenth wedding anniversary.

By now, we had both retired so our financial position had changed rather drastically. As I said in the Preface, we are no longer able to afford holidays but, as we never cease to remind ourselves, living in Wadhurst is 'one long holiday' - for so it is. We could not be happier, we have everything we need for daily living so the fact that our holiday diaries have come to an end is a small price to pay.

I can think of no better ending than to quote Dag Hammarskjöld:

> For all that has been, thanks.
> For all that will be, yes.